Chocolate on Trial

Slavery, Politics,

and the Ethics of Business

Lowell J. Satre

Ohio University Press
Athens

Ohio University Press, Athens, Ohio 45701

www.ohio.edu/oupress/

Printed in the United States of America

Ohio University Press books are printed on acid-free paper ⊗ ™

13 12 11 10 09 08 07 06 05   5 4 3 2 1

Cover image: Dead slave with staff. Charles A. Swan, *The Slavery of To-day or, The Present Position of the Open Sore of Africa* (Glasgow, UK: Pickering & Inglis, 1909).

Frontispiece: William Cadbury led his company's efforts in the first decade of the twentieth century to stop the use of slaves on Portuguese-owned cocoa plantations. Reproduced courtesy of Cadbury Trebor Bassett.

The author has elected to retain certain early twentieth-century terms, such as "native" and "tribe," that appear in many of the primary sources consulted in the writing of this book. Although such terminology has been superseded in current scholarship, its use in this work is intended to reflect the language and outlook of the principal figures described herein.

Library of Congress Cataloging-in-Publication Data

Satre, Lowell J. (Lowell Joseph), 1942–
Chocolate on trial : slavery, politics, and the ethics of business / Lowell J. Satre.—1st ed.
p. cm.
Includes bibliographical references and index.
ISBN 0-8214-1625-1 (cloth : alk. paper) — ISBN 0-8214-1626-X (pbk. : alk. paper)
1. Chocolate industry—Great Britain—History. 2. Slave trade—Portugal—Colonies—History. 3. Slave labor—Africa, West—History. 4. Business ethics—Great Britain—History. 5. Business and politics—Great Britain—History. 6. Cadbury Ltd.—History. I. Title.
HD9200.G72S38 2005
331.11'734'09671509041—dc22

2005005901

To all enslaved men, women, and children,

and to those who work to abolish slavery.

CONTENTS

ILLUSTRATIONS

MAPS

1 Henry W. Nevinson and Modern Slavery

Flog him! Flog him! A good flogging! . . . Boa chicote!
Henry W. Nevinson

AN ENGLISH JOURNALIST and his native carriers, fevered and sore-footed, walked east twenty miles a day on the narrow, dusty path through Angola's Hungry Country. Antelopes, porcupines, and warthogs roamed amid the scruffy trees and bitter grasses growing in deep, white sand. Green parrots and cranes flew overhead, and in the evening, leopards roared. Butterflies, ants, and bees—indeed, all creatures—were "crazy for salt."[1] Bees drove the writer from his tent after he treated his feet with saltwater, and they caused the carriers to go "howling along the path by creeping up under their loin-cloths." While there was wildlife, the travelers saw few humans. Villages marked on their maps no longer existed.

Yet evidence of recent human passage through the area abounded, with graphic indications that the slave trade was alive and well in the Hungry Country. Human bones littered the sides of the trail, so many that it "would take an army of sextons to bury all the poor bones which consecrate that path." The bones in the dust were those of slaves who could no longer march, who were too weak to walk. Some captives were simply left to die; many others were killed by a blow to the head. The journalist wrote that when he raised the head of a recently killed slave, "the thick, woolly hair came off in my hand like a woven pad, leaving the skull bare, and revealing the deep gash made by the axe at the base of skull." Shackles that had bound hands and legs to prevent escape hung from the lower limbs of trees; if needed, they could be recovered by later trading parties. Such shackles were disconcertingly simple to make. A native carved an "oblong hole" out of a piece of wood, into which arms or legs fit (often securing two slaves), and a round peg driven through small holes secured the limbs. But should even these simple shackles prove difficult to come by along the trail, the slavers, whoever they were, had little need to worry about runaways surviving to tell their brutal tale—there was no place for the slaves to run to in the Hungry Country. After all, the evidence of their failure to escape was abundant.

The journalist, Henry Woodd Nevinson (1856–1941), was on assignment for *Harper's Monthly Magazine*, gathering information that would be the basis for a series of articles and a subsequent book describing slavery in Portuguese West Africa. The Hungry Country through which the reporter and his party trekked extended for some two hundred miles from the River Cuanza nearly to the fort at Mashiko in the interior of Portuguese Angola. Nevinson landed on the coast of Angola in December 1904. He first visited Luanda, a worn-out capital of decaying forts with rusty guns whose mix of the religious and the secular, of the old and the new, testified to a glorious past fallen on hard times. Portugal had abolished slavery in all of its colonies, including Angola, in the 1870s, but plantation owners and others still desperately craved workers. To satisfy this constant demand for labor, a state-supported system of "contract labor" emerged, wherein government agents certified that natives could, of their own free will, sign contracts committing themselves to five years of labor at a set wage. Government officials assumed responsibility for the proper treatment of workers, who allegedly were free to return to their homes at the end of their contracts should they so desire. During his trip throughout West Africa, Nevinson sought evidence to confirm or deny the suggestion that such contract labor was not, in fact, voluntary, but simply another form of slavery.

In his description of the journey, Nevinson wrote about alighting from a mail steamer at Lobito Bay, about two hundred miles south of the capital, and making his way inland a few miles to Catumbela, an old town that had long been the terminus for slave trade from the interior. Later, he went to the nearby Angolan port of Benguela, second in importance only to the town of Luanda and formerly the center of the slave trade to Brazil. At Benguela, he joined a South African Dutch, or Boer, ox-wagon train (there was a Boer settlement in southern Angola) for a two-month, 450-mile trek into the interior through Bihé country. The trip was both strenuous and dangerous. The incessant fording of streams and steep climbs through the rugged countryside provided ample opportunities for serious or even fatal accidents. West of the high plateau, the terrain was beautiful, a "land of bare and rugged hills, deeply scarred by weather, and full of the wild and brilliant colors—the violet and orange—that bare hills always give," and it was teeming with wild animals, including elands, lions, zebras, and buffaloes, as well as eagles, vultures, hawks, flamingoes, parrots, cranes, aureoles, honey guides, and great bustards.

Beyond these mountains, the landscape opened onto a plateau. Near Caconda, a largely abandoned town, lay a fort with a Portuguese officer and thirty native soldiers, a few trading houses, and a Catholic mission in which several priests ministered to the natives with a church, workshops, a school, and a garden. A sisters' mission similarly catered to the needs of girls. Nearby were several small native villages, and Nevinson believed that the missions had "bought" the boys' and girls'

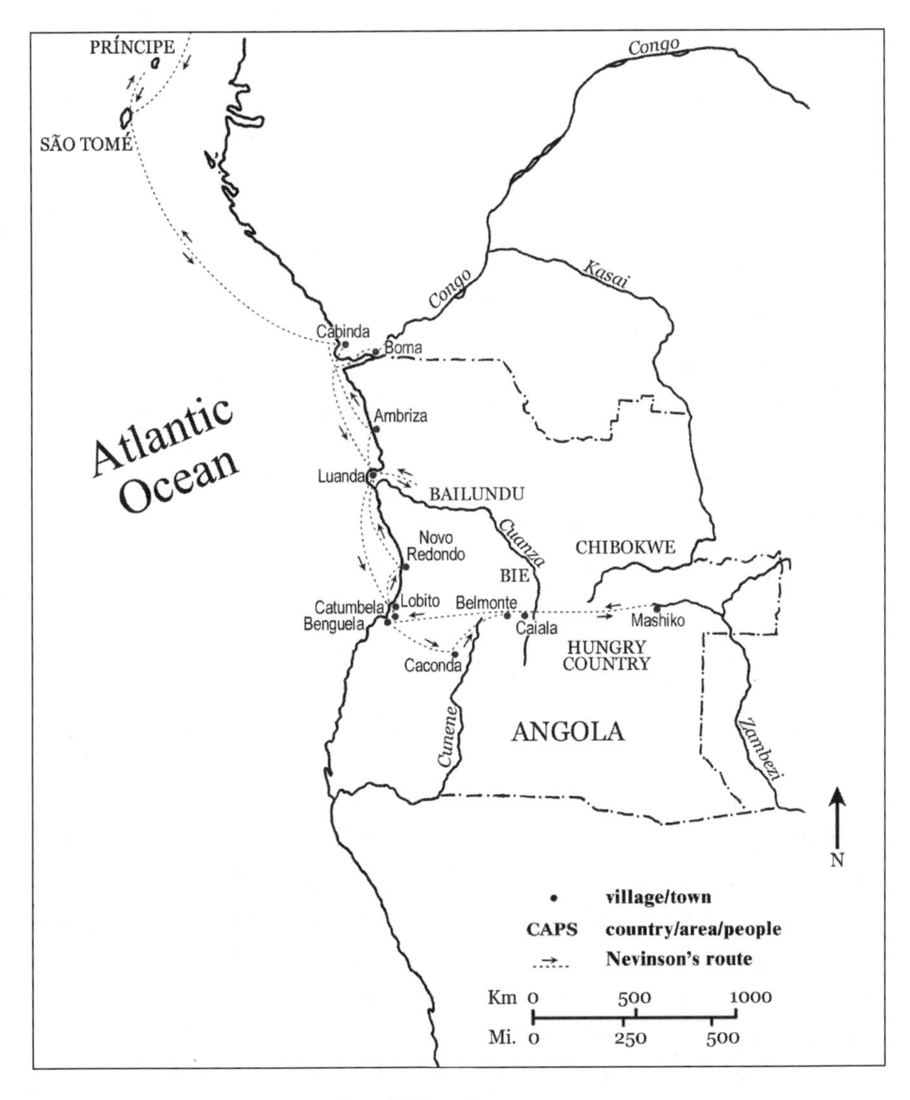

Map 1. Angola. Map by Lowell and Ellen Satre.

freedom from "slave-traders," then trained them and settled them in these surrounding villages. The missionary fathers, however, refused to discuss the issue with him.

After leaving Caconda, the ox wagons spent three weeks struggling through bogs and fording five rivers in order to reach the Bihé district. In addition to a Portuguese fort at Belmonte and the nearby town of Caiala, a few trading houses were scattered throughout the area. According to Nevinson's account, slaves worked at the trading houses, which were centers of slave trading, and on the few plantations, most of which grew sweet potatoes used to make rum, a primary trading currency. There were few animals in this almost treeless plateau, the climate was cool, and many Bihéans, or Ovimbundu, lived in huts grouped together in stockaded villages off the path. A chief, dressed in his "kingly" garb, dispensed justice and passed on traditions to his subjects. The Bihéans offered wisdom through a veritable cache of proverbs and sayings, and they reveled in music, particularly with drums and the *ochisanji*, a sort of portable piano.

Slave owning was common among the Bihéans. A man might trade his sister's children to pay off a debt or to slake the thirst for rum. Occasionally, a family member would be sold to a Portuguese trader supplying contract laborers for the government. The Ovimbundu engaged in all manner of trade, bearing heavy packs on their heads or shoulders as they walked the narrow paths into the interior, six hours a day for two months, far beyond the Hungry Country. They exchanged beads, salt, and cotton cloth for rubber and beeswax, while guns, gunpowder, and cartridges provided valuable barter for the purchase of slaves.

After Bihé, Nevinson forded the River Cuanza and crossed into the Hungry Country, which in his narrative he termed the "Worst Part of the Slave Route," with its gruesome evidence of bones and shackles. Following his journey through the Hungry Country and a bit beyond, he retraced his steps to Belmonte, in Bihé, where he took the course of the old slave path that ended at Catumbela and Benguela on the coast. The views from the mountains were a "radiance of jewels," akin to nature landscapes that the "Umbrians used to paint as backgrounds to the Baptist or St. Jerome or a Mother and Child." The path through the mountains was at times so steep that it was like a "goat-path in the Alps." This was an especially active route during the dry season, when thousands of carriers in the large trading parties made their way into the interior. Rum was a major trade item, even though in 1890 it had been banned from being brought into the Bihé by the European colonizing powers.[2]

Though Nevinson spent several months in Angola, he never encountered a large slave caravan. He suggested several reasons for this. He noted, for example, that he was trekking at the end of the wet season, when traders were only starting their journeys inland for slaves. Further, slave traders were aware of Nevinson's presence and purpose and may have taken steps to cover up their trade. It was possible, as well, that alternative paths to the north of the main route might have been used for the slave caravans. And in 1902, a native uprising at Bailundu, in response to the greed, pillaging, and violence of traders and government officials, had for a time brought about a dramatic decline in the human trade and forced the government to recognize native grievances. A few slave traders were imprisoned, some slaves were freed, and forts were ordered not to tolerate the "chained gangs" on the routes. Also, slave trading in the watershed area of the Congo had proved increasingly dangerous for traders from Angola, as Belgians protected their own market through a ring of forts. Moreover, slave caravans were occasionally difficult to recognize, as traders camouflaged the slaves as carriers.

While not so open or flagrant by 1905, the iniquitous slave trade persisted. Near Caiala, in Bihé, Nevinson happened on a party of about twenty boys with light packs, guarded by two men with *chicottes* (whips made from the hide of a hippopotamus) hiding in the bush, and he suspected that they were a small slave caravan. In another case, Nevinson's carriers referred to a party they were meeting as *apeka* (slaves). All told, there were seventy-eight people in that caravan, with armed men at the beginning, middle, and end watching over a party of mainly young boys. With the aid of one of his carriers, Nevinson talked to a "beautiful woman of about twenty or [a] little more" who reported that she had been captured far in the interior by another tribe and sold to a "white man for twenty cartridges." Torn from her husband and three children, the youngest still nursing, she was heading for *okalunga*, a term natives used to signify hell or death. He spotted her again a few days later on the road to Benguela, one of forty-three "voluntary laborers" marching to the "Emigration Agent" under guard of a company of soldiers.

A particularly venal episode centered on a disreputable Portuguese trader who claimed extraordinary compensation from villagers for the loss of property during the Bailundu War of 1902. Although the natives appealed to an official at Belmonte, they were ordered to pay twenty times the damages suffered. To help pay off the debt, parents sold children into slavery. Just before Nevinson visited the village, a distraught father committed suicide after having "pawned the last of his children." The trader also forced the chiefs to dance in his compound. "So the matter stands, and the villagers must go on selling more and more of their wives and children that the white man's greed may be satisfied," Nevinson wrote in disgust. Occasionally, slaves attempted to flee this living hell. Near Catumbela, a large Luvale man, bloody from his failed effort to gain freedom, was guarded by the owner's slaves, armed with long knives and "ready to cut him down if he tried to run again." His punishment, according to Nevinson's carriers, would be death by flogging in front of the owner's other slaves.

Nevinson did not adhere to the theology of Christian missionaries, but he admired their resolution and their benevolent work among the natives. All too often, they preached a gospel so complex that even the learned of the church could not agree on its tenets, and while the natives understood the words of a sermon, they generally did not understand the doctrine. Nevertheless, the repetition of the few hymns translated into a tribe's language—one chorus was "repeated seventeen times without a pause"—offered a kind of innocent joy. The missionaries lived in simple poverty, shared what little they had, and worked medical miracles, mending bones and treating the "terrible sores and ulcers which rot the shins and thighs, tormenting all this part of Africa." Although few natives were drawn to the missionaries by "persuasive eloquence or religious conviction," they did gain from the missionaries the "two charms of entire honesty and of inward peace." In one of his most powerful observations, Nevinson remarked: "In a country where the natives are habitually regarded as fair game for every kind of swindle and deceit, where bargains with them are not binding, and where penalties are multiplied over and over again by legal or illegal trickery, we cannot overestimate the influence of men who do what they say, who pay what they agree, and who never go back on their word. From end to end of Africa common honesty is so rare that it gives its possessor a distinction beyond intellect, and far beyond gold." Yet Nevinson saw that the missionaries were caught on the horns of a dilemma. While they disapproved of slavery, they dared not express their feelings publicly, lest they be "poisoned and . . . driven out of the country, leaving their followers exposed to a terrible and exterminating persecution." A local trader who disliked an American mission in Bihé occasionally sent his slaves to destroy it. For missionaries to complain to the *chefe* (the government agent) at the fort in Belmonte was useless. Should the chefe render justice, the other traders would report him to officials on the coast, and he "would be removed, as all Chefes are removed who are convicted of justice."

Nevinson believed that he had revealed an essential cause of the terrible suffering endured by the natives in Angola: Portuguese authority was ineffective. Portugal's civil and military officials, and its traders as well, operated outside the law, and whatever authority officials exercised was either misused or abused. The curator general of Angola was responsible for ensuring that the contract binding a worker for five years was legal and that its provisions—including those related to hours of work, wages, food, and clothing, as spelled out under Portuguese laws and regulations of 1875, 1878, and 1903—were appropriate. The standard contract stated that the native had "come of his own free will to contract for his services."[3] The contract had to be signed by both laborer and employer in the presence of a magistrate or a representative of the curator. The contract was renewable after five years if both parties so desired, and magistrates were required to visit the districts to make sure that the contracts were honored and that any children born to the laborers were free. Legally, Nevinson stressed, the *serviçal* (contract laborer) was protected. The reality, however, was otherwise.

An agent, or a "labor merchant," scoured an area for slaves, often far in the interior. He bargained with a chief or chiefs who, in exchange for guns and cartridges, kegs of rum, or bales of cotton, provided a specified number of men, women, or children. Often the agent, with a large gang, sold his services to one of two tribes at war, his payoff being the right to purchase captives. The labor merchant ultimately procured them in many places, through many deals. Nevinson enumerated several reasons why natives might end up as slaves: "Some had broken native customs or Portuguese laws, some had been charged with witchcraft by the medicine-man because a relative died, some could not pay a fine, some were wiping out an ancestral debt, some had been sold by uncles in poverty, some were the indemnity for village wars; some had been raided on the frontier, others had been exchanged for a gun; some had been trapped by Portuguese, others by Bihéan thieves; some were but changing masters." Many slaves did not survive the march to the sea, their bones adding to the landscape. Of those who reached the ports, recalcitrant ones could expect to be beaten. In Catumbela, at the end of his long journey, Nevinson heard from the courtyards "the blows of the palmatoria [paddle used to beat the palm of the hand] and chicote and the cries of men and women who were being 'tamed.'"

Where were all of these slaves going? Some remained in Angola, clearing brush on plantations, toiling at trading houses, or mating as concubines. But most of them, around four thousand per year, were shipped to the islands of São Tomé and Príncipe, where they would spend the rest of their lives on cocoa plantations.

The whole process at Benguela was oriented toward providing labor for these islands. A few days before a steamer arrived, the town stirred to life. The curator took his place in a large room in the tribunal building, and an agent "herded" before him "gangs" of slaves. An official asked the slaves if they were willing to work in São Tomé under the regulations set down in a 1903 decree. Nevinson's outrage flowed through his pen: "No attention of any kind is paid to their answer. In most cases no answer is given. Not the slightest notice would be taken of a refusal." A legal document for five years of labor was then completed. Nevinson wrote, "[Each slave] receives a tin disk with his number, the initials of the Agent who secured him, and in some cases . . . the name of the island to which he is destined." A slave was also given a paper with personal information, which was deposited in a tin cylinder. As Nevinson elaborated: "The disks are hung round their necks, the cylinders are slung at their sides. . . . All are then ranged up and marched out again, either to the compounds, where they are shut in, or straight to the pier where the lighters, which are to take them to the ship, lie tossing upon the waves." But they were no longer slaves, for the curator had made them into serviçais (the plural form of serviçal). Nevinson commented bitterly: "The climax of the farce has now been reached. The deed of pitiless hypocrisy has been consummated. The requirements of legalized slavery have been satisfied. The government has 'redeemed' the slaves which its own Agents have so diligently and so profitably collected. They went into the Tribunal as slaves, they have come out as 'contracted laborers.' No one in heaven or on earth can see the smallest difference, but . . . by the excuse of law [Portugal] smooths her conscience and whitens over one of the blackest crimes which even Africa can show."

In Nevinson's estimation, greed led to the slavery he saw in Angola: "The only motive for slavery is money-making, and the only argument in its favor is that it pays." Angola itself was a functioning slave state, with at least half the population in slavery. The price of a male slave in Benguela was about £20, the value of a male or female in São Tomé about £30. The list of those benefiting was long—the government that charged various duties for each slave, the agents who delivered laborers to the islands, the steamship company Empresa Nacional that shipped them, the doctor who kept them alive, the captain who got them to their destination, and the port that received them.

This labor system was not without its critics in Angola and Portugal. Though some were disturbed over the institution of slavery, many in Angola complained that labor essential for the development of the province was going instead to create wealth for rich plantation owners on the islands. A newspaper in Luanda, *A Defeza de Angola*, bravely "exposed" the "whole system." Those who questioned the institution of slavery feared the threat of physical violence. Conscientious officials found themselves replaced, forced out by the powerful local economic interests. Nevinson, who suffered from fever occasionally during his tour of Angola, was poisoned just before he sailed for São Tomé. While he was not certain that the poisoning was deliberate, all evidence pointed toward that conclusion, as he had often been warned that his investigation put him at risk. During his last few days in Angola, he made plans to send his papers to England should he die.

The ship on which Nevinson sailed carried 150 slaves from Benguela, picking up others at Novo Redondo and Luanda for a total of 272, not including an estimated 50 babies. Dressed in bright new clothes provided "to give them a moment's pleasure," the natives stayed on the lower deck, seldom talking, "and over the faces of nearly all broods the look of dumb bewilderment that one sees in cattle crowded into trucks for the slaughter-market." Natives feared the worst: for many, the name São Tomé had become synonymous with okalunga—hell. Although Portuguese law required that serviçais be given the opportunity for repatriation after five years, with funding provided by deductions from the workers' monthly pay, none of them ever returned from the islands.

From the upper deck, first-class passengers looked down on the serviçais "with interest and amusement." At Novo Redondo, a mother with a very young infant struggled to mount the unsteady steps in the rolling sea, providing Nevinson's narrative with a poignant scene:

> At last she reached the top, bruised and bleeding, soaked with water, her blanket lost, most of her gaudy clothing torn off or hanging in strips. On her back the little baby, still crumpled and almost pink from the womb, squeaked feebly like a blind kitten. But swinging it round to her breast, the woman walked modestly and without complaint to her place in the row with the others.
>
> I have heard many terrible sounds, but never anything so hellish as the outbursts of laughter with which the ladies and gentlemen of the first class watched that slave woman's struggle up to the deck.

A few days later, a slave leaped overboard. A boat quickly captured him, and when he was returned to the ship, beaten and bruised, the passengers yelled, "Flog him! Flog him! A good flogging! . . . Boa chicote!"

The voyage from Benguela to São Tomé took eight days. The small equatorial island was often shrouded in mist and clouds, which occasionally cleared to reveal mountains and "the white house of some plantation and the little cluster of out-buildings and huts where the slaves were to find their new home." On June 17, 1905, the laborers were landed and then assembled according to the plantations for which they had been requested. Gangers (foremen of groups of workers) led them in the walk to the plantation. "For them," Nevinson wrote, "there are no more journeyings, till that last short passage when their dead bodies are lashed to poles and carried out to be flung away in the forest."

The islands of São Tomé, about thirty miles by twenty, and the much smaller Príncipe, to the north, lie in the Gulf of Guinea some one hundred fifty miles off the west coast of Africa. Nevinson stressed that population figures were hard to come by; São Tomé's slaves numbered between twenty thousand and forty thousand and Príncipe's a bit over three thousand. The prosperity of the islands was based on the production of cocoa beans. The cocoa trees, set on "fine volcanic soil," thrived in "a hot-house climate—burning heat and torrents of rain in the wet season, from October to April; stifling heat and clouds of dripping mist in the season that is called dry." There were about 230 *roças* (plantations) on São Tomé and 50 on Príncipe, some owned by individuals, others held by corporations. The wealthy owners normally lived in Lisbon, Portugal.

Conditions on the roças differed considerably, depending on "the wealth of the owner and the superintendent's disposition." All shared a basic plan: cocoa-tree groves, an area containing huge pans for drying cocoa beans, the planter's house, slave quarters, and a hospital. The size of the labor force on a roça varied, with the largest numbering about a thousand serviçais. One morning, Nevinson visited a "model" plantation on São Tomé, "a show-place for the intelligent foreigner or for the Portuguese shareholder who feels qualms as he banks his dividends." The roça featured brick huts for the slaves, neatly tended cocoa trees, modern machines, electricity-generating engines, and a "clean and roomy hospital with its copious supply of drugs and anatomical curiosities in bottles." The plantation doctor remarked in passing that the death rate was "twelve or fourteen per cent. a year among the serviçaes." The chief cause was "Anæmia" brought on by "unhappiness." The doctor testified that the life span of the serviçais was decent if they could be kept alive through the first few years, when misery and homesickness took a terrible toll. According to a British consular report, Príncipe's adult death rate for 1901 was slightly over 20 percent per annum. The superintendent of a large, well-managed São Tomé plantation acknowledged that its child mortality rate was 25 percent per year.

The serviçais were paid once a month, with men commanding a higher wage than women. The pay was considerably less than the minimum required by the decree of 1903, and the owners did not even deduct a portion for the required repatriation fund, as they knew none of the laborers would ever be returned to their homeland. The workers were paid in cash and often were required by the owners to spend their money at the plantation store, on items such as cloth, food, and rum. As noted earlier, the law required that labor contracts had to be renewed after five years, and the curator approved and signed renewals in batches, either at the plantation or at his office. The serviçais were never consulted.

Laborers were valuable, and owners worked diligently to keep them from escaping, with dogs providing security in the evenings. Nevertheless, some slaves escaped—especially on Príncipe—and fled into the interior, where they were hard to track down. By law, apprehended runaways had to be returned to the owners, who flogged them and returned them to work. While most hunting parties sent out to capture runaways were unsuccessful, Nevinson related one planter's account of an instance in which the fleeing slaves, men and women, were spotted hiding in the trees: "'It was not long, I can tell you, before we brought them crashing down through the leaves on to the ground. My word, we had grand sport that day!'" Eighteen slaves fled from Príncipe via a canoe in early 1905 and made their way to the island of Fernando Po, but Spanish authorities there returned them to Príncipe.

Although corporal punishment was used, Nevinson believed that self-interest tempered the violence inflicted on slaves. As he put it: "The cost of slaves is so large, the demand is so much greater than the supply, and the death-rate is so terrible in any case that a good planter's first thought is to do all he can to keep his stock of slaves alive." Nevinson asserted that not only did plantation owners need to replace serviçais who died, they also required additional laborers to expand cocoa-bean production to attempt to satisfy the insatiable market so that "England and America can get their chocolate and cocoa cheap." This unquenchable thirst for labor on the cocoa islands drove up the price of the slaves and dictated the Angolan slave trade; the government "[urged] its Agents to drive the trade as hard as they can, and the Agents do their very utmost to encourage the natives to raid, kidnap, accuse of witchcraft, press for debts, soak in rum, and sell."

A flurry of treaties to prohibit slavery in the heart of Africa, signed in the nineteenth century by European nations including Portugal and Britain, had usually proved worthless. Commercial interests begged to be satisfied, Nevinson pointed out, and by signing a paper, the slave became a "free" serviçal, and all interested parties—government, business, and humanitarian—were satisfied. Even Great Britain, which had actively opposed the evil trade by stationing a warship off the coast of Benguela, had lost much of its moral authority by reason of reports of its recent abuse of labor in the Australian colonies and in the South African mines.

Nevinson contended that those who saw the creation of wealth on the fertile islands as a measure of success approved the use of well-treated serviçais, even though the word *serviçal* itself was simply a legal term for *slave*. Portuguese capitalists and others accepted the belief that Africans would not work on the islands "without compulsion." "But they forget," he added, "that legal terms make no difference to the truth of things. They forget that slavery is not a matter of discomfort or ill treatment, but of loss of liberty. They forget that it might be better for mankind that the islands should go back to wilderness than that a single slave should toil there. I know the contest is still before us. It is but part of the great contest with capitalism, and in Africa it will be as long and difficult as it was a hundred years ago in other regions of the world."

Nevinson left São Tomé on June 30, 1905, arriving in England on July 21. His articles on slavery, which contained many photographs (including scenes of a skull lying by a trail and a shackle dangling from a tree limb), appeared in *Harper's Monthly Magazine* from August 1905 through February 1906 under the title "The New Slave-Trade." His book *A Modern Slavery*, mainly a compilation of his *Harper's* articles, was published in 1906.[4] While appalled by the slave trade and slavery that he witnessed, Nevinson found Portuguese West Africa a varied, interesting, and beautiful country, and—unusual for his time—he regarded the natives as hardworking and intelligent people who cared greatly for the welfare of their families. He never referred to them as being inferior to Europeans. He did not wish to "civilize" the natives but to free them to practice their own unique and important way of life.

From 1905 to 1914, because of his determination to eradicate the slavery he had exposed in Portuguese West Africa, Nevinson found himself in the middle of a controversy that encompassed England's political, diplomatic, economic, humanitarian, and journalistic interests.[5] He made public a wealth of information that confounded the British government and forced Cadbury Bros., one of England's great chocolate manufacturers, to justify before a court of law its purchase of cocoa beans from the islands of São Tomé and Príncipe.

2 The Firm of Cadbury and the World of Slave Labor

I should be sorry needlessly to injure a cultivation that as far as I can judge provides labour of the very best kind to be found in the tropics: at the same time we should all like to clear our hands of any responsibility for slave traffic in any form.

William A. Cadbury

If Thomé were at the bottom of the sea, the slavery question would be settled in Angola for ever.

Father Rooney to William A. Cadbury

HENRY NEVINSON WAS not the only person to inquire into the nature of labor in Portuguese West Africa. While visiting São Tomé in June 1905, he met Joseph Burtt (1862–1939), a young Quaker commissioned by Cadbury Bros., the English chocolate confectionery manufacturer, to investigate allegations that plantations on the island were using slave labor to produce the cocoa beans purchased by the company. This book is about the controversy surrounding the labor utilized on São Tomé in the production of cocoa, the basis of chocolate goods. The terms *cocoa beans* and *cocoa* are used to denote the raw material, whereas *chocolate* refers to the product made from cocoa, in either liquid or solid form.[1]

Linguistic evidence indicates that the first people to domesticate the *cacao* (Anglicized as cocoa) plant were the Olmecs of Central America in the first millennium BCE. The Maya drank chocolate and incorporated it into their marriage ceremonies; the Aztecs reserved the consumption of chocolate drink for the social elite. Both the Maya and the Aztecs used cocoa beans as currency. It was the Maya who introduced cocoa to the Spanish.

Cocoa trees initially grew only in Central America, but in the nineteenth and twentieth centuries, Europeans transplanted them to colonies located near the equator, as the trees require a hot climate, sufficient rainfall, and a relatively low altitude, ensuring warm evenings. The pods, which contain thirty to forty beans or seeds, grow directly from the tree's trunk or large branches and mature in about six months. The ripe pods cut from the tree are split open and the beans removed. The beans ferment for a few days, during which they briefly germinate, and are then placed in large pans; the beans are turned regularly while they dry at high temperature. These beans are sacked and shipped to manufacturers for the final processing. A nineteenth-century cocoa shop owner roasted the beans and then removed their thin covering to leave the kernel, or nib, which he ground into a powder. Liquids and various additives would be mixed with the powder to create a chocolate drink.

The eighteenth-century Swedish scientist Carl Linnaeus, who liked the chocolate drink, classified the cacao tree as *Theobromo cacao* (*theobromo* being the Greek term for "food of the gods"). Europeans did not favor the drink until sugar and spices, including cinnamon, were added to cut some of the bitterness. Chocolate was initially consumed only by the elite of European society, but by the seventeenth and eighteenth centuries, the drink had made its way into English coffeehouses. Until the nineteenth century, chocolate was regarded as a medicine that seemingly cured every bodily ailment. It was a complicated drink to mix, partly because a large quantity of cocoa butter had to be removed in order for it to be palatable. In 1828, C. J. Van Houten, a Dutch chemist, developed a hydraulic press that efficiently extracted the cocoa butter, producing a cake of cocoa ready for use. This process reduced the cost of chocolate, making it more available for mass consumption. Due to a series of innovations in the manufacture of chocolate in the nineteenth century, what had been little more than a gruel of cocoa and additives, including large quantities of starch, evolved into a delicious drink and an attractive candy bar by 1900.[2]

At the turn of the twentieth century, the British cocoa and chocolate business was dominated by three Quaker-owned firms—Cadbury, Fry, and Rowntree—although European companies continued to claim a large part of the British market.[3] The Quakers (officially the Society of Friends) had emerged as a Christian religious body in the seventeenth century. As a persecuted minority, Quakers were excluded from politics and certain social circles, yet many became prosperous businesspeople, excelling in banking and trading ventures. They often supported each other and were extraordinarily active in the celebrated antislavery movement of the eighteenth and nineteenth centuries.[4]

John Cadbury (1801–1889) opened a tea and coffee shop in Birmingham in 1824.[5] In 1861, sons Richard (1835–1899) and George (1839–1922) took over the struggling company, which had by then become a chocolate firm. Success finally came in the 1860s after the company began using one of Van Houten's presses. Responding to public concern over adulterated foods, the Cadbury firm began selling a pure "Cocoa Essence" drink in 1866 and shortly thereafter utilized the cocoa butter by-product as the base for various chocolate candies, which were marketed in neatly decorated boxes.

When the business outgrew the shop on Bridge Street in Birmingham, it was moved four miles south of town to a purpose-built factory designed by George Cadbury. Located in a rural setting, the factory was named Bournville after the Bourn Brook, which bordered the area (the brook actually had several names). Besides, the name *Bournville* had a pleasant French sound to it, and France was the country that produced the most prestigious chocolate of the period. The company built sixteen homes for the foremen; a communal bath and recreational facilities, plus dining quarters, were added for the workers. Because of the rapid growth in the sale of chocolate products, the Cadbury company expanded these premises several times by the end of the century.

In 1900, a workweek at Cadbury's factory was forty-eight hours long, and the company required promptness and efficiency from its employees. File cards recorded the work history of each, and rule violations could lead to dismissal. Like many progressive employers of the time, Cadbury Bros. operated under a "marriage bar," which meant that women had to leave the firm's employment when they married. For the protection of young single women, there was a strict separation of the sexes in the factory. But in spite of such close control over the employees, factory jobs at Cadbury were much sought after. While demanding, the owners took a paternalistic interest in their workers' entire lives. Members of the Cadbury family seriously adhered to the Quaker tenet in providing aid to those less fortunate. In 1895, George Cadbury, a particularly devout Quaker who spent a lifetime engaged in adult religious education for the poor, began, at his own expense, the construction of 143 houses in Bournville for members of the working classes. These semidetached homes, available also to workers not employed at the Cadbury factory, were initially sold with the aid of low-interest loans, but occupancy soon became restricted to leases. In 1900, George Cadbury turned over more than three hundred homes to the newly created Bournville Village Trust. The village eventually included shops, recreation facilities, garden allotments, a school, and a lecture hall. No public houses for the sale of alcohol were permitted. Bournville quickly came to be regarded as one of the most successful model villages in Britain, which at the turn of the twentieth century was engaged in the Garden City movement, designed to improve the living conditions of its people.[6]

Many Cadbury employees, however, including the large number of single women that the firm employed to keep expenses down, were unable to live at Bournville Village because they could not afford the relatively high rent. Nor were Cadbury's purpose-built factory and employee amenities unique, as confectionery competitors overseas were often in the forefront of providing facilities for their workers.[7] Nevertheless, in 1900, this highly successful and influential British company employed 3,310 workers, the women outnumbering men about two to one, in a widely admired factory setting.[8] In April 1898, the chancellor of the exchequer, Sir Michael Hicks Beach, remarking on the dramatic increase in the consumption of the "admirable [cocoa] beverage," thanked the firm of Cadbury in all but name for its remarkable achievement.[9]

Even after the expansion of manufacturing facilities in the late nineteenth century, George and Richard Cadbury continued to run the firm as a private company. Based on an earlier agreement between the two brothers, the firm became a private limited liability company following the sudden death of Richard in 1899. George Cadbury was named chairman of the committee of management of Cadbury Brothers Limited, while Richard's sons, Barrow and William, and George's sons, Edward and George Jr., became managing directors with responsibility over specific sections of the business.[10]

In addition to his holdings in the Cadbury firm, the elder George Cadbury was a newspaper proprietor. He purchased several suburban Birmingham papers in the 1890s, and he gained notoriety in 1901 when he purchased the *Daily News* (London), in order to give the Liberal Party a mouthpiece during the South African War and to provide an organ for the antiwar convictions of the Quakers. In the forefront of social reform and a critic of Conservative Party policies, the *Daily News* assailed the Conservative government in 1904 for approving the use of Chinese coolie labor in the South African mines; it regularly headlined its stories with phrases such as "Yellow Slavery" and "Chinese Slavery."[11] George Cadbury also used the *Daily News* sponsorship of the Sweat Shop Exhibition to focus attention on sweated trades (where people worked in deplorable conditions at extraordinarily low pay) in England and to campaign actively for old-age pensions. Alfred G. Gardiner, the editor of the *Daily News*, gathered around him a group of brilliant journalists, many of whom were personally interested in solving England's social ills. The *Daily News* consistently lost money, but George Cadbury accepted that burden as a part of his charitable work.

While he did not interfere in the day-to-day operation of the newspaper, he did expect it to reflect sound Liberal ideals and social policies, and he occasionally put pressure on journalists whose writings appeared to threaten his goals.[12]

The political world to which George Cadbury contributed his support was in transition. The Liberal and Conservative Parties, though still dominant, were divided into factions. In 1886, a significant number of party members left the Liberal Party when William Gladstone, its leader, came out in favor of home rule for Ireland. The Liberals who broke from the party, wishing to maintain the union of Britain and Ireland, included several of the old Whig aristocrats and some reform-minded members of Parliament (MPs); the most notable among them was Joseph Chamberlain, who was widely regarded as one of the most forceful and focused politicians in Britain. Chamberlain's power base was Birmingham, where he had gained financial success as a screw manufacturer and had served a very successful term as mayor. The breakaway group of Liberal Unionists joined with the Conservatives (often called the Tories) under Lord Salisbury as prime minister to form a government in 1895. This government, consisting of Conservatives and some Liberal Unionists—including Chamberlain, who served as colonial secretary, and the Duke of Devonshire—was often labeled Unionist. To make things even more confusing, Unionists were often called Conservatives or Tories. In 1903, Chamberlain called for tariff reform to strengthen Britain's economic base. He proposed that a tariff be levied on all goods entering Britain except for those originating in the empire, a system that would bind the colonies economically to Britain. Chamberlain's proposal split the Unionist Party between those who continued to adhere to the free trade doctrine and those who advocated a tariff. The Liberal Party was also divided between those who were enthusiasts for the empire (often called Liberal Imperialists) and those who promoted more social reform at home. There were also a reasonable number of Liberals who opposed war, among them George Cadbury. In general, it is fair to view Liberals in the early twentieth century as proponents of social justice, free trade, and responsible imperialism, whereas the Unionists, or Conservatives, stood for the preservation of civic institutions, the union of Britain and Ireland, and the extension of the empire. Joining this political menagerie were the Irish Nationalists, who called for home rule for Ireland, and, in 1900, the new Labour Party, which drew on support from labor union members and middle-class sympathizers. Liberals controlled governments from 1880 to 1886, 1892 to 1895, and 1905 to 1915, while the Conservatives held power from 1886 to 1892 and 1895 to 1905.

In early 1901, when William A. Cadbury (1867–1957) visited Trinidad, where the company owned a small cocoa-bean plantation, he was told that slave labor was used on the island of São Tomé.[13] Shortly thereafter, this unsubstantiated comment was given credence when the Cadbury company received an offer of a plantation for sale in São Tomé that listed as assets two hundred black laborers worth £3,555. The roça Traz-os-Montes, on the western border of the roça Água Izé, obtained these laborers "through contracts with the African chiefs in Angola at the rate of about £7. 4. 0 p. annum." The plantation used black laborers to work the soil, since they were "acclimated, and do much better service than might be expected from European labourers." They were fed primarily bananas and clothed at minimal cost, "and their treatment when ill is of slight importance." The Cadbury company, which had no interest in purchasing the roça, recorded in its board minutes of April 30, 1901: "This seems to confirm other indirect reports, that slavery, either total or partial, exists on these Cocoa estates. We agree to assist in the investigation, and if need be the publication of the facts of the case through the Anti-Slavery Society or otherwise, and W. A. C. [William A. Cadbury] is directed in the first place to see Joseph Sturge or William A. Albright and seek advice in the matter."[14] Sturge and Albright were Quakers who were active in antislavery circles. It was appropriate that the board assigned William Cadbury this task of investigating reports on the use of slaves on São Tomé cocoa plantations, as he was in charge of buying materials for the firm.[15]

William Adlington Cadbury was thirty-four years old when the company board requested that he inquire into labor on São Tomé's plantations. Educated at Friends' schools, he spent two years at J. J. Seekings's engineering shop in Gloucester and in 1886 followed that experience with eight months at the machine shop and drawing office of Stollwerck's chocolate company in Cologne, Germany. William Cadbury began working at Bournville in 1887. An engineer and a buyer of materials, he was regarded as thorough, serious, and stern, although he was also a "great romantic" who loved nature. He was good at simple sketches, in pen or pencil, of the sea and mountains and of plants and animals, the latter occasionally cartoonlike. He also enjoyed playing cricket and football.[16]

The Cadbury company had good reason to be troubled about labor conditions on the island of São Tomé. Management opposed the abuse of workers, yet in

1900, the firm had purchased over 45 percent of its cocoa beans from the island.[17] The company was concerned about its ignorance of conditions on São Tomé and Príncipe, and even before William Cadbury's 1901 trip to the West Indies, the firm had attempted to gain information about these Portuguese islands through the British consul for the area.[18] William Cadbury, following the information that the company received about the estate for sale, wrote as ordered to Joseph Sturge. He told Sturge that he hoped to gain more facts than those contained in the single bill of sale and admitted that one "looks at these matters in a different light when it affects one's own interests, but I do feel that there is a vast difference between the cultivation of cocoa and gold or diamond mining, and I should be sorry needlessly to injure a cultivation that as far as I can judge provides labour of the very best kind to be found in the tropics: at the same time we should all like to clear our hands of any responsibility for slave traffic in any form."[19] In a similar letter to William Albright, Cadbury stressed that he was reluctant to publish the bill of sale from the plantation "without any confirmation as to its details, as the wording of the paragraphs are not sufficiently clear to be taken as a statement of fact."[20] That he should find the bill of sale "not sufficiently clear" in regard to the laborers makes little sense, as the document specifically identified human beings as property.

Thus, in his initial letters concerning São Tomé's labor, William Cadbury demonstrated that while he was against the use of slave labor, he did not equate the labor of São Tomé to that of other forms of slavery reported in Africa. At the same time, he wanted to be absolutely fair to the responsible parties on the cocoa plantations and in Portugal. His attitude of fairness, combined with a minimizing of the serious nature of labor abuse on the islands, helps to explain why nearly eight years would pass before the Cadbury company took decisive action in this arena. Nevertheless, for much of that period William Cadbury's life was to be preoccupied with the issue of slavery, even to the point of providing a witness-stand defense of his company's honor.

William Albright was a member of the board of directors of the British and Foreign Anti-Slavery Society (hereafter referred to as the Anti-Slavery Society). On William Cadbury's request for advice, Albright turned to the society's secretary, Travers Buxton (1865–1945), for information about labor on São Tomé.[21] Buxton was a member of a family involved throughout much of the nineteenth century in the movement to emancipate slaves. Thomas Fowell Buxton had helped to establish the Anti-Slavery Society in 1839, and his grandson, Sir Thomas Fowell Buxton, a former MP and onetime governor of the colony of South Australia, was serving as president of the society in 1901.[22] Educated at Oxford University and trained as a barrister, Travers Buxton never practiced law but served on various humanitarian committees, becoming secretary of the Anti-Slavery Society in 1898. A proper Edwardian, he was "courtly and grave in manner" and carried himself with an air of "calm and dignity."[23]

William Cadbury and Travers Buxton corresponded regularly over the next few years about slave conditions in West Africa. Although there is no record of Buxton's immediate responses to Cadbury, he must have stressed that reports during the previous twenty years gave ample evidence of a dynamic West African slave trade to the São Tomé cocoa plantations. The Anti-Slavery Society received written reports from missionaries to Africa, who were mainly Protestants; these and other correspondence were often printed in the *Anti-Slavery Reporter*, and the scenes they depicted sound remarkably similar to those described later by Nevinson. For example, Sir Frederick Goldsmid reported that in 1883 he was on board a steamer from Luanda to São Tomé carrying about sixty men, women, and children who had been bought in Benguela for about £4 or £5. Each bore "a ticket tied round the neck," and all were landed at São Tomé and Príncipe. About the same time, the Earl of Mayo recounted witnessing eighty-two Africans taken to the islands under a contract that was "virtually Slavery." While generally "treated well," the laborers despaired the loss of their homeland, which they would never again see.[24] The explorer Henry Morton Stanley, who all too often brutally mistreated his own African porters, was especially critical of the Portuguese for practicing slavery in their colonies.[25] In 1891, Héli Chatelain, a missionary from Switzerland who spent considerable time in West Africa, described the slaves he saw transported from Angola to São Tomé: "Some of them looked healthy and strong; the majority showed signs of bad fare; some, again, were starved to skeletons, and had the ghastly, feverish, piercing, half insane look that is peculiar to their condition; the most of them had the hard, vacant, indifferent expression of men who know they are going to what they most dread, while they are ignorant of where and in what shape their sad destiny awaits them." In São Tomé, often regarded as a "paradise of Nature," slaves expressed to him one great wish—to return to their homelands.[26]

The *Anti-Slavery Reporter* of November 1900 carried the translation of an article that had appeared in the French paper *Le Signal*, in which a commercial traveler described the slave trade he observed in Angola: "All this [trade] is done with the protection of the Portuguese Government; the route passes by five Portuguese forts; the slaves are sold at Bihé. All the officials possess them. They also buy their concubines there."[27] The *Reporter* of January and February 1901, in addition to a description of "melancholy" slaves on the islands, printed several accounts of slaves marched from the interior of Angola; one writer noted: "I have never seen such slave gangs bound west as pass us day after day since crossing the Quanza, and the many dead and decomposing bodies by the roadside tell their sad tale—knocked on the head to end their misery, or hamstrung and left."[28] In 1902, a missionary wrote about his experience on board an Empresa Nacional steamer carrying some 400 serviçais to São Tomé. The ship's doctor told him that the shipping line carried about 250 serviçais on each ship, for a total of approximately 6,000 per year. "He and others," the missionary noted, "said the death rate on the Island of San Thomé is very high indeed, but causes no compunction to the planters, since the supply is, for some years at least, at the present rate, almost unlimited."[29]

Given this extensive evidence, it is surprising that the Cadburys had not recognized this slavery early on, especially since several of their Quaker friends were active in humanitarian organizations—and Quakers, when gathered together, normally engaged in discussions related to the plight of people both at home and abroad. Indeed, George Cadbury, the chairman of the company, became a member of the Anti-Slavery Society no later than 1893, and from 1900 to 1908, he contributed the sum of £5 10s. annually, while Barrow and William Cadbury gave lesser amounts.[30] Certainly, George Cadbury would have received the *Anti-Slavery Reporter* during that period.

A second organization, the Aborigines' Protection Society (APS), of which George Cadbury was also a member from 1900 to 1908, worked to protect natives in various parts of the world, especially in areas associated with the British Empire. This society was formed in 1837, a spin-off of the British government's Select Committee on Aborigines, which had been appointed to report on native peoples in the empire and to provide them with protection. Several charter members of the Aborigines' Protection Society had served on the Select Committee, including Thomas Fowell Buxton, who was chair of the committee and later president of the APS. In 1901, this society was headed by Henry Richard Fox Bourne (1837–1909), who had served in the War Office in the 1850s and 1860s and then edited the *Examiner* (London) and the *Weekly Dispatch*. A prolific writer, his books included *Memoir of Sir Philip Sidney*, *English Seamen under the Tudors*, *A Life of John Locke*, and *Foreign Rivalries in Industrial Products*. A Liberal, he became secretary of the Aborigines' Protection Society in 1889. Fox Bourne was a stubborn, pugnacious, and single-minded man who devoted himself to helping the oppressed. Businesspeople and governmental officials feared but usually respected him for his uncompromising attitude.[31]

The Aborigines' Protection Society and the Anti-Slavery Society shared several members in common on their committees.[32] Fox Bourne and Buxton frequently wrote to one another and corresponded with the firm of Cadbury as well as with the Portuguese and British governments regarding the use of slave labor in Portuguese West Africa. In late December 1902, Buxton asked the Portuguese legation in London about reports that the Anti-Slavery Society had received in regard to the slave trade and slavery in Angola and the islands. In February 1903, a Portuguese minister responded, indicating that both old and recent Portuguese decrees made certain that there was no slavery and that the "facts" included in the society's letter were without foundation. Vigilant action by officials in West Africa, he said, ensured that "Portugal may justly boast of having completely suppressed the wicked traffic which nowadays only has an existence in the imagination of certain philanthropists."[33]

It appears that throughout 1901 and 1902, William Cadbury concentrated only on gathering information and was reluctant to become actively involved in the inquiry. As he wrote to Buxton in June 1902 about accounts of the Angola slave trade, "I do not feel myself called upon to take any initial step in the matter, though I am willing to help in any organised plan that your Society may suggest for the definite purpose of putting a stop to the slave trade of this district."[34] Finally, Cadbury arranged a visit to Lisbon in March 1903, hoping thereby to be "able to do something in the matter with the authorities in Portugal" or "at least be able to inform myself a little more fully of the existing circumstances."[35] Cadbury was accompanied on his trip to Lisbon by Matthew Stober, a Scottish missionary to central Angola for the Angola Evangelical Mission. Stober had made contact with the Anti-Slavery Society in 1902, expressing his horror over the slave trade in that Portuguese colony.[36] William Cadbury met Stober in February 1902, and Cadbury's three-page, typed summary of the conversation reveals that the missionary provided a devastating review of the slavery in Angola and on the islands, where "the estimated life is 3½ or 4 years" because the workers died as a result of "the system" and not the climate.[37] At that same time, William Cadbury wrote to Joseph Fry, head of the Fry chocolate firm in Bristol, recounting for him the disturbing facts about labor conditions in São Tomé, informing him of the pending trip to Lisbon, and requesting that Fry and his company "support us in our endeavors to bring these matters before the [Portuguese] authorities." He ended the long letter on a hopeful note: "We are informed, we believe with some authority, that the Portuguese have a considerable respect for the modes of British Colonial administration, and that British influence is likely to have more weight than any other." He also indicated to Fry that his uncle, George Cadbury, promised to use his influence with the *Daily News* to publish "some of the facts of the [São Tomé] case," if that were necessary.[38]

Cadbury did not speak Portuguese, so Matthew Stober was to aid in interviewing parties in Lisbon. Stober also had a number of contacts there who were knowledgeable about Portuguese colonial affairs.[39] Together, the two men interviewed several São Tomé cocoa plantation owners who resided in Lisbon and also Gen. Manuel Gorjão, minister of marine and colonies. They were told by some that the new labor decree issued on January 29, 1903, would secure the end of labor abuses in São Tomé. These new regulations required that laborers be paid a minimum wage, 40 percent of which would be placed in a repatriation fund. The regulations also furnished protection against illegal labor recruitment. The planter Francisco Mantero, who claimed to have helped bring about the new regulations, insisted that the treatment of the laborers on the island was proper and that problems of any kind were caused by wasteful and dissolute natives. He admitted, however, that the conditions in Angola might be bad. One person interviewed, a colonial bank manager, resented the fact that Britain dared to question Portugal on its labor conditions—after all, he maintained, Britain harbored the likes of people such as Joseph Chamberlain, the Unionist colonial secretary from 1895 to 1903 who had supported aggressive British expansion in Africa, and Cecil Rhodes, the imperialist who had reportedly condoned the abuse of natives. Cadbury also learned that any child born on a plantation became the property of the owner and thus effectively a slave.[40]

A priest named Father Rooney, who served a Roman Catholic mission with stations in Angola and São Tomé, had visited the island for about a year. Rooney talked of "the most wretched state of the natives arriving in the islands . . . how at times they all conspire not to eat and that not infrequently suicide occurs." He did not expect that the new regulations would control the slave dealers in Angola, and according to Cadbury, his parting words were, "'If Thomé were at the bottom of the sea, the slavery question would be settled in Angola for ever.'"[41] Cadbury met A. G. Ceffala, manager of the Eastern Telegraph Company's station in São Tomé, who told stories of the condition of laborers and agreed to write Cadbury occasionally with more specific examples.[42]

Stober and Cadbury also talked to Sir Martin Gosselin, the British minister to Lisbon. Gosselin, a Roman Catholic who had served as British representative to the Brussels Slave Trade Conference between 1889 and 1890 and had been head of the African department at the Foreign Office, proved exceptionally knowledgeable on Portuguese labor practices. Gosselin, too, lacked faith in the new labor regulations and viewed the São Tomé situation as "the same as any slavery of past days"; he thought that the greatest cruelty occurred in Angola, where "petty kings treated the people as cattle and for liquor or money will readily trade their own people."[43] While denigrating the new regulations, Gosselin nevertheless encouraged Cadbury to give the Portuguese government a year to see if improvements in laboring conditions occurred before sending out an agent.[44] Unbeknown to William Cadbury, the British government was at that moment attempting to facilitate the recruitment of native labor in Portuguese Africa for the mines in South Africa. Having no desire to alienate the Portuguese in the midst of these delicate negotiations, the British Foreign Office was probably pressuring Gosselin to avoid any immediate confrontation with Portugal over labor problems in São Tomé.[45]

William Cadbury heard a great deal of testimony in Lisbon, most of which graphically confirmed earlier reports of an extensive and brutal slave trade in Angola and the regular use of slave labor on the cocoa plantations of São Tomé and Príncipe. He claimed to be surprised to learn that English firms purchased a significant percentage of the cocoa beans produced on the islands (Cadbury alone purchased almost 20 percent of the island's cocoa in 1902), with lesser amounts going to the United States and to Europe.[46] He told Gosselin that the two firms of Cadbury and Fry would look elsewhere for their beans should labor conditions not improve. In Gosselin's words, Cadbury stated that "this might mean paying a somewhat higher price at first; but they were ready to make this sacrifice, if by so doing they could put a stop to a disguised slave Trade."[47] Yet when William Cadbury reported to the company on March 20, 1903, he was markedly upbeat: "We have been most favoured and I cannot but feel that the things are going to mend a little—much will depend on how strenuously it is followed up, and the onus of this will lie on the British—perhaps most of all on our two firms."[48] Four days later, he wrote, "I believe no good would come just now of making further complaint . . . General Gorjão [minister of marine and colonies] will help us if any Portuguese can and I hope he may be in office long enough for his work to tell."[49]

What accounted for William Cadbury's optimism? As we have seen, he was predisposed to the idea that this form of slavery was not as evil as the slavery found elsewhere in Africa. He hoped, in spite of many warnings to the contrary, that the new labor regulations would safeguard the laborers; he obviously wanted to believe that the Portuguese government officials were sincere in their promise to enforce the new rules. Cadbury had found the Portuguese to be exceptionally polite, although in his communications with them he was always dependent on his interpreter. Perhaps he was impressed by the planter Francisco Mantero's invitation to send a Cadbury representative to São Tomé to witness firsthand the proper treatment of labor.[50] Coincidentally, on March 16, 1903, the *Morning Leader* (London) reported that some Portuguese army officers and merchants had been sentenced to transportation (deportation to a penal colony) for several years "for causing the recent revolt in Loanda, in Portuguese Africa, by slave trading and cruelties to natives."[51] The Cadbury board of management followed William Cadbury's recommendation; at the board's April 7 meeting, the company agreed not to publicize the details of Portugal's past abuses, since authorities were implementing new regulations of January 1903 that were "modelled on British lines." William Cadbury was to contact the Fry company and the Anti-Slavery Society and to "bring up the subject again in this meeting when he thinks fit."[52]

As a result of William Cadbury's trip to Lisbon and the planters' invitation for representatives of the chocolate firms to visit the islands to evaluate for themselves the conditions of the laborers, Cadbury directors decided to appoint an agent to journey to Portuguese West Africa. The agent, they surmised, might be able to measure the effectiveness of the "recently introduced regulations which are a considerable improvement on any in the past."[53] Joined by Fry of Bristol, Cadbury Bros. asked the Aborigines' Protection Society and the Anti-Slavery Society to recommend someone who could serve the companies in that capacity.[54] For the next several months, the humanitarian societies and the firm of Cadbury used their extensive contacts in the social, governmental, and business worlds to identify possible candidates. Early on, the company insisted that the person be fluent in Portuguese; Gosselin had advised William Cadbury on June 18, 1903, that "the person sent out should have a knowledge of Portuguese, so as to render him independent of an interpreter."[55] In July 1903, Cadbury's board agreed that the firm would pay an agent £1,000 for a year's service, although one year later, the directors voted to compensate the agent privately out of their personal funds.[56]

It quickly became apparent, however, that it might be difficult to find a person qualified to go to Africa on this mission. In July 1903, Fox Bourne reported that one of the officials in the Foreign Office had told him even they had been unable to find a "competent person" to send out as a vice-consul.[57] Logically, Cadbury Bros. might have turned to Matthew Stober. He spoke Portuguese and at least some native languages of Angola, and he was certainly a knowledgeable individual. But Stober may have been too outspoken in his criticism of Portuguese practices for William Cadbury's taste.[58] Fox Bourne recommended a delay. He had talked to Arthur Nightingale (1859–1926), British consul in Luanda, who was under orders by the Foreign Office to visit São Tomé on his return trip to Angola and to investigate conditions on the islands. Nightingale hoped that no other inquiry would occur until after he issued his report. Moreover, Fox Bourne reported that Nightingale thought little of value would come out of a private visit, as the agent "would probably fall ill before he could see or do anything of importance" and would need to know Portuguese and native languages. Nightingale also believed that the planters, "if only in their own interests," attempted to treat the slaves "humanely" and argued "that the real curse is the importation which now goes on and which the new regulations will do little to improve." Nightingale thought that the core of the problem, which the British should address, was the brutal slave trade on the continent. Fox Bourne added that since Nightingale "approves of 'forced labour' within what he considers reasonable limits," his opinions were even more credible. He then recommended that the firms wait for the publication of Nightingale's account before dispatching an agent, "meanwhile putting all the pressure we can upon the Government to use its utmost influence in securing reforms in Angola itself."[59]

Arthur Nightingale knew well the treatment of labor in the Portuguese colonies. As consul, he had recently issued a report emphasizing the large numbers of slaves in the islands and the exceptionally high death rate among them, especially in Príncipe.[60] Before becoming a consul, he had managed a plantation of about five hundred laborers near Luanda and had gained a reputation for cruelty in his treatment of the natives.[61] Nevinson met Nightingale while in West Africa, and he indicated that the consul's vivid description of the slave system continuing in Angola led Nevinson to trek into the interior of Angola rather than journeying into the Congo.[62]

William Cadbury reported to Martin Gosselin in September 1903 that the firms of Cadbury and Fry had postponed sending out an agent; they had not found anyone suitable, and their "friends in London" had recommended that the companies delay sending an emissary until receiving a report from Nightingale.[63] Meanwhile, disturbing news continued to pour in. Ceffala, the chief of the Eastern Telegraph Company office in São Tomé whom Cadbury had met in Lisbon, wrote several letters stressing the high mortality rate of the laborers and the total absence of repatriation.[64] Gosselin told William Cadbury in 1904 that no repatriation of serviçais had occurred before 1903 and that the new 1903 regulations would not be effectively applied until at least 1908, due to the five-year span of labor contracts.[65] A close friend in Lisbon wrote Cadbury in July 1904 that the frequent personnel changes in the Portuguese government meant that enforcement of the 1903 labor regulations was improbable.[66] Cadbury Bros. and the humanitarian societies had hoped there would be a British consul for the islands to help enforce those regulations, but the British government did not appoint one.[67] The Cadbury firm also knew by May 1904 that the British Foreign Office had not sent Nightingale to the islands after all but directly to Boma, the capital of Leopold II's Congo, to replace Consul Roger Casement, who returned to Britain to report on the treatment of natives in the Upper Congo.[68] Arguably, the Foreign Office never intended to send Nightingale but was instead stalling to avoid antagonizing the Portuguese.[69] Indeed, in October 1904, when Fox Bourne pressed the Foreign Office on the importance of a visit to São Tomé, the official "made light of the question and gave me to understand that, in its present mood, the Foreign Office will take no more trouble in the matter than it can help."[70] The response was a portent of the Foreign Office attitude for the next several years.

In spite of all this uncertainty and conflicting opinion, Cadbury Bros. remained interested in sending an agent to the islands. William Cadbury grew restless over the lack of action in the Portuguese colonies. In March 1904, he reminded Martin Gosselin that the latter had encouraged the company to give Portugal time to implement the labor laws of January 1903; he noted, "This we have done, and there is no apparent result."[71] The firms of Cadbury and Fry agreed that an agent should be sent out under the auspices of the chocolate firms, as they had received "a distinct invitation to come over and see for ourselves what are the facts in the case." A commissioner representing the companies, William Cadbury suggested, would be more acceptable than one sent by the Anti-Slavery Society, as some had suggested, which "would be received with great suspicion and probably opposition in the islands."[72] Fry strongly urged that Rowntree of York and Stollwerck of Cologne (longtime business friends of the Cadburys)as well as Walter Baker of Boston, by far the largest chocolate firm in the United States, be invited to join in sending an agent.[73] On October 22, 1904, Cadbury Bros. sent a letter to several chocolate firms, explaining the perceived problems of labor on the cocoa plantations and reviewing the firm's actions on the issue over the previous two years. The Cadbury company requested support for sending out an investigator and asked for recommendations.[74] Rowntree endorsed taking steps to improve the lives of the serviçais but also perceptively noted difficulties that the chocolate firms could face in setting up an inquiry. Should the companies undertake a study and find that slavery existed, they would have to either request that the British government put pressure on Portugal or call for a boycott of the slave-produced cocoa beans. Rowntree disliked the idea of one government interfering in the affairs of another; besides, the British government itself had been guilty of tolerating the abuse of laborers in its own South African colony. At the same time, however, for the British Quaker-owned companies to engage in a successful boycott would be very difficult, for it would mean convincing enough other chocolate firms to stop the purchase of São Tomé cocoa so as to drive down significantly the price of the island's beans. A boycott by the chocolate companies would also mean "a very serious pecuniary loss to those manufacturers who entered upon it." Instead, Rowntree recommended that the study be carried out by either of the two humanitarian societies, since their contacts with the press and their respect in society would make their report more effective than one coming from the chocolate companies themselves.[75]

For the next six years, the major British chocolate firms, most notably Cadbury Bros., would be faced with the very problems that Rowntree so carefully outlined. Fry, responding to Rowntree's lengthy letter, stressed that possible financial loss should not deter action by the companies, for that would mean "countenancing a great wrong."[76] While the Cadbury firm gained the support of Fry, Rowntree, and Stollwerck for sending out an agent, Baker, although "heartily in sympathy with any efforts," declined to participate and stressed that chocolate firms in the United States had imported only 4 percent of São Tomé's production in 1901.[77]

As Cadbury Bros. negotiated with other firms about sending an agent to Africa, Henry Nevinson, in September and October 1904, entertained and accepted a £1,000 offer from the American magazine *Harper's* to undertake and write articles about an "adventurous journey." After considering various possibilities, he hit on slave trade in Portuguese West Africa and, in preparation for the sojourn, consulted several people, including Fox Bourne and Buxton.[78]

Nevinson was born in Leicester, England, in 1856. His parents were devoted members of a puritanical and evangelical branch of the Church of England. When Nevinson became an adult, however, he was a skeptic who looked askance at any Christian church. His reading material at home had been severely restricted, but his horizons broadened at Shrewsbury School, and he immersed himself in classical Greek, while also learning Latin and rudimentary French. Following four years at Christ Church College, Oxford, he studied German literature at Jena University. After returning to England from Germany, he settled in London's East End and served at Toynbee Hall, Samuel Barnett's settlement for the working class. During the 1880s and 1890s, Nevinson founded and commanded a cadet corps for working-class boys and belonged, for a few years, to H. M. Hyndman's Social Democratic Federation. Married and with a family, he taught history and literature at various schools and dabbled in journalism. His *Life of Friedrich Schiller* was published in 1889, and a well-received volume entitled *Neighbours of Ours*, about members of the tough but respectable East End working class, came out in 1895. That work was followed a year later by *In the Valley of Tophet*, a series of sketches of life in the Black Country, the manufacturing area around Birmingham. An avid bicyclist and hiker, Nevinson often walked through the night in the countryside. He visited Greece for the first time in 1894, and in 1897, he accepted an assignment from Henry W. Massingham, editor of the *Daily Chronicle*, to report on the Greek revolution against the Turks on the island of Crete, where he found himself in some physical danger. The following year, Nevinson covered the Spanish-American War from Madrid, and in 1899 and 1900, he reported on the South African War from the besieged town of Ladysmith, Natal. He became literary editor of the *Daily Chronicle* in 1899, a position he held, while undertaking other assignments, until 1903.

Nevinson left the *Daily Chronicle* in late 1903 to join a group examining conditions in Macedonia. On his return from Greece in 1904, he helped to raise money in England for the Macedonian Relief Fund. His volume of short stories, *Between the Acts*, appeared in 1904. These stories were applauded by *Harper's*, and as a result, the owner and the editor of that American journal asked him to write a series of articles.[79] Thus, by 1904, the forty-eight-year-old Nevinson was a recognized journalist and writer who respected the working poor and identified with the oppressed in their struggles against tyrants.

Travers Buxton told Nevinson about the Cadbury company's interest in sending a representative to Portuguese West Africa. In October, Nevinson wrote William Cadbury that he was leaving soon for Angola, São Tomé, and Príncipe and that he was working for *Harper's*. He indicated he wished to meet with Cadbury and noted, "[I] should be very pleased if I could be of any assistance to you, & also if you could give me one or two introductions to planters."[80] After seeing Nevinson on October 20, 1904, Cadbury reported to Buxton that the journalist "seemed just a little disappointed that we were not off-hand willing to accept him as our own commissioner, but I cannot see how we could do this, seeing that he knows no word of Portuguese, and is not prepared to stop more than 6 months in Africa altogether."[81] Cadbury mailed Nevinson a copy of the Portuguese labor regulations and a letter of introduction to Ceffala, the Eastern Telegraph manager on São Tomé.[82]

By the time of his interview with Nevinson, William Cadbury had tentatively decided to hire Joseph Burtt as the company's agent to the colonies.[83] Burtt, a handsome forty-one-year-old, was born in Kettering, in England, worked at a bank during his late teens, and helped to establish a commune in Gloucestershire in the late 1890s, where he lived in "poverty and joy" for a year. He also helped to care for his invalid father, built a house, and laid out a garden.[84] He applied for an assistant secretary position in the Anti-Slavery Society in 1903 but withdrew his application, even though he appeared certain to get the post, because he regarded London life as "not only foolish, but positively wrong." Travers Buxton had looked forward to working with him but understood that Burtt's "hyper-conscientious" reasons for withdrawing would have to be accepted.[85] While Buxton told Burtt of the Cadbury firm's interest in sending a commissioner to Africa, there is no record indicating that Buxton ever recommended him as a candidate.[86] Writing in 1949, William Cadbury referred to Burtt as a Quaker and "an intimate friend for many years and welcome in any company for his good humour and charming personality—with a passion for justice to the oppressed." Cadbury added that the "San Thome crusade appealed to him," and since Burtt was a bachelor, he readily agreed to spend time with a family in Oporto to learn Portuguese and to undertake the lengthy journey to Africa.[87] Under the terms of the agreement, Burtt, who had already spent three and a half months in Portugal, would return for an additional three months to ensure that he was fluent in Portuguese. Before leaving on the mission, he would return to England to visit his ill mother. He would take with him to Portugal and its colonies a letter of introduction from the four chocolate firms. Contrary to Rowntree's opinion, William Cadbury insisted that an agent sent by the companies was preferable to one dispatched by the humanitarian societies, who would be suspected by the planters as a "spy": Burtt would go as "the friend of the planters" and "be perfectly unprejudiced on one side or the other." Cadbury hoped that neither of the two humanitarian societies would publicize Burtt's visit, as it "might seriously prejudice the planters to him, and lessen the value of his visit."[88]

At least two people reminded William Cadbury that Burtt's task was exceptionally demanding. Baron Carl de Merck, a Bavarian nobleman living in Lisbon and a good friend of Cadbury's, was a cocoa-bean and rubber trader for Henry Burnay & Co. in the Portuguese capital.[89] Merck enjoyed meeting Burtt but questioned whether he was confident enough "in his own judgment" and "a practical man." Merck found him too indecisive and insufficiently fluent in Portuguese.

The emotional trader liked Burtt and considered him to be a "thoroughly nice gentlemanly fellow, even quite sweet as the Americans may say" but doubted that he was "strong enough."[90] Cadbury assured Merck that Burtt had the companies' confidence. Burtt's disinterestedness in the chocolate business made it certain that his judgments would be unbiased; moreover, he got along very well with the Portuguese, whom he had found very friendly. Cadbury also stressed how difficult it had been to find someone qualified who could commit himself for a year or more to such an endeavor. Burtt had long been studying social issues in England, and "he will look upon African questions with as fair a mind as any man whom I know," Cadbury wrote.[91] Meanwhile, the ever wary Fox Bourne warned William Cadbury that Burtt "will need to be constantly on his guard against the too roseate information the Portuguese planters may be apt to give him."[92] Cadbury told Fox Bourne that he expected Burtt to find the conditions of the workers on some plantations "as satisfactory a nature as in many of our own colonies" but that his main quest would be to determine if they were slaves. Cadbury believed the allegations that no serviçal had ever been repatriated, but that fact needed to be confirmed.[93]

William Cadbury's perspective on Burtt's mission was peculiar. On the one hand, Cadbury represented a company that prided itself on its concern for its

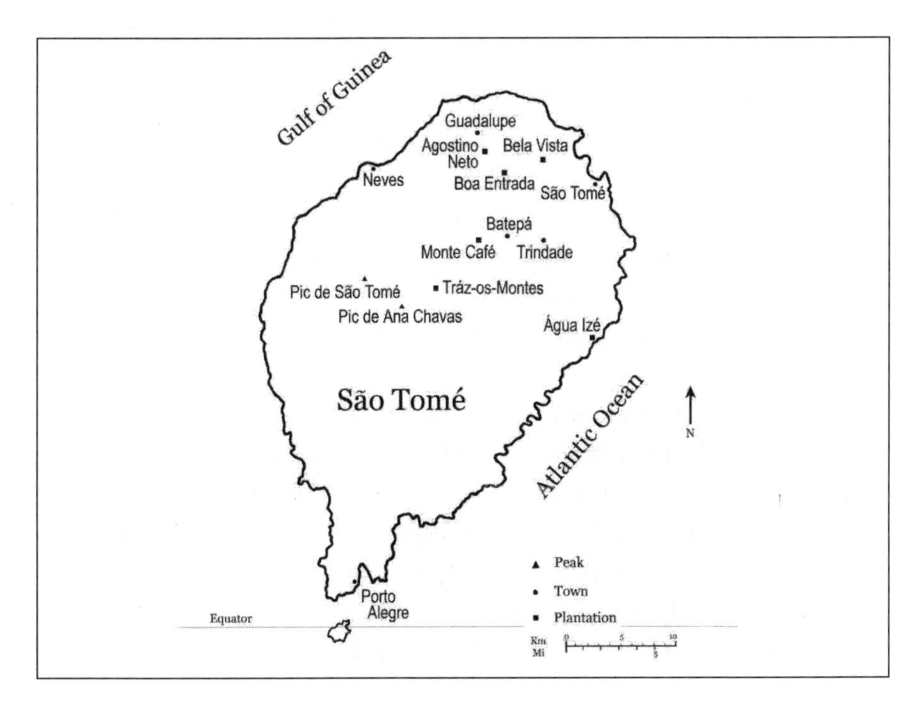

Map 2. São Tomé. Map by Lowell and Ellen Satre.

workers. It had built a modern factory, had helped to finance the construction of a model village, and was associated with the Quakers, who long enjoyed the reputation of being in the forefront of humanitarian responsibilities. But on the other hand, four years had passed since early 1901, when Cadbury first heard rumors of the use of slave labor on the islands. Virtually all reliable information he had accumulated during that period pointed to a brutal trade in humans in Angola and a captive labor force on the islands, where workers died in great numbers and those who survived were never free to leave. In spite of this, Cadbury wanted his agent to go out as a "friend" of the planters and to take his time.

Burtt left Lisbon for Africa on June 1, 1905, arriving at São Tomé on June 13. He remained on that island and on Príncipe for almost six months, making Ceffala's cable station his headquarters.[94] He met Henry Nevinson, who was near the end of his own trip, on June 18. In his diary, Nevinson described Burtt as "an innocent man with much luggage. Heard fr[om] Hart that the planters had ordered everything to be carefully arranged for his visits."[95] After walking with Burtt to a fishing village a few days later, Nevinson concluded that he was a man still searching for meaning in life and quite impressionable. Burtt was, he surmised,

> about the youngest man of 43 that could live—the mind of a youth, confused & interesting & full of dreams & theories. Has been at a Communist [communalist] settlement in Gloucestersh[ire] but now is in a state of reaction, despising the working man & reverencing the working capitalist. Supports the slave system as good for Africans & thinks Portugal is doing very good work here. Thinks the plantations greatly increase human happiness & so on. All very crude & youthful stuff, full of contradictions & very astonishing. Longs for "life," & hankers much after literature. I warned him of Benguella & then was rather sorry, for he is full of fears, wh[ich] he bravely admits.[96]

Three days later, the two men visited Boa Entrada, a model plantation whose doctor "admitted a deathrate of over 12% among the adults."[97] The following day, Nevinson left São Tomé, arriving in England on July 21, 1905, after a stop in Lisbon. His articles on the slave trade began appearing in *Harper's* the following month. Burtt would spend the next two years traveling, not returning to England until April 13, 1907. His report would not be made available to the British public until October 1908, over seven years after the Cadbury firm first heard about slave labor on these islands.

3 Portugal and West Africa

> My opinion is that taking it all round, the serviçaes are well treated and cared for, that they are not unhappy, and that there is no hardship in the way they are worked.
>
> It must be remembered that they are drawn from some of the lowest types of humanity, and have none of the instincts of Civilisation; and that morally they are improved rather than deteriorated by their more regular life and work.
>
> *W. S. R. Brock, vice-consul, 1894*

> The *serviçaes* are not allowed to quit the limits of the plantations; they have no change of scene; no change of duty; no change of food; no remission of their wearisome routine save that brought by sickness or death. What the fathers and mothers are doing today the children know they, too, will be doing in the same spot, in the same way and under the same compulsion if they live to become fathers and mothers themselves.
>
> *Roger Casement, consul, 1902*

SÃO TOMÉ'S EARLY history is a chronicle of violence of exploitation, rebellions, and raids. Portugal laid claim to an uninhabited São Tomé in the 1470s, and a substantial population quickly developed on the island. São Tomé soon became a shipping depot for slaves procured from the nearby African continent, and some of these slaves remained on the island. In 1492, Spain drove out its Jews, many of whom fled to Portugal, where some were enslaved. Children of the enslaved Jews were seized and shipped to São Tomé in 1493; their descendants seem to have survived into the sixteenth century. Portugal also sent many of its convicts to São Tomé. A free black population emerged, as some of the slaves or their offspring were freed.[1] By the 1490s, slaves from Benin grew sugarcane on the island, and by 1518, São Tomé had five thousand to six thousand slaves working some sixty sugar mills.[2] By the middle of the sixteenth century, the island's European and mulatto planters led the world in the output of sugar. The production declined, however, because of competition from the New World, specifically Portuguese Brazil, whose sugar was of a superior quality. The island also experienced a series of destructive raids on plantations and the town by escaped slaves and by French and Dutch forces.[3] From 1580 to 1640, Portugal and its empire was under the control of Spain. In 1641, the Dutch, who attacked many Portuguese colonies in the seventeenth century, seized control of the island for three years.[4] In the early history of São Tomé, the Portuguese apparently accepted blacks and mulattoes, permitting and even encouraging sexual relations between blacks and whites. In contrast, the Portuguese of Angola held an extremely negative view of Africans and governed by force.[5]

Portugal controlled Angola from the fifteenth century, primarily through *degredados* (exiled convicts), who served as soldiers, slave traders, merchants, and government officials. Commanding labor resources determined economic success in the area. Human beings, not animals, transported goods, and masters and merchants hired or enslaved porters. This use of labor was not so much developed by the Portuguese as inherited from the Africans. Meanwhile, terribly high death rates among whites discouraged the migration of free settlers. Effective occupation of Angola was slight, and the few Europeans in the colony were concentrated in Luanda. With liquor as currency, slaves were sold and shipped out through the small port towns of Luanda and Benguela. The Portuguese in Angola became "Merchants of Death" as the eighteenth-century capitalist economy "freed individuals to pursue private material gain without formal regard for the lives and welfare of others."[6] All told, sparsely populated Angola exported at least three million slaves to the Americas from the 1500s to the 1800s.[7]

Although São Tomé served as an important depot for the slave trade to the Americas until the 1840s, the island fell into disrepair and suffered a marked depopulation after the late sixteenth century. In 1844, the islands of São Tomé and Príncipe together had slightly over 12,000 people, 185 of whom were white.[8]

Portugal's empire in the eighteenth century focused on Brazil. Trade with its huge South American colony and Great Britain brought a measure of prosperity to Portugal, including a nascent industrial base. While Portugal lost control over Brazil in the 1820s, it continued to maintain close trade relations with the new nation. At the same time, Portugal attempted to develop its domestic resources and its remaining colonies, primarily those in Africa. By the 1850s, a liberal bourgeois government triumphed over the old feudal landholding class in Portugal, and commerce expanded, especially with Great Britain. Portugal opened its ports to most nations, but the government retained control over shipping between the colonies and the home country. Many national leaders also looked to the central portions of Angola and Mozambique in southern Africa as a means to strengthen the material and political resources of the state.[9]

Portuguese imperial fortunes in Africa were closely tied to those of other European countries, especially Great Britain. Europeans had traded in sub-Saharan Africa since the fifteenth century, but their landholdings were minimal. Well into the nineteenth century, most European colonies, with the exception of those of the British in southern Africa, were confined to coastal regions or enclaves. European trade with the interior was normally conducted through African intermediaries, as Europeans found themselves far too susceptible to deadly diseases and unable to dislodge powerful tribes. The Europeans knew little of the continent's remote areas. During the course of the nineteenth century, however, a series of technological changes made it possible for them to gain entrance into the hinterland and to acquire control of territory at a relatively low cost in lives and money. Well-publicized activities of explorers such as John Speke and Richard Burton as well as the missionary-explorer David Livingstone spurred interest in Africa. Europe's technological and industrial expertise produced weapons, particularly quick-firing rifles, that gave Europeans a marked military superiority, steamboats that facilitated access to the interior, and quinine that protected Europeans against the worst ravages of malaria.[10] Explorers and Christian missionaries stimulated European interest in Africa in the mid-1800s, but by the last quarter of the century, the greatest impetus for Western incursion into Africa was economic. Industrializing nations cast covetous eyes on the huge continent, looking for raw materials for their industries, foodstuffs for their growing populations, and markets for their manufactured wares. Nevertheless, cost-conscious European political leaders and businesspeople would gladly have exploited the continent's resources without the added financial burden of governing.

The scramble for African land by Europeans from the 1880s until World War I was stimulated by Britain's entrance into Egypt and by King Leopold II's hunger for overseas territory. As sovereign of the relatively new nation of Belgium, Leopold wished to gain prestige for himself and his small country by joining the ranks of the imperialists. By the 1870s, under the aegis of his own African International Association, Leopold began eyeing the huge Congo basin. In the early 1880s, Leopold's agents and an official representing France raced to explore and claim regions of the Congo. Germany, which hitherto had held no territory overseas, was next to enter the colonial race, gobbling up four territories, including South-West Africa, in the early 1880s. Encouraged by the land claims of Leopold and Germany's Otto von Bismarck, other European nations quickly followed suit. Thus, by the 1880s, five European nations were involved in the race to gain colonies in the African subcontinent: France, Britain, and Portugal, all of which had long held scattered territories, were joined by the colonial newcomers Germany and Belgium. Citing economic and security needs and national pride, Europe effectively divided up the entire African continent by 1912, with only Liberia and Ethiopia remaining independent of European control.[11]

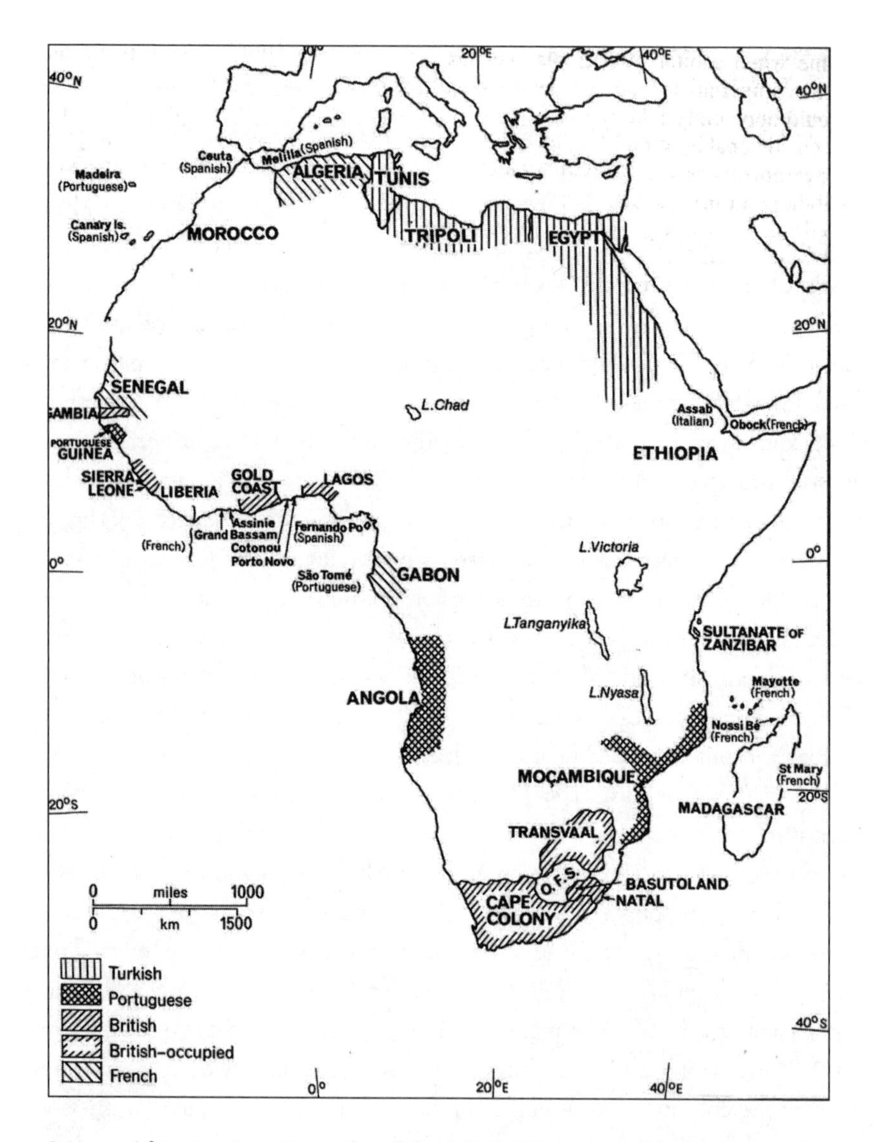

Map 3. Africa in 1879. Reproduced from Peter Duignan and L. H. Gann, eds., *Colonialism in Africa 1870–1960*, vol. 4 (Cambridge: Cambridge University Press, 1975). Reprinted with the permission of Cambridge University Press and consent of Peter Duignan.

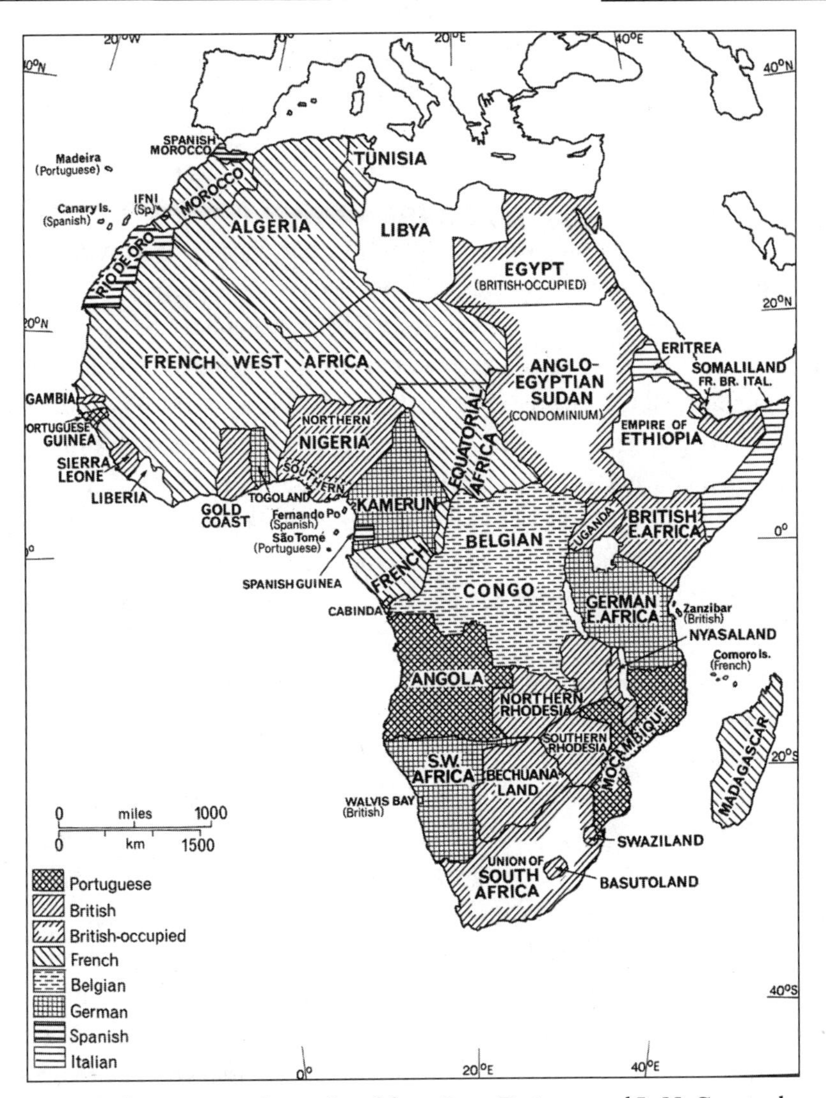

Map 4. Africa in 1914. Reproduced from Peter Duignan and L. H. Gann, eds., *Colonialism in Africa 1870–1960*, vol. 4 (Cambridge: Cambridge University Press, 1975). Reprinted with the permission of Cambridge University Press and consent of Peter Duignan.

England had maintained close ties with Portugal since the fourteenth century, entering into an alliance in 1373, when the Portuguese monarch was involved in a dynastic dispute with the Spanish principality of Castile. English forces aided Portugal against Castile in the 1380s, culminating in the Treaty of Windsor of 1386.[12] While relations between the two countries were often stormy, the alliance, frequently revived and often altered, persisted into the twentieth century.[13] King Charles II of England married Catherine of Braganza in 1663, and as part of the alliance, he supplied soldiers to help defend Portugal against Spain. The Methuen Treaty, a commercial agreement in 1703, cemented these ties and proved beneficial to both Portugal and England. Portuguese wines gained a privileged position in England, and the latter's woolen textiles captured the market in Portugal. As the weaker of the two parties, Portugal often was dragged into conflicts as an ally of Britain, as happened in the wars against France during the revolutionary and Napoleonic eras. At the conclusion of the Napoleonic Wars, Britain forced Portugal to abandon slave trading north of the equator. Britain frequently interfered in Portuguese dynastic politics during the first half of the nineteenth century, and it facilitated Brazil's peaceful break from Portugal, thereby gaining economic influence in the South American nation.[14]

London also freely intervened in the development of Portugal's other colonies when it would be to Britain's advantage. Lack of its own monetary resources forced Lisbon to cooperate with the British in the economic development of Portuguese enclaves in India. Britain looked unfavorably at Portugal's quest to expand its control in southern Africa and specifically refused the Portuguese claim of control over the estuary of the Congo River in the 1850s and 1860s. Arbitration with Britain, however, awarded Portugal control over Delagoa Bay in Mozambique, and in 1884, Britain negotiated a treaty that recognized Portugal's control over the Congo and its interior while providing Britain trading access to the Congo and Zambezi Rivers. This treaty, which represented an attempt by Britain to utilize its ascendancy over a weak Portugal and thereby forestall the entrance of more powerful European nations (especially France) into the Congo region, was never ratified. Objections by British merchants who feared Portugal's inability to administer the mouth of the Congo, by humanitarians who were appalled by Portuguese abuse of native laborers, and by other European powers forced London to abandon the agreement. In 1884, Bismarck summoned European nations to a conference in Berlin to lay out some of the rules for colonial expansion, thus setting off the scramble for Africa. The conference prohibited the export of slaves from the Congo basin and called on Europeans to civilize the natives. Also, France, Portugal, and especially the king of Belgium's private African company acquired control over most of the Congo basin.[15]

Portugal began to expand its empire in the late nineteenth century, largely for economic reasons. The Europe-wide depression that began in the 1870s and lasted for some two decades caused a decline in prices, a reduction in profits, and much greater international competition in agricultural and industrial goods. Portugal was hit particularly hard by this depression and turned to its colonies in Africa for economic salvation, as did many European nations.[16] While Portugal often lacked the resources to stake effective claims to territory, its empire ultimately survived and, indeed, thrived because of the intense rivalries of its much more powerful neighbors, Britain and Germany. But in the process, the British government's abrasive actions often alienated and infuriated the Portuguese government and people.

Although the Berlin Conference of 1884 recognized Portugal's claim over some territory on the Congo estuary, Lisbon chose to concentrate on southern Africa. Even before the Berlin Conference, the government in Lisbon took steps to protect its markets in Angola, thus enabling Portuguese merchants to send significant quantities of foodstuffs, cotton textiles, and other manufactured goods to the colony over the last quarter of the nineteenth century. The shipping company Empresa Nacional de Navegação, set up in 1881, quickly dominated colonial trade, and the Banco Nacional Ultramarino, founded in 1864, enjoyed a monopoly on investments in the colonies and became a major landholder in Angola by taking over property when owners could not make payments.[17] In general, however, Portugal's African colonies in the period from 1870 to 1914 showed only marginal success, with the exceptions of São Tomé and the southern part of Mozambique.[18] São Tomé's prosperity, perhaps unmatched by any other European colony during the period, was made possible by the presence of a steady and reliable labor force. For the period from 1905 through 1910, São Tomé led the world in the production of cocoa, with about 17 percent of the world's output.[19]

In the decade following the Berlin Conference, Portugal traded claims on the African coast to France and Germany in exchange for their giving Portugal a free hand in southern Africa. In 1885, Portugal began its long wars of pacification in the backlands of Angola and Mozambique, intending to create one large, potentially profitable colony stretching across south-central Africa. For any country, this was an ambitious undertaking; but for a poor nation with little capital, it meant constantly living on the brink of financial and diplomatic bankruptcy.

Intent on laying claim to territory in the eastern part of Africa for the construction of a railway, Cecil Rhodes, the diamond magnate and supreme manipulator of the Cape Colony, joined forces with other South African economic and political leaders in 1890 to pressure Lord Salisbury's government to deliver an ultimatum to the Portuguese government. Their goal was to induce Lisbon to halt its efforts to acquire parts of latter-day Rhodesia and also Nyasaland (Malawi), where Scottish missionaries sought British protection. By threatening war, Britain forced the Portuguese government to give up its claims over much of the interior of Africa. In early 1890, enraged Portuguese citizens stoned the house of their own foreign minister as well as the British legation in Lisbon and threatened British subjects in Oporto. The Portuguese government was forced to resign, and republicans gained more support in the monarchical Iberian nation. Britain also discouraged the laying of the Delagoa Bay railway, which was to stretch from the Transvaal to Lourenço Marques on the coast in Mozambique, fearing that the Boers could become economically independent of British colonies in southern Africa. While Britain and Portugal arrived at an agreement in 1891, the latter's financial difficulties grew worse. In addition to a rising national debt fed by unbalanced budgets, subsidies for the laying of colonial railways and waging wars against natives proved costly.[20]

Britain's search for security in southern African threatened Portugal's empire in both Angola and Mozambique. Tension between the Boer republics and the British government worsened after the 1895–1896 Jameson Raid, a Rhodes-sponsored armed invasion of the Transvaal that failed miserably and won sympathy for the Boers from Europeans and Britons who objected to Britain's aggressive machination. In an attempt to reduce support for the Boers, the Salisbury government signed an agreement with Germany in 1898 concerning the financial status of the nearly bankrupt Portugal. Under the treaty, Germany and Britain would guarantee Portugal a loan, with its own colonies in southern Africa serving as collateral. Should Portugal default on the loan, Britain would acquire southern Mozambique, including Lourenço Marques and the terminus of the Delagoa Bay railway. Lord Salisbury, who did not want to break up Portugal's African empire, thought it unlikely that Lisbon would ever contract a loan under these terms, and he was correct, as the Portuguese turned to Paris for money. Although this treaty was "stillborn," it represented a cold and calculated move on London's part to use the Portuguese Empire as a bargaining chip to gain security for Britain.[21]

The South African War between Britain and the Boer-controlled Transvaal and Orange Free State erupted in October 1899. On October 14, Britain, anxious that the Boers not gain arms via Lourenço Marques, reaffirmed the treaty of alliance with Portugal and guaranteed the integrity of Portugal's possessions.[22] Alfred Milner, high commissioner in South Africa and the man most responsible for this conflict, wanted to blockade Delagoa Bay to make certain that no supplies reached the Boers. That plan did not come to fruition, and Salisbury rejected another proposal that Britain lease the bay at up to £100,000 per week during the war, calling the scheme "startling" and all but impossible to implement.[23]

The slave trade remained a crucial part of Portuguese colonial commerce throughout the nineteenth century. Slave merchants in Angola, through trading and raiding parties sent deep into the country's interior, continued to export large numbers of slaves to South America even after 1836, when the Portuguese government attempted to abolish the transatlantic slave trade. Believing that slave labor inhibited colonial prosperity, the Marquês de Sá da Bandeira, a Portuguese political leader and humanitarian, issued decrees limiting the colonial slave trade in the 1830s. He did not, however, enjoy sufficient political support at home or in the colonies to enforce these laws, and it was not until the 1850s that he pushed through a series of decrees that effectively limited the slave trade in Portugal's African possessions and provided for the gradual abolition of slavery.[24] To satisfy the transitional labor needs of the colonies, the *libertos* (freed slaves) were required to work several years for their former masters. The government also set up a board of protection to safeguard the libertos. In a decree of 1853, Portuguese authorities permitted an Angolan landowner to export his slaves to his property in Príncipe, with the proviso that they first be baptized and then freed. Although ostensibly free, they were forced to work for their new master on the island for seven years without pay before receiving their complete liberty. During this period, the owner was required to provide the freed slaves with food, shelter, clothing, health needs, and Christian instruction. A board to protect the libertos was also established on São Tomé and on Príncipe. According to a historian of Portugal's African empire, "In this insignificant grant decree were the beginnings of a contract labour system. Here also was the beginning of the system of exporting slaves from Angola to São Tomé, which was to erupt fifty years later into a notorious scandal and controversy."[25]

The 1858 decree ended slavery throughout the Portuguese colonies, to be effective within twenty years. The final 1878 labor regulation was "an advanced milestone in Portugal's native policy. . . . It flatly abolished forced labour and endeavoured to replace it with a system of free labour instead. It was designed to protect the rights and interests of the African and to guarantee for him a basic human standard."[26] The code, however, was fatally flawed, as it required that all Africans be engaged in useful labor. The slaves of Angolan masters were simply transformed into serviçais—for life. Others who were deemed to be not usefully working could and often were forced to sign on as contract laborers. The government, under pressure from the settlers, found vagrants to help fill the labor needs of the colony as contract laborers.[27] Moreover, because Portuguese control of remote areas of Angola was nonexistent, the slave trade in the interior continued. The Ovimbundu of the Bihé and Portuguese traders continued to ply their commerce in humans, marching the captives to the ports of Benguela and Catumbela, where most slaves became serviçais and were shipped to São Tomé for the remainder of their lives.[28]

Demand for labor on the islands had been growing since midcentury, with the establishment of coffee and cocoa-bean plantations. The coffee plant was first introduced to the islands in 1787, the cocoa tree in 1822.[29] The development of coffee and cocoa cultures on São Tomé and Príncipe was slow, however, as the islands lacked roads, harbors, credit facilities, and a labor force. But the islands did possess plenty of fertile land, and by the 1850s, coffee emerged as an important crop; cocoa became a significant export in the 1880s.[30] Agents in Europe brokered the São Tomé cocoa beans, and Cadbury Bros. began purchasing them in 1886.[31]

Planters in São Tomé, who had made no attempt to improve the miserable lot of their slaves or their libertos, lost laborers after the abolition of slavery in the 1870s, for many of the freed slaves simply left the plantations and moved into the interior to set up their own farms. To satisfy the needs of the plantation owners, the large-scale importation of contract laborers began in the late 1870s.[32] Although blacks and Creoles owned much of the land well into the nineteenth century, individuals and corporations from Portugal had gained control of most of the land by 1900, fraudulently in many instances.[33] The roças concentrated on cocoa and coffee, but they frequently grew other crops as well, including palm, maize, and various fruits.

While Portuguese authorities attempted, however ineffectively, to safeguard workers from abuse in the latter half of the 1800s, the government disregarded even that minimal humanitarianism by the turn of the twentieth century. A committee set up in 1898 to examine the problems of Portuguese Africa, which was chaired by an aggressive imperialist, abandoned earlier nineteenth-century liberal thinking and argued that the "state, not only as a sovereign of semi-barbaric populations, but also as a depository of social authority, should have no scruples in *obliging* and, if necessary, *forcing* these rude Negroes in Africa . . . to work, that is to better themselves by work, to acquire through work the happiest means of existence, to civilize themselves through work" (emphasis in original). Hence, the decree of November 9, 1899, stated: "All natives of Portuguese overseas provinces are subject to the obligation, moral and legal, of attempting to obtain through work the means that they lack to subsist and to better their social condition. They have full liberty to choose the method of fulfilling this obligation, but if they do not fulfill it, public authority may force a fulfillment."[34] Farmers, women, leaders, and certain others such as the elderly and the very young were exempt from the regulation, but African men who were not gainfully employed could be forced to work for the state or for private individuals. The regulations provided for a minimum wage and decent treatment by the employers, and the contract was limited to five years.[35] Many justified coercion by citing the belief that the natives did not wish to work, partly because their material needs were minimal and could be easily satisfied.[36]

All European powers in the nineteenth and early twentieth centuries sought regular and inexpensive labor for their colonies. Expanding Western industrial economies hungered for rubber, oil, copper, tin, diamonds, gold, and other ores and minerals for their factories, as well as food for their swelling populations. They pursued these resources in colonial possessions or developing regions of the world, particularly in Africa and in Central and South America. Capitalists sought an efficient, inexpensive, and docile labor force to plant and harvest crops, mine minerals, and transport goods, while colonial governments required workers to build roads, bridges, harbors, and offices and to lay rails. The ending of slavery and the slave trade in the nineteenth century forced employers to look elsewhere for labor. Indentured labor was one alternative, leading to the transfer of millions of people throughout the world.[37] Colonial regimes also needed revenue to cover expenses and thus resorted to a variety of taxes to generate both labor and income. Poll, hut, or house taxes were imposed in the French Congo, English-controlled Sierra Leone, Griqualand West, Basutoland, Nyasaland, Northern and Southern Rhodesia, and Portuguese Mozambique, as a means of forcing the natives to engage in productive paid work so that they could then pay the levies. Nonpayment of the taxes could lead to forced labor and, in some cases, hut burnings and even shootings. Natives were drafted by governments to build roads, haul goods, collect rubber, and mine gold; in French Madagascar, public works projects were carried out through the use of the *corvée,* a tax imposing labor for a certain number of days per year.[38]

❧

As a British official in central Africa in the 1890s, Sir Harry Johnston used both diplomacy and military force to forestall a Portuguese intrusion into the area and to enable Britain to seize control over Nyasaland. As was common among colonialists, he regarded European rule as essential for the welfare and benefit of

Africans. On the whole, he respected Africans, even though he judged them as unequal to whites.[39] In a long letter to the *Times* of December 22, 1902, Johnston spelled out the need for a huge workforce to rebuild South Africa following the recently ended South African War. He was interested in "young able-bodied men between the ages of 15 and 35." He was reluctant to import Indians or Chinese or to employ whites who, though more productive than natives, had "to be paid for at such a much higher rate as to put the question out of court" and were prone to strike during periods of increased output. He looked particularly to Portuguese and British territories north of the Zambezi River as a source of labor. Many natives in that area were already working on plantations and in mines and in laying railways. In his remarkable letter, Johnston estimated the number of "surplus" natives and evaluated the physical strength of members of the myriad tribes throughout central Africa who might be willing to toil in South Africa. Experience had shown that natives from Portuguese East Africa were "suitable for hard muscular work," whereas the natives from the interior of Angola were "muscular and . . . quite broken in to hard work, as many of them carry on extensive porterage between the coast and the interior." The Portuguese government had been "most obliging in allowing extensive recruiting for labor to go on in South-East Africa." Johnston emphasized that the natives needed good and plentiful food, "warm and stout clothing," decent shelter, reasonable hours, and "fairly good pay," as their experiences would determine if other laborers would be willing to offer their services. While Johnston stressed the need for proper treatment of the natives, he viewed labor as a necessary commodity. He gave no hint of the atrocities inflicted on Africans by King Leopold II's agents—even though he knew of the brutal mistreatment and did not approve of it—as they extracted rubber from the Congo River basin at the cost of millions of lives.[40] And he never once addressed the issue of the maltreatment of workers in Portuguese Africa or elsewhere, past or present.[41]

By the late nineteenth century, cocoa beans were one of the commodities in demand in the Western world. The Spanish in Fernando Po and the Germans in Cameroon, São Tomé's neighbors on the Gulf of Guinea, also used coerced labor on their cocoa plantations. Yet coerced labor was not an inexpensive system.[42] By the 1890s, the Congo Free State's thirst for labor drove up the cost of slaves marketed as serviçais at the Angolan ports, with slave traders competing for laborers in a relatively small common market.[43]

British explorers, humanitarians, and officials followed the plight of laborers in Portuguese Africa after the abolition of slavery in the 1870s and were well aware of continued abuses. The explorer Verney Lovett Cameron, who crossed Portuguese Africa between 1873 and 1875, reported an extensive slave trade throughout the area.[44] Henry M. Stanley, Lord Mayo, and the Anti-Slavery Society all cited evidence of slavery in the 1880s.[45] The Anti-Slavery Society pointedly castigated the British government for negotiating the treaty with Portugal in 1884 giving the latter jurisdiction over the Congo.[46] In contrast to these critical appraisals, Harry Johnston wrote in 1884 that the town of São Tomé was in good repair, the roças were well maintained, and their owners and families were knowledgeable of the greater world. The island was "the ideal of a black man's paradise, and the negroes of Sao Thomé the happiest in the world." His views of Angola were only slightly less enthusiastic. An efficient "apprenticeship" program—a form of coercion necessary because the native "will never work unless he is obliged"—provided Portugal's colonies with "cheap and plentiful" labor.[47]

In the 1870s, British officials made representations on the slavery issue to Portuguese governors and diplomats, who vociferously denied that there was any slavery in their colonies.[48] In July 1882, A. Cohen, the British consul in Luanda, wrote to Lord Grenville, the foreign secretary in Gladstone's Liberal government, about his recent visit to São Tomé. After commenting on the considerable production of coffee and cocoa beans, Cohen summarized the means by which the Portuguese had secured labor since emancipation. The workers, he wrote, were captured in the interior and taken to ports, where they were "sold to agents of the planters at San Thomé at prices varying from 4£ to 6£ in goods; registered and contracted by the Government Authority for a period of five years, on the expiration of which term a return passage [was] to be provided to those who wish[ed] to repatriate. Inasmuch, however, as the offer [was] never made, or the opportunity afforded, they [could] never leave the island, and so [became] permanent indentured labourers." While Cohen reported that the workers were well provided with medical treatment and food, he noted that the climate and toil and change in life took a very high toll, pushing the mortality rate toward 20 percent per year.[49] From 1875 to 1900, nearly fifty-six thousand serviçais, mainly from Angola, were shipped to the islands.[50]

On June 4, 1894, Joseph Pease, a Liberal MP from Northumberland, asked Edward Grey (1862–1933), the undersecretary of state in Lord Rosebery's short-lived, 1894–1895 Liberal government, if the latter had any information about Portugal's possible violation of the Brussels Act of 1891 in regard to slavery in São Tomé. Grey, who appears often in this story, remarked that Portugal had abolished slavery. He continued, "If in spite of this there were a slave traffic, of which we have no knowledge, the slaves would become free when landed in the islands." He asked that Pease refer any pertinent information to the Foreign Office.[51] The following day, Pease, an industrialist and sportsman of Quaker background, sent Grey two pieces of evidence.[52] A recently received letter from a "well-known Liverpool firm" (most likely John Holt) testified that slaves "are being constantly bought in the hinterlands of the Province of Angola, & not a single Portuguese steamer leaves the ports of Benguella or Novo Redondo without its contingent of slaves for Loanda or San Thomé. . . . Of late years the supply of able-bodied men has not been equal to the demand, & scores of little children—from five to six years of age upwards—are carried off to plantations." Pease also included a copy of a letter from Algernon Littleton, a retired captain in the Royal Navy, dated June 5, 1894. Littleton had sailed the west coast of Africa in the mid-1880s and reported that the recruiting of labor for the islands amounted to slavery. While well treated, the slaves were not able to return to their homes, and the death rate, according to a doctor, ran 15 percent annually. Littleton doubted that anything had changed in the preceding ten years.

The Foreign Office then asked the consul in Luanda to respond to Pease's inquiry. Vice-Consul W. S. R. Brock, a merchant, replied in a letter of August 28, 1894. In an important demonstration of the attitude of British officialdom toward slavery in Portuguese Africa, Brock contended that much of the information offered by the Liverpool shipping firm and by Littleton was out of date. He also referred to Consul Cohen's review of 1882 as being fairer than more recent evaluations but still that of a "prosecutor." He regarded Lord Mayo's statement in *De Rebus Africanis* as a typical humanitarian response and described a letter in the Anti-Slavery Society's *Reporter* of March 28, 1884, as too much "a bitter feeling against the Portuguese generally, [wandering] so far from the subject that it warrants even a stronger expression than gross exaggeration." Children, he added, were never recruited, except in the sense that they accompanied their mothers. He continued: "My opinion is that taking it all round, the serviçaes are well treated and cared for, that they are not unhappy, and that there is no hardship in the way they are worked. It must be remembered that they are drawn from some of the lowest types of humanity, and have none of the instincts of Civilisation; and that morally they are improved rather than deteriorated by their more regular life and work." Brock acknowledged that the labor issue was complicated: "The native hates work and cannot be got to see the necessity of it. The climate is such that white men cannot long sustain manual labour under the burning sun, whereas the native can, being physically constituted in a different way." To change the labor system would devastate Angola and "would mean absolute ruin to the island of San Thomé," an island that was a "bright spot" for Portugal.[53]

Nearly four months later, W. Clayton Pickersgill, consul in Luanda and a former missionary in the Congo, added a supplementary note to Brock's letter. Pickersgill had read the material cited by Brock and thought that the writers whose assessment Brock had questioned "exhibit a picture of the present day working of the system of contract labour . . . which is absolutely true, as regards all important features." The serviçais, who were paid very little, could command much more in the competitive labor market. Abuse occurred especially because curators and other magistrates openly sided with those who purchased the labor, rather than with the natives. Pickersgill also contended that contractual abuse was rife throughout Angola, and the authorities were intimately involved with the custom. The system overwhelmed even those who did not agree with it. A chantey among the serviçais ran:

> *In San Thomé*
> *There's a door for entrance,*
> *But none for going out.*

Pickersgill had never heard of a single instance of a worker returning from São Tomé. The manager of a coffee plantation had told him that one could recontract five hundred laborers without any of them "appearing personally." Some serviçais fled the plantations only to realize that they were on an island from which they could not escape and returned broken. Pickersgill concluded:

> If I were asked to suggest a remedy for this evil, I should point out that the Portuguese Government does not administrate more than one-third of the territory which has been apportioned to it; and that there does not exist, either amongst the colonists or the officials, any sort of objection to a trade in slaves, provided that it is carried on with some show of humanity.
>
> As long, therefore, as there is a wilderness with creatures in it who are no man's care, so long will they be regarded as game; and the only

> sure way to put a stop to poaching is for the Government to occupy the country which it claims to possess.

Foreign Office officials refused to act on Pickersgill's comments. Thomas Sanderson, the permanent undersecretary, commented, "I think for the present we had better leave it alone." Foreign Secretary Lord Kimberley added, "A very old difficulty. I agree."[54] A Liberal government that preached the moral utility of the empire declined to pursue this humanitarian issue with the Portuguese government.

Two years later, Lord Salisbury, prime minister and foreign secretary in the Conservative government between 1895 and 1900, asked that Pickersgill investigate a report from a German doctor who alleged that laborers on the islands were kept in a "state of practical slavery." In February and March 1897, Pickersgill spent four weeks on São Tomé, visiting several cocoa and coffee plantations and finding the treatment of the serviçais reasonable in regard to food, clothing, and medical attention. The "ugly fact," however, was that 20 percent of the laborers died in the first year of service, and 50 percent were dead by the end of the five-year contract. A Foreign Office official wrote that in a similar instance in 1894, it had been "decided to take no notice." He asked, "Are we still to follow that policy?" To this, Salisbury responded, "Leave it alone."[55] In the 1890s, leaders of neither political party were willing to address the issue of slave labor in their ally's West African colonies. With few exceptions, that attitude persisted to the time of World War I and thereafter. Diplomatic and economic considerations, as we will see, outweighed humanitarian concerns.

❦

From 1897 until 1903, when William Cadbury visited Lisbon for the first time, reports kept Foreign Office officials well informed of the continued labor abuse in Portuguese West Africa. Consular reports from Luanda told of the shipment of laborers from Angola to the islands. This exportation of workers displeased plantation owners in Angola, who could not compete with the richer planters on the islands. Arthur Nightingale, acting consul in Luanda, wrote in 1899: "A good healthy man and woman cost at the present time about 50£ sterling placed in San Thomé: this seems very much like quoting for cattle or any other marketable commodity. Such quotations are made, and contracts are signed to deliver so many pairs at so much per pair." Nightingale, however, approved of the labor law of 1899 requiring vagrant natives to work for the state or for private contractors in order to benefit both the colony of Angola and the natives. The law would, he contended, "compel many thousands of natives to work who at present are content to live in wretched grass huts, existing on manioc roots, rats, and such-like vermin. It would greatly benefit the black man himself, he would become healthier in his habits, and would learn to know the power of money and the benefits to be derived from his labours, he would learn to dress himself in decent clothes."[56] In June 1902, Nightingale reported to Lord Lansdowne, the Conservative foreign secretary from 1900 to 1905, that when a governor-general of Angola had recently attempted to halt the exporting of people to São Tomé, planters on the islands forced Lisbon to remove the restrictions. Nightingale described various tricks used by traders in the interior to acquire slaves, and he included in his report a letter from an employee of the British Museum who had recently been in the interior near Benguela and witnessed trade routes "strewn with skeletons and corpses in every state of decomposition." Many had starved to death, "while others when unable to keep up with the caravan [were] brutally murdered—a sharp blow with the keen little native hatchet at the back of the neck usually giving the quietus." Nightingale stressed that though it was no easy task to gain labor from African natives, the use of slavery by the Portuguese was unacceptable, and European nations should not tolerate such a practice.[57] One month later, he contended that only strong external pressure would convince the Portuguese government to stop the Angolan slave trade.[58] Roger Casement, the British consul at Boma (Leopold's capital in the Congo) and earlier a consul at Luanda, described the monotonous life of contract laborers: "The *serviçaes* are not allowed to quit the limits of the plantations; they have no change of scene; no change of duty; no change of food; no remission of their wearisome routine save that brought by sickness or death. What the fathers and mothers are doing today the children know they, too, will be doing in the same spot, in the same way and under the same compulsion if they live to become fathers and mothers themselves." Young people married on the plantation, with the owner choosing the bride and groom—"not necessarily in accordance with the wishes of the individual, but often with an eye to the prospective breeding properties of those thus summarily united."[59] Both Nightingale and Martin Gosselin, the minister to Lisbon, argued that the new labor law of January 29, 1903, would not provide reform, as it was drawn up in the interests of the islands' planters; furthermore, those provisions for the protection of the serviçais would not be enforced.[60]

After William Cadbury's trip to Portugal in March 1903, officials in the Foreign Office expressed fear that the labor conditions on the islands would become a matter of public debate in England, something they hoped to prevent. One official noted that since there were no British subjects involved, the government found "no direct ground for interference. But it is quite horrible that the matter may be taken up in the press & in Parliament & an attempt made to create a feeling against Portugal similar to that arroused [*sic*] against the Congo Free State. It might prevent a movement of this kind assuming considerable proportions if the question were discussed, perhaps unofficially, with the Portuguese Minister [Soveral]."[61] When Lansdowne met with the Marques de Soveral, the latter denied that there were any problems on the islands. In June 1903, Lansdowne told Nightingale to stop at São Tomé after completing his leave in London, as the Foreign Office wanted him to visit the islands occasionally.[62] Nightingale, however, was unable to travel to the islands on his return because he was required to go directly to Boma to take Casement's place there. There is some doubt that the Foreign Office ever intended for Nightingale to go directly to São Tomé, lest Britain upset the Portuguese government.[63] Nightingale, however, apparently drawing on other sources of information, wrote the Foreign Office a long letter from Boma in May 1904, reconfirming the brutal treatment of workers in São Tomé and indicating that there was no evidence that the new regulations of 1903 had made a difference. He stressed that if there were to be repatriation from the islands to Angola, Portuguese authorities would have to provide land for the workers there and make certain that the back wages were properly paid. He added, pessimistically, "But I am afraid that all this would be too great an undertaking for the Authorities in Angola. . . . The St. Thomé planters form a strong political element in Lisbon, and as long as they are able to influence the party in power I feel sure the 'slave traffic' in Angola will continue to flourish as heretofore."[64] In a rare moment of humor, Gosselin reported that a major planter on São Tomé had told him that he needed many more laborers but could not get them "for love or money," to which Gosselin added, "I think we may fully believe the statement that serviçaes cannot be raised in Angola by the former of these two means."[65] In October 1904, the Foreign Office decided, partly at Gosselin's suggestion, that Lisbon officials should not be immediately approached about the serviçais because the power of the São Tomé planters would bar any reform; "we should merely make ourselves disliked without doing any good," the London officials added.[66]

In November 1904, Brock, acting consul in Luanda during Nightingale's absence, requested approval of a trip into the interior of Angola to see if the 1903 law was being applied and to investigate the extensive trade in guns and powder affecting Angola and German territory to the south. The Foreign Office turned him down, fearing that his report could irritate the Portuguese and noting that there was a "danger of learning inconvenient facts which might oblige us to make representations to the Portuguese Govt. which we don't want to do."[67] Nevertheless, Brock traveled into the interior without Foreign Office approval, and he reported that the 1903 law seemed to be having a positive impact. While the slave trade still existed, the white officials were not participating as they had before, and raiding for slaves was decreasing. Slave dealers still kept the best slaves for themselves, sending the rest to the islands.[68] In 1905, Col. Colin Harding, the acting administrator of North-West Rhodesia and commandant of the Barotse Native Police, published his account of the slave trade in the interior in words very similar to those of Nevinson, whose articles were being issued at the same time:

> Every day I am seeing traces of the slave trade. The wayside trees are simply hung with disused shackles . . . skulls and bones bleached by the sun lie where the victims fell, and gape with helpless grin on those who pass, a damning evidence of a horrible traffic. . . . One poor fellow had not been dead long. Lying by the remains of the fire he had ignited before his death, his gaping skull resting on his fleshless hands, his spirit had passed away without pain and without a struggle. No one ever recognised his life, no one mourns his death. Other remains are found; here the skull is battered in by the trader's axe and the body clearly exhibits signs of the greatest torture and pain in the throes of death. Every sick man in a slave caravan who cannot walk is despatched in this way.[69]

Meanwhile, the Bailundu War erupted in Angola in 1902, costing some two thousand lives, both African and white, although Christian missionaries were spared. The Bailundu had long been involved in slave trade and the production of wild rubber, an increasingly significant part of the Angolan economy. Portuguese incursions into the central Angolan plateau after 1890 reduced the authority of the Bailundu leaders, whose traditional economic and political control began to crumble. Many factors contributed to this war: the presence of unscrupulous Portuguese merchants, who often resorted to rum and trickery as tools of trade; the loss of land; a fall in the price of rubber; the spread of diseases; and the insatiable demand for slave labor on the islands, in the Congo, and on the Angolan plantations and public works projects. After the war, several Portuguese traders and officials were found guilty of helping to cause the uprising and were sentenced to transportation and fined. While trade in serviçais dropped over the next two years, there is no indication that labor practices improved in the long run; the uprising was a failure.[70] From 1904 to 1909, warfare between natives and Portuguese military forces was common. In one case in late 1904, members of the Cuanhama tribe in southern Angola killed an estimated 130 to 250 white Portuguese soldiers.[71]

At the turn of the twentieth century, the European demand for commodities, ranging from foodstuffs to minerals, created an almost insatiable thirst for labor in western and southern Africa. Many European officials and traders, who openly regarded natives as inferior and in need of the discipline of hard work, justified the use of coerced labor as a benefit for the Africans. Among the West Africans brutally captured and enslaved for the well-being of Europeans were those who worked the cocoa plantations of São Tomé.

4 Evidence Amassed

> So great is the dread of the island plantations, that when a servical leaves Angola his family go through a service for the dead on his behalf.
>
> *Joseph Burtt*

> The fact of the matter is that the system is neither more nor less than slavery but that we do not dare to say much as we might thus offend the Portuguese with whom we desire to stand well.
>
> *Edward A. Walrond Clarke, Foreign Office*

HENRY NEVINSON LANDED in England in July 1905, following his journey to Angola and the islands of São Tomé and Príncipe. In August, his first article on labor in Portuguese West Africa appeared in *Harper's Monthly Magazine;* follow-up stories appeared monthly, and his book *A Modern Slavery,* a compilation of the articles, was published the following year. In a March 1906 article for the *Daily Chronicle,* a Liberal London morning newspaper, he expressed the hope that a decision by the English manufacturers to stop purchasing São Tomé cocoa beans might have "some effect upon the Portuguese heart." He also called for British intervention based on the Berlin and Brussels Acts of 1885 and 1890 and on "the right of common humanity."[1] The press, the Foreign Office, humanitarian societies, Cadbury Bros., and Portuguese planters and officials followed his revelations and his appeal for action.

Several newspapers and journals reviewed Nevinson's writings. In its August 4, 1905, edition, the leftist-oriented *Clarion* simply quoted excerpts from the first installment in *Harper's.*[2] Henry N. Brailsford, a brilliant socialist journalist, commenting on *A Modern Slavery* for the *Tribune,* a Liberal daily, asserted that "there are few works in our libraries which convey the picture of distant miseries with a sincerity so evident and a skill so masterly."[3] Edmund Dene Morel (1873–1924; hereafter referred to as E. D. Morel), leader of the Congo Reform Association, commented in the *Daily Chronicle* that Nevinson's moving book "is marked throughout by wonderful self-restraint, which only breaks down here and there in passages of mordant bitterness."[4] In October 1906, the *British Friend*, a Quaker journal, warned that Nevinson had made clear that "the old agreements for preventing slavery have broken down, that the forces of capital are able to make them of no account, and that the ideals of freedom and justice which once stirred the minds of men are now too commonly sneered at as sentiment. . . . Failing effective interference, it would be a consolation to know that the great English firms which manufacture cocoa were agreed in declining to purchase that which is grown by slave labour."[5] Already, without naming names, concerned Quakers were calling on coreligionists who headed huge chocolate firms to boycott Portuguese-supplied cocoa. In a book review that was a portent of future newspaper condemnations of the major English chocolate companies, the *Daily Mail*, a halfpenny, large-circulation, Conservative morning newspaper, criticized the "Quaker houses who largely advertize their preparations of cocoa but singularly enough never mention that the main ingredient is obtained by slave labour."[6] Almost all of the notices of the book carried extensive quotations from Nevinson, so readers quickly grasped his vivid descriptions as well as his anger over the exploitation of the African laborers.

The Foreign Office sent the first four *Harper's* issues to the Marques de Soveral, the Portuguese minister to London, who informed Foreign Secretary Lansdowne in October 1905 that his Portuguese government denied all the charges.[7] Sir Eric Barrington, a Foreign Office official, warned Soveral in March 1906 "that the philanthropists were much excited & that it [would] be very disagreeable if public feeling were aroused by the fact that the Portuguese Govt. were encouraging something painfully akin to the slave trade."[8] For the most part, however, Foreign Office personnel clearly did not want Portugal's abuse of serviçais to become a public issue, and they examined Nevinson's articles with concern. Edward A. Walrond Clarke feared that members of Parliament, citing Nevinson's descriptions of the slave trade, would raise questions in the House of Commons, the lower house of Parliament.[9] In February 1906, an official wrote, "We have repeatedly called the attention of the Portuguese Govt. to these abuses though it has not been thought polite recently to press the matter unduly."[10]

Both the Anti-Slavery Society and the Aborigines' Protection Society had for several years encouraged the British Foreign Office to demand that Portugal stop the use of slave labor in its colonies. Quoting evidence from Nightingale, Colonel Harding, and missionaries in Africa, Fox Bourne, secretary of the APS, penned a strong letter of condemnation to the Foreign Office on July 25, 1905, concerning the thriving slave trade in Angola, especially in areas bordering Rhodesia and the Congo. When officials at the Foreign Office attempted to minimize the seriousness of the trade, Fox Bourne would have none of it. He had the evidence, and he knew how the Foreign Office operated. In a second letter one month later, he stressed that the British government should force Portugal to stop slave trading, under the terms of the Brussels Act of 1892.[11] The humanitarian societies were quick to publicize Nevinson's articles, and Fox Bourne, who met with Nevinson in early September 1905, thought that the societies would be able to put the *Harper's* articles to good use.[12] After reviewing the last of Nevinson's installments, he wrote in his society's newsletter, *The Aborigines' Friend:* "Mr Nevinson has done good service in calling attention to it [slavery] by his graphic and manifestly truthful account of his own painful experiences. It remains for others to carry on the work of protest and exposure—it may be hoped, with his assistance—and especially, if it can be done, to enlist the effective sympathies of our Government in putting such pressure on the Portuguese Government as will bring about necessary reforms. Our country has treaty rights warranting that course."[13]

Fox Bourne planned to contact the Foreign Office early in 1906, as he hoped that Henry Campbell-Bannerman's Liberal government, which had just taken office, would be more sympathetic to the humanitarians.[14] However, times had changed since the last Liberal government fell in 1895. Edward Grey, the new foreign secretary, along with Herbert Asquith as chancellor of the exchequer and Richard Haldane at the War Office, were Liberal Imperialists who commanded substantial power within the new Liberal cabinet.

Liberal imperialism was the ideological brainchild of Lord Rosebery, the prime minister who had succeeded Gladstone at the head of the Liberal Party in 1894. Rosebery and his acolytes saw the empire as the future of Britain's economic, political, military, and moral power in the world, and they did not want party motives, morality, or ideology to stand in the way of the empire's development in that capacity. Grey and the other Liberal Imperialists regarded foreign policy as above party politics, indeed, above party ideology. They believed that the conduct of foreign policy could and should remain unchanged, no matter which party was in power. Thus, Grey made few changes in policy when he took over the Foreign Office. He consulted minimally with his cabinet colleagues and depended heavily on professional advisers in his office. As a Liberal Imperialist, he tended not to regard foreign policy as a moral issue.[15] Such an attitude was hardly calculated to appease the sensibilities of an old Gladstonian Liberal such as Fox Bourne, particularly in regard to slavery in Portugal's African colonies.

Grey knew about slave labor in Portuguese West Africa. He had dealt with it in the 1890s, when he served as undersecretary at the Foreign Office, and the staff there had provided him a detailed summary of the issue when he became foreign secretary in December 1905.[16]

On March 14, 1906, Fox Bourne, accompanied by Nevinson, met with two Foreign Office officials, Eric Barrington and Undersecretary Lord Fitzmaurice. Fox Bourne expressed his desire to submit a paper that would detail Portuguese government treaty violations concerning the slave trade. In response to Barrington's minutes of the meeting, the circumspect Grey wrote, "We need not refuse his memo: but we must not be committed as to the use we are to make of it."[17] Nevinson, in his autobiography (an account that is confirmed in his diary), recalled a less than pleasant meeting with Barrington, who

> accosted me savagely with the words, "Are you the author of these very unpleasant articles on Portuguese Slavery? Did you write that purple report?" I replied that I was glad he found the articles unpleasant, but the report was hardly purple enough. Assuming the official sneer, he then asked, "Do you want us to reduce these wealthy islands to a wilderness, on your bare word?" I replied that a wilderness would be better than the abominations I had seen. With rising indignation, he demanded, "Would you have England police the world wherever you find slavery?" Imitating the official manner, I replied that the answer was in the affirmative, and the interview ended in courteous animosity.[18]

In April 1906, Fox Bourne sent to the Foreign Office a letter outlining the Portuguese decrees and various nineteenth-century treaties obligating Britain and Portugal and occasionally other European governments to take steps to halt the slave trade from the west coast of Africa. Article 9 of the General Act of the Berlin Conference of February 26, 1885, required that European colonial powers stop slave trading in the Congo basin. While Angola and the islands were technically outside the conventional basin, Fox Bourne stressed that many of the slaves used in those possessions were acquired from the Congo basin.[19]

Meanwhile, William Cadbury had been communicating with Nevinson, receiving reports from Joseph Burtt (the company's agent in West Africa), and corresponding with the secretaries of the humanitarian societies and other friends about slavery in Portuguese West Africa. Shortly after returning from Africa, Nevinson dropped a note to Cadbury about meeting Burtt in São Tomé, observing that "he seems to be a thoroughly good fellow, and I have no doubt he will be able to tell you all you want to know."[20] In October 1905, Nevinson wrote Cadbury, "I have no heroic remedy for the state of things. A real change can only come from a complete change in the disposition of the Portuguese people. But I think all true reports must have some influence on the best of them."[21]

The high-strung Baron Carl de Merck, the cocoa broker in Lisbon, initially questioned Nevinson's judgment. In an October 1905 letter to his friend William Cadbury, he remarked: "I do not think much of the man's report. I have even found it one of incredible presumptions. . . . Unless a man is very well read, of an universal mind and thoroughly able to put himself in the place of others, how can he judge!"[22] Two months later, he was noticeably moved by Nevinson's November and December articles. Merck, who dealt regularly in international finance (having acted as a broker for Cecil Rhodes and the Rothschilds in the failed 1892–1894 negotiations for the purchase of the Delagoa Bay railway), possessed a conscience and understood the terrible exploitation of the Africans. He wrote:

> But, Cadbury, how awful those two last chapters in Harpers November & December! I do not think it will be necessary to send Burtt to Angola. Those words of the man can only be true and what a terrible picture of misery & slavery they paint. Of course, Burtt has confirmed to us, what I all the time have been upholding, that the labourer in Thomé is well treated. But the way he gets captured and is sold and sent there is terrible.
>
> Of course it will be the same to him everywhere that in order to exist, where the white man comes, he forces the Negro to work. . . . What is to be done! I do not believe Portugal will be ever forced to alter that state of affairs, but it has impressed me very much.[23]

On a return visit to Lisbon in January 1906, William Cadbury met Henry P. Fletcher, who was the secretary of the U.S. legation; São Tomé plantation owner Francisco Mantero; and Merck. Cadbury reported on this trip to the annual meeting of the Anti-Slavery Society in early 1906. The present Portuguese government, he stated, exhibited no inclination to implement the reforms promised in 1903, and even concerned Portuguese citizens had no expectation of improving the plight of the laborers except "by encouraging tribal wars!" He believed, however, that because of the high cost of labor, the plantation owners generally treated their workers humanely.[24] Earlier, Cadbury had told Fox Bourne that little had changed in Lisbon over the three years since his previous visit, adding that "[it] is not likely to be until some public opinion is brought to bear upon it." The repatriation act, of which so much good had been expected, was, in his words, "practically a dead letter."[25]

William Cadbury was also receiving Burtt's letters from Portuguese West Africa. While in Príncipe, the company's agent succumbed to what he believed was sleeping sickness, the scourge of the island, and suffered from a "constant headache and stiffness in the neck."[26] A month later in Angola, he became violently ill again, and after five days of high fever, he checked into a hospital, where he found the people pleasant but the food "incredibly bad."[27] Due to his vulnerability to illness, Burtt requested that Cadbury Bros. send someone from England to go with him on his inland journey. W. Claude Horton, house surgeon at Birmingham General Hospital, accompanied Burtt on his expedition into the interior of Angola in 1906.[28] Burtt and Horton hired fifty carriers for the trek to Bihé and expected to employ new carriers for a later journey.[29] By September, they had passed through the notorious Hungry Country and were restocking their food supplies. According to Horton, Burtt had once again become extremely ill but was improving: "He has been riding all day in a tipoia [a small hammock] till the last few days and now does a little walking each day. He has had eczema all over his body and has also been a bit feverish."[30]

Cadbury felt a need to explain one critical aspect of his agent's investigation to the humanitarian societies. He informed Fox Bourne that Burtt carried letters of introduction to all the large roças and to the governor of São Tomé. Cadbury felt certain that such an "open" visit would help provide Burtt with "unbiassed" information, believing that the Cadbury company's openness would be reciprocated by the plantation owners and their managers.[31] Cadbury wrote Travers Buxton, secretary of the Anti-Slavery Society, that Burtt's six months on the islands resulted in cordial receptions by the plantation owners, some of whom made their books available to him and gave him freedom "to go anywhere by himself."[32]

On the whole, Burtt found that while the laborers were reasonably well treated, their lives were meaningless and monotonous. Although their basic material needs were met, they could not leave their plantations except by permission. Religious instruction was a mere formality, and the agent quoted a worker laconically summarizing a priest's message: "'He tells us to multiply and eat well, and sleep well, that we may work well for Dona Claudina [the mistress of the roça].'"[33]

William Cadbury informed his uncle George that Burtt "entirely confirms the reports that no imported labourer has ever been returned to the mainland of Africa, and children who are born on the estates are the absolute property of the owners."[34]

If Burtt's letters about São Tomé painted a grim picture, his evaluation of the conditions in Angola was, if anything, bleaker. After several months on the mainland, he wired Cadbury Bros. a coded message that "the condition [of the general state of Angola] may be described as worse than stated by H. W. Nevinson."[35] In this case, Burtt confirmed the commonly accepted view that conditions in Angola were much more dismal than on the islands. Apologists for São Tomé's plantation owners, as well as William Cadbury and Foreign Office officials, often used this assessment to soften criticism of the islands' labor system.

In November, Cadbury also heard from E. M. Mathias, who had worked for telegraph companies in Portuguese West Africa for six years. Mathias said that Nevinson's articles had not done justice to the evils of domestic slavery in São Tomé. He identified two "culprits" in the labor system: the curators, who were appointed to protect the serviçais but were so poorly paid that they readily accepted bribes from owners to recontract the laborers, and the plantation owners, many of whom used unscrupulous methods to acquire and develop the plantations.[36]

Virtually all the information William Cadbury gathered in 1906 about the status of serviçais in Portuguese West Africa—from Burtt, Nevinson, Merck, and Mathias—pointed to a labor force recruited by slavers, abetted by government officials, and maintained by force. Moreover, there was no indication, as Cadbury himself learned in his conversations in Lisbon, that the situation would improve in the near future. Yet even in the face of these grim evaluations and with growing public pressure to stop buying São Tomé cocoa, William Cadbury refused to consider a boycott. One can only guess that he had determined that his own course of action—to prod the stubborn and proud but amiable Portuguese people in the direction of reform—would benefit the plantation owners, the serviçais, and his own company.

In 1904, when his firm was searching for an agent to investigate Portugal's colonial labor practices, Cadbury had been reluctant to hire Nevinson because of his inability to speak Portuguese and his unwillingness to commit for a lengthy period overseas. Burtt confirmed some of Cadbury's misgivings about Nevinson. By early 1906, he had read several of Nevinson's articles and had been informed of Merck's opinion that Burtt's visit to the continent was not necessary after Nevinson's powerful descriptions of the mainland. However, Burtt wished to continue, contending that Cadbury needed a second opinion to Nevinson's for two reasons: "The first is [Nevinson's] utter lack of sympathy with and understanding of the Portuguese character, and the second is the nervous and overwrought condition of his mind brought on by his arduous toil and sufferings in the interior. The English people at Loanda assure me that his fears of assassination were entirely imaginary. Brock who travelled home with him, says it was purely a delusion though a common one to persons who have been overdone in Africa." At the same time, Burtt respected aspects of Nevinson's reporting. He downplayed the reporter's lack of facility in the Portuguese language, noting that "his knowledge of French and keen powers of observation would in measure compensate for this." He also thought that "if the articles are in places overdrawn, personally I imagine few people could have given a more vivid and on the whole truthful idea of the procuring of labour for the plantations than Nevinson has done."[37] He expressed admiration for Nevinson's description of labor recruitment on the continent. Some of Burtt's most descriptive letters focused on Angola. For example, he understood that Angolan natives had been enslaved "for so many generations"—indeed, "the child drinks it [slavery] at its mother's breast"—that "submission flows in the blood." He continued: "So great is the dread of the island plantations, that when a servical leaves Angola his family go through a service for the dead on his behalf."[38] Nevinson could hardly have described the situation more bluntly. Burtt looked askance, however, at Nevinson's view of the islands. After reading the article entitled "Islands of Doom," he wrote to Cadbury to express his concern that because Nevinson "writes authoritatively on matters of which he knows practically nothing," his unsubstantiated remarks would be accepted as "facts" in the United States and England. Burtt believed that Nevinson had not spent enough time on the roças to support his accusations.[39]

Was Burtt writing what Cadbury wanted to hear? He probably was. As both Merck and Nevinson observed, Burtt was a pleasant but naive young man who wanted to do good in the world. He certainly knew how Cadbury felt about Nevinson, and he naturally wanted to please his employer. Thus, he echoed Cadbury's own evaluation of the journalist, although even Burtt had to admit to an admiration for Nevinson.

In October 1905, the Foreign Office, always under pressure from the humanitarian societies to investigate labor conditions on São Tomé, directed Arthur Nightingale, who was returning to Luanda after his temporary assignment in

Boma, to visit the two islands and to report to Lansdowne.[40] Three months later, writing from São Tomé, Nightingale complained about traveling conditions on the islands: "What with the rough mountainous paths, the scorching tropical sun, drenching tornadoes, badly prepared food (in some places), and vicious mules to ride, life has not been a bed of roses for me of late." He recommended that the British government appoint A. G. Ceffala, the superintendent of the telegraph station in São Tomé, as vice-consul to the island, to help gather information and to aid English companies.[41] Nightingale's report was slow to arrive, however, and Fox Bourne and several MPs asked the Foreign Office about the reason for the delay. Fox Bourne was willing to give the Foreign Office a "reasonable time" for the report, but his Aborigines' Protection Society hoped "to stir in the matter as soon as may seem proper."[42] In addition to inquiring about Nightingale's account, Fox Bourne's letters to the Foreign Office demanded that the British government, on the basis of international treaties, protest to Portuguese authorities about the traffic in humans in their African colonies.[43]

Meanwhile, MPs from both of the major political parties were beginning to raise questions about the reports of slavery in Portuguese West Africa. While Unionists obviously hoped to benefit politically by associating the Liberal Party with a toleration of slavery in Portuguese colonies, Liberal MPs over the next several years would also press the Liberal government to take steps to halt this use of slavery. The issue did not fall neatly into partisan politics. On July 5, 1906, Unionist MP Sir Gilbert Parker asked Grey about "allegations of slavery carried on in the islands" and questioned how the government intended to bring it to Portugal's attention. The foreign secretary replied that the British government had occasionally addressed the Portuguese on the issue of laboring conditions on the island, and he assured Parker that Nightingale's report on his recent visit was "expected shortly." When Parker inquired if the report would be presented to the House of Commons, Grey replied, "I must see it before I can decide that." Parker also asked what was being done to address the issue of slave cocoa being imported into Britain. Walter Runciman, who replied for the Board of Trade, remarked briefly with words that Grey had recommended: "I do not see that any steps can be taken respecting purchases of cocoa by British merchants."[44]

At long last, Nightingale's report on São Tomé arrived at the Foreign Office on August 20, 1906. The report began with historical background. With the abolition of slavery in the 1870s, Nightingale wrote, the term *slave* had simply been altered to read *serviçal* or *contract labor,* and there had been little change in the life of most workers. In spite of a law to the contrary, children under the age of fifteen were regularly "contracted." Only in 1900 had Angolans begun protesting the export of labor to the islands, claiming that "the province was being drained of its most valuable asset merely for the benefit of the planters in São Thomé and Principe." The price for a contract laborer had soared from only £4 to £6 in the early 1880s to between £30 and £35 by 1900, and in 1906, it was about £25 in São Tomé. Nightingale pointedly called this system slavery: "The prices mentioned above clearly prove that the 'serviçal' is in reality a slave, and becomes the property of the person who contracts him, much the same as if he were a horse or some other marketable commodity." While contracts provided for under the decree of January 1903 were indeed drawn up, laborers themselves were simply not consulted. What was needed was not new laws but the enforcement of existing laws.

In all, Nightingale spent from November 24, 1905, to February 9, 1906, on the two islands, visiting twenty-one roças on Príncipe and thirty-nine on São Tomé. The death rate was considerably higher on Príncipe than on São Tomé because of the presence of the tsetse fly, which transmitted sleeping sickness. The mortality rate at the Príncipe roça of Porto Real d'Oeste averaged about 20 percent per annum for the six-year period between 1900 and 1905. Although there was no education provided for children, Nightingale believed that on the whole "the labourers are well treated in every respect, and great credit is due to the planters for the care they bestow upon the people." There was, however, a "black spot, and it is a big black spot . . . the non-repatriation of the Angolan labourer. That is the one great evil, and it behoves [*sic*] the Portuguese Government to put an end to the present mode of recruiting labourers in Angola as soon as possible." Nightingale clearly sided with the planters, who provided significant revenue to the state but in turn received only "heavy import duties and export duties."[45] While Nightingale, a British official, condemned the means by which the government recruited and retained the serviçais, he clearly admired and respected the Portuguese plantation owners for their labor system in general. Labor, of course, was the key to economic success in all of the European colonies.

Once Foreign Office officials had finally received Nightingale's report, they had perforce to deal with it. When the office received a document or letter, a clerk would write a précis of it. Others would comment on the document or even on the précis, suggesting possible action. These comments were normally followed by the initials of the writer. Higher-ranking officials were the last to study the document, with the secretary of state initialing at the end that he had seen it and sometimes adding his own remarks.

Foreign Office officials were clearly preoccupied with the expected reaction of the Aborigines' Protection Society to Nightingale's report. They felt that they had to walk a very fine line, having to respond to the queries of the society without demanding too much of the Portuguese government. The summary of the report began with a list of Fox Bourne's concerns over the treatment of the serviçais. Guy H. Locock, who wrote the précis, stated that Nightingale offered "ample proof that the Servicaes are not harshly treated in the islands, and we might inform the Aborigines Protection Society of the measures taken to ensure the well-being of the servicaes & of the general . . . purport of the Report." Another official remarked: "The Regulations [of 1903] appear excellent & if properly carried out it will be difficult to make representations to the Portuguese Govt. with regard to the islands. We might however urge them to take steps to suppress the slave trade on the mainland." Barrington added: "The Aborigines Protection Society are very anxious to be allowed to see this report, and it might be politic to show it or the greater part of it to the Secretary or let him have a slightly bowdlerised copy for the confidential information of the Society on the distinct condition that no part of it is to be published. This might prevent their friends in Parl[iamen]t. from pressing for its presentation which would annoy the Portuguese." Grey wrote: "No representations should be made to the Portuguese at present. Such portions of Consul Nightingale's report as relate to the present condition of affairs might be communicated, *but not for publication*, to the Aborigines Society. The portions, which relate to past history, may give rise to unnecessary controversy & annoyance" (emphasis in original).[46]

Why was the Foreign Office so determined not to offend the Portuguese government, since the evidence of labor abuse in Portuguese West Africa—from both official and humanitarian sources—was both plentiful and convincing? One Foreign Office minute on the Nightingale report offers the most convincing reason: the government was unwilling to press Portugal on the issue until it had secured labor for the Transvaal, its own colony in South Africa.[47] Throughout the latter part of the nineteenth century, native labor from Portuguese Mozambique had been exported to French and British possessions in the surrounding area. The laborers were initially sent to Natal and to the Kimberley diamond mines, but by the 1890s, they were recruited for the gold mines in the Transvaal, which became a British colony as a result of the South African War (1899–1902).[48]

By December 1901, the Portuguese governor-general of Mozambique and Alfred Lord Milner, the British high commissioner of South Africa, had arrived at a modus vivendi, or temporary agreement, over labor recruitment for the mines.

Under this agreement, the Witwatersrand Native Labour Association was responsible for recruiting native labor for the many gold mine owners in the Johannesburg area. The temporary agreement was always in danger of breaking down, and South African mining interests desperately sought larger and more reliable sources of labor, especially following the South African War. In 1904, the Conservative government approved the importation of Chinese coolie laborers into South Africa to help work the mines. This use of coolies, however, proved to be politically explosive, as Liberal and Labour politicians equated the conditions and terms under which coolies toiled to slavery; they also saw the coolie labor as a threat to potential white workers from Britain. Therefore, the British government attempted to conclude negotiations with Portuguese officials to secure Mozambique labor. This source could provide workers who were paid little, were tightly controlled, and had few rights. The complicated negotiations, which strengthened Portugal's control over native laborers in Mozambique and generated revenue for the Portuguese colonial government, were not completed until the signing of the Mozambique-Transvaal Convention in April 1909.[49] Until that time, the British Foreign Office, whether under a Conservative or a Liberal government, was unwilling to pressure the Portuguese government to reform its labor practices in West Africa. The government in London, like its counterpart in Lisbon, was determined to secure a reliable labor force for a valuable colony. To a great extent, the gold mines of the Transvaal were equivalent to the roças of São Tomé. Greed and profit dictated both Portuguese labor policy in São Tomé and British labor policy in Johannesburg. Cadbury Bros. was little more than a sideshow to the transactions in South Africa.

The Foreign Office sent Fox Bourne an edited version of Nightingale's report, hoping that it would satisfy the secretary of the Aborigines' Protection Society and weaken his public call for reform. Although Fox Bourne was not permitted to print any of the report, he could and did freely show it to members of his committee and to Travers Buxton, the secretary of the Anti-Slavery Society.[50] After reading the edited report, however, Fox Bourne told the Foreign Office that Nightingale's account had confirmed all of the APS's worst fears, and he called on the government to pressure Portugal to live up to its treaty obligations. One official did not think much of Fox Bourne's long letter, but another, Clarke, perceptively noted: "The fact of the matter is that the system is neither more nor less than slavery but that we do not dare to say much as we might thus offend the Portuguese with whom we desire to stand well."[51] Eric Barrington drafted an inoffensive reply to Fox Bourne indicating that the government would continue to pursue the matter and would approach the Portuguese "whenever an opportunity occurs."[52]

Much to the displeasure of the Foreign Office, Fox Bourne arranged to have Liberal MP Brampton Gurdon ask the government if Nightingale's report was going to be published and what action it intended to take in regard to Portugal and slave labor.[53] Foreign Office authorities found themselves in a dilemma. They had sent only a portion of the report, in confidence, to the Aborigines' Protection Society. Unfortunately, Undersecretary Fitzmaurice noted in his minutes, they had informed Fox Bourne that it was but an extract, and now he wanted all of it. Fitzmaurice added, "I do not see how we can publish the historical part at the beginning without offending the Portuguese Govt." If they did not publish it in full, he continued, the office could be "accused of suppressing part of the Report. . . . It seems hardly fair on Mr. Nightingale to publish as his Report an edition which has been so encluded [*sic*] as largely to alter its complexion."[54] In another confidential memorandum, a Foreign Office official wrote that "in the version which had been communicated to the Aborigines Protection Society all reference to the mainland traffic . . . had been omitted, and the publication of the whole text of the Report would lay His Majesty's Government open to the charge of having suppressed facts which entirely altered the tenour of the Report."[55] In October 1906, however, Grey wrote that "we cannot keep back the report forever," and he made it known that he wanted a memorandum drafted for the Portuguese government that reflected reports from Nightingale and Brock, who had submitted one on the Bihé area of Angola, as well as information "expected from Messrs. Cadbury."[56] On October 29, 1906, Grey, responding to the question from Gurdon, stated that Nightingale's report had been received but that "it was not written in a form for publication, and it deals only with part of the question. I may say generally that the conclusion is that the labourers in San Thomé Principé [*sic*] are well treated, but it is doubtful whether the provisions for repatriation under the new regulations have hitherto been made effective. This and other information, which has been received or is expected soon, will be brought to the notice of the Portuguese Government, in the hope that they will take steps to remedy the evils that exist. When this is done and a reply has been received I will see whether Papers can be laid."[57]

These parliamentary inquiries over São Tomé also sparked debates in the Portuguese Côrtes, or parliament, where speakers expressed their displeasure over British interference in Portugal's affairs.[58] A month earlier, in September 1906, the Portuguese government issued a memorandum claiming that slavery had not existed in its colonies since 1875 and that workers' rights were always protected. Island laborers were under a legal contract for no more than five years and protected by government authorities. While repatriation was "assured," laborers often renewed their contracts because they were well provided for, even in old age, when plantation owners found tasks suitable for them.[59]

The British government, headed by a Liberal Party that was heir to William Gladstone's ideal of openness and honesty, had by this time so tampered with a document as to make it unfit to publish. This same government, representing a nation that had led the fight throughout the nineteenth century to rid the world of slavery and slave trade, found itself in league with a nation (itself a signatory of many treaties and agreements ending slavery) that regularly relied on de facto slavery in its colonies. The evidence of slavery was overwhelming. Yet Portuguese officials and planters, as well as Britain's Liberal foreign secretary, Edward Grey, all hid behind semantics, arguing that there could be no slavery in the Portuguese colonies because it had been abolished in the 1870s; moreover, subsequent regulations had guaranteed this. Grey knew better (his doubts were often expressed in Foreign Office documents), but his public comments regarding Portugal were so tempered as to lose any force they might have had. Ultimately, of course, the Liberal government's policy concerning Portugal was driven by its need to ensure a labor force for its South African possession.

The Foreign Office felt obligated to provide Lisbon with a copy of Nightingale's report. Soveral, the Portuguese minister to London, complained bitterly to Grey in November 1906 about Nightingale's "inquisitional questions" and threatened the consul with indictment.[60] Grey found it "curious that they [the Portuguese officials] should be objecting to something which they have not seen."[61] By December 1906, Sir Francis Villiers, the British minister to Lisbon (the knowledgeable and popular Martin Gosselin had died suddenly in February 1905), had discussed the report with Luis de Magalhães, the Portuguese minister for foreign affairs.[62] Magalhães assured Villiers that there was no possible basis for the allegations. Although he admitted that it was very difficult for the government to completely control the huge province of Angola, wrongdoers, when apprehended, had been punished. The Foreign Office instructed Villiers to inform Magalhães that the British public was very concerned about the labor conditions in Portugal's colonies and that if the allegations were correct, there would be great pressure on the Portuguese government to make amends.[63] A copy of Nightingale's report was finally sent to Soveral in January 1907.[64]

George and William Cadbury wished to meet with Edward Grey. The two Cadburys would have had ready access to the foreign secretary, since George Cadbury helped to fund Liberal Party candidates and also owned the *Daily News*, the main Liberal morning newspaper in London. In correspondence to Grey dated October 19, 1906, George Cadbury spelled out the company's concerns since 1902. Cadbury Bros. and other chocolate firms had sent an agent to the Portuguese colonies to study labor conditions. While the agent had not completed his report, his letters indicated that laborers in São Tomé were recruited in Angola and forcibly marched to the coast. After signing a contract, they were shipped to the islands, where they remained forever. The serviçais were reasonably well treated on the plantations, but their mortality rate was excessive. George Cadbury asked Grey for an interview "when possibly you may be able to help us in considering the next step to be taken." He elaborated: "We are, as English cocoa makers, anxious to act together, and are prepared to make some sacrifice in the interests of the natives. We should be glad, however, to be assured that any step we take will be in harmony with any premeditated action of the British Government, and be of real use in helping to solve the great African labour question."[65] The interview he requested occurred on October 26, 1906, and lasted for twenty minutes. On the following day, George Cadbury wrote to thank Grey for his time and asked him if the summation he included correctly reflected the meeting, as he wished to communicate it to other interested parties: "Shall we be correct in stating that you will be willing to receive the report of our commissioner, and will then consider whether you can properly make some representation to the Portuguese Government on the subject; also that before that time at least you think it would be inadvisable for us, as cocoa makers, to make any public protest. We should be glad to agree to such a suggestion and we do not doubt our friends also will agree."[66]

On November 6, 1906, the Foreign Office wrote to George Cadbury that Grey "would be glad if you would refrain from calling public attention to the question until he has seen the report of your Commissioner and has had an opportunity of speaking to the Portuguese Minister on the subject."[67] On November 7, Cadbury Bros. sent Grey a draft of a letter the company intended to mail to the other cocoa manufacturers and "a few of our intimate friends" describing the interview.[68] A week later, Barrington told the Cadbury directors that "Sir E. Grey approves the terms of the document in question."[69]

The interview and the subsequent exchange of letters satisfied both parties at the time. The Foreign Office wanted to dampen any public criticism of Portuguese colonial labor practices, at least until after the British had arrived at an agreement with Lisbon concerning Mozambique labor in South Africa. Meanwhile, the Cadbury company gained at least the tacit approval of the British government for the firm's endeavors to improve labor conditions in the Portuguese cocoa plantations while continuing to purchase cocoa beans from the islands. William Cadbury, however, feared that Grey would not be able to accomplish much, but he realized that "as we had agreed to see him I cannot see that we can do more than accept his advice—if his representations fail we must then take further action."[70]

Both Cadbury Bros. and the Foreign Office continued to collect information on the dire state of affairs in Portuguese West Africa. The Foreign Office received a letter from the Admiralty dated July 6, 1906, written by John Harvey, commander of HMS *Dwarf*. His ship had recently called at Príncipe and São Tomé. He described the town of Príncipe as in a "deplorable state of ruin." The plantation workers on Príncipe, he added, "struck me as the most miserable looking beings I have ever seen in East or West Africa; large barracks are built for their accommodation, which certainly gives it the appearance of a slave compound."[71] On November 2, 1906, William Cadbury sent Grey a copy of a lengthy article that appeared in the Hamburg newspaper *Fremden Blatt* on July 28, 1906. Written by Professor Aug. Prister, a chemist who had spent time in Africa, the article graphically portrayed the slave trade and the conditions of life in Angola. He described Angola as a beautiful country cursed by the slave trade, where women were treated as slave breeding stock. Men and women commanded such high prices in São Tomé that few were available in Angola, and European firms building a railroad from the coast near Benguela into the interior were forced to hire workers from elsewhere. "Our ladies," he added, "who drink the good cocoa and chocolate, have no notion how the Portuguese planters get their workmen." Yet the European governments, with consulates in Luanda and in view of the trading in humans, did nothing. And Angola continued to suffer under the Portuguese who, after four hundred years, had accomplished naught: "There are no streets, no schools, no industry, no trade—it is the peace of a cemetery. . . . In a country of thousands of square miles with a climate of the finest kind, they cannot even grow potatoes for the handful of Portuguese who live there, for they are imported from Lisbon."[72]

One of the parties to whom William Cadbury regularly reported was his friend and confidant E. D. Morel. They began corresponding in 1903, and a close working relationship and a marked degree of mutual respect quickly developed.[73] For example, Cadbury consulted Morel in 1903 over the selection of an agent to visit the Portuguese colonies.[74] Morel began work in 1891 as a clerk for Elder Dempster, the Liverpool-based shipping company. The firm, owned by Alfred Jones, traded extensively in central Africa and was involved, among other things, with the export of ivory and rubber from the Congo. (Both Nevinson and Burtt traveled on Elder Dempster ships while in West Africa.) Morel, who by 1895 was head of the Congo department, eventually realized that the natives in the Congo were not compensated fairly for their work. Evidence mounted that they were being brutally exploited by European traders under the aegis of King Leopold's private company. Morel resigned from Elder Dempster in 1901 to become a journalist. With support from Alfred Jones and John Holt, he set up the *West African Mail* in 1903 and worked to expose Leopold's oppressive regime in Africa. Holt, the owner of a Liverpool shipping firm that bore his name, heavily influenced Morel and also developed ties with William Cadbury. Early in his career, Holt had worked in West Africa, becoming a defender of the natives and a staunch advocate of free trade. He was particularly critical of companies that restricted commerce through the exercise of monopoly power.[75]

Morel's crusade against King Leopold's brutal colonial rule was given a boost when Roger Casement, British consul in the Congo Free State, was ordered by the British government to visit the interior in 1903; the devastating report he penned thereafter, depicting the death and destruction caused by European traders, was published in early 1904.[76] Morel formed the Congo Reform Association (CRA) in the same year.[77] As editor of the *West African Mail* (renamed the *African Mail* in 1907) and secretary of the CRA and with a family to support, Morel was often short of financial resources. Holt regularly provided funds to him, and William Cadbury first contributed £100 to the CRA in February 1904.[78]

After exchanging several letters, William Cadbury and Morel first met on June 26, 1905, at which time Cadbury offered to contribute £1,000 to Morel for his work. Following the meeting, Cadbury indicated that he approved of Morel's policy regarding the Congo—"it must be right to publish proved facts regardless of the cost"—and he told Morel, "I am glad to have met you, we have right on our side & a fight like this makes life worth living." In retrospect, Cadbury's statement appears ironic, considering how reluctant he became to publish facts on São Tomé. Morel, meanwhile, wrote Cadbury immediately after their initial get-together: "I have just got home, and thinking over our conversation, I am afraid I took very calmly your extraordinarily generous statement that you wished to give £1000 to the cause. The fact of the matter was that I did not quite know what to say—I felt rather overwhelmed."[79] In December, after Cadbury helped to set up a committee to provide financial support for the CRA, Morel wrote him, "You're a brick of bricks."[80] From 1908 to 1912, Cadbury contributed about £400 per year to Morel, and he provided more than £1,000 at a testimonial in 1911. He continued to support Morel's family even after Morel died in 1924.[81]

E. D. Morel and William Cadbury regularly corresponded over the years about common concerns. After the publication of Nevinson's first article on São Tomé in August 1905, Morel expressed fear that Portuguese matters might distract from the much worse situation in the Congo.[82] Years later, Nevinson wrote that although Morel worried "that Angola might divert attention from the Congo," he became a good friend.[83] Through Morel, Cadbury met the Reverend John Harris and his wife Alice, Baptist missionaries in the Congo who had provided investigators with considerable information and photographs of the atrocities there. Effective public speakers, they began working for the CRA in 1906 and later were employed by the Anti-Slavery Society.[84]

Although the Aborigines' Protection Society had pointed out abuses in the Congo throughout the 1890s, its resources were limited and its concerns exceptionally broad. Moreover, while Morel and Fox Bourne respected each other's devotion to humanitarian efforts, they often clashed over tactics. Morel's biographer refers to Fox Bourne as "an irritable and utterly dedicated humanitarian, who had worn himself out defending the interests of natives all over the globe." Fox Bourne appreciated Morel's energy and concern over the Congo, but he resented his attempt to reshape and use the Aborigines' Protection Society for his new Congo Reform Association. In February 1904, he chastised Morel for "the reckless haste with which you are rushing a plan which you have sprung upon men who have been working at the Congo question long before you took it up, and whom you now expect, on the spur of the moment, to bow to your decision and submit to your leadership."[85] In spite of Fox Bourne's caustic letter, Morel believed that relations between the Congo Reform Association and the Aborigines' Protection Society were good, as three members of the latter group served on his board. He often observed that people in organizations found consensus difficult. He wrote to Cadbury in October 1905: "If I had not over and again gripped things and involved my own responsibility, acting at once, and running the risk of being disavowed, we should not be so far advanced as we are now. I have the greatest respect for F-B but he is over seventy, old and in bad health, constantly away. Then the APS work on old fashioned methods; there must always be Committee meetings, for anything at all—result, delay, opportunity passes etc."[86] Cadbury also found Fox Bourne wanting and described him as a "meddlar."[87]

For his part, Cadbury did not wish to play any public role in the CRA, preferring to remain an invisible supporter; when he was asked in December 1905 to become a committee member of the CRA and then asked in November 1906 to join a CRA delegation to see Grey, he declined, stating that he needed to concentrate on the São Tomé inquiry.[88] Morel surely welcomed Cadbury's attitude, which freed him to run his association without interference from his major contributor. E. D. Morel was known to be a difficult person to work with; he was egotistical and "increasingly difficult to satisfy." His biographer adds, "Certain of his own righteousness, Morel was equally convinced of the wickedness of his opponents."[89]

As 1906 drew to a close, little had been accomplished regarding the allegations of slave trade and slavery in Portuguese West Africa except for the amassing of additional incriminating information. Nevinson had published his articles and his book *A Modern Slavery*. The Foreign Office had received damning evidence from its own consul, Nightingale, and from a naval commander, but it chose to remain silent in order to buy time to finalize a labor agreement with Portugal in South Africa.

William Cadbury had revisited Lisbon in January 1906, once again meeting with officials, and he had also gained from Burtt a cache of letters attesting to the shocking slave trade in Angola. Nonetheless, he remained scornful of Nevinson's reporting, distrusting his graphic prose and resenting his air of certainty. He told Fox Bourne in February 1906 that Burtt had spent about eight months on the islands, "obtaining the very fullest particulars from personal investigation, which is more than Mr. Nevinson did—most of his facts are mere hearsay."[90] In February 1907, Cadbury wrote Travers Buxton that Burtt was "making a much more thorough investigation than Nevinson" and that his report was "quite as severe as anything Nevinson has written, though without the embellishment."[91]

Cadbury obviously found it difficult to recognize that Nevinson was a journalist, and a very good one. Journalists tend to examine events over a short period, then make judgments on the basis of available evidence. For William Cadbury—who was a deliberative and thorough person whose entire day was carefully planned as well as a member of the Society of Friends, in which issues were carefully discussed at length—Nevinson's stories must have appeared rash.[92] Meanwhile, Nevinson remained involved in the great slave issue, haunted by what he had witnessed in West Africa and afflicted by physical infirmities and discomforts he acquired in Angola that would plague him for many years. As a working journalist, however, he was out of Britain in late 1905 and for much of 1906, reporting on the revolutionary turmoil in Russia. Meanwhile, the old and ill Fox Bourne battled on, sending his well-argued missives to the Foreign Office, all the time doubting if the government was willing to put any meaningful pressure on its ancient ally. One more piece of evidence remained to be put forward, the report of Joseph Burtt.

5 Joseph Burtt's Report

> The root of the whole matter lies in S. Thomé and Principe. The islands want labour, and are ready at any time to pay down half a million sterling for it, without asking questions.
>
> *Joseph Burtt's report, 1906 draft*

> If this is not slavery, I know of no word in the English language which correctly characterizes it.
>
> *Joseph Burtt's report, 1907*

THE WRITING, EDITING, translating, and publishing of Joseph Burtt's report preoccupied the firm of Cadbury throughout 1907. As negotiations between the chocolate companies and the Foreign Office over the final version of the report stretched well into that year, humanitarian societies, concerned citizens, a chamber of commerce, and the press grew impatient. Because the Foreign Office requested that the companies not make the report public, Cadbury Bros. sought to restrict public discussion of Portuguese labor practices and purposely discouraged journalists from publishing critical articles. This effort was, however, a shallow pretense, since George Cadbury, one of the principal chocolate company owners, was also the proprietor of several newspapers, including the *Daily News*, that had been in the forefront criticizing the government over the abuse of Chinese coolie laborers in South Africa. By the time Burtt's report was finally made available to the Portuguese in late 1907, two years had elapsed since the appearance of Nevinson's *Harper's* articles, and it was over a year after the publication of his book *A Modern Slavery*. In December 1907, William Cadbury and Burtt held a series of discussions with Portuguese planters and government officials concerning the implications of the report. However, the Burtt report was not made available to the general public in Britain until October 1908.

Burtt returned to Britain on April 13, 1907. He had sent ahead a draft of his report, copies of which Cadbury Bros. provided to the Foreign Office and to cooperating chocolate manufacturers.[1] Burtt began meeting with key people as soon as he arrived home. On May 2, he convinced the board of directors of Rowntree that "beyond all doubt . . . the negro labourers in the Cocoa plantations of S. Thomé and Principe are in the condition of practical slavery, and that the methods by which this negro labour is obtained from the mainland of Africa is cruel and villainous." Rowntree's directors feared that a boycott of São Tomé cocoa might not be successful but that continuing to buy this cocoa could mean complications. If the British companies chose to expose conditions on the plantations, they needed to be able to inform the public that the cocoa firms did not use slave-produced beans. And to wage an effective campaign against the plantation owners, the press would have to be involved. Joseph Rowntree ominously warned: "The firms of Cadbury and Rowntree have many political enemies who would rejoice to have an opportunity of denouncing in the press what they would call the hypocrisy of the Cocoa houses who, after exposing slavery in Thome, continued to use 'slave grown cocoa.'"[2] The Rowntree and Cadbury families supported the Liberal Party financially and through newspapers that they owned. In the heated political atmosphere of the first decade of the twentieth century, the opposition Tory Party and its press would obviously relish any opportunity to attack both the Quaker-owned chocolate firms and the Liberals.

On April 25, 1907, a week before his interview with the Rowntree directors, Burtt discussed his report with Edward A. Walrond Clarke and Charles H. Lyell at the Foreign Office. Officials found the report "very moderate in tone" and not nearly so dramatic as claimed by the Cadbury firm the previous December.[3] The Foreign Office clearly wanted to minimize the report; a week later, Edward Grey suggested to Cadbury Bros. that the Foreign Office provide the Portuguese government with "a slightly expurgated version of Mr. Burtt's report omitting such portions as might give unnecessary offence to them." At the same time, the British government planned to assure the Portuguese that if they took steps to stop the abuses in the near future, London would attempt to persuade Cadbury officials not to print Burtt's report. If such steps were not forthcoming, however, the Portuguese government should expect publication of the report, "which would certainly be followed by an agitation in the press and the public." Grey then asked Cadbury Bros. "whether [it] approve[d] of the above communication being made to the Portuguese Government, and whether, in the event of satisfactory assurances being received from them respecting the discontinuance of the abuses now complained of, [it] would consent to Mr. Burtt's report remaining unpublished."[4]

Burtt told Fox Bourne of his discussions at the Foreign Office. Alarm bells immediately rang in Fox Bourne's mind, and he at once wrote a pointed letter to William Cadbury. This explicit letter set forth the difficulties that the Cadbury company would face if it acquiesced to the Foreign Office request to delay publication of the report:

> I told him [Burtt] I should write to you urging . . . the inexpedience, as it seems to me, of your giving any promise to Sir Edward Grey that you will delay publication of Burtt's report until you have the sanction of the F.O. I am most anxious that Burtt's report, as well as Nightingale's, should be made public as soon as possible and that thus the ground should be cleared for putting all the Parliamentary and other legitimate pressure we can, by way of inducing it to take vigorous action before the Session closes. Otherwise, there will be grave risk of nothing being done till next year.
>
> The F.O. can, of course, suppress indefinitely Nightingale's report. But it has no power, unless you give it, over Burtt's report and I am convinced by previous experience in such cases that it will procrastinate as long as it can.
>
> Do let us push the matter to the front before the evidence (much of which *you* have collected at great outlay and with such zeal) can be thrown aside as "ancient history." And do not let us give our Foreign Office any excuse for sheltering itself under vague promises from the Portuguese Government, which it will delay making as long as possible and which, when made, threaten to be as worthless as previous edicts and ordinances have been made, unless public and international opinion can be brought to bear upon it.[5]

William Cadbury assured Fox Bourne that it was proper for Grey to use Burtt's report as the basis for talks with the Portuguese. Grey knew that the Cadbury firm expected the Portuguese to carry out reform within a reasonably short time, but at the same time, Cadbury Bros. felt compelled to give Grey enough time to act. The chocolate firms insisted that they would not give up their rights over the report.[6] While William Cadbury appeared to brush aside Fox Bourne's concerns, the company had substantial reservations about the Foreign Office appeal of May 2 that publication of the report be postponed or perhaps canceled if Portugal promised to make real changes in the near future. In a draft letter to the

Foreign Office that was never mailed, Cadbury Bros. contended that the abuse of labor in Portugal's colonies, which enjoyed the support of the government in Lisbon, was "in almost every sense as bad as the old-time slavery." The firm feared that Portuguese officials could not be trusted because they so regularly flaunted the enforcement of reform measures.[7] At its May 14, 1907, meeting, the Cadbury management committee (composed of George Cadbury; his two sons, Edward and George Jr.; and his two nephews, William and Barrow) agreed to the publication of Burtt's report if the Foreign Office did not act "within six months." On July 30, the committee decided that if "diplomatic representations prove ineffective we will after a reasonable time give up using Cocoa from the islands of St Thomé and Principe."[8]

Burtt and the Cadbury directors eventually agreed to the Foreign Office request to amend the report.[9] But the Foreign Office officials were disappointed in Burtt's revised report, for he had not only "cut out the passages we had suggested" but also "left out most of the names of his informants, & generally such chapter & verse as would enable his statements to be verified." When officials told Burtt that his deletions "weakened the force of the report to a most serious extent," he argued that he had to protect his sources.[10] Burtt finally provided the Foreign Office with a confidential supplement, but under no circumstances was it to be revealed to Portuguese authorities.[11] While Foreign Office officials were disappointed in Burtt's failure to provide sufficient documentation, Lyell noted that if the report were indeed accurate, "the system described is a far more flagrant breach of the Brussels Convention than anything we have heard of from the Congo."[12]

Representatives of the Cadbury firm met with Foreign Office officials to finalize the report on June 27, 1907. According to the company's understanding, if the Foreign Office could not show tangible results of Portuguese reform "say by the end of the year," then, "in the interests of the black population of a large section of South Africa, it [might] be necessary to publish the report."[13] William Cadbury also informed Nevinson that the firms of Cadbury, Fry, and Rowntree had asked the Foreign Office to convey their concerns to the Portuguese government and had set a time limit for meaningful reform. Should that fail to materialize, the companies felt free to publish Burtt's report and, if necessary, call for a boycott of Portuguese cocoa beans.[14] Nevinson appreciated the chocolate firms' efforts: "If it comes to the boycott, I am convinced that the system cannot continue, and in any case your Firms will have . . . done much to restore our moral influence in the world."[15]

By June 1907, Fox Bourne decided to publish a short statement about Portuguese labor practices in West Africa. In a five-page draft, he offered evidence of slave trade and slavery as submitted by Nevinson and by British consuls, including Nightingale, Casement, and Pickersgill. He also commented on Nightingale's postponed report and on Grey's concerns, as well as on Burtt's forthcoming account that was to substantiate earlier evidence. Without telling them what to do, Fox Bourne stressed that the English chocolate firms, some of which purchased raw materials from these slave-based plantations and whose own agent had carefully investigated the state of affairs, "should be in no doubt as to the wickedness of the traffic. That wickedness . . . is on a par with the slavery by which the West Indian sugar industry and the cotton industry of the United States were maintained in former days. The first of these abominations was done away with nearly seventy years ago; the second lasted only two decades longer."[16]

Fox Bourne sent copies of the article to officials at Cadbury, Fry, and Rowntree, with a letter explaining that the Aborigines' Protection Society expected to publish it soon. The society, he noted, had no knowledge of the extent to which any of the companies purchased materials from the islands, but he hoped that the firms would be supportive of the APS's cause. After five years of dealing with the Foreign Office over this issue with no action, the society believed that more dramatic steps needed to be taken. Fox Bourne added: "Our only warrant for inviting your cooperation is a firm conviction that there should be no further delay in such efforts as this Society can make towards putting an end to a monstrous evil, for the tolerance and development of which Great Britain is to a large extent responsible."[17]

In a letter to William Cadbury five days later, Fox Bourne insisted that British consumers and producers of chocolate were at the time implicitly guilty of supporting the production of "slave grown cocoa." He explained that the Aborigines' Protection Society had been virtually forced to take public action, since Foreign Office officials admitted that in spite of evidence against Portugal, the British government "sees difficulties in putting pressure on the Portuguese Government for some months to come, and would like an indefinite postponement."[18]

The three large, Quaker-owned chocolate firms did not want Fox Bourne to publish his article. Therefore, six directors—Francis and Roderick Fry, Arnold and Seebohm Rowntree, and William and Edward Cadbury—met for one and a half hours on June 27, 1907, with Fox Bourne, the secretary of the Aborigines' Protection Society. These formidable business directors, who were bound together as members of the Society of Friends, formed an impressive and cohesive group. They were captains of the English chocolate industry. While competing with one other, their three firms had cooperated by 1907 on certain components of the business, such as advertising, pricing of goods, and hiring.[19] In addition to all six directors being the leaders of powerful, influential, respected, and philanthropic companies, two of them had gained recognition for studying the low pay and wretched labor conditions among members of the working class. In 1901, Seebohm Rowntree wrote *Poverty: A Study of Town Life*, a classic examination of destitution in York, the hometown of the Rowntree company, and Edward Cadbury coauthored *Women's Work and Wages* in 1906 and *Sweating* in 1907.[20]

The company representatives emphasized to Fox Bourne all they had been doing about São Tomé labor. However, according to William Cadbury's notes of the meeting, Fox Bourne, who no longer trusted the Foreign Office on this issue, believed there was no choice but to refuse to purchase cocoa beans from the islands. Finding that they could get nowhere with the obstinate and uncompromising Fox Bourne, the companies' directors requested a meeting with the committee of the Aborigines' Protection Society.[21] Thus, on July 4, 1907, William and George Cadbury, along with Seebohm and Arnold Rowntree, attended a second meeting with Fox Bourne, who was accompanied by board members Brampton Gurdon, E. Wright Brooks, and others. William Cadbury regarded this second conference as a confrontation at which Fox Bourne accused the chocolate firms of hypocritical behavior and argued that the only right course of action for the companies was a boycott.

The directors of the three chocolate companies focused on several points at their meetings of June 27 and July 4 with Fox Bourne and his board members. They informed Fox Bourne and his committee that they had told Grey the companies would stop the purchase of the São Tomé cocoa if he so recommended, even if such an action cost the firms money. The companies predicted that a boycott would put a few hundred of their employees out of work or on short time for a period. However, despite the fact that the company directors would "each get a halo for [his] self sacrificing virtuous act" of boycotting São Tomé cocoa, nothing would have been accomplished, according to William Cadbury, except gaining "the comfortable assurance that we have wiped our hands of all responsibility in the matter." The chocolate companies opted to follow what seemed to be a sensible alternative that was proposed by the Foreign Office: the British government would apply diplomatic pressure on the Portuguese to stop the use of slave labor. As a part of that diplomatic initiative, the Foreign Office wanted the chocolate companies to present Burtt's report directly to the Portuguese planters. If, at this crucial moment, Fox Bourne chose to issue a graphic statement critical of the Portuguese plantation owners and government, the Foreign Office's dealings with Lisbon would become all but impossible: "If you consider that you have no other course but to *immediately* create a very bitter feeling against the Portuguese by the publication of such a statement as you have drafted, it should at least be clear to you that you make it practically impossible for the Government to take any action short of armed force, or for us at any time again to approach the Lisbon cocoa planters by whose courtesy it has been possible to obtain Joseph Burtt's report."[22]

After the July 4 meeting, the Aborigines' Protection Society, obviously under tremendous pressure from the three chocolate firms (several of whose members were subscribers to and board members of the APS), agreed to withhold public comment for a reasonable period while the government took the opportunity to carry out its initiative with the Portuguese. The society, however, reserved for itself "the liberty of communicating on occasion with the Foreign Office and of collecting and publishing such further evidence as may come in its way."[23] Fox Bourne assured William Cadbury that he had "never thought of questioning [his] integrity & honest zeal in this matter or that of the firms concerned." He hoped that the policy Cadbury Bros. was following would be effective, but given Foreign Office practice, he found that unlikely.[24]

Fox Bourne and William Cadbury exchanged a few letters in relation to their confrontation. Cadbury obviously believed that Fox Bourne had made improper use of some information and had failed to recognize that, due to the small portion of the world's supply of cocoa originating in São Tomé, a boycott by English firms could not be effective except in a "moral" way. He was also disturbed by what he regarded as an unsubstantiated statement by Nevinson claiming that a U.S. chocolate firm had stopped buying São Tomé cocoa because of revelations of slave labor on the islands. In addition, Cadbury declared that a lawyer friend of his, on reading Fox Bourne's article and cover letter, thought that the secretary of the Aborigines' Protection Society harbored an assumption that the actions of the chocolate firms over São Tomé were hypocritical.[25] Cadbury was a member of an influential family with political connections and an official in a firm with extraordinary resources. He and his associates, who enjoyed paternalistic relationships with their workers, would have expected deferential respect from subordinates. Indeed, in this long story of São Tomé cocoa, William Cadbury proved willing on several occasions to exercise his authority to berate those who questioned his strategy. Fox Bourne did not easily back down, however, and responded to Cadbury's charge of hypocrisy: "You must excuse my saying that, if your lawyer advised you that remarks I had used resolved themselves into a charge of hypocrisy against you, I think a lawyer, were I to consult one, would advise me that the letter I am now replying to charges me with deliberate untruth & falsification of facts. It is because I put no such interpretation on your letter that I now write in friendly terms." As to the statement attributed to Nevinson, Fox Bourne stressed that "neither I nor the Society should be held responsible for all the statements made by him."[26] Fortunately, the next letters were not so barbed.[27]

Why were the chocolate firms and particularly William Cadbury so opposed to the publication of Fox Bourne's small pamphlet? There was, after all, nothing particularly new there, as Nevinson, numerous consuls, missionaries, and other people in the colonies had written of Portuguese colonial slavery. Fox Bourne and Travers Buxton and their organizations had revealed much of this tale of woe to the Foreign Office and to MPs for years. At bottom, the deliberative and driven William Cadbury was perturbed that anyone dared to object to his plan for bringing about reform. While Fox Bourne's pamphlet would not have enjoyed a large circulation, copies would have been sent to newspapers (which would comment on it in their pages), to some MPs (who would thus have the basis to ask additional questions in Parliament), and to members of the humanitarian societies. In the last case, many were Quakers who were already growing uneasy, inasmuch as chocolate firms continued to purchase cocoa beans produced by slaves.

By 1907, Henry Nevinson was also growing impatient with the lack of action by the Quaker chocolate manufacturers. He continued to gather additional information on the slave trade from people acquainted with Angola, including the missionary Matthew Stober. He met Burtt on April 29, shortly after he had returned from Africa and conferred with Foreign Office officials. According to Nevinson, Burtt related that Grey wanted the Cadbury company to "keep quiet till he [Grey] has made private representations to Portugal." Burtt did not believe that these representations would be of value or that a boycott would be effective, "as the amount is not enough to matter" (in 1907, Cadbury Bros. imported nearly 7.4 million pounds of cocoa beans from São Tomé, about 13 percent of the island's total exports); rather, he felt publicity was needed to bring the matter to a head.[28] But publicity, of course, was what William Cadbury was discouraging. On May 28, Nevinson met with representatives from Cadbury, Fry, and Rowntree, including William Cadbury and Burtt. He suggested forcefully that a boycott would have a powerful "moral effect" and later recorded in his diary that the representatives "listened quietly but I felt a hostile air." At that meeting, William Cadbury argued that the core of the slave problem was in Angola, whereas Burtt saw the islands as the primary problem because of the high prices that the plantation owners were willing to pay for labor.[29]

Most observers recognized that labor-related conditions were much worse in Angola than on the islands. Nevinson, however, refused to distinguish between the two colonies, as Africans were enslaved in both. He would not accept limitations on human rights (his reporting from India, Ireland, and Russia, for example, focused on the inability of people to control their own lives), and he demanded that the chocolate firms make a meaningful and positive response by boycotting the Portuguese plantation owners. If Nevinson was on the one extreme of insisting on the right of self-determination for African laborers, there were many businesspeople and government officials in Britain and elsewhere in Europe who believed that the natives, for their own welfare and development, needed to be engaged in what Europeans perceived as productive work, even if that required coercion. Along this spectrum, the directors and owners of the three large English chocolate firms would clearly have held views close to Nevinson's. They were, after all, Quakers and humanitarians. William Cadbury, however, wanted to believe that the Portuguese government officials were well-meaning individuals and that the roça owners ultimately cared about the welfare of their laborers. In spite of overwhelming evidence to the contrary, he was unable or unwilling to accept that plantation owners and managers were not interested in reform.

The slavery issue and the role played by the Cadbury company was a common topic of discussion in the journalistic circles in which Nevinson moved, especially at the *Nation*, where editor Henry Massingham gathered writers and other guests for regular luncheons at the National Liberal Club to discuss current topics.[30] Among those present were members of the Rowntree family as well as the writer Henry Brailsford, who encouraged Nevinson to focus his attention on the slavery issue. Joseph Rowntree, of the York chocolate company, had purchased the *Speaker* in 1906, transforming it into the *Nation* in March 1907, while his nephew, Arnold Rowntree, served as an officer in the Rowntree newspaper holdings.[31] By July 1907, Nevinson, who had begun writing for the *Nation* in February of that year, was collecting material for another article on slavery to appear in the *Fortnightly Review*. Given the open discussions on the topic, the chocolate firms heard of his plan. The company officials feared that this article might force them to give up São Tomé cocoa and therefore complicate the Foreign Office's diplomatic approaches to Lisbon.[32] Thus, the Cadbury company devised a potential counterattack through the newspapers, particularly the Cadbury-owned *Daily News*.[33] The chocolate firms sent Richard Cross, an officer at the *Nation* and an attorney for Rowntree, to attempt to dissuade Nevinson from publishing the article.[34] Cross wrote William Cadbury that "if Nevinson knows what we are really doing there will not be much difficulty in persuading him to hold over his article, and I propose to see him in London . . . this week. . . . The Rowntrees are quite prepared to let me state that if diplomatic representations prove ineffective they will after a reasonable time give up using cocoa from the two islands. I suppose I shall be right in saying as much on your behalf but I should like you to tell me in your own words how far you propose to go in this respect."[35]

Cross was naive if he thought that Nevinson did not know what the chocolate manufacturers were doing. The journalist had met not only with the firms' representatives but also (and regularly) with Burtt and Fox Bourne. Cross saw Nevinson at the National Liberal Club on August 1, 1907, where he gave him a copy of Burtt's report.[36] Following the meeting on August 1, Nevinson described Cross as "altogether admirable—honest, straight, and intelligent. I am also convinced they are doing the only good thing, but I do not see the least reason in suppressing what I have got to say, especially as Burtt's report, which he kindly gave me, reads like an abstract of my book and no more. A plain statement of the case can only be to the honour of the Firms that go right, and I want to spread the movement abroad too if possible."[37] Cross and Nevinson communicated several more times.[38] On August 20, Cross told William Cadbury that Nevinson "speaks with great admiration of what the Cocoa Firms are doing, and though he means to go on with his article he will not be in any way offensive but rather the reverse."[39]

In spite of pressure to the contrary, Nevinson published "The Angola Slave Trade" in the September 1907 issue of *Fortnightly Review*. He opened with a vivid description of the horrendous sight of the bodies he had seen in the Hungry Country. A correspondent had just told him, Nevinson added, that the conditions of the Angolan slave trade in 1907 were no better than what he himself had witnessed in 1905. He also recounted brutal corporal treatment meted out to runaway slaves on the island of Príncipe. Noting that the islands produced one-fifth of the world's cocoa beans and that English manufacturers gained about one-fourth of their beans from São Tomé, Nevinson continued: "One-fifth of all the chocolate eaten and cocoa drunk in the world is the produce of slave labour, and the cocoa and chocolate makers of Great Britain have been indirectly employing one-third of the slaves on the islands." He praised the British chocolate manufacturers for investigating the conditions in Portuguese West Africa; he detailed Portuguese laws that consistently failed to protect laborers; and he spelled out the activities of the British government, including the Foreign Office's particularly "cautious" attitude. What could be done? Nevinson mentioned that a New York firm had notified him that it had stopped purchasing São Tomé cocoa because of his report. He hoped that if Portugal did not quickly mend its ways, "other great firms, famous for their integrity and high social ideals, will follow the same course. A boycott proclaimed by well-known British and American makers would have an incalculable effect upon the public opinion of the world. . . . Meantime, the thing for us ordinary consumers to remember is that one-fifth of all the cocoa and chocolate we take is now produced for us by a form of black labour as truly slavery as anything on our own possessions before the emancipation, or on the plantations of the Southern States before the American Civil War."[40] One journal noted of Nevinson's article: "It is a strange instance of the topsy-turvydom of our economic arrangements that the cocoa and chocolate which are turned out in this country by philanthropic manufacturers with the most scrupulous care for the welfare of their employees, should have been grown under the most infamous and revolting conditions of murderous slavery."[41]

Far more disturbing to William Cadbury than Nevinson's article was the publicity generated by a meeting of the African Trade Section of the Liverpool Chamber of Commerce in late September 1907. At the center of that affair was the selfsame Henry Nevinson who, accompanied by the missionary Matthew Stober, testified to the group about slavery in Portugal's West African colonies. After hearing Nevinson's remarks, the African Trade Section called on the British government "to take at once such steps as lie in their power to abolish the system" and asked the chocolate firms to consider boycotting the cocoa.[42]

The Foreign Office, fearing that heightened publicity would complicate the government's presentation of the Burtt report to the Portuguese, was not pleased with the proceedings, which received considerable publicity in the newspapers.[43] After gaining approval from the Foreign Office, William Cadbury spoke to the Liverpool Chamber of Commerce on October 21 on behalf of the three chocolate manufacturers. He detailed the steps taken by the companies, including sending Burtt to West Africa. He stressed that the British government, which had always been apprised of the companies' activities, would shortly present Burtt's report to the Portuguese government and that representatives of the firms would meet with the planters in Lisbon to discuss Burtt's account. Cadbury added that while the Foreign Office had originally asked the companies not to bring the labor issue before the public, recent publicity in Britain and Portugal meant that such a restriction was no longer necessary. Cadbury admonished the chamber for making it difficult for the Foreign Office to carry out its policies in Portugal and for disturbing the Portuguese, who were proud of the economic success of São Tomé and viewed criticism as "prompted by commercial jealousy." A boycott, like that suggested by the chamber of commerce, would deprive the chocolate manufacturers of their greatest source of influence, the power of purchase. Besides, should the English firms stop buying cocoa from the islands, companies from other nations would quickly step in and procure the beans, and nothing would be gained. In closing, Cadbury added that the companies had been in contact with the Aborigines' Protection Society and the Anti-Slavery Society and that "they have concurred with us in our course of action up to the present."[44] Following Cadbury's presentation, the chamber of commerce unanimously passed a resolution of support for the chocolate companies' efforts.[45]

John Holt created the greatest sensation at these meetings by openly criticizing the chamber's president, Alfred Jones, for daring to question the motives of the chocolate companies while himself acting as representative of King Leopold, who was brutally exploiting the people of the Congo.[46] Both Holt and Jones headed shipping companies that operated in West Africa. Holt had first gone to West Africa in 1862 and spent a total of twelve years there, often under trying conditions.[47] He and his friend Mary Kingsley, the anthropologist and writer, believed in the inherent worth of natives and were critical of domineering colonial regimes that denied West Africans their individuality and humanity. He was a proponent of "minimum" or "indirect" rule by colonial governments. A free trade advocate, Holt found it increasingly difficult to deal directly with the natives, since monopolistic regulations as well as intermediaries of various companies denied his shipping firm access to the markets. He contended that natives should be engaged only through the free exchange of their labor and not through coercion, as in the case of Portuguese West Africa or Leopold's Congo. In addition, Holt believed that Nevinson's recommendation of a boycott of São Tomé cocoa would be little more than a temporary measure. What was needed, he argued in a letter to the *Liverpool Daily Post*, was an expansion of cocoa production in areas of West Africa where free labor was utilized, as in the British colonies of Gold Coast and Nigeria, as well as Gabon and the Cameroons.[48] He encouraged the Cadbury company to create a "Cocoa Growing Association" to promote a cocoa supply from British colonies.[49]

Holt, Kingsley, and E. D. Morel are collectively referred to as the "Liverpool School," and Holt and William Cadbury were major financial supporters of Morel and his Congo Reform Association.[50] Both Holt and Morel advocated peasant landownership and enterprise. The Aborigines' Protection Society and Fox Bourne had stressed native property rights for many years and may have influenced Morel in that matter.[51]

While the chocolate companies gained approval from the Liverpool Chamber of Commerce and two chocolate-related trade associations for their endeavors in West Africa, several parties questioned the Cadbury firm's statement to the chamber.[52] Without being specific, William Cadbury reported to Morel that at a Society of Friends meeting in London on November 1, 1907, "there was a very divided feeling about our action, many I regret to say considering that we were acting hypocritically, although perhaps nobody quite said that word."[53] Also, the London representative of C. J. Van Houten, the large Dutch chocolate manufacturer, made it known in a letter to the *Liverpool Daily Post* that his company did not use São Tomé cocoa.[54] In early October, a Birmingham resident announced that a "cocoa crusade" had been established earlier in the summer "to stop the sale of slave-grown cocoa in England, America, and other civilised countries."[55] Of a more damaging nature were the public statements made by the humanitarian societies. At Liverpool, William Cadbury stated that the firms had contacted the Aborigines' Protection Society and the Anti-Slavery Society, which in turn were in accordance with the firms' stance. Fox Bourne pointedly informed Cadbury Bros. that "no such concurrence was expressed" in July 1907, when the chocolate manufacturers had pressed him not to publish his article on São Tomé.[56] Both humanitarian societies quickly informed the public, through their own newsletters and by a letter to the press, that while they had been contacted by the Cadbury firm, they had not necessarily approved of the companies' action but had simply agreed for the time being to postpone additional activities.[57]

William Cadbury's scheme to bring about reform in São Tomé and Príncipe through quiet persuasion was collapsing by 1907. Press coverage of the situation on the islands continued to mount; Nevinson, Fox Bourne, and even Burtt thought that publicity, not silence, would lead to reform. After six years of activity (some critics would have said inactivity), Cadbury had little to show for his efforts. Even some Friends expressed misgivings about the Cadbury company's continued purchase of Portuguese cocoa. Also, the big Quaker-owned cocoa firms found their business increasingly subject to political forces.

In 1907, MPs questioned the Liberal government about conditions on São Tomé and Príncipe, especially in regard to the number of serviçais imported and their rate of repatriation, as well as the status of treaties between Britain and Portugal regarding slave trade. When Grey was asked on July 18 whether there were any papers concerning island labor that could be presented to Parliament, he indicated that there was nothing "which could be usefully laid before the House," no doubt a phrase carefully crafted to avoid publishing the emasculated and embarrassing Nightingale report.[58] On July 22, an MP asked if the government would "consider the desirability of prohibiting slave-grown produce into this country," to which Prime Minister Henry Campbell-Bannerman responded, "It is not considered desirable to take any steps in the direction indicated."[59] In a House of Commons budget debate two months earlier, Conservative Andrew Bonar Law reproached Chancellor of the Exchequer Herbert Asquith for retaining an import duty on cocoa that benefited the few, including chocolate manufacturers, who used their wealth to ensure that others could not gain the same advantages.[60] Bonar Law was pointing out the inconsistency of a Liberal Party that espoused free trade while continuing to levy an import duty that inhibited trade.

Bonar Law deliberately pinpointed the Liberal newspapers owned by the Quaker chocolate manufacturers who also favored free trade. In the rough and tumble world of the London press, attacks on opposition newspapers and their owners were commonplace. The Tory press was all too happy to question the motives of Liberal newspapers after the Liberal triumph in the 1906 election made Campbell-Bannerman a prime minister presiding over a mixture of imperial enthusiasts and social reformers. When the São Tomé labor issue became clearly associated with the Quaker chocolate firms and newspaper proprietors, the Tory papers seized the opportunity. They charged that George Cadbury and Joseph Rowntree were part of a "cocoa press" or "cocoa trust," being little more than philanthropists using their newspapers "to further their own business interests."[61]

On September 3, 1907, the Conservative *Daily Graphic* printed a letter under the headline "Slave-Grown Cocoa" from a Theo Broma, writing from the London Commercial Sales Rooms, Mincing Lane. The name of the writer itself was a play on words, *Theobroma* being part of the Latin nomenclature for the cocoa tree. The writer asserted that thousands of bags of cocoa beans grown in São Tomé were shipped from Lisbon to Liverpool for the Quaker chocolate manufacturers. He concluded: "Their attention has been called over and over again to the fact that they make their chocolate and cocoa powder from slave-grown cocoa, but they do not appear to care one pin. In Mincing Lane we consider they have Nonconformist consciences in excelsis."[62] In a letter to the *Daily Graphic* six weeks later, Cadbury Bros. spelled out what the company had been doing on the issue. Until recently, company officials, at the request of the Foreign Office, had not responded to these allegations. Now, however, they were free to do so, and they asked for a retraction: "This allegation is untrue, libellous and offensive to ourselves and the other two firms concerned and calculated to do us serious damage. . . . We must ask that you kindly insert in your paper a withdrawal of the allegation contained in the last paragraph of the letter, and an apology." In the October 24 edition, the *Daily Graphic* agreed that the Cadbury company had recently explained its actions regarding São Tomé to the Liverpool Chamber of Commerce, and the newspaper apologized to the chocolate firms.[63]

Many Portuguese were aware of the controversy over labor in West Africa. In the early twentieth century, a number of Portuguese Angolans criticized the labor recruitment system and demanded that Lisbon make changes.[64] Governors-general of Angola attempted to enforce the letter of the law, including that of January 29, 1903, but they were overridden by powerful cocoa interests in Lisbon, as the government wished to secure a steady supply of labor for the prosperous islands. The Luanda weekly, *A Defeza de Angola*, ran several articles in May 1904 critical of the methods of recruiting Angolan labor for São Tomé, contending that it was cruel and also deprived Angola of valuable workers.[65] For their efforts, the editor of the weekly and his reporters were physically assaulted.[66] Consul Horatio Mackie reported in 1907 that the drain of labor to the islands was detrimental to the development of Angola. The British company that was constructing a railway in Angola to the Katanga mines was forced to import two thousand Indian laborers for the project. Fearing for the health as well as the potential enslavement of such workers, British officials eventually determined that Portuguese law did not apply to British subjects in Portuguese territory.[67]

The most powerful Portuguese statement against the labor system appeared in a 1903 article by Judice Biker, the governor of Portuguese Guinea, who "documented the whole sordid procedure." As one historian contends, Nevinson "did nothing more than elaborate in cold and angry detail the substance of the charges made by Biker and by other Portuguese and foreign critics. The difference was that

Nevinson, one of the most famous correspondents of his time, had a larger, more receptive audience."[68] It should be acknowledged, the historian notes, that the call for reform by some of the Portuguese Angolans—especially the plantation owners—was as much "selfish" as "philanthropic," for they needed the laborers on their own estates, but even so, "their attack on the export system was as forthright as any English criticism."[69]

At the same time, some Portuguese fiercely denied that there were any labor problems in Portuguese West Africa, especially on the islands. In 1903, Soveral, the Portuguese minister to London, gave the standard response to allegations of slavery in Angola: it simply did not exist, as past laws and the recently proclaimed decree of January 1903 had eliminated it. Moreover, the offices of the curator provided "a perfect warranty for the avoidance of abuses in the employment of labour hands in Portuguese Africa." Finally, he cited foreign visitors to Portuguese West Africa, including Harry Johnston, who had testified to the good conditions there.[70] In 1906, the Portuguese government issued a memorandum proclaiming the extraordinary care that officials took to ensure the rights of native laborers: "The contract entered into by native labourers from the Angola province for the agricultural colony of San Thomé has always received from the central, as well as from local Governments, the most scrupulous care and special attention." While the Portuguese government required that the natives engage in useful labor, it had "always taken special and attentive care to protect and favour the natives in its colonies, seeking to inspire them with an understanding of the duties of work, without prejudice, with all the guarantees of free men, rendering them useful to themselves, the colonies and to the country." The document added that "official reports" and the "impartial testimony of foreign visitors" verified that "the labourer engaged for San Thomé lives there in the best conditions, happy and satisfied; he rears a family, he voluntarily renews his contracts and prefers to remain there rather than be repatriated, to such a degree that, on some properties, it is a common thing to find old labourers no longer capable of active service who stay on in the position of superannuated servants doing small services compatible with their age and strength."[71]

In 1907, Henrique Monteiro de Mendonça published *The Boa Entrada Plantations*, a defense of the São Tomé labor system. Mendonça, owner of Boa Entrada, painted an idyllic picture of the conditions on his estate, using both words and photographs. He was extremely critical of Nevinson and the humanitarian societies, and he pointedly reminded the reader that Portuguese colonies provided British South Africa with labor, especially for the gold mines. However, even Mendonça, who owned what was widely regarded as the best-run roça on the island, admitted that the mortality rate on his estate was high.[72]

The British and Portuguese royal families maintained close contact with one another. Portugal's crown prince, along with the minister of marine, visited England in September and October 1907.[73] This visit was one in a series of calls between the two royal families that strengthened ties that had been frayed in the 1890s. Carlos, the king of Portugal, attended Queen Victoria's funeral in 1901 and returned to England in 1902. King Edward, who was a close friend of Soveral, spent six very successful days visiting Portugal in April 1903. He was enthusiastically received by chambers of commerce there when he spoke of the need to protect the integrity of Portugal's colonies.[74]

In February 1907, the Foreign Office asked Consul Mackie in Luanda to gather information in Angola on the labor recruitment for the islands. Since Nightingale's visit to the islands in early 1906 had particularly irritated Portuguese officials because it was unannounced, the British told Lisbon of Mackie's proposed investigation.[75] In September 1907, Mackie spent a few days in various parts of Angola, sailing on three steamships and observing the administration of the labor-contracting system and its ties to the islands. He found neither evidence of abuse nor laborers who were upset with their obligation to work. He emphasized, however, that his report could not be regarded as complete because he saw but a small part of a large country; furthermore, because government officials knew of his visit, favorable situations could have been "prearranged." He recommended that Portugal set up a commission to determine directly from the natives how they felt about the recruiting process.[76] In November 1907, Villiers, the minister to Lisbon, informed Grey that the Portuguese government, based on information gained by Ayres da Ornellas, the minister of marine who had recently visited Africa, intended to issue new regulations giving government officials more direct control over labor recruitment and repatriation.[77]

Missionary Héli Chatelain had no doubt that slavery and its trade was continuing in Angola, where he had served for many years. A U.S. citizen of Swiss origin, Chatelain was waiting in Europe until he was certain he could safely return to Angola. In a conversation with Clarke at the Foreign Office, he asserted that none of his complaints about the slave trade directed to Portuguese authorities for twenty years had ever been acknowledged. He had, however, been threatened by such officials, who claimed that they had always "fooled the British in the past, so they would in the future." He personally knew Portuguese administrators who owned slaves and often bought and sold them. Authorities forced Chatelain to return any slaves who came to his mission to the nearby fort, where they were restored to their masters, and many "were beaten at the fort so as to teach them not to run away again." Officials fined Chatelain for his objections to the slave trade, and "the whole white population talked openly that I should be killed and the mission station burned down."[78]

A bizarre and troubling incident involved a general named P. Joubert Pienaar, who fought for the Boers during the South African War and later settled in Angola. He found slavery there unacceptable, and because of his protests, he and many members of his family were compelled to flee.[79] In 1906 and 1907, he corresponded often with British Foreign Office officials about the slavery issue in Angola and his alleged mistreatment by Angolan officials.[80] In a visit to Clarke at the Foreign Office in October 1907, Pienaar spelled out his determination to invade Angola in the spring of 1908 "through Barotesland . . . so as to drive the Portuguese into the sea." Expounding on a scheme not unlike the 1895–1896 Jameson Raid into the Transvaal, Pienaar insisted that he had the support of the "kaffirs" (a disparaging term for Bantu, a native people of southern Africa), who "would rise like one man against the Portuguese." After driving the Portuguese out of Angola, he "intended to hand the country over to King Edward." Walter Langley, assistant undersecretary of state, regarded Pienaar as dangerous, lest he enter any British colony bordering on Portuguese Africa; Langley proposed to alert the Colonial Office to Pienaar's plans.[81] The *Cape Times*, British newspapers, and humanitarian societies' newsletters carried Pienaar's account of brutal slavery and slave trading in Angola and the islands, which was remarkably similar to Nevinson's.[82] Lisbon newspapers were disturbed by Pienaar's allegations of slavery.[83] William Cadbury understood from his sources, including Chatelain and Burtt, that Pienaar was a disreputable, dishonest person and not to be trusted, and so Cadbury wrote letters to Buxton and Fox Bourne urging that their societies not publicize the man's allegations. Pienaar was pointing to articles in the *Reporter* and the *Aborigines' Friend* as "credentials."[84]

A "fashionably dressed" Pienaar appeared in the United States in April 1908, announcing that he had called off his invasion of Angola because he was unable to get the support of the British Foreign Office. The Foreign Office had warned him in December 1907 that because he was a British subject, his proposed actions violated the Foreign Enlistment Act. According to a *Daily Telegraph* reporter, Pienaar was trying unsuccessfully to raise money to stop the slave trade.[85] On April 30, 1908, in an article headlined "Quaker Filibusters," the *Evening Standard* (London), a Conservative newspaper, carried the Pienaar story, along with references to the firms of Cadbury and Fry. Two weeks later, however, the paper, obviously under legal pressure from Cadbury Bros., issued an apology: "We need hardly say that we had no intention of suggesting that these firms (or, indeed, any members of the Society of Friends) had any connection whatever with 'General' Pienaar or his wild-cat schemes."[86]

The publicity surrounding the Liverpool Chamber of Commerce episode and Pienaar's strange mission disturbed William Cadbury while he was preparing a visit to Lisbon to present Burtt's report to the planters. He believed it was going to complicate his mission to press the need for reform on the planters, who were sensitive to any type of rebuke.

Joseph Burtt's report went through several revisions. He wrote and signed the earliest one in Luanda, dated December 24, 1906; he made other revisions in 1907. While all of the editions condemned the labor practices in the Portuguese territories, the initial version contained the strongest language. In this first draft, Burtt referred to the labor contract signed in Angola as a "farce," writing that the "native is taken from his home against his will, is forced into a contract he does not understand, and never returns to Angola. The legal formalities are but a cloak to hide slavery." One paragraph on education that did not appear in the final version reads:

> With one or two exceptions, no education or religious teaching is given to the servical. Some few are taught handicrafts, such as carpentering and blacksmithing. A common argument in favour of the system is that the life at S. Thomé is a school in which the native is led from his savage state into the higher paths of civilization, and at S. Thomé he has the benefit of living with white men in a better moral environment. If the plantations of S. Thomé are intended to elevate the black race, it is strange that no attempt has been made to give even the most elementary education, and persons who know Africa will be somewhat sceptical as to the benefits arising from the black servant's association with his white master.

Two other paragraphs in this draft but omitted from the final report dealt with the attention the planter gave the laborers. The argument that the planters treated their laborers with care because they were so valuable was "limited in application.

Passion may be stronger than self interest. Generally the planter is the employee of others, and one death on a plantation, where death is so common an occurrence, seems a matter of but little moment." The next paragraph illustrated the extraordinary power of patronage:

> The arm of the Portuguese law is short; it is, moreover, pulled by many strings. A man without influence may fear it, but not the planter with a powerful patron at Lisbon, as the following case illustrates:—Rumours reached a curator, who is the official representative of servical interests, that the labourers were maltreated at a plantation. He was about to take proceedings to stop the injustice and punish the offenders, but the plantation having a powerful patron at Lisbon . . . cried out for help, and not in vain. The curator was withdrawn to Lisbon, and the investigation was quashed. Such things explain the phrase I once heard an educated Portuguese vehemently exclaim, "There is no law." Again and again since have I verified the truth of that bald statement.[87]

In describing Benguela, the first draft stated: "Benguella is a city of slavery, and a person on the look-out meets with significant details." The final report read: "I met there with abundant evidence of the kind of compulsory labour I have referred to."[88] Burtt's early version described the work of commercial houses and plantations in Mossamedes (a village south of Benguela) as being done by serviçal labor. A runaway slave was usually turned in, earning a little money for the man delivering the runaway to his master. In the draft report, Burtt used this terminology: "He is then handed over to the police, and beaten according to the wish of his master, once, twice, or even three times a day." The final report ended after the words "his master."[89]

Burtt's several conclusions were significantly different, although both the initial and final versions were strong. In the draft of December 1906, he closed with the following:

> Among suggestions that have been made for the betterment of existing conditions the following appear the most practicable:—
>
> > Making known to the English public the existence and extent of slavery in Angola, and the islands of S. Thomé and Principe.

> The procuring of labour from the Portuguese colony on the east coast of Africa, where labour is voluntary.
>
> The enforcement by the Government of native labour for fixed periods of time.

> The root of the whole matter lies in S. Thomé and Principe.
>
> The islands want labour, and are ready at any time to pay down half a million sterling for it, without asking questions.
>
> A vast region of forest, plain, and mountain, is mainly peopled by a weak, gentle race, without national spirit, or power of combination for protection.
>
> What are the barriers between supply and demand? Two hundred miles of sea, a weak and corrupt Government, with a few forts spread over half a million square miles of territory.
>
> The wonder is, not that there is so much slaving in Angola, but that there is so little.
>
> So long as it is possible to get a high price for black labourers, so long will slavery exist.[90]

At this stage, Burtt already had some strong ideas that were apparently not in tune with William Cadbury's. First, he urged that the English public be informed of the magnitude of slavery in the Portuguese colonies; Cadbury did not permit the release of Burtt's report until October 1908, almost one year after its publication in Portuguese. Second, Burtt stressed that the primary cause of slavery was the incessant need for labor on the islands; William Cadbury and many others claimed that the root of the problem was in Angola, where the laborers were initially enslaved, and not on the islands.

The final edition closed with these lines: "But now that I have to state my conclusions, I must use the words which most nearly portray actual facts. I am satisfied that under the serviçal system as it exists at present, thousands of black men and women are, against their will, and often under circumstances of great cruelty, taken away every year from their homes and transported across the sea to work on unhealthy islands, from which they never return. If this is not slavery, I know of no word in the English language which correctly characterizes it."[91]

By the summer of 1907, Burtt was in Portugal overseeing the translation of his report into Portuguese and meeting with Merck, British officials, and other visitors, including the missionary Charles Swan. Burtt found a Portuguese press that was "bitter and unreasonable" in its attack on England, and he warned William Cadbury that the two of them would have to use "utmost moderation" in their upcoming meeting with the planters "or we shall arouse in these hot blooded southerners a fury that will be deaf to reason." Burtt found it necessary for security reasons to telegraph some of his information under an unidentifiable address and without using names.[92] To complicate matters further, Portugal was in the midst of a major political crisis. The king gave the newly appointed prime minister, João Franco, dictatorial powers, thereby arousing the fury of republicans. The politically naive Burtt expected that a "wealthy and determined Premier desirous of reform," combined with a crown prince who had just returned from a tour of Portugal's West African colonies including São Tomé, "should both be of service to us."[93]

Foreign Office officials feared that little would come from Burtt's report because the final version omitted too many names and details. Lyell acknowledged that slavery existed but said, "I am afraid we are not under any illusions that it will be seriously shaken by Burtt's report in its weakened form."[94] After reading the report, the minister to Lisbon, Francis Villiers, remarked: "It did not impress me much, & I doubt if it will impress the Portuguese at all."[95] Burtt sent a copy to J. G. Baldwin, British consulate general at Lourenço Marques, Mozambique, who told him that "it confirms everything I thought, although in your natural desire to avoid exaggeration, you have not evidently made out the worst of the case." What troubled Baldwin was not the attitude of the Portuguese, whose values were not the same as those of the British anyway, but rather the "smug manufacturers of cocoa who for years have made fortunes out of the blood of the African natives & who use those fortunes to advertise their unctuous rectitude in the columns of 'tied' newspapers. However, you know my views & I can only wish you the best of luck in your efforts to bring them to a better sense of their responsibilities."[96]

As late as October 1907, the Foreign Office was under the mistaken impression that Cadbury Bros. would not issue Burtt's report if the Portuguese government undertook substantial reform in the serviçal system. The company, however, believed that it was "honour bound to present this report to the planters who asked for it at the earliest possible moment" and obligated to give publicity to the situation by releasing the report to the Portuguese press.[97] The Foreign Office did insist that the firm of Cadbury present the report to the Portuguese government before releasing it to the planters.[98]

Villiers gave copies of Burtt's report to the Portuguese minister for foreign affairs on October 25, 1907. The British Foreign Office, after extensive correspondence with Cadbury Bros., recommended that the deputation from the chocolate firms not proceed to Lisbon until mid-November.[99] William Cadbury traveled alone to Lisbon, arriving about November 19, by which time Burtt had distributed some fifty copies of his report to the planters, "delivering personally the most important."[100] Cadbury met with Villiers, who was optimistic that something good would come from applying pressure on the Portuguese government, and with Ornellas, the minister of marine and colonies, who had accompanied the crown prince on his recent tour of Portugal's West African colonies. Ornellas indicated that he intended to apply in Angola the same regulations for contract labor that he had used as an administrator in Mozambique. Cadbury reported that while Ornellas appeared "suspicious" at first, the minister later "firmly pledged . . . immediate reform."[101] Cadbury also received a lesson in Portuguese government from his friend Merck, a partner specializing in rubber and cocoa for Burnay, "the biggest merchants in Portugal." Merck explained that by making Franco a dictator and approving of his actions, the king had offended "every section of the public and the press, who consider it an insult to their intelligence and liberty to be told by the King that they are unfit to rule. Thus we cannot possibly expect any serious attention from Franco and his ministers (his own nominees) when their very existance [*sic*] is threatened with momentary danger." Merck emphasized that the only argument that would make an impression on the planters was that unless conditions in Angola dramatically improved, the chocolate firms would stop buying the beans: "No attempt to explain our moral position will be in the slightest understood, as public morality is here absolutely unknown." Any attempt to explain the principle of a fair wage to the planters "would simply be considered evidence that we were liars or fools." Merck contended that the planters would "never undertake to interest themselves in Angola, because all money invested there will be sunk on account of the absolutely rotten government: the reason S. Thome thrives is because a ring of planters run it absolutely in their own interests and the Government is practically excluded from any possibility of mismanagement."[102] After receiving William Cadbury's letter of November 26, 1907, referring to Merck's recommendation of a boycott, Cadbury's board wired back that "we have decided to refuse to buy unless [the proprietors abolish the present state of slavery]. We await Frys & Rowntree's replies after they have seen the correspondence."[103] Obviously, the three Quaker-owned chocolate firms gave very serious consideration to boycotting São Tomé cocoa in late 1907, but they did not implement the plan at that time, very possibly because William Cadbury opposed such action.

The planters' reactions to Burtt's report soon began to appear in Lisbon newspapers. Cadbury remarked that the response was "vituperative" and in "absurdly bad taste," leaving little opportunity for deliberation.[104] The proprietors issued a thirty-page response, denying that there was any labor problem in the colonies, citing the positive reports of many travelers over the previous thirty years, and questioning Burtt's abilities. The planters' primary defense, Cadbury stated, was that "the natives must be civilised in the school of work & civilization." Besides, they contended that they "*have a right to transfer labour from colony to colony at will without foreign interference—this is not emigration while under one government and therefore no repatriation is needful*" (emphasis in original).[105] Villiers said the planters' reply used crude language that offended Cadbury, but the latter was ready to negotiate in a "most amicable and moderate way."[106] Merck reported that the remarkably hostile reply from the proprietors was the work of the Conde de Valle Flôr, one of the most successful and ruthless planters—a man with profits of £200,000 over the preceding year who almost managed to block Cadbury's meeting with the planters. Francisco Mantero, a proprietor on the islands and secretary of the Planters' Association, however, opposed Valle Flôr's action, and the meeting went forward.[107]

William Cadbury and Joseph Burtt met with a large delegation of planters on November 28, 1907. Cadbury explained that during his first visit to Lisbon in 1903, planters had asked him to personally investigate laboring conditions in West Africa. While unable to go there himself, he had sent his trusted friend Burtt. In this brief talk to the planters, Cadbury noted that laborers on the islands enjoyed relatively good treatment, although their mortality rate remained far too high. He emphasized the need for the free contracting of laborers and insisted that until repatriation was a fact, "no argument will persuade the world that this is free labour." Near the end of his speech, Cadbury warned the planters: "Much as we should regret to lose the opportunity of buying your excellent cocoa, and even knowing that it would entail to us financial loss, speaking at least for my own firm, our conscience would not allow us to go on purchasing raw material for our business, unless we are assured that in the future it is to be produced by free labour." Cadbury closed by praising the planters for their success and applauding the greatness of the Portuguese as colonizers: "We plead for strong and immediate action, and confidently trust that the agriculturalists, who have by their courage and energy done so much in one generation to raise the island of S Thomé to a colony of the foremost rank, will assist their able administrators to banish from their estates the remnants of a bad system, and establish in the ancient colony of Angola a standard of true freedom, worthy of the nation which first explored the shores of Africa, and is counted among the greatest colonising Powers of the earth."[108] Following his remarks, he responded to the planters' detailed statement. Altogether, including lunch, the meeting lasted eight hours.[109]

In the Cadbury Papers collection, there is a poem marked "Private" and written on stationery from the Braganza Hotel in Lisbon in what appears to be William Cadbury's handwriting. It reads:

> *A pou hungry African josser*
> *Employed on that excellent roça*
> *of Boa Entrada,*
> *Broke into the larder*
> *Of kind-hearted Mr. Mendoça*
> *I fear you will call him a glutton,*
> *He demolished a saddle of mutton,*
> *Proceeded by licking*
> *The bones of a chicken,*
> *And ended by bursting a button.*
> *You imagine his awful disgrace!*
> *But no—just the opposite case:*
> *Mr. Burtt had been round*
> *And there could not be found*
> *A single chicotte in the place!*

Following the poem are the words "Not part of the official statement to the Planters of St. Thomé & Principe dated XI.28.07." At the end of what must have been an exhausting day, Cadbury had penned a poem about Burtt's presence and power on the islands: not even a chicotte, a strip of hide used for whipping a serviçal, was left on the plantation.[110]

In early December 1907, Villiers reported that the Portuguese government had decided new regulations guaranteeing proper labor recruitment with repatriation were needed and would be in place before the end of the year.[111] Shortly after the conference with Cadbury, the planters issued a flowery statement that attested to their humanitarian concern for the laborers and listed the steps they were taking to ensure that the repatriation fund was correctly administered. They reviewed the actions that the Portuguese government had pursued for the proper recruitment of labor in Angola. The summary closed with this statement: "The particulars of information collected by Mr. Burtt in S. Thomé and Principe and accepted in good faith by him were not always an exact expression of truth."[112] Cadbury believed that his discussion with the planters had been useful, since they subsequently indicated a willingness to cooperate with the Portuguese government in bringing about the proper treatment of the laborers.[113] Cadbury Bros. thanked Ornellas, the minister of marine, for his "promise of very definite reform in Angola" and then sent out an optimistic news release in mid-December that was picked up by many newspapers.[114] One writer asked a question that would reappear over the next few months: why was Burtt's report not made available to the English public?[115]

When Travers Buxton expressed concern to William Cadbury about the stability of the Portuguese government, a clearly upbeat Cadbury responded that the "latest news states that Franco's position is stronger than ever, and his Colonial Minister, Senhor Ornellas, is an exceedingly good man, and we have every confidence in him doing his best for us as long as he remains in power."[116] The day before William Cadbury's letter to Buxton was written, Cadbury's board of directors "agreed to cease to use S. Thome cocoa if the planters fail to carry out their promises (it will be probably a year or two before this will be shown.)"[117] Clearly, the Cadbury firm was willing to give the Portuguese a generous amount of time.

Burtt's report, published for the Portuguese and a select few in England, appeared more than six years after Cadbury Bros. first learned that slave labor was used in the growing of cocoa beans in São Tomé and Príncipe and four years after the company decided to hire an agent to visit Portuguese West Africa. What were the specific purposes of Burtt's mission? That is not an easy question to answer, since the minutes of Cadbury's board meetings are very brief and sketchy. Moreover, very early on, the board had assigned the issue to William Cadbury, who made many of the decisions in this regard and only occasionally reported to George Cadbury or to the board. The purposes of Burtt's mission were never spelled out and can only be extracted from relevant letters, all of which, ironically, were from William Cadbury to Fox Bourne. A second question, of course, involves the extent to which Burtt achieved these purposes.

In May 1903, William Cadbury wrote that the firm hoped an agent might determine the effectiveness of Portugal's "recently introduced regulations."[118] The new labor regulations of January 1903 had been in place for one and a half to two years by the time of Burtt's visit. While Burtt wrote little of these regulations, he stated in his conclusions that the "official machinery" provided by the government decrees to protect serviçais "has not been brought into being, and the most serious evils, which it was to have prevented, flourish unchecked."[119] William Cadbury stated in June 1905 that one purpose of Burtt's trip was to determine "whether the people are actually slaves or not," although Cadbury was almost certain that they were.[120] Burtt clearly established, as had Nevinson and many others, that the laborers on the islands' plantations were slaves. By 1907 and indeed much earlier, it was obvious to the Cadbury firm that slavery existed on the islands and that the Portuguese planters and government had done virtually nothing to alter that fact. There was, however, a third purpose for the trip. In the midst of his bitter dispute with Fox Bourne in July 1907, an indignant William Cadbury insisted emphatically that the goal of Burtt's investigation was not to prove the existence of slavery (Cadbury already knew that); rather, he said, Burtt "went out for the purpose of convincing the Portuguese" that slavery existed.[121] If that was truly the objective of the trip, then it makes sense that Cadbury Bros. would be willing to give the Portuguese an opportunity to accept the facts and to take appropriate steps to eradicate the slavery. At the same time, Cadbury was naive, at best, if he believed that any meaningful change would come about, given the many years of adamant refusal by the Portuguese planters and much of the Portuguese government to recognize labor problems on the islands. Moreover, this objective does not explain why William Cadbury would permit Burtt's trip and his subsequent report, which he saw as so vital for the welfare of the serviçais, to take such a long time to come to fruition. Certainly, there was no clearly stated goal for Burtt's trip, and that may have been why Cadbury found himself so at odds with Fox Bourne, Nevinson, and others.

Pleased with Burtt's effort, Cadbury's board agreed to give him "a present of £500 as an expression of satisfaction with the way in which he has fulfilled his engagement."[122] Aside from the report that Burtt produced, however, the Cadbury company had in four years accomplished nothing for the slaves who produced the cocoa beans.

6 Careful Steps and Concern—or Dragging Feet and Hypocrisy?

> Instead of expressing confidence in the definite pledge of the Portuguese Government, let them [the chocolate firms] refuse to purchase cocoa from the Portuguese planters of San Thomé and Principe until these pledges are redeemed. So long as they continue to purchase the cocoa, so long must they share the responsibility for the conditions under which it is produced.
>
> *Chronicle of the London Missionary Society*

THE YEAR 1907 closed with the publication of Burtt's report in Portugal and the ensuing meetings between William Cadbury and Portuguese government officials and planters. Optimistic as usual, Cadbury hoped for reform, and he was willing to give the Portuguese at least a year to accomplish that. Lisbon bought some time by sending a colonial official named Francisco Paula Cid to investigate its West African labor practices. Humanitarians, particularly Fox Bourne, thought little of Portuguese efforts and pressured the firm of Cadbury and the British government to take stronger steps to stop the abuses in Portuguese West Africa. Aging and ill, Fox Bourne had been secretary of the Aborigines' Protection Society for nearly twenty years and surely longed for one final success in the war against slavery. Nevinson and his growing band of supporters joined with the humanitarian societies to hold conferences in London in October and December 1908 to highlight problems in Portuguese West Africa, and newspapers stepped up their attacks on Cadbury Bros. for purchasing São Tomé cocoa. The Foreign Office continued to urge the humanitarian societies to be patient with the Portuguese government, which faced a major crisis in February 1908 with the assassination of the king and his heir. Meanwhile, William Cadbury and other company officials became increasingly sensitive to anyone who questioned the firm's continuing purchase of cocoa beans from São Tomé. Fox Bourne's strong stand prompted Cadbury to respond angrily and then break off further correspondence. In the spring of 1908, William Cadbury announced that he would personally visit São Tomé to see if meaningful progress was being made in improving conditions on the plantations.

In a letter of December 17, 1907, to Cadbury's directors, Fox Bourne revealed that he was completing another pamphlet, this one dealing primarily with the mainland slave trade in Portuguese West Africa.[1] William Cadbury's lengthy response maintained that some good had come from his recent visit to Lisbon, in spite of its stormy beginning. The Portuguese, he said, were particularly hostile because of the publicity surrounding the Liverpool Chamber of Commerce meeting. He expected much from Ornellas, the colonial minister, and believed that the Portuguese needed to be given an opportunity to carry out their promises. Therefore, Cadbury contended that the "present moment is exceedingly inopportune for again bringing prominently before the public the abuses of the past"; instead, he argued, one should focus on progress. He hoped that Fox Bourne would make discreet use of Burtt's report in his publication.[2]

What appeared from Fox Bourne's pen a few days later was not the pamphlet but a six-page article entitled "Central African Slave Traffic" in the newsletter of the Aborigines' Protection Society, a story he had previously withheld in deference to the wishes of the chocolate companies. Now, after so much time and with so many people still in bondage, the gloves were off. Fox Bourne recounted the wealth of information on slavery accumulated over the past several years, ranging from consular reports to investigations by Nevinson and Burtt. Yet even with all this evidence, the British government had achieved no "good results." If little could be expected from the government, Fox Bourne argued, it fell to the producers and consumers of chocolate to "uphold the traditions of their country as an opponent of slavery" and to act accordingly by boycotting São Tomé cocoa.[3]

On February 3, 1908, Cadbury's officials responded to Fox Bourne with a strongly worded letter, arguing that the article and its call for a boycott "stirs up all the bad feeling of the past which gives very little credit to the Portuguese for any honest intentions." The officials thought that the Aborigines' Protection Society had gone back on its word, and they demanded that Fox Bourne not cite Burtt's report in the forthcoming pamphlet. The Cadbury firm sent copies of this letter to Burtt, the Anti-Slavery Society, John Harris, and the firms of Fry and Rowntree.[4] William Cadbury considered Fox Bourne's letter a deliberate attempt to complicate the reform endeavor and "make all friendly action impossible."[5] In his response to Cadbury Bros., Fox Bourne contended that the Aborigines' Protection Society had not violated the agreement reached in July 1907 because the society had waited until the Cadbury company concluded negotiations with the

Portuguese. Moreover, the society was not publishing new information but was simply repeating and confirming the very real problems that Cadbury Bros. and others had identified.[6] On February 8, William Cadbury sent an even angrier letter to Fox Bourne. He argued that the APS's call for a boycott offered no opportunity for the Portuguese to carry through on reform and constituted an "insult" to both the Portuguese government and to Foreign Secretary Grey, who had worked so hard on the issue. Cadbury officials, he stated, "entirely dissociate ourselves from your Society."[7]

Why was William Cadbury so distressed with Fox Bourne's position on São Tomé? The frustration stemmed in part from the fact that Fox Bourne was a stubborn man. In his two meetings with the APS secretary in July, Cadbury had found it impossible to get him to change his mind. He admitted that Fox Bourne honestly thought the only possible action would be for the chocolate companies to stop purchasing beans from the Portuguese. Certainly, Fox Bourne's stance was grounded on a strong moral foundation, but so too, of course, was William Cadbury's. Accordingly, Cadbury could never quite accept the idea that Fox Bourne's moral base had the same certainty as his. At the same time, Cadbury felt sorry for the man because he was ill—although Cadbury did remark that "unfortunately" Fox Bourne was "not too ill to go on writing and making mischief." Cadbury also discouraged Morel from printing a "scathing" editorial in his newspaper because he did not want to attack Fox Bourne "publicly."[8]

Fox Bourne knew that William Cadbury had many relatives and friends on the two humanitarian society boards, but, apparently, not even the possible loss of contributors could dissuade the secretary. Furthermore, the old reform crusader was no lightweight in his arguments, which he supported by a wealth of information from many sources. He was well connected and sought out by those who had a story to tell. Foreign Office officials, who, like Cadbury, did not generally see eye to eye with the humanitarian leader, always felt obligated to respond to him. At times, remarks—often handwritten—in Foreign Office documents indicated a reluctant agreement with Fox Bourne.

Yet Cadbury was also well aware that his company would suffer financially, at least in the short run, if it suddenly stopped buying São Tomé cocoa. Though in many ways staging a boycott would be the easiest thing to do, he believed that it would accomplish nothing beyond fostering a smug self-satisfaction for having taken action. He thought that with the removal of the British companies' financial clout, all possible influence over planters and officials would be lost. The planters could simply sell their beans to companies whose officials did not have the same moral compunction as did those of Cadbury, Fry, and Rowntree. Like Morel, Cadbury believed that trade, if used properly, could be an important tool to bring about meaningful moral and humanistic reform, and he was not about to lay down that tool easily. In Fox Bourne's view, however, Portugal had been given every opportunity to mend its ways. The evil of slavery had to be met by moral outrage and direct citizen, government, and corporate action against the vile perpetrators, with the most immediate course being the boycott.

On February 1, 1908, two gunmen in a plaza in Lisbon murdered Portuguese King Carlos and his heir, Luís Felipe, effectively marking an end to any realistic expectation that reform would come soon. The assassination also led to the fall of Premier João Franco, to whom the king had granted dictatorial power in 1907. The Portuguese people had not liked their king. He was seen as a hedonist, squandering resources on himself while doing nothing to modernize his nation or to meet the daily needs of his desperately poor people. Increasingly inclined to republicanism, the citizens showed remarkably little remorse over their loss.[9] The British Foreign Office was concerned about the political turmoil in Lisbon, and though it sent some naval ships to Lago, it made certain not to appear to intervene in Portugal's domestic affairs.[10]

Ornellas, minister for marine and colonies, had promised William Cadbury in late 1907 that the Portuguese government would issue new regulations reforming the recruitment of laborers in Angola and providing for their repatriation and that steps would be taken to secure local compliance with the new rules.[11] Early in 1908, the Anti-Slavery Society and the Aborigines' Protection Society both pressed the British Foreign Office and Portuguese authorities to make certain that these pledges were carried out. On January 10, 1908, Travers Buxton, secretary of the Anti-Slavery Society, wrote to the secretary of the Portuguese legation in London, with a copy to the Foreign Office, summarizing what he understood to be the proposed reforms and promising that his committee would evaluate the Portuguese government's efforts.[12] On February 19, Fox Bourne penned an even stronger letter to the Foreign Office, detailing the pledges made by the Portuguese government. He stressed that all officials, especially those in Lisbon, had to be held responsible for halting the terrible recruiting system in Angola. He demanded the "complete abandonment of this survival of slave trading and slavery" and called for the British government to ensure that the Portuguese leaders fulfilled all of their "treaty obligations to Great Britain."[13]

While the Foreign Office assured MPs on February 10, 1908, that Portugal was in the process of issuing new labor regulations that would provide effective government control of recruiting and the implementation of a repatriation scheme, all was not well in Lisbon.[14] Instead of issuing new regulations, the new Portuguese government opted to send a representative to West Africa to investigate the situation there and to submit an official report. Foreign Office officials, as well as Cadbury Bros. and humanitarians, immediately suspected that Lisbon was once again taking steps to hinder meaningful improvements in the lot of the serviçais. All feared that the man to be sent out as commissioner, naval Lt. Capt. Francisco Paula Cid, would be ineffective, since as governor of the district of Benguela in Angola as well as São Tomé and Príncipe, he had tolerated the longstanding recruiting and laboring practices of those colonies.[15] Lest they alienate the overly sensitive Portuguese authorities and planters, British Foreign Office officials could do little more than assure humanitarians that they expected Cid's forthcoming report to lead to meaningful reform.[16] The dilemma facing the Foreign Office was apparent in Guy Locock's minutes on Fox Bourne's letter of May 1, 1908: "I do not see that we can make any more representations to the Portuguese at present. They are sending out an official to enquire into the whole system, and if we worry them with further representations it would very probably only have the effect of making them unwilling to proceed with the plan of reforms. Of course it is easy to understand Mr. Fox Bourne's point of view. He is profoundly suspicious of the Portuguese professions, and really in view of Portugal's record with regard to slavery I do not think he is wrong in doing so." One Foreign Office official proposed that Villiers, the minister to Lisbon, thank the Portuguese government for the appointment of Cid and encourage officials to take immediate steps to "remedy any shortcomings" evident in the administration of labor in Angola. Another official commented, "This will have to be done very tactfully as the Portuguese are extremely sensitive."[17]

In June, Cadbury Bros. mailed to the Foreign Office an article from the *Voz de Angola* dated April 23, 1908, that confirmed the company's apprehensions over Cid's mission and increased the possibility that the firm would soon have to discontinue its purchases from the islands. The article claimed that when he was governor in Benguela, "[Cid,] though acquainted with the unspeakable injustices to which the natives were (and still are) subjected, never raised his voice to plead for justice, never recorded the iniquities of the slave traffic, nor used the least influence to repress that traffic." According to the writer, Cid had "been party to the horrors of a hidden slavery that de-populates Angola, that wounds the pride of a cultured people, and enriches half a dozen ambitious men at the expense of shaming Portugal."[18] Yet in spite of these misgivings, William Cadbury, writing two months later, remained hopeful "that we shall hear of some definite step taken before the end of the year."[19]

The Cid mission to West Africa was the Portuguese government's response to Cadbury's visit to Lisbon in late 1907. Cid departed in April 1908, and it would be a year before he filed his report. Meanwhile, humanitarians railed against the lack of any progress in Portuguese labor conditions, while the Cadbury company sought to minimize damage done to the image of their company.

Nevinson stepped up his assault on Portuguese labor practices in early 1908, first with an article in the *Daily Chronicle* on March 30. One U.S. chocolate manufacturer, he wrote, had stopped purchasing São Tomé beans after reading his own exposé in *Harper's*. He also emphasized that under the Acts of Berlin and Brussels, Britain had the right to intervene in West Africa. While Britain's "reputation for humanity and justice" had declined in the previous decade, the country could still put pressure on Portugal. If Portugal resisted, Nevinson added, "I suppose we are still strong enough at sea to send a cruiser to arrest one of these legalised slave ships on its course, and bring the abomination to an end."[20] On April 3, he attended the annual meeting of the Anti-Slavery Society, but he received little support for his critical remarks about Portuguese labor, as the gathering may have been dominated by friends of William Cadbury. When Nevinson was suddenly asked to move a resolution expressing thanks to both the British Foreign Office and the Portuguese government for Portugal's agreeing to take steps toward meaningful reform, he refused, contending that the Portuguese had failed in the past to implement their own rules.[21] On April 6, at the annual meeting of the Aborigines' Protection Society, Nevinson moved a resolution calling on the British government to work under treaty provisions to assure correct treatment for the natives in Africa and to secure their rights, with particular reference to those in Angola and São Tomé. In the preceding few years, promises made by the Portuguese government to improve the lot of the laborers had failed. "As a means of combating the existing evil," Nevinson called for a British boycott "in the consumption of cocoa and chocolate obtained from districts in which natives torn from their homes pass the rest of their lives in slavery, and in which the death rate is appalling."[22] The *Manchester Guardian* reported that Nevinson concluded his remarks with this statement: "It was the great cocoa merchants and manufacturers . . . who prevented reform, as their profits under the present system were enormous, and they were unwilling to sacrifice them."[23] Cadbury Bros. immediately protested that the report was incorrect, and after the chocolate firm issued a writ of libel against the *Guardian*, the newspaper issued an apology "for unwittingly having been the medium of circulating an inaccurate statement to which we ourselves would in no way subscribe." The newspaper also printed a letter from Nevinson, who had been approached by Richard Cross, the attorney for Rowntree, about the *Guardian* column; in it, he argued that he had not held the cocoa manufacturers responsible but had condemned the "slave-dealers and plantation owners, who make immense profits off the traffic."[24]

Nevinson expected that the chocolate firms would issue a writ of libel against him for the *Guardian* article, and he gathered evidence from other reporters to support the contention that he had been misquoted.[25] William Cadbury was not pleased with Nevinson's reappearance in the matter. Nevinson, Cadbury wrote, "is back in England, and made a disturbance at the annual meeting of the Anti-Slavery Society. Harris writes me that he (Nevinson) is feeling very sore at the success of [Morel's Congo Reform Association] and the fact that he and Fox-Bourne are left out in the cold—I am sure we will have considerable further trouble."[26] Morel told Cadbury in July that Nightingale regarded Nevinson as an "ass" because the latter had taken seriously the testimony that people in Príncipe had shot escaped laborers for "fun," when the truth was they had simply been "pull[ing] Nevinson's leg."[27]

In April 1908, Fox Bourne published *Slave Traffic in Portuguese Africa: An Account of Slave-Raiding and Slave-Trading in Angola and of Slavery in the Islands of San Thome and Principe*. In this sixty-seven-page pamphlet, he created a moving description and summary of the Portuguese slave trade by quoting accounts of government officials, explorers, missionaries, and writers (most notably Nevinson but not Burtt) and by citing correspondence of the Aborigines' Protection Society with the Foreign Office and others. An appendix included a memorandum from the APS to an international conference being held in Brussels in late April 1908, imploring the European powers to take steps to halt the huge arms trade in uncontrolled areas of the Congo that helped to feed the slave trade throughout West Africa.[28] The pamphlet was the basis of articles in several newspapers.[29] The editorial in the Cadbury-owned *Daily News*, titled "A Modern Slave Trade" and written by Henry Brailsford (who according to Nevinson had threatened to resign if the article were not run), held that the Portuguese had failed to protect the workers by application of legitimate contracts or by repatriation. Brailsford charged that the "system, in plain words, is slavery, and slavery aggravated by slave-raiding and a bad climate. . . . The law . . . has never been enforced because the Colonial Government itself profits enormously by the export of slaves to the islands." The English, through earlier treaties and economic incentives, had sought to abolish slavery in Portuguese possessions to no avail: "Two generations have passed [since abolition], and still the system, under new names and new subterfuges, survives. English public opinion, if this scandal in Angola continues, will not be more tender to Portuguese slavery than it is to King Leopold's commercial barbarism."[30]

By this time, William Cadbury was once again corresponding with Fox Bourne, thanking him for the copy of the pamphlet and "for the strong memorandum to the International Conference." Cadbury had complimented Fox Bourne earlier in the month for an article in the *Aborigines' Friend* on the slave traffic, and he told Morel on April 27 that the "attitude of F.-B. and even Stober to us has become a little less bitter, and I think they are realising that after all we have as much right to a free conscience in the matter as they have, and that slamming at us is not necessarily helpful to reform in Angola." Cadbury admitted that while he had trusted Colonial Minister Ornellas, he could not say the same of his successor, Vice-Admiral Augusto Vidal de Castilho. So much had happened recently in Portugal—the assassination, a new ministry, and elections—that his company would have to reconsider its plan of action should no reform occur by December 1908. The firm could tell the Portuguese government that it would reduce purchases of cocoa beans by one-fifth and still retain influence. Already, he said, the company was buying less, though "[we] are not making any fuss about it."[31] Morel, replying to Cadbury, doubted that there would be any economic impact on the Portuguese if the British firms simply stopped buying cocoa beans from the islands. He added, "I have always understood that your ceasing to purchase would not affect the economic point much, but would be chiefly of a sentimental character." Cadbury replied, "I think that if we stop buying cocoa it would have some moral effect, but in actual bulk our purchases are nowhere."[32] In effect, Cadbury was admitting that his company's continuing purchase of São Tomé beans, the core of his plan to induce the Portuguese to halt their slave practices, had no meaningful economic basis to it. Ironically, if it made no difference that Cadbury Bros. stopped buying cocoa from São Tomé, then it must have made no difference that the firm continued its purchasing. William Cadbury had, perhaps unwittingly, placed his company in a no-win situation. Only "moral" persuasion might work, and Portuguese planters had never responded to that type of pressure.

Throughout 1908, the Aborigines' Protection Society and the Anti-Slavery Society continued to flood the Foreign Office with information on and questions about the labor situation in Portugal's West African colonies. Fox Bourne focused on justifying British intervention in Portugal's labor affairs based on various treaty obligations requiring both countries to halt slave trade and slavery in West Africa.[33] On prodding from Fox Bourne over Britain's right to intervene and to apprehend Portuguese ships believed to be carrying slaves, Foreign Office officials determined that while the treaties of 1842 and 1871 provided for such intervention, it would be ineffective because a vessel boarded by the British would be taken to the nearest Portuguese colony, where a Portuguese judge would preside. "What prospect," someone noted, "would there be of a Portuguese Court finding that the serviçaes were slaves?"[34] The Foreign Office always responded to queries, but Walter Langley, assistant undersecretary of state, admitted in an interview on August 17 that the office was frustrated, as it could not hope to enforce the treaties. (How different Britain's view of the world was by 1908 compared to the mid-nineteenth century, when Lord Palmerston would have sent a gunboat to Angola to apprehend any slaving ships and still demand that Portugal supply labor for the British colonies.) Langley also contended that hard evidence was very difficult to come by. Missionary accounts and even Burtt's report, he said, were not strong because they gave "no names or particulars." He welcomed any "facts" that the Foreign Office could present to the Portuguese government. Even then, however, he and his colleagues had to be careful not to offend the Portuguese, as that might "[injure] our cause."[35]

The government also faced questions in Parliament in 1908 over slave labor in the Portuguese colonies, the availability of the Burtt report, the issuing of new regulations, the progress of Cid's trip, and treaties applicable to the subject.[36] In a July debate on funding for the Foreign Office, Charles Dilke, a Liberal, admonished government officials for failing to address properly the issue of slave trade in the Portuguese colonies, instead allowing "themselves to be put off with promises" that were never kept. The government, circumspect in its response to similar queries from the humanitarian societies, responded to these many questions in like fashion. In reply to Dilke, Grey did little more than indicate that the government had communicated its concerns to the Portuguese authorities and "urged them to do all in their power and with as little delay as possible to put things into a satisfactory condition."[37] On July 27, the British government admitted that the consular agent it had recently appointed for São Tomé was the manager of a large plantation on the island.[38]

Other groups and individuals were troubled by the accounts of labor abuse in Portuguese colonies. In January 1908, the English and the Scottish Co-Operative Wholesale Societies inquired directly to the Foreign Office about Portuguese plans to carry out labor reforms in São Tomé.[39] The Anti-Slavery Committee of the London Yearly Meeting of the Friends, convened in March 1908, addressed the reports of slavery in Portuguese West Africa but took no action, since the Quaker chocolate makers had "carefully investigated" the situation and had "obtained promises of amendment from members of the late Government of Portugal as well as from planters."[40] In its April 1908 *Chronicle*, the London Missionary Society expressed fear that the slavery of São Tomé was equal to that of the Congo Free State. The society called for action by the chocolate firms: "Instead of expressing confidence in the definite pledges of the Portuguese Government, let them [the chocolate firms] refuse to purchase cocoa from the Portuguese planters of San Thomé and Principe until these pledges are redeemed. So long as they continue to purchase the cocoa, so long must they share the responsibility for the conditions under which it is produced."[41] A representative of one of the chocolate firms—Nevinson thought it was Richard Cross, an attorney for Rowntree—complained to the editor of the *Chronicle* about the article, but the following month, the London Missionary Society encouraged readers to request a copy of Burtt's study directly from Cadbury Bros. and to read Nevinson's book and Fox Bourne's pamphlet.[42] The *Chronicle* summed up the situation: "The real crux of the whole question is that the Portuguese Government has little authority over the dealers and planters in Angola, and the past regulations are likely to be of small avail where large money interests are concerned. If regulations could have reformed the traffic, it would have been reformed by now."[43]

The Protestant missionary Héli Chatelain, who had long toiled in Angola, emphasized in a letter to Travers Buxton, secretary of the Anti-Slavery Society, that Lisbon lacked the political will and power to enforce any new labor regulations and that only extraordinary coercive measures by a great power such as Britain would be of any value:

> The Foreign Office ought to know that even tho' not "born in Portugal" the "System" (interested in upholding slavery) which is as powerfully entrenched in Lisbon as in West Africa is stronger than any Minister (a transient shadow) stronger than Parliament (a powerless talking machine) stronger than the King (a real shaky reed) stronger than anything Portuguese, yet weak as a babe before a British or American man-of-war.

> All protests of societies like yours and all diplomatic notes (as such) make the Portuguese abetters of slavery chuckle; they are met with protests or promises of investigation and reform and that is the end of them. After 23 years' experience of Angola and Lisbon I am more convinced than ever that Portugal is unable to cut the cancer out of her body, unless aided by an outside Power.[44]

The *Manchester Guardian*, reacting to the announcement of Cid's mission and to the release of Fox Bourne's pamphlet on slavery, printed an editorial in May that, like Chatelain's statement, called for the British government to force reforms on its "ancient ally," which was obligated under treaties to halt slavery and slave trade in its West African colonies. The newspaper regarded the Portuguese government as "the tool of the planters, employing the power of the State to fill their pockets."[45]

Matthew Stober, the missionary to Angola, visited some of the chocolate firms and encouraged them to take immediate steps against the Portuguese planters.[46] Stober, whom William Cadbury found too forceful, raged furiously against the continuing slavery and slave trade. He contended that the much vaunted regulations of 1903 had failed miserably: of the thousands of natives engaged in 1903, few were living five years later. He stressed that a set of new regulations, issued by the Portuguese government in April 1908, did nothing but perpetuate the old system. The state continued to aid and abet the exploitation of the natives, making possible the use of recruiting agents, "the worst of men—men without conscience" who quickly amassed slaves. He also regarded the appointment of Cid as a farce. Stober said that even though there were good people in Angola who protested against the evil, meaningful relief would come only through the good efforts of the chocolate manufacturers and through international pressure. He was none too pleased with the slow endeavors on the part of companies that advertised the idyllic conditions of their own factory workers but purchased cocoa beans produced by slaves. "Are not both," he asked, "entitled to the same rights?" Even if it meant financial losses, the chocolate firms should stop the purchase of these slave-produced beans and encourage the development of "free native labour" in West Africa.[47]

Behind the scenes, Francis Villiers, the minister to Lisbon, warned Portuguese Foreign Minister Wenceslau de Lima that there was a good possibility humanitarian interests in Britain could stage a campaign over Portuguese slavery similar to that being waged over the Congo.[48] Villiers understood that Liberal MP Charles

Dilke and others involved in the agitation regarding the appalling abuse of natives in Leopold's Congo were now forming a committee to monitor the treatment of labor in the Portuguese colonies. Foreign Office functionaries were perplexed as to what they should do, since the British government could hardly expect critics to be satisfied with Portuguese promises of reform. One official feared that "a violent campaign" would force chocolate manufacturers to boycott Portuguese planters and "deprive us of our best weapon." He thought that Villiers should continue pressing the Portuguese government over the repatriation of laborers and that the Foreign Office should notify the humanitarian societies of London's endeavors. The assistant undersecretary stressed that the Foreign Office could not prevent public criticism but that it could inform the Portuguese government of the possibility of such a campaign.[49]

On October 1, 1908, William Cadbury and Joseph Burtt left on an investigative trip to Portuguese West Africa. As early as the spring of that year, Cadbury had hinted to several people that he intended to make the journey to study for himself whether the Portuguese were carrying out the reform that they had promised to institute when he met the plantation owners in Lisbon the previous December. Cadbury especially hoped to witness laborers signing contracts, something neither Burtt nor Nevinson had been able to do, and to gain additional information on mortality rates and the repatriation of the natives.[50] To facilitate the inquiry, he hoped to be accompanied by someone such as Charles Swan, who had been a missionary in Angola and could speak both Portuguese and the natives' language. As it was, by July he had selected his friend Joseph Burtt instead. Cadbury explained to his company board that if the firm were to discontinue its purchases from São Tomé, "it would be a courteous action to the Portuguese to have taken the trouble to make this final personal investigation."[51] The very proper Cadbury, when writing to the Portuguese colonial minister for letters of introduction, professed a respect for the Portuguese, while insisting that they reform their labor system for the benefit of all, including the chocolate makers.[52] In a 1908 letter to an acquaintance, Cadbury noted that the decline in the demand for cocoa beans, which had therefore decreased their price, gave the firm far more leverage to force reform. During an earlier period of extraordinarily high prices, a boycott would have been ineffective, as other firms would have quickly secured the stock. He argued that all roças ought to adopt paid labor and that those plantations with sleeping sickness or high mortality rates should close. He warned his friend Merck that the costs for owners would go up and that profits in São Tomé, which had been "enormous in comparison with other cocoa growing districts," would fall.[53] As Cadbury hinted in his letter, the price of cocoa had dramatically increased from 1906 to 1908 because major São Tomé planters, along with Lisbon agents, had forced up the price by withholding a significant portion of São Tomé cocoa from the market. The most notable of these agents was Merck's employer, Henry Burnay and Company—a banking and commodity-dealing firm with a direct interest in several estates on the island. The scheme to jack up the price of cocoa collapsed in 1908.[54]

William Cadbury's friends feared that the proposed trip was much too dangerous. While Morel understood the reasons for the trip, he feared that Cadbury might die from a disease and that, as a result, the reform movement for West African labor would lose its primary leader. Just before Cadbury's departure, Morel wrote, "May you be protected in every possible way during the next six months . . . I shall be with you often in heart and thought."[55] Merck contended that Cadbury owed more to his "wife & children" than to the "negroes in St. Thomé." He believed the problem lay in Lisbon, not the islands, and finally advised Cadbury to "give up using Thome Cocoa. The effect will be ever so much more efficacious than your Donquixotic journey."[56] Several newspapers carried notices of Cadbury's trip, and employees at Bournville gave him a bon voyage party.[57]

William Cadbury publicly stressed that he was traveling to Africa to determine the extent of Portuguese reform, but behind the scenes, Cadbury Bros. was already taking steps to buy less São Tomé cocoa. The firm had recently bought heavily from the islands, even when prices were high, but on April 7, 1908, Cadbury's directors instructed its cocoa buyer, Edward Thackray, to decrease the purchase of cocoa from São Tomé.[58] The chocolate company had apparently been searching for some time for an alternative source of cocoa beans. In October 1907, John Holt recommended to William Cadbury that the company consider encouraging the development of cocoa bean production in the Gold Coast, a British West African colony.[59] In July 1907, a government agricultural instructor in Trinidad accepted a position with the Cadbury firm in West Africa to educate natives in the production of better quality cocoa beans. He was joined by a second expert in 1908.[60] In March 1908, Cadbury reported to Morel that he had heard good things about "British administration in the Gold Coast" and that the natives there "[are] exceedingly prosperous, and that the Englishman has no chance to get the upper hand." Cadbury also asked Morel for information on the Gold Coast.[61] By May 1908, Cadbury Bros. had allocated money to establish experimental cocoa plantations in the Gold Coast, and by late 1908, company representatives had purchased a few bags of excellent cocoa beans.[62] William Cadbury made arrangements to visit the Gold Coast while on his trip to the Portuguese colonies.

In spring 1908, the Anti-Slavery Society, disturbed over the "inconclusive and dilatory measures" proposed by the Portuguese government to deal with laboring conditions, called for a London conference in October to make plans to bring about real change. Members of philanthropic and missionary societies, representatives of the chocolate firms, and MPs were invited, as were other concerned leaders.[63] Secretary Buxton immediately contacted William Cadbury, asking for his cooperation. Cadbury expressed strong reservations: he preferred that the meeting be private and that the press not be invited. Buxton wrote that Cadbury did not want the press to "make wild and sensational statements as these would seriously impair his efforts to come to a settlement—on business lines, Portugal being extremely sensitive to British criticism."[64] Instead, he wanted the conference postponed until early 1909, as he thought it only fair to give the Portuguese a year to implement the reforms that were promised to him in Lisbon in December 1907. Cadbury also informed Buxton that he intended to visit Angola and São Tomé.[65] He declined to participate in the conference or even to submit a letter in his absence, since he did not wish to compromise his own trip. Cadbury feared that the British press would misrepresent what he said: "I have seen quite sufficient of the mischievous handling of statements by the press to know that it would be possible to turn any words of mine into a handle for lessening the effect of my visit."[66] Buxton, deferring to Cadbury's wishes, did not open the meeting to the press, nor was the conference advertised. It was to be a private session open only through invitation, with a news release issued at its conclusion.[67] The conference would, however, be held in October as originally scheduled, for invitations had already been extended and the meeting could not be easily postponed.[68]

Cadbury Bros., with the approval of the other chocolate manufacturers and the Foreign Office, agreed to make the Burtt report available for publication by the Anti-Slavery Society and by Morel's *African Mail* just before the conference.[69] When it was published in October 1908, the report generated significant publicity. The Cadbury-owned *Daily News* headlined its article "A Terrible Indictment/Grim Report on Indentured Labour/Slavery in Angola/Firm Action of British Manufacturers." The *Western Morning News* (Plymouth) feared that the report showed conditions in São Tomé to be worse than those in Leopold's Congo and added that if Portugal did not mend its ways, the chocolate companies should halt their purchases. "It would be better," the newspaper commented, "to pay a little more for our cocoa than trade upon the blood and tears of human chattels." While noting that Britain's hands were by no means clean in terms of its own labor usage, the paper urged Grey to take "stringent measures to purge the taint of slavery from what is virtually a British industry." The *Manchester Guardian* pointed out that though natives were not seriously mistreated on the islands, the main accusation was that "once on the islands, [they] are never allowed to return." The recruitment of laborers on the continent and especially their march to the coast smacked of "all the horrors of the slave-trade." The *Guardian* commended the cocoa manufacturers for investigating these allegations and lauded William Cadbury's present trip to West Africa to determine what "promises" had been kept by the Portuguese.[70]

Morel published Burtt's report in the October 9 edition of his *African Mail* and took the opportunity to praise the British chocolate manufacturers as "humane, level-headed business men" who began investigating the allegations of slavery when first hearing of them in 1903 and then sponsored Burtt's trip. Since Burtt's return, Morel wrote, "the British cocoa manufacturers have done all that mortal man could do to bring the Portuguese to a sense of the gravity of their responsibilities." The *African Mail* was not pleased that the Anti-Slavery Society decided to hold a conference, which would inevitably raise emotions and cause "serious difficulties to Mr. William Cadbury in his self-imposed mission" to Africa.[71]

Edmund W. Brooks, a Quaker businessman and humanitarian who had been involved in relief missions overseas, was offended by Morel's criticism of the timing of the antislavery conference. An active board member of both the Anti-Slavery Society and the Aborigines' Protection Society and secretary of the London Yearly Meeting's Anti-Slavery Committee, he believed that the chocolate companies should have known about the labor conditions long before 1903, as the slavery had been going on "for many years before that date." Members of the Society of Friends, he stressed in his letter to Morel, were concerned about how long the issue had dragged on. The conference was imperative to help "enlighten" the public. "I do feel," he said, "that the action of the Cocoa Manufacturers is open to criticism of an adverse character." Why, Brooks asked Morel, had Burtt's report "been kept covered up all this time, during which at least 5/6,000 slaves have been done to death?" The firms of Cadbury and Rowntree had known of the problem long enough: there was "no justification for their continuance therein, years after all the facts of the case have become known to them." According to Brooks,

Cadbury Bros. should do what George Cadbury had promised Fox Bourne years earlier—that is, stop purchasing São Tomé cocoa when the slavery was confirmed. "That is the position which they ought to take up, and when they have done that, then and then only, will their hands be clean, and they will be able to join with others in an earnest endeavour to put an end to the iniquities now existing under the Portuguese Government."[72] Brooks, like Fox Bourne and Nevinson, could not fathom why the Cadbury company continued to purchase tainted goods from plantation owners who clearly would not change their totally unacceptable labor practices.

Brooks was correct in expressing serious reservations about the Cadbury firm's strategy of continuing to purchase slave-produced cocoa. The chocolate companies had been slow to act, and they knowingly bought beans from the islands while tens of thousands of Angolans were enslaved and thousands of them died. William Cadbury first heard reports of slave labor in São Tomé in 1901, not 1903. Burtt had sailed in June 1905, but his report was not placed before the Portuguese until November 1907; copies were not made available to the British public until October 1908. By contrast, after visiting West Africa in 1904 and early 1905, Nevinson wrote a blistering exposé of slavery and the slave trade within the year. Hence, Nevinson and many humanitarians were losing their patience with Cadbury and the other chocolate manufacturers.

Morel, who did not take criticism lightly, supplied the Foreign Office with copies of his letters on the timing of the conference. Not only was he always quick to champion William Cadbury, he was also piqued because he had not been invited to the conference.[73] Morel responded to Brooks with a ringing defense of William Cadbury's activities. "I have," he wrote, "a great affection and respect for Mr. W. A. Cadbury the man, and complete confidence in his judgment." Cadbury had taken a strong stand against powerful people and was "about to face it in the camp of the enemy in Africa—possibly at no little physical risk to himself." But when Morel wrote Brooks that "I am not concerned with and have no relations with the Cocoa-manufacturers as such," he was not being honest.[74]

Morel, we have seen, was receiving a handsome regular subsidy from William Cadbury for his efforts at the *African Mail* and in the Congo Reform Association. Also, in the summer of 1908, Cadbury sent several lengthy documents regarding his views on São Tomé to Morel, who wanted this information so that he would be able to represent Cadbury properly when writing about the slave issue in the *African Mail.* Cadbury also indicated on July 10, 1908, that he anticipated a short history of the São Tomé matter would have to be written after he returned, and in a letter to Morel, he added, "Perhaps you will be the man to write it for us." In this exchange of ideas, both men—as Morel also expressed his ideas on native workers—clearly gave careful thought to Portuguese labor. Cadbury believed that there was no justification for importing any more laborers into Príncipe, which was a "death trap." He thought that Africans should work either under relatively short contracts without the presence of their families or under longer-term contracts and with family members in decent housing; under all circumstances, they should work with "absolute freedom to go and to return." Morel, for his part, could find little in defense of the Portuguese labor system. If the labor regulations were really enforced, there would be no workers for the islands, as natives from Angola would refuse to relocate there. Moreover, repatriation had clearly failed. Morel thought that Cadbury had followed the "fair and wise course up to the present" and stated he would be "delighted to write the book you suggest." He also told Cadbury he was "convinced that your journey will lead you to the conclusion, which appears to me to be inevitable—not to buy San Thome cocoa."[75]

If Morel was dissatisfied with the timing of the conference scheduled for October 1908, Nevinson was upset with "the exclusion of the Press, which would necessarily give the meeting a suspicious air of secrecy." Morel was pleased that little publicity had been given to it; Nevinson was disturbed that the lack of general press representation deprived the meeting of publicity that it so much needed and deserved.[76] As it was, sixty to seventy people, including Nevinson and journalists Henry Brailsford and Harold Spender of the *Daily News*, attended the conference at the Westminster Palace Hotel on Thursday afternoon, October 22. Lord Monkswell—an active member of the Liberal Party, an attorney, and the president of the Congo Reform Association—presided over the gathering, which involved members of the humanitarian societies, several religious ministers, and representatives from the chocolate firms. Nevinson, who in his diary referred to the "full audience of lords & fatted people, mostly hostile to me," provided a vivid description of the slave trade and slavery in Portuguese West Africa, the trade in humans having increased since his visit there four years before.[77] He thanked the chocolate firms for their efforts to identify the problems but expressed disappointment that they had not stopped their purchase of cocoa beans from the islands. He believed the only effective course would be a boycott—or the British government sending a naval vessel "to fire across the bows of mail steamers carrying its cargo of slaves. We have in the past many times gone to war for worse causes than this." Ultimately, Nevinson stressed, the Portuguese would have to utilize free labor by paying decent wages and guaranteeing repatriation.[78]

Fox Bourne gave a detailed account of Britain's right to intervene in Portugal, referencing a series of treaties in the early 1800s whereby Britain pumped several hundred thousand pounds into the Iberian nation in exchange for its agreement to abandon the trade in slaves; he also cited Portugal's reaffirmation of its earlier obligations by signing the Berlin and Brussels Acts. Britain, he stressed, had to enforce these treaty obligations so that "Portugal is at once clearly made aware that it will no longer be at liberty to break faith with the civilised world"; further, the Portuguese had to understand that "Great Britain . . . does not intend to be trifled with any longer and is ready to effectively claim as an indisputable right the equitable treatment of African natives."[79] Nevinson recorded in his diary that Fox Bourne "spoke badly." Foreign Office official Clarke commented on Fox Bourne's remarks in a departmental minute: "Mr. Fox Bourne who is the meanest looking little anatomy of a Uriah Heep, was naturally the person who advocated the most bellicose courses. I once advised him to go out himself to Angola like Mr. Burtt and Mr. Cadbury & investigate things for himself but he was thrown into a fever of apprehension at the mere proposal."[80]

Henry Brailsford, Nevinson's journalist colleague, directed the most pointed questions to the chocolate manufacturers who were present. Why, even after they were well aware of the charges of slavery, had they continued to import cocoa from the island at an ever greater rate? Was this, he asked, the proper means for the firms to prepare for a boycott? Nevinson noted that there was "much ill-feeling" about the question, and the chairman, obviously uncomfortable with Brailsford's query, excused the manufacturers from responding. No Cadbury family member attended, but Walter Barrow, solicitor to their firm, remarked that the company's imports from the islands had increased at the same ratio as its total cocoa imports from all sources.[81] Journalist Harold Spender, a member of the Congo Reform Association, called on those present to inspire the public to put pressure on Grey to act, since in São Tomé, unlike in the Congo, England was directly "involved." Another speaker agreed that after William Cadbury's return, interested parties should rally public opinion to pressure the Foreign Office to act.[82]

The meeting concluded indecisively, although Monkswell lamely indicated that he would most likely contact the Foreign Office about the issue. Because reporters were not present, the conference did not generate the many critical evaluations that normally occur after a meeting of this sort. The *Manchester Guardian*'s perceptive editorial, however, pointed out that all actions taken since 1902 to stem the slavery had failed to generate a positive outcome: the number of slaves on the islands had increased, as had the amount of Portuguese cocoa imported into

Britain. While the Foreign Office "counselled patience," slaves on the plantations continued to die at an alarming rate. Clearly, the Foreign Office was obliged to take more constructive steps.[83]

The *Guardian* editorial generated a series of letters from "A Manchester Shipper" who contended that the newspaper had failed to recognize that the laborers were well treated on the islands, as attested to by the fact that very few of them wished to be repatriated. From personal contact with the planters, both in the suburbs of Manchester and in Africa, he alleged that "when judged by all the recognised standards of Christianity and humanitarianism they have no need to fear comparison with many employers of labour in this country." Moreover, the writer argued that the Anti-Slavery Society should concentrate its attention on the abuse of laborers in the Transvaal, be they from Mozambique or China.[84] Nevinson, who replied to the letters from the "Manchester Shipper," argued that "[the laborers are] slaves for the simple reason that they are bought and sold and are taken to the islands quite independently of their own consent. Those conditions, and not ill-treatment, are what constitute slavery." But conditions on the islands were also desperate, as evidenced by the armed men and savage dogs employed on the plantations to try to secure the serviçais, some of whom still managed to flee into the interior of the islands where they preferred "to live naked and starving in the forest."[85]

In December 1908, a second antislavery conference convened in London. Nevinson and John St. Loe Strachey (1860–1927), editor of the *Spectator*, played important roles in setting it up. In June 1908, Nevinson became an editorial writer for the *Daily News*. Thus, the abrasiveness of Nevinson joined with the "militancy" of Henry Brailsford for a stormy sixteen months. Nevinson was never an easy man to work with, and editor Alfred Gardiner was compelled to cope with several threatened resignations. According to a historian of the British press, "Cantankerous and devoid of humour, Nevinson clashed to one extent or another with every editor for whom he worked."[86] Contrary to what he wrote in his autobiography, Nevinson recorded in his diary that Gardiner defended Brailsford when the latter wrote an editorial on Angola in May 1908, and Nevinson admitted that George Cadbury was more than willing to discuss with them the major issues, including that of slavery.[87] There is no evidence that George Cadbury tried to block the journalist's appointment to the *Daily News*. When he was first hired, Nevinson noted that the "Cadburys had raised no objection & made no conditions exc[ept] that they must first see anything on the slavery that I wanted to put into the paper. Otherwise I should be quite free." While he regretted "the loss of freedom & the free lance" that came with joining the staff of the *Daily News*, he was "assured money & position, a certain influence, & the securing-up of energy. The slavery is the only important thing, & at present the Firm [Cadbury] seems to be running fairly straight."[88] On August 11, 1908, he met George Cadbury, "70 but quite alert; apparently straight . . . spoke of Angola & how William C[adbury] had wished to give it up altogether, but then the slaves [would] have no friend."[89]

On November 7, 1908, the ever suspicious Morel reported in a letter to William Cadbury's wife that Brailsford and Nevinson had recently called "a secret meeting of journalists in order to place before them a plan of campaign for attacking the cocoa manufacturers." Morel had met Nevinson at a dinner, and without indicating his knowledge of the plan, he warned Nevinson not to launch an attack on the Cadbury company. Morel thought him "weak and with no balance of judgment," while believing that Brailsford had a "much more dangerous and subtle brain."[90] In his diary, Nevinson described taking a walk with Morel, when the latter insisted "on the virtue of Willm Cadbury & his efforts in the cause, his agony day by day, his attempts to move the others &c."[91] On November 9, two days after the first letter, Morel said that the meeting of the journalists had taken place but that "the tone has quite changed"; instead of an attack on the chocolate firms, there would be a public meeting in early December to support William Cadbury. Morel, who was invited to this second conference, claimed that the "various warnings they have received on all sides have had their effect in considerably modifying the outlook of the conspirators!"[92] Harold Spender, who attended the meeting of the journalists on Friday, November 6, also found them "in quite a different mood."[93] Brailsford and Nevinson had had a "very satisfactory" conversation with George Cadbury the day before. Cadbury explained why a boycott was not in place but indicated he had gained the support of two other chocolate manufacturers for a possible boycott. Nevinson recorded privately that Cadbury "asked us only not to attack Portuguese as long as William is out there, in his own paper, but agreed it was a good thing to rouse public opinion here outside his paper: we told him we were going to hold a meeting, & he raised no objection. He thanked us both for the time we took on social reform in our leaders [editorials], & we parted in great amity. I told HNB [Brailsford] we had both been too suspicious, & he agreed, adding he had been worse than I, which is true."[94]

John St. Loe Strachey, who chaired the organizing committee of the conference, had owned and edited the *Spectator* since 1898. A Liberal Unionist and steadfast free trader, Strachey made the *Spectator* the most influential Unionist weekly of the early twentieth century. A fellow editor regarded him as a man of "unswerving rectitude" with "a carefully-studied air of moderation and sweet reasonableness," while another writer stressed that he was mainly concerned with the "moral health" of people.[95] From 1908 to 1914, Strachey used his influence to focus public attention on improving the welfare of laborers in Portuguese West Africa, and he threw open the pages of the *Spectator* to Nevinson and others to campaign for the end of slavery.

The committee of journalists worked hard to ensure a good turnout at the public meeting set for December 4, 1908. To secure the signature of Travers Buxton on the letter announcing the meeting, Spender emphasized to Buxton that the organizing committee would look with "approval" on the activities of the chocolate manufacturers to gain reform in São Tomé.[96] Although Buxton agreed to sign the letter, he stressed that because the members of his Anti-Slavery Society had decided to withhold "public agitation" until they heard the outcome of the missions by the Portuguese commissioner Cid and William Cadbury, they might "prefer to support the meeting passively, and not be speakers, altho' entirely sympathetic with its general object."[97] The Anti-Slavery Society was playing it safe. Such qualified statements bothered Nevinson, but he still assured Buxton that there "will be no attack of any kind on our Cocoa Firms. As you know, I have never attacked them, though they have not yet done wh[at] I expected. I think they will."[98] The letter announcing the meeting appeared in the *Times* on November 21. After recounting evidence of slavery and slave trade in Portuguese West Africa, the letter contended that the forces of reform "will be strengthened in suppressing this abominable traffic if the wide spread support of British public opinion is gained." Therefore, "all who view with horror the continuance of a system under which men, women, and children are bought and sold for labour" were invited to the meeting to be held at Caxton Hall, Westminster, on Friday, December 4. An impressive list of writers, journalists, social reformers, politicians, and humanitarians signed the letter, including Samuel Barnett, the founder of Toynbee Hall in East London; novelists John Galsworthy and H. G. Wells; Labour politician J. Ramsay MacDonald; philosopher and journalist Leonard T. Hobhouse; classical scholar Gilbert Murray; C. P. Scott, editor of the *Manchester Guardian;* and Nevinson, Strachey, Fox Bourne, and Buxton.[99]

Nevinson and Strachey negotiated with Buxton and George Cadbury over the exact wording of a resolution to be offered at the meeting, calling for a possible boycott of São Tomé cocoa.[100] Both journalists stressed to Cadbury that the resolution was not intended to be hostile to the chocolate firms; Nevinson reminded him that "you hoped public opinion would be aroused as much as possible upon the subject of the Angola Slavery, and you will be pleased to see that some steps are being taken with this object."[101] George Cadbury replied that he would very much have preferred that public opinion not be stirred up while his nephew was still in West Africa, but he added that the firm would boycott São Tomé cocoa if William Cadbury's report was "unfavourable."[102]

Nevinson found it a "frightful exertion" to coordinate the meeting and to keep all the participants agreeable to the resolutions.[103] He had to convince a wavering Robert Horton, a dissenting minister, to move the resolution about the cocoa boycott. Nevinson described Horton as an "old & sleepy" man who had apparently "lost his cleverness." He believed that Horton had been approached by the "slimy serpent" John Harris, a colleague of Morel's at the Congo Reform Association and a defender of the Cadburys.[104]

Strachey, presiding at the December 4 conference, extolled the virtues of the chocolate companies and particularly William Cadbury but maintained that the firm of Cadbury's case would be strengthened by raising public pressure to end the intolerable labor practice. Nevinson recorded that several speakers gave effective talks, including a woman missionary associated with the Angola Evangelical Mission who offered examples of the Portuguese government's toleration of the illegally recruited labor.[105]

The meeting itself, held before a full hall—and an audience that included Walter Barrow, solicitor to the Cadbury company, and Foreign Office official Walter Langley—was not without minor complications.[106] There were interruptions by individuals protesting the English exploitation of colonial laborers and others defending Portugal. Nevinson believed that his own speech recounting the horrors of the slave trade and slavery was totally ineffective: "I was very bad—cold and dull with my facts, no charm or personality at all. I had better have thrown notes & facts away. My glasses bother me too. It was a hideous failure just when I ought to have succeeded." He complained that Morel, who came with "his shifty face," managed to have the word "immediately" removed from the resolution encouraging support for a boycott.[107] Two resolutions were passed with some objections. The first stated that "a deputation shall call upon the Foreign Office to use its utmost influence with the Portuguese Government in order to secure its [slavery's] abolition, in accordance with past assurances and existing treaties." Ironically, Horton, who had earlier been reluctant to offer a motion, used some of the strongest language of the day—"that every person who drank a cup of cocoa might almost feel a choking sensation, and every child that sucked a stick of chocolate was sucking human blood."[108] He introduced the second resolution, which thanked the firms for exposing "the evils" of Portuguese labor, encouraged all chocolate manufacturers to boycott São Tomé cocoa unless Portugal took meaningful steps to halt slavery, and called on consumers "to support the firms who take this action."[109] The press thoroughly covered the proceedings. A long article in Strachey's *Spectator,* however, offended Nevinson because he was not mentioned by name.[110]

Following the conference, Strachey arranged a meeting with Grey, who insisted that the group involved be few in number and that no publicity be given to the session. Buxton was upset that he was not included in the delegation, necessitating profuse apologies from Nevinson and Strachey.[111] On December 10, Nevinson, Strachey, Horton, and Rudolph Lehmann, MP, had a long conversation with Grey, during which they presented the resolutions passed by the conference. Nevinson described Grey as "very clear & straight; saw at once the point to attack is the recruitment on the mainland."[112] Grey acknowledged that the recent Caxton Hall meeting and any additional public meetings would strengthen diplomatic representations in Lisbon, and "he entirely approved of the threat of boycott which indeed he regarded as the best & almost the only possible instrument."[113] The foreign secretary explained that a possible diplomatic move might be to propose to the Portuguese that the British consul in Luanda be permitted to ascertain the conditions under which laborers had been recruited in Angola. If all was well, the Portuguese would have a sound defense, whereas illegal activities would rightly require correction, "and we should be in a much better position for pushing our representation."[114] Three weeks later, per Grey's instructions, Villiers impressed on Portuguese Foreign Minister Wenceslau de Lima the intensity of the reformers in England, gave him a copy of the first resolution passed at Caxton Hall, and charged that the Portuguese apparently gained laborers "by force, and that the contract which they signed . . . was one which they did not sign voluntarily and did not understand."[115]

Thus, the year 1908 ended without any resolution among interested parties as to how reform might be pressed on the Portuguese. Nevinson, with some of his journalist colleagues and Fox Bourne, openly espoused the view that chocolate companies should boycott São Tomé cocoa beans. Meanwhile, the chocolate firms agreed that the continued purchase of the islands' beans gave the Birmingham and other Quaker-owned firms greater leverage in pressuring the Portuguese planters and government to end the use of slave labor. The British Foreign Office, as ever, remained reluctant to demand much of the Portuguese. William Cadbury and Joseph Burtt were traveling in Portuguese West Africa, hoping to find evidence that the Portuguese were finally implementing changes to their labor system. But while all the discussions and activities occupied the energies of many during the year, a newspaper editorial of September 26, 1908, became the single focal point of the entire controversy.

7 Defending Reputations

> The Angolan in the native state is an absolute animal—he has neither home nor family—please grasp this fact firmly. . . . The islands . . . are a veritable paradise for the blacks.
>
> *John A. Wyllie*

> And the worst of all this slavery and slave-driving and slave-dealing is brought about by the necessity of providing a sufficient number of hands to grow and pick cocoa on the islands of Principe and Sao Thomé, the islands which feed the mills and presses of Bournville!
>
> *The Standard*

> Our object is to put a stop to the conditions of slavery—not merely to wash our own hands of any connection with them.
>
> *Cadbury Bros.*

FROM THE ONSET of the controversy over São Tomé cocoa, Cadbury Bros. was determined to guard the company's name from any hint of wrongdoing. The company wished to protect its good reputation, a valuable asset that it utilized regularly in its advertisements. Cadbury also understood, after its contact with the British Foreign Office in October 1906, that it should not draw public attention to slavery on the Portuguese island until a later time. The company used this request to downplay the slavery issue as a justification for remaining silent on the matter until the Liverpool Chamber of Commerce meetings of September and October 1907.

Cadbury officials also distrusted journalists. This attitude may have originated, at least regarding the cocoa matter, with William Cadbury's antipathy toward Henry Nevinson as a reporter. George Cadbury purchased the *Daily News* because he disliked many of the stories in the press and wanted to ensure that the Liberal point of view was heard. As proprietor of the *Daily News*, he had a propensity to control or at least to examine the stories dealing with São Tomé. Whatever the reasons—and they were many and complex—the Cadbury board carefully monitored and immediately responded to news items that were deemed to be unfavorable or inaccurate in relation to the company. This situation probably harmed Cadbury's image in the long run, for it eventually led to the libel trial that focused attention on the firm's extensive history of purchasing slave-produced cocoa beans.

As noted earlier, the *Manchester Guardian* and the *Evening Standard*, under legal pressure from Cadbury Bros., issued letters of apology in April and May 1908 for articles that allegedly misrepresented the firm. In June 1908, *John Bull*, a paper edited by the muckraking MP Horatio Bottomley, ran two articles admonishing the three chocolate firms—Cadbury, Fry, and Rowntree—for defending their continued purchase of São Tomé cocoa beans by stating that other firms would buy up the stock if the English did not. The newspaper charged that "any abuse, however vile, might be defended on that plea." *John Bull* admitted that the world was not perfect: "Business men have to shut their eyes to some things they would willingly change if they could, but after all there are limitations to this complaisance. Messrs. Cadbury, Fry and Rowntree are men of deservedly high reputation. . . . Is it worthy of such men to buttress up a horrible system of slavery upon the flimsy pretexts alone available?"[1] The Cadbury company was up in arms once again: its board minutes recorded the decision "to take legal action in this or any future case, if we have clear ground to go upon."[2] On June 27, *John Bull* ran a long letter from the firm of Cadbury recounting the many steps taken by the chocolate manufacturers to correct the situation. A "retraction" by *John Bull* followed the letter: "This document speaks for itself, and we think it only right to say that we are satisfied that Mr. Cadbury and the other gentlemen who signed it are really anxious to put an end to the abominations to which we have directed attention, and that if they have not already closed their business connection with these Portuguese cocoa planters it is because they really believe that the actual course they have taken is more likely to bring about reform and better treatment for the labourers upon the plantations."[3] Then, in January 1909, the *Chronicle of the London Missionary Society* stated that the "moral suasion" used by the three firms for five years had led to "no improvement in the lot of the natives," and it called for the firms to boycott São Tomé. The following month, after Cadbury Bros. accused the *Chronicle* of using a "somewhat contemptuous reference" to the "serious" effort made by the chocolate companies, the newspaper opined that its remarks were "in no way intended to be contemptuous" but added that "*five years have passed since the British cocoa firms took the matter up, and yet the lot of the natives is to-day as terrible as ever*" (italics in original). The *Chronicle* had little faith in more promises by the planters.[4]

On September 26, 1908, five days before William Cadbury departed on his journey to West Africa and two weeks prior to the publication of Burtt's report in England, the *Standard*, a Conservative London morning newspaper, published an editorial (see Appendix) questioning the sincerity of the Cadbury company's reform effort. The *Standard* praised William Cadbury for undertaking the trip, "which does not come too soon." Not only did his company produce fine chocolate, it also displayed remarkable concern for its workers in Bournville, where it provided a factory and village dedicated to their welfare. Nevertheless, the paper added, "white hands of the Bournville chocolate makers are helped by other unseen hands some thousands of miles away, black and brown hands, toiling in plantations, or hauling loads through swamp and forest." The *Standard*, confusing William Cadbury with his newspaper proprietor uncle, George Cadbury, indicated that the former had long expressed concern over laborers of various races: "He is understood to be largely interested in a newspaper which is the champion of the down-trodden coloured person groaning under the oppressions of British justice. To his alert conscience the thought of Chinese labour imported into South Africa was a loathing and an offence." Even though the Chinese workers were "under no compulsion to go," earned a decent wage, and were protected by both the Chinese and British governments, Cadbury's newspaper was not satisfied: "The hint, the suspicion, the remote possibility of slavery is enough to stir the anger of such a sensitive soul, and Mr. Cadbury's journal denounced the accursed thing without stint or measure."

Given William Cadbury's great concern, the *Standard* expressed astonishment that his "voyage of discovery has been deferred so long." One would have expected the company itself to have verified carefully the conditions on the plantations, yet that was not done. Others had performed that task, most notably Henry Nevinson. After applauding Nevinson's journalistic qualifications of "penetrating observation," "trained judgment," and breadth of experience, the *Standard* based much of its editorial on a vivid paraphrase of his book, while tying the slave labor on São Tomé to Quaker ideals: "It is not called slavery; 'contract labour' they name it now; but in most of its essentials it is that monstrous trade in human flesh and blood against which the Quaker and Radical ancestors of Mr. Cadbury thundered in the better days of England." After depicting the farce of repatriation, the *Standard* concluded: "And the worst of all this slavery and slave-driving and slave-dealing is brought about by the necessity of providing a sufficient number of hands to grow and pick cocoa on the islands of Principe and Sao Thomé, the islands which feed the mills and presses of Bournville! . . . There is only one thing more amazing than his [Nevinson's] statements: and that is the strange tranquility with which they were received by those virtuous people in England whom they intimately concerned."[5]

The *Standard* editorial reflected several powerful interests that were in conflict in early twentieth-century England. Both the *Standard* and the *Daily News* sought to influence governments and to mold public opinion in the highly competitive London newspaper arena. The *Standard* was owned by C. Arthur Pearson, a Conservative newspaper proprietor who also held the *Daily Express* and the *Evening Standard*. Joseph Chamberlain referred to him as "the greatest hustler I have ever known," and a biographer contended that Pearson was "intellectually . . . unfitted to guide, much less to form, public opinion."[6] Howell A. Gwynne, the editor of the *Standard*, had been a correspondent for Reuters, and Nevinson had come to respect his "judgment and tolerance" during the South African War.[7] Both Gwynne, a good friend of imperialists Cecil Rhodes and Alfred Milner, and Pearson ardently supported Chamberlain and his "tariff reform" plan of 1903. Chamberlain's proposal broke from the near sacred principle of free trade and advocated levying import duties on goods entering Great Britain except for those that came from its colonies. The *Daily News*, by contrast, was extraordinarily critical of Milner and Chamberlain's South African War, and it bitterly attacked the Conservative government's approval of contracting Chinese coolie labor to help rebuild Johannesburg's shattered economy following the war. George Cadbury purchased the *Daily News* in 1901, during the war, to give Liberals a voice in London. The Cadburys, the *Daily News*, and the Liberal Party were avid proponents of free trade, campaigning hard against Chamberlain's tariff reform and the specter of an expensive small loaf of bread compared to a cheaper large one. Hence, the warring sides took their positions: Liberals versus Conservatives, expansionists versus responsible colonialists, free traders versus tariff reformers, and newspaper versus newspaper.

Nevinson's account of slavery was at the core of the *Standard*'s accusations against the Cadbury company. A week after the editorial appeared, Gwynne told Nevinson that he would pursue more of the story, "Libel or not," as he was "much moved about it, & wouldn't let it drop." After consulting Fox Bourne and at least one other person, Nevinson wrote a letter to the *Standard*, which appeared on October 6, 1908, nearly two weeks after the newspaper attacked William Cadbury.[8] After thanking the paper for "drawing attention" to slavery in Portuguese West Africa, he revealed that William Cadbury had related to him, before Nevinson traveled to Africa in 1904, that the firm "had been inquiring into the system for some two or three years previously" and had agreed with other chocolate manufacturers to send a "special commissioner" to "investigate." Nevinson met that commissioner, Joseph Burtt, in São Tomé, and after spending eighteen months in Africa, the latter had submitted a report. Though that report was not yet public, Nevinson had read a copy, and he stated that it "entirely agrees with my own account in every important particular." He welcomed Cadbury's upcoming visit to West Africa. Nevinson closed by stating that the Cadbury-owned *Daily News* had "denounced this slave system as strongly and openly as yourself" in an article published on May 6, 1908.[9]

Cadbury's board of directors was extremely disturbed over the "grave accusations . . . made against the Company" by the *Standard*, and it turned the affair over to its solicitor and William Cadbury for appropriate "measures."[10] Newspapers had rebuked the company in the past for its purchase of São Tomé cocoa, but when threatened with legal action by the Cadbury firm, they had always backed down and issued apologies. The *Standard*'s editorial, however, was different. It was both broader and more pointed than previous editorials and news stories that Cadbury Bros. had deemed libelous. The London newspaper implied that the company, in spite of its often expressed ideals of honesty and responsibility, came up remarkably short. The *Standard* ridiculed William Cadbury as a "philanthropist and friend of humanity," and it mocked company owners as "those virtuous people" who cared not a whit for the "grimed African hands" whose sweat was "so essential to the beneficent and lucrative operations at Bournville." Enough was enough. Cadbury Bros. sued the *Standard* for libel, claiming that because of the article, the company's officials "have been and will be injured in their credit and reputation." In the writ issued October 5 and delivered November 30, 1908, the plaintiff, the firm of Cadbury, declared that the words used by the defendant, the *Standard*, meant that Cadbury's officials "were hypocrites, who, professing to be philanthropists and to be concerned in the improvement of conditions of life and work amongst the working classes, acquiesced in a system of brutalising servitude enforced by wanton cruelty amongst the natives of Portuguese West Africa, and that they were fit objects for odium and contempt."[11] For the next fourteen months, both parties to the case prepared their arguments. Thus, the resources and energies of Cadbury Bros. and the *Standard* shifted away from improving the lot of the serviçais and instead focused on a legal battle in which virtue was at stake.

On their trip to the Portuguese West African colonies, which they began in October 1908, William Cadbury and Joseph Burtt first stopped at the islands of São Tomé and Príncipe. They visited the Boa Entrada plantation—"the show place of the island and very justly so," according to Cadbury. The manager, he wrote, "frankly supported our demand for repatriation, and told us it was as needful for S. Thome as for Angola."[12] According to Arthur Nightingale, who had stopped at Boa Entrada in 1906, the plantation encompassed 5½ square miles and employed 527 laborers; the annual death rate was 6 percent among the older laborers and higher for recent arrivals.[13] Altogether, Cadbury and Burtt inspected some eight plantations on the two islands, spending two days on Príncipe and three weeks on São Tomé.[14] Cadbury, however, was disappointed that the governor-general and the curator of São Tomé failed to furnish him with "authentic and official vital statistics."[15]

Cadbury's daily log of his trip included a series of sketches of ships and of rock and land formations, as well as a drawing of the island of Príncipe. Between October 2, 1908, and February 15, 1909, he mailed home nineteen letters, mainly to Emmeline, his wife of six years. These personal letters, which included several of his sketches, showed him to be an observant, interested, and caring person who loved and missed his wife and three children. Through the communications to his wife, Cadbury also instructed the company to send gifts, often chocolate, to his hosts. (These handwritten letters were afterward typed and submitted to Cadbury Bros.) His vivid depictions of conditions and his comments about people were descriptive and often critical; on the whole, his letters were more graphically written than the published report of his journey.[16] While at Luanda, he joined in a game of cricket with the men from the *Britannia*, a cable-repair ship in the harbor, and later dined with British consul Mackie; the restaurant staff "put a little red ensign in the pudding and made quite a festive time for us."[17]

Cadbury was unable to witness any contracting of serviçais, which was one of the main reasons he had undertaken the trip. The curator in Benguela reported that the process of signing on laborers had been "temporarily suspended" beginning on October 11, 1908, which, Cadbury added, "exactly coincides with our stay in this part of the world." The government, he said, "has been successful in frustrating the object of my visit."[18] Both Cadbury and Mackie suspected that serviçais were being smuggled to the islands during the evening.[19] Mackie introduced Burtt and Cadbury to the governor-general of Angola, who was hostile and "hardly disguised the fact that he regarded Mr. Cadbury's presence in Angola with disfavour." It was evident from discussions with the governor-general that the new labor regulations of 1908 were of limited value.[20] Cadbury also found that Francisco Cid, the official appointed by the Portuguese government to examine labor conditions in its West African colonies, was traveling with individuals directly involved in the slave trade. Cadbury feared that "there is no hope of any change until much greater pressure [is] put upon the powers that be."[21]

After Angola, Burtt and Cadbury stopped at the Gold Coast, where Cadbury met with company officials working on improving and expanding cocoa-bean production. He approved the purchase of fourteen acres of land at Mangoase as the site for a model plantation. He and Burtt also visited with two chiefs in the interior, one of whom raised and sold cocoa beans.[22] Cadbury found the cocoa beans provided by Mate Kole, the chief of the Krobos, to be of excellent quality, and he later arranged to send the chief "two cocks and four hens of the best breed possible for the tropics."[23]

In early January 1909, Cadbury's board of directors decided that the conditions of labor in São Tomé had "not been reformed," and as a result, the company determined to stop immediately the purchase of cocoa beans from the islands and to use up all existing stores by the time William Cadbury returned.[24] Cadbury landed at Plymouth, England, on March 9, 1909.[25] One week later, the firms of Cadbury, Fry, and Rowntree announced publicly that they would no longer purchase cocoa from the Portuguese islands of São Tomé and Príncipe because of the "failure of the Portuguese Government to fulfill the pledges of reform," although they would be willing to reexamine that position when adequate progress was made to guarantee the proper treatment of the serviçais. Stollwerck, the German chocolate firm, quickly agreed to support the boycott, although Ludwig Stollwerck complained to Arnold Rowntree that when he had advocated the boycott eighteen months earlier, he had been "treated somewhat coldly!"[26] Within the next few days, several other chocolate manufacturers in Britain and on the European continent made it known that they would not purchase São Tomé cocoa either; a few stressed that they had never bought it. Some distributors, such as the Co-operative Wholesale Society and the Army and Navy Stores, stated that they would not sell chocolate made from São Tomé cocoa.[27]

Many newspapers printed the boycott announcement and carried substantial articles on Cadbury's West African trip.[28] George Cadbury's *Daily News* congratulated the firms on the boycott decision, adding: "The planters have been proof against all the appeals of humanity. We shall see whether they cannot be reached through the pocket." Both the *Daily News* and the *Spectator* called on the public to support the boycott.[29] The *Manchester Guardian* approved of the boycott but feared that the British government had not done everything within its power to halt the trade. Why should British warships, which stopped suspect ships on the east coast of Africa, "be forbidden to interfere with the immense slave traffic carried on under their guns between Angola and San Thome and Principe?"[30] The *Nation* hoped that public opinion in the United States, "which is still, we are sure, keen on the question of slavery," would pressure U.S. firms to join the boycott.[31] *John Bull*, congratulating itself for having drawn attention to the slavery issue, found that the firms had granted the Portuguese government "such an abundance of time to redeem its pledges as almost to put them under suspicion of moral blindness." Fortunately, *John Bull* added, the companies had agreed to stop any purchases from the islands after William Cadbury discovered that conditions on the island were indeed what had been reported for years.[32] The *Yorkshire Herald* berated the chocolate manufacturers for having reacted so slowly and chastised the Cadbury company for its "gross act of inconsistency" in using its newspaper to attack the labor system in South Africa but doing remarkably little about Portuguese labor practices.[33] The *Friend*, a Quaker journal, believed that the firms had kept "their judicial bearing throughout a difficult investigation."[34]

Both Travers Buxton and Nevinson were pleased with the boycott.[35] Nevinson, in a signed article in the *Daily News* titled "A STEP TO FREEDOM," viewed the boycott as a great event: "If only the peoples of Angola could hear and understand what has to-day been done, what a shout of joy would go up from that oppressed and hopeless land! At last, then, the crying of their silence has been heard, and mercy has listened to their tale of ancient wrong." But the parties, he stressed, should not be satisfied with half measures that might improve the lives of the workers: "The one and only cure is to stop the buying and selling of men and women, to stop the compulsory labour—in short, to stop the slavery."[36] Writing in the *Nation*, a passionate Nevinson remarked: "Slavery is not a question of treatment, good or bad. It is a question of the sale of men and women at a price, and of their compulsory labor." Even if, he added, "there was no cruelty at all, and if the laborers on the plantations were as carefully tended as infants in a ducal nursery, the system would be slavery all the same."[37] Nevinson congratulated William Cadbury for "a great piece of work accomplished, and it does you great honour in every way."[38]

Hilda Grundler, a missionary whom Cadbury met when he visited West Africa, thanked him for the clear statement on the boycott. Writing from Luanda in May 1909, she expressed the hope that the recent expulsion of four white slavers from the interior was a harbinger of change in Angola. A recent experience at a plantation in the interior, however, pointed out how demented some people could be, she said. A caravan passing through from the interior offered the plantation owner a beautiful young mother "in exchange for rum." The proprietor ordered that her elaborately formed "head gear"—a "sort of birds' [*sic*] nest and entwined with beads threaded into the hair"—be cut off; but the deal fell through, "so the poor thing, shorn of her wonderful beauty, was given back to the caravan, and taken further to be bartered for again at the next *White* man's station" (emphasis in original). Grundler continued to be impressed, even more so after ten years in the area, with "the utter immorality of the Whites in this part of the world." Her observation pertained not only to the Portuguese but also to other Europeans who settled in the area "following the examples around them, and succumbing to that often repeated maxim 'It is the custom out in these parts.'"[39]

Beginning in 1901, executives of chocolate firms, journalists, humanitarians, and government officials had become aware of the existence of slavery in Portuguese West Africa. Months of protracted study, inquiry, explanation, communication, and promise extended to years. Via countless meetings, letters, and editorials, accompanied by earnest hand-wringing, Westerners who were free to think, talk, and write about sins elsewhere in the colonial world debated the issue of slavery. But during all these critical months and years, what had become of the slaves? Were they any more free, any more respected, any more able to work? Could they rest, enjoy life, or choose where to live and work and play because of the efforts of the Europeans? The answer is no. After years of Western rhetoric, there was no appreciable change in the lot of slaves in Angola or on the islands. Not until after the boycott began in 1909 was there any substantial improvement in the recruitment of the serviçais and in their lives on the plantations.

William Cadbury worked on completing his report as soon as he returned to England. His March 17, 1909, letter to Burtt, whom he addressed as "Joe," asked for information on a Latin name for the tsetse fly, figures on laborers shipped to Angola, and a man's name that he needed for his account.[40] Morel, at Cadbury's request, helped to write the conclusion to the report.[41] By May, however, William Cadbury, on the advice of his counsel, decided that the report, *Labour in Portuguese*

West Africa, could not be released because it might be "construed as a breach of court etiquette (contempt of court)" in regard to the upcoming libel trial against the *Standard*. While Cadbury was permitted to send a rough copy to the Foreign Office, as well as to other interested parties such as Travers Buxton, the document was not made public.[42]

Fox Bourne died one month before the boycott was announced. Ill though he was, he had continued to press his case to the Foreign Office. Perhaps his "finest letter" was the one he wrote for the Anti-Slavery Conference in October 1908 and sent to Grey on November 4, 1908.[43] In this letter, Fox Bourne carefully spelled out the international agreements Portugal had signed during the nineteenth century, stressing Britain's obligation to enforce them. It was Fox Bourne's ability to pinpoint legal and moral responsibility that made his arguments powerful and all but impossible to refute. In his letter, he took on Portuguese officialdom:

> While purveying of slaves is chiefly in the hands of private individuals, let it be remembered that recognised officials, some of them in high stations, and licensed agents of the Portuguese Government are responsible both for the "ransoming" of the helpless captives, and for their conveyance to and distribution among the Portuguese cocoa plantations and sugar plantations.
>
> It is pretended, of course, by the perpetrators of these crimes and their apologists, that indentured labour is not slavery. But no honest person can doubt or deny that intended labourers, as forcibly procured as are the natives of the interior parts of Africa, as forcibly driven over perhaps a thousand or more miles to the coast and there forcibly indentured, are other than slaves in the fullest sense of the term.[44]

Fox Bourne's thorough research and encyclopedic knowledge, aided by his mastery of several European languages and his network of correspondents, gave him a formidable base from which to operate. A writer in the *Times* remarked: "He never flamed up; he glowed with a constant fire of steady indignation, which he fed laboriously with Blue-books and facts verified and sifted. By his quiet manner, his catholicity of mind—which had been cultivated if not created by much writing upon many topics—his suggestion of pity even in his most severe denunciations, he commanded the respect of candid persons, many of whom, indeed, accepted his conclusions upon trust, so convincing were the evidences of his sincerity."[45] The *Manchester Guardian* believed that Fox Bourne, single-minded to a fault, "incurred many enmities in the course of his work. But he went straight on his course without fearing any man."[46] The Aborigines' Protection Society did not survive his death. Instead, it merged with the Anti-Slavery Society, with which it had so much in common, in June 1909.[47]

Following the boycott of Portuguese cocoa by English and continental confectionery manufacturers, São Tomé beans continued to find a market, just as William Cadbury had feared. A cocoa broker told Nevinson in June, two months after the boycott began, that the price of the island's beans had gone up a bit, "owing to shortage somewhere else."[48] German brokers moved into the Portuguese market, and U.S. firms bought heavily in São Tomé cocoa.[49] The Anti-Slavery Society decided in May 1909 to send Burtt to the United States to educate the American public on slave-grown cocoa beans and to pressure the huge U.S. firms to stop purchases from the islands.[50] The society raised funds for the trip primarily through appeals in English newspapers and contributions from Americans.[51] The English chocolate firms, while pleased with the deputation to the United States, declined to contribute to the fund, as they wished to make certain that Burtt could honestly testify to the Americans that he was on a humanitarian mission and did not represent any English "commercial interests."[52] Burtt's suggestion that he take an African boy with him on the journey was turned down by the Anti-Slavery Society, for fear that the "colour feeling" still ran very high in the United States.[53] Burtt, who married in July 1909, was accompanied on his visit to the United States by his wife, Emmeline. John Daniels, secretary of the American Congo Reform Association, handled local arrangements for the tour, which began in Boston about October 1. For six weeks, Burtt addressed public and private audiences in many of the eastern cities, large and small, in what appears to have been a successful appeal, although James Bryce, the British minister to Washington, declined to introduce Burtt to Secretary of State Philander Chase Knox.[54] Many U.S. publications carried articles about slave-produced cocoa, most notably *Leslie's Weekly*, a New York magazine. Burtt also personally contacted several U.S. chocolate manufacturers, including Baker, the largest in the world, which maintained that it had not bought São Tomé cocoa for a year; the company contributed $100 to the travel fund. The trip was cut short, however, when Burtt had to return to Britain to testify in the *Standard* libel trial, scheduled for late November.[55]

The Portuguese government was exceptionally displeased with the Anti-Slavery Society's deputation to the United States, for Lisbon claimed that Portugal was taking effective steps to implement reform.[56] However, Portuguese efforts over the previous year and a half—since William Cadbury's meeting with the planters in Lisbon—had not inspired confidence. Even Angolan and Portuguese newspapers severely criticized both the new regulations of April 1908 and the Cid mission as promising no appreciable improvements.[57]

By 1908 or 1909, the British Foreign Office had lost faith in any possibility of reform, although it would not admit this for diplomatic reasons. Consul Mackie, in Luanda, went into the interior of Angola to investigate the treatment of the native laborers, and his report of March 1908 painted an appalling picture of raids to acquire laborers, brutal treatment of natives, ruthless beatings and executions of slaves who ran away and were apprehended, the presence of wooden fetters to keep captives from fleeing, the collusion of Portuguese officials, the failure of even the most zealous Portuguese reformers, and the lack of government authority throughout the district. Mackie concluded that "the system under which labour is recruited in my district is closely akin to slavery."[58] Francis Villiers, Britain's minister to Lisbon, informed the British Foreign Office in November 1908 that repatriation efforts had failed, with only one person listed as returning home. The minister stressed that repatriation was often impossible for the natives, many of whom originally lived hundreds of miles in the interior of Angola in homes that "in many cases ceased to exist."[59] Mackie tactfully wrote to the Portuguese commissioner Cid in December 1908 suggesting changes, including ensuring repatriation, that would help provide for meaningful contract labor.[60]

MPs flooded the Foreign Office with questions about slavery in Portuguese colonies in February and March 1909, just before the chocolate manufacturers announced their boycott. Questions in Parliament raised by Leverton Harris, who was unusual in that he was a Unionist MP and a Quaker, were designed to embarrass both the firms for purchasing slave-produced cocoa beans and the Liberal government for tolerating it.[61] When Harris and another MP asked Grey why the government could do nothing under treaty provisions about the vicious contract system, the foreign secretary lamely replied that the initial step in enforcing a treaty was "always diplomatic negotiation. We are in that stage now." When pressed further on the question, Grey stated that the British government was still "waiting for the result of [Portuguese] inquiries. . . . It is a very old subject, and has been receiving consideration with a view to further communications."[62]

In January 1909, the Portuguese government altered the rules regarding medical assistance and hygiene for the serviçais.[63] In March and April, Mackie reported to Grey that the governor-general of Angola had expelled four Portuguese merchants for involvement in slave trading. Mackie emphasized that he was not certain what this meant, although the first two merchants may have been guilty of violating the Portuguese government's strict orders not to trade in slaves while Cadbury visited the area.[64] About the same time, however, Portuguese officials expelled an American missionary for "inciting the natives to rebellion" when he resisted government efforts to remove a native from his mission.[65] Cid returned to Lisbon in early 1909, and a new set of regulations stemming from his investigation was issued in June. The government pledged to define and restrict recruitment of labor in Angola, to place recruiting agents under government supervision, to provide support facilities for natives moving from the interior to the coast, and to guarantee repatriation.[66] The Anti-Slavery Society and Burtt pointed out that while the regulations were an improvement, the question of enforcement would be critical. Moreover, the regulations were still inadequate, as many areas of concern were still not addressed—including issues relating to the children of serviçais, who remained the property of plantation owners.[67] In July 1909, Portugal announced that it was halting all exportation of workers from Angola to the islands for a period of three months (only those already under contract would proceed to the islands), but it would continue to recruit laborers from Mozambique for service in the west.[68]

Recruitment from Mozambique began in 1908 under contracts limited to one year, with immediate repatriation.[69] In August 1909, seventy-three workers from Mozambique who were laboring in São Tomé revolted because the curator had told them that they were on three-year, rather than one-year, contracts. *O Século*, a Lisbon newspaper, reported that at least one laborer was killed. The Portuguese government intervened, repatriated the laborers, and canceled the license of the emigration agent who was involved.[70] Meanwhile, the repatriation of Angolan natives remained exceptionally slow, and serviçais from Angola were still arriving on the islands in November 1909, probably because they had been contracted before the July deadline.[71] Mackie remained very pessimistic about whether the new regulations would help the serviçais, as there was no reason to believe that the Portuguese government could properly recruit them or repatriate them.[72] In 1909, the British government appointed Francisco Olivare Marin as unpaid British consul to São Tomé, to look after "the British native residents, many of whom were in a destitute condition and desirous of being repatriated." Because

Marin was the nephew of Francisco Mantero, a powerful plantation owner, Cadbury's directors had little faith in the appointment.[73]

In November 1909, the twenty-year-old king of Portugal engaged in a goodwill tour of England designed primarily to cement ties between the two nations. King Manuel and his accompanying officials attended luncheons, visited theaters and shops, and went on hunting trips. Amid the entertainment, Edward Grey met with Carlos du Bocage, minister of foreign affairs, and arranged for the renewal of an arbitration treaty between the old allies. Bocage did not discuss the issue of labor in West Africa with Grey, but the Portuguese minister assured an interviewer that Britain was well aware of the strong steps being taken by Portugal to "prevent abuses." All was well between England and Portugal, he encouragingly added.[74] While Bocage and the young king might have dismissed any possibility of differences arising between the two countries, apologists for Portugal were trying desperately to minimize the damage caused to the plantation owners by the boycott and by critics in Britain.

Officials in Lisbon were rightly concerned about the impact of the boycott on the market for São Tomé cocoa. The island was, after all, their most prosperous colony. Merck thought that the planters would institute reforms as soon as possible so as not to lose business, and he expected that plantation owners would increasingly import labor from Mozambique.[75] The *Times* correspondent in Lisbon, after talking to Merck, reported in March 1909 that Wenceslau de Lima, the foreign minister, was meeting with the planters about the boycott.[76] On several occasions, Lima reiterated to Villiers, the British minister to Lisbon, that the Portuguese government was in the process of formulating plans to assure that there were no abuses of the laborers and to punish anyone involved in the slave trade; Villiers replied that the British government recognized Portugal's "good intentions" but noted that "what was wanted was to see these carried into effect."[77] Unfortunately for the Portuguese, governments were short-lived, and offices changed hands frequently among a small group of politicians. Shortly after Cid's return, two governments fell within three weeks, and Lima, who had just served as foreign minister, emerged as prime minister.[78] Indeed, there were twenty-two foreign ministers over a thirty-year span.[79] The *Times* reported that a duel was fought in mid-March 1909 between the finance minister and a man who had accused him of defrauding the Treasury.[80]

While Portuguese officials struggled to institute reform during a period of enormous political instability, several apologists for the planters on São Tomé emerged. Francisco Mantero, a plantation owner and secretary of the Planters' Association, explained to William Cadbury that most serviçais who thus far had returned to Angola received no compensation from the repatriation fund, since most had been hired before 1903 and were always paid in full.[81] In 1910, Mantero would publish *Manual Labour in S. Thomé and Principe*, a three-volume defense of the islands. A. de Almada Negreiros, a Portuguese colonial civil servant in São Tomé, submitted a short typescript titled "Manual Labour in the Portuguese Colonies" to the Anti-Slavery Society in March 1909; the document contended that instead of "wast[ing] away in vice and decay" in Angola, the workers on the islands were well treated and enjoyed a far better life in São Tomé. This exemplary treatment, which he illustrated by citing testimony from a large number of witnesses and experts, most of whom had visited the islands in the late nineteenth century, was a defense regularly offered by the planters. Another common argument Negreiros used was that British critics should concentrate their attention on the mistreatment of Indian laborers in South Africa or on the Africans from Mozambique who toiled in terrible conditions in the Rand.[82] Nevinson dismissed Negreiros, who was associated with the Lisbon newspaper *O Século*, as "an old enemy of mine" who had "spread every kind of scandal & abuse against me. I think he has even challenged me to a duel. I tear up his letters now and send them back unanswered. Probably he is paid by the planters or Lisbon Govt."[83] Morel refused to print a letter from Negreiros that was "full of vulgar abuse and childish accusations" directed against William Cadbury, whom Negreiros accused of making remarks that were "derogatory" to "the honour of Portugal."[84]

Lt. Col. John Alfred Wyllie (1855–1939) was a much more eloquent and persistent defender of the São Tomé planters. Born in Edinburgh, he attended the Royal Military College at Sandhurst as well as Gray's Inn, London; instead of becoming a barrister, he entered the army in 1875 and was on the India Army list from 1877 to 1909. While on the Indian subcontinent, he served as a magistrate and involved himself in rubber plantations. He later lived in Spain and Portugal, where he mastered the languages and wrote about agriculture. He visited both São Tomé and Príncipe, and in 1907, he translated Monteiro de Mendonça's *The Boa Entrada Plantations*, a defense of the labor system.[85]

Beginning in 1909, Wyllie and Nevinson frequently engaged in public debates over Portuguese labor practices. One of these exchanges stemmed from a June 4, 1909, article in the *Times* that was very critical of the British perspective on Portuguese labor. According to the reporter who wrote the article, the planters expected that the boycott would have little impact on their marketing of cocoa beans, as other buyers would quickly emerge. The Portuguese government was already taking steps to implement certain of Cid's suggestions, but repatriation remained difficult, "as labourers who have married and founded families in St. Thomé, and have experienced the comforts of a regular life and personal security, will not readily return to that degraded state of barbarism which awaits them in the interior of Angola." Many in Portugal continued to believe that the boycott was motivated by commercial and not humanitarian motives on the part of the English chocolate companies. The recent publication of the high death rate of laborers in the Rand gold mines and the increase in barriers to the repatriation of Mozambique miners in the Transvaal exposed British duplicity. In this relatively long article, the correspondent contended that any "foreign testimony" about Portuguese colonial labor was suspect after the "harrowing tales recently published by Mr. Nevinson," which, he implied, were incorrect.[86]

Never one to take criticism lightly, Nevinson defended his position the following day. The claim that workers lived in such an idyllic state that they had no desire to leave was, according to him, all too common a claim by slaveholders. As for the British chocolate companies, he believed that they could defend themselves against the accusation that they boycotted for reasons of trade.[87] Wyllie did not reply to Nevinson's letter until September 28, after returning from a trip to the islands. He stated that critiquing the "facts, fictions, and conclusions" of Nevinson's *A Modern Slavery* "would require . . . a volume equal to the original." Wyllie's basic contention was that the plantations of São Tomé, which were admirably run, should never be confused with the admittedly deplorable conditions on the mainland. The planters, "as kindly and intelligent a body of men as can well be found," should not be held responsible for "atrocities committed by savages, black, brown, or white, in the *Hinterland* of Angola or on the borderland of the Congo Free State." He was particularly disturbed that the boycott had spread to the United States, especially after Portugal suspended recruitment from Angola. Wyllie asserted that if British humanitarians were truly touched by the buying and selling of workers, they would boycott rice from Burma, where there was forced labor. As to repatriation, it was not the planters' fault that the Angolans had no place to return to, "for want of a record of his original habitat. The Angolan in the native state is an absolute animal—he has neither home nor family—please grasp this fact firmly. . . . The islands . . . are a veritable paradise for the blacks." The high mortality rate of the serviçais, he added, was caused almost exclusively by "alcoholism and geophagy" (the eating of earthy substances).[88]

Two days later, Nevinson countered Wyllie's many arguments. Although recruitment in Angola may have been ended in the preceding few months, Nevinson emphasized that the recently published letter and book by the missionary Charles Swan, as well as evidence from other observers, graphically pointed out that the number of natives from Angola brutally seized for their labor had dramatically increased well into 1909. As to Wyllie's charge that the Angolan had "neither home nor family," Nevinson suggested that "the Angolan, in common . . . with nearly all Africans, has a particularly strong instinct for home and family. Nor is it accurate to say that repatriation from the islands is impossible for want of a record of the *serviçal's* original *habitat*. His birthplace and the name of his chief are supposed to be given, and, as far as I have seen, are given, on the 'register' which the *serviçal* receives in a tin cylinder when he leaves the mainland for the islands, from which at the time of my visit none had ever returned."[89] On October 16, responding to a comment in the *Spectator*, Wyllie asserted: "It is not the labourer that is paid for, it is his labour. To ignore this distinction . . . is to ignore the only stable basis of relations between master and servant in all lands where, for climatic reasons, coloured labour must replace white."[90] In a private letter, Wyllie angrily declaimed that "when a pack of fanatics British and American persist in attributing to my S. Thomé friends tales of atrocity rivalling in luridness those of the Congo itself, I am up in arms at once. I know them to be lying, and tell them so to their faces if I can." As was common during the period, Wyllie did not see the blacks as being in any manner equal to the whites, and he believed that any attempt to treat them as such was absurd: "I regard the abolition of slavery in the United States as the biggest blunder a nation ever committed. The black man's function in creation is the service of the white man, and all that was necessary was to have abolished the cruelty and oppression incidental to the system, not the system itself."[91]

Although most British in the early twentieth century opposed slavery, many joined Wyllie in regarding black Africans as inferior to whites. This belief grew throughout the last quarter of the nineteenth century, fed by social Darwinism and by the concept that the British were an imperial or governing race, obligated by their superior intelligence and technological sophistication to spread the blessings of their civilization to other parts of the world. Science by no means reached an agreement on the concept of race, and in the early 1900s, there was, if anything, more acceptance of race as a measure of ability than in the previous century. Popular travelogues, comments by anthropologists, and exhibitions focusing on the empire, particularly after the 1880s on sub-Saharan Africa, reinforced these opinions.[92] The literature of the period perceived Africans as suited for manual labor, effectively becoming the "new proletariat." In works of fiction, life for Africans was portrayed as onerous, both before and after slavery.[93] Colonial officials viewed Africans as ignorant and simple, needing the firm hand of administrators to become productive subjects.[94]

Nevinson was primarily responsible for making slavery in Portuguese West Africa a public issue in Great Britain through his publication of articles in *Harper's* between 1905 and 1906. He kept the matter alive for the next several years by issuing *A Modern Slavery* in 1906 and by producing numerous letters, articles, and speeches on the topic.[95] Certainly, he was joined in his denunciation of the dreadful labor system by journalists, humanitarians, and politicians, but Nevinson was the driving force; he was the conscience of Britain. He felt a moral obligation to respond to defenders of the Portuguese planters, such as Wyllie. Because of his conviction over the central role that he played in the issue, Nevinson was easily offended when he believed he was not adequately recognized for his contribution. His air of certainty, which bordered on pomposity, bothered William Cadbury, who likewise believed that he himself bore the primary responsibility for bringing about change in the Portuguese labor practices.

The differences between Nevinson and Cadbury had been evident since they first met in 1904. Cadbury believed that Nevinson failed to contact the proper officials when he was engaged in his investigation. While Cadbury understood that Nevinson was "quite unselfish in his motives," he asserted that the latter's actions had made him appear as a despicable "spy" to the Portuguese. The British, he wrote, would treat likewise a foreigner who spoke no English but inquired into and reported on British "mis-administration" in the colony of Nigeria.[96]

The disagreements between the two men became more pronounced in 1909, especially after Cadbury returned from his West African journey. On March 27, the *Spectator* implied that Nevinson's account of his trip to West Africa for *Harper's* had spurred the firm of Cadbury to mount its own investigation and that Nevinson's exposé had been the equivalent of Morel's work in the Congo.[97] These pointed assertions by Strachey, the editor of the *Spectator,* struck a raw nerve in William Cadbury, who had always refused to acknowledge that Nevinson played any part in sparking the Cadbury company's inquiry into Portuguese labor practices; Cadbury also brooked no comparison between Nevinson and Morel, who was his friend and confidant. In a series of letters to Strachey, he stressed that he had first heard rumors of slavery when visiting Trinidad early in the century. Shortly after Cadbury returned from Trinidad, Matthew Stober, the missionary in

Angola, contacted him, and "the credit of rousing my enthusiasm in the matter is certainly due to him." Cadbury Bros. then became interested in sending an agent to West Africa, but when Cadbury met Nevinson a bit later, the latter proved unwilling to devote sufficient time to the project. On his expedition, Nevinson had spent relatively little time on the islands. Cadbury contended that Nevinson did not understand the Portuguese people, as he did not speak their language and had not visited their country when studying the labor issue. Nevinson, he added, "has done everything to poison the minds of the British public against the Portuguese; he has made statements about the Portuguese which they will never forgive as they know they are absolutely untrue, and to them his name is ranked with Pienaar's who is described out there as a criminal of the lowest class; I often tell them that this is unfair to Nevinson, as he is honoured at home as a journalist, and his mis-statements were from the fact that he was obliged to accept all information at second hand, and was very unwell during part of his visit." Cadbury believed that Nevinson conceived the supposition that English firms "should buy up the islands and run the property on proper lines." This rumor, Cadbury stressed, perturbed Portuguese who contended that humanitarian concern over labor was but a ploy to drive down the value of the plantations and to facilitate their inexpensive purchase by the British. If Nevinson had done his homework with "responsible people" in Lisbon and "patiently studied their side of the question," Cadbury asserted, he "might have done much lasting good to the cause, because I know he means well." While not saying so directly, Cadbury was contrasting Nevinson's trip to that of Burtt, who spent considerable time in Portugal learning the language and making arrangements with planters to visit their roças and then writing a report that Cadbury believed was a model of reasonable commentary. Cadbury criticized Nevinson's participation in the Caxton Hall meeting in December 1908, and he argued that Nevinson had declared incorrectly that a U.S. firm had dropped the purchase of São Tomé cocoa after having read Nevinson's initial reports. Finally, Cadbury questioned Strachey's comparison of Nevinson's activities to those of Morel. He warned Strachey that should Nevinson persist in making his misleading statements, "I am afraid my firm will have to take still further action," obviously implying a libel suit against Nevinson. Cadbury recognized that he and Nevinson approached the issue with contrasting styles: "I think on the whole it is best to realise that Mr. Nevinson's tactics will always be totally different from my own, and I shall not interfere with him if he has only the good taste to leave our firms to do what we conscientiously believe to be right."[98]

Strachey readily accepted Cadbury's explanation of how and when he had been apprised of the conditions of workers on the islands, but Strachey also maintained that Nevinson had been most cooperative in regard to the Caxton Hall meeting and the deputation with Grey that followed: Nevinson "was a good deal easier to manage than some of the others with whom I worked." Strachey recognized the importance of "Morel's action in the Congo," and yet he noted, "I feel that Nevinson, though he might not as you say have always been as judicious as Morel, has always acted with great self denial and singleness of purpose." Strachey wrote that he would "urge [Nevinson] to be very circumspect in what he writes and says for the future. Though so impulsive a man I have always found him amenable to an appeal to reason if put to him in a proper way." Strachey closed one of his letters by thanking Cadbury for his devotion to the cause: "We all owe your firm, and especially you, a deep debt of gratitude in the matter."[99]

According to Nevinson's diary, Strachey told him on April 16 that "Willm. Cadbury had been saying nasty things about me as one who was always driving at them, & making out they [would] not have boycotted but for me, & then claiming all the glory. . . . Probably he will attack me in his book."[100] A few days later, John Harris of the Congo Reform Association told Nevinson that "Cadbury was very angry about Caxton Hall meeting."[101] As we have noted, Cadbury had not wanted the meeting to take place until after his return from Africa.

William Cadbury also suspected that Nevinson had close ties with the *Standard*. On April 16, 1909, he warned Burtt about the journalist: "No doubt Nevinson will be writing to you; please *be exceedingly careful about anything you say to him:* the 'Standard' justification has come to hand, and it is not difficult to trace his finger in some of the clauses" (emphasis in original).[102] Six weeks later, Nevinson talked about the libel suit to Gwynne, the *Standard* editor. Gwynne thought that the suit might not "come into Court after all" and admitted that while he had "no legal evidence," he remained upset at the Cadbury company's response to slavery and was "driven by indignation after my book."[103] Harrison, an attorney for the *Standard*, shared evidence with Nevinson that had been provided by Cadbury Bros. indicating both the chocolate firm and the Foreign Office had found that Nevinson's reporting, though correct in general, was but "sensational literature" and of little help in the campaign for reform. Harrison explained that he might call on Nevinson to testify at the trial should the Cadbury firm attempt to "impugn [Nevinson's] integrity &c."[104] There appears to be no evidence, however, that Nevinson encouraged Gwynne to attack the Cadbury company, and Nevinson preferred that the case not come to trial.[105]

As mentioned earlier, Nevinson was not an easy person to deal with and he often quarreled with his editors.[106] A journalist who spent much time abroad, he also threw himself into many causes at home. In addition to his involvement in the slavery controversy, he became an ardent supporter of women's suffrage, marching in processions and writing articles and speeches for a radical cause that occasionally turned violent. In December 1908, after vocally protesting a speech by the Liberal chancellor of the exchequer David Lloyd George and being thrown out of the meeting by stewards, Nevinson was temporarily suspended from the staff of the *Daily News* by its editor, Gardiner, who had been sharing the platform with Lloyd George. Nevinson and Brailsford resigned from the staff of the *Daily News* in September 1909 after an editorial in the paper "excused" the government for the forced feeding of women's suffrage inmates. The two journalists announced their resignation publicly in the *Times* on October 5. Nevinson, at Gardiner's request, remained for another month as an editorial writer.[107]

Current and convincing evidence of the continuation of the slave trade in Angola appeared in 1909, including a detailed article written by a knowledgeable correspondent to the *Times* explaining that Congo natives, in revolt against Belgian authorities, swapped slaves for guns and powder via Portuguese traders, who then shipped the slaves to the islands.[108] By far the most notable account came from Charles Swan, a longtime missionary in Angola. Unbeknown to the public, William Cadbury, at a personal cost of £400, sponsored Swan's late 1908 and early 1909 trip to Angola; the trip was designed to supplement information Cadbury gained on his own journey, which occurred at the same time.[109] Swan contacted many missionaries from U.S. and English societies in Angola, all of whom signed a statement attesting that the slave trade was still commonly practiced and that those captured were often destined for São Tomé, from which they never returned. Swan also conversed personally with natives on board steamers going to the islands, who told him how they had been "forcibly taken from their homes and handed to the whites in payment of 'crimes,' &c." Swan presented the information he had collected, including the names of those involved in the slave trade, to the Foreign Office. His letter in the *Times* of June 22, 1909, vividly depicted evidence of the ongoing slave trade:

> My own connexion with the colony extends over 23 years, but in no one day previously have I seen so many indications that the awful traffic

> goes on unabated as I saw during my first day's journey from the coast in October last. The awful mixture of rum bottles, shackles, and bleaching bones was enough to make one sick at heart. There was also the emaciated body of a young lad who had been left to die that morning; there he lay with the shackles for his feet and hands, and the stick with which he had helped himself along to his unknown future, till his weary limbs refused to move, and the spirit took its flight. My men picked up 92 shackles for legs, arms, or neck, without ever leaving the path to look for them; most of these were comparatively new, and a very great many of them still contained the sap of the wood. Can any proof be more positive that the trade is not a thing of the past, as is constantly affirmed?[110]

In August, Swan's *Slavery of To-day or, The Present Position of the Open Sore of Africa* was published, replete with his own photographs of the slave trade, two of which are reproduced in this book.

Because of the libel trial, William Cadbury attempted, unsuccessfully, to keep his relationship with Swan secret. Swan wrote to him on May 10, 1909: "With regard to your request that I 'destroy all these letters,' am I to understand that you wish me to destroy all letters I have received from you since we began to correspond?"[111] Two weeks later, Cadbury explained that the *Standard* "will not hesitate to try and make capital out of any action of mine—I should like it to be impossible for them to say that I have seen or in any way influenced your report or your action."[112] Cadbury's attempted cover-up failed, however, and the *Standard*'s attorneys contacted Swan in July 1909.[113]

The passages that follow summarize and assess the Cadbury firm's situation in 1909, just before the libel trial against the *Standard* began. Cadbury Bros. had been aware of the possible use of slave labor on São Tomé since 1901. Company officials—especially William and George Cadbury—determined that an investigation had to be mounted to confirm that the serviçais were slaves. William Cadbury personally met with planters and government officials in Lisbon in 1903, and they invited the company's officers to witness for themselves the conditions on the islands. Based on that invitation, the directors of Cadbury commissioned a Quaker friend, Joseph Burtt, to learn Portuguese and then to proceed to West Africa to scrutinize Portuguese labor practices. Shortly after Burtt left on his trip in 1905, Henry Nevinson returned to England from his own voyage to West Africa and published a searing indictment of Portuguese labor practices, describing them as "modern slavery." Burtt, who returned to England in 1907, submitted a report that confirmed Nevinson's judgment. William Cadbury and Burtt delivered the report to the British government in the summer of 1907 and to the Portuguese planters and officials in November 1907. The document was not made available to the British public until October 1908. Despite the fact that Nevinson and the humanitarian societies—especially the Aborigines' Protection Society, headed by Fox Bourne—called for prompt action on the part of the chocolate firms and the British government to force the planters to discontinue immediately the forced labor system, William Cadbury believed that the Portuguese had to be given an opportunity to mend their ways. Amid continual reports, even from the Foreign Office, that not all was well in West Africa, Cadbury decided to travel with Burtt to West Africa in late 1908 to determine to what extent the Portuguese had implemented the reforms they had promised after Cadbury and Burtt's visit to Lisbon in 1907. On William Cadbury's return from West Africa in March 1909, Cadbury Bros. and the other major Quaker-owned British chocolate manufacturers, Rowntree and Fry, announced that no substantial progress had been made and that therefore they would immediately cease buying São Tomé cocoa beans. Since 1906, the Cadbury firm had kept the Foreign Office informed of its activities, and it was convinced that government officials were pressuring the Portuguese to bring about positive change.

There is every evidence that the Cadbury company was truly concerned about the allegations of slavery in Portuguese West Africa and worked diligently, if slowly, to bring about change. The company spent substantial resources in attempting to determine the plight of labor in the Portuguese colonies; Burtt's 1905–1906 trip cost between £3,000 and £4,000, much of which was borne personally by Cadbury's directors. In addition, William Cadbury devoted an extraordinary amount of time to the cause. A very deliberate person, he was determined to give the Portuguese, whom he found well mannered and well meaning, every opportunity to recognize the shortcomings of their system and to mend it. Moreover, he argued consistently from the beginning of the controversy that Cadbury Bros. was not willing simply to boycott São Tomé cocoa, as the firm would then lose any influence over the Portuguese government and the planters, who would turn elsewhere to market their goods.

Cadbury's concern for the lives of its own employees, in the factory and in the community, was admirable and progressive. That the company extended this concern to its suppliers, domestic and foreign, was perhaps even more significant. In

October 1906, Cadbury's board, wishing to avoid associating as much as possible with businesses that engaged in "sweating" (unacceptable work settings), agreed to "ascertain" the laboring conditions of its domestic suppliers. This practice could be called an "ethical purchasing policy," which the company would apply more stringently after 1913. Cadbury deliberately excluded foreign suppliers from this policy in 1906 because it was so dependent on overseas firms for basic materials, and the company apparently felt that it could not effectively enforce such a rule in a vast, worldwide market.[114]

Although Cadbury Bros. claimed that the company's actions regarding São Tomé were based solely on humanitarian concerns, contemporary critics insisted—and many present-day scholars agree—that the cocoa manufacturer took into consideration other factors when making its decisions.[115] For example, some cocoa brokers at the time thought that Cadbury and Fry postponed the boycott until their own needs could be met.[116] There were sound economic reasons for the Cadbury company not to boycott the Portuguese product in 1907. Edward Thackray, a cocoa buyer for Cadbury, admitted in 1909 that the price of cocoa two years earlier was exceptionally high and that sources were limited.[117] William Cadbury stressed that 1909 was a far better period in which to begin a boycott, as the price for the beans had dramatically declined by then. George Cadbury told Nevinson in October 1909 that the boycott had "lost him nothing in money," for the firm had been able to purchase beans from Bahia (Brazil).[118] There is little doubt, therefore, that Cadbury's directors were cognizant of how costly a boycott could be to the company.

Nevinson, Fox Bourne, and others believed that Cadbury and the other Quaker chocolate manufacturers moved too slowly in regard to rectifying labor conditions in São Tomé. This charge has considerable merit. It is surprising that the directors of Cadbury did not learn of the allegations of labor abuse in Portuguese colonies well before 1901. They moved in humanitarian circles, and many Quakers served on the boards of antislavery societies whose publications, we have seen, had been warning for several years, even before the turn of the century, of the brutal labor-recruiting activities in Portuguese West Africa. In addition, some members of the extended Cadbury family had contributed to the Anti-Slavery Society since 1884. George Cadbury made financial donations to the society beginning in 1892, as did William Cadbury beginning in 1900. Both were also occasional members of the Aborigines' Protection Society after 1901.[119] Furthermore, from 1901 on, William and George Cadbury regularly corresponded with secretaries of both societies, so they had the opportunity to be well informed on all aspects of slavery. George

Cadbury owned the *Daily News* from 1901, and that newspaper had demanded that the government take immediate action to halt the abuse of Chinese coolie laborers in South Africa. For a paternalistic firm that prided itself on providing safe working conditions and reasonable wages for its factory hands, it is amazing that company officials would take eight years before determining that laboring conditions warranted stopping the purchase of cocoa from São Tomé. The motivations and indeed the entire reputation of the firm of Cadbury would be fully examined in court in late 1909.

Plate 1. Traders used shackles to prevent the flight of slaves. When no longer needed, the shackles were hung in a tree, as in this October 1908 photograph from Angola. Reproduced from Charles A. Swan, *The Slavery of To-day or, The Present Position of the Open Sore of Africa* (Glasgow, UK: Pickering & Inglis, 1909).

Plate 2. This shackle, according to Joseph Burtt, was used on the neck of a woman slave on the march from Angola's interior to the coast. Reproduced from *Leslie's Illustrated Weekly*, October 14, 1909.

Plate 3. Joseph Burtt entitled this photograph "Beasts of Burden." Armed men guarded heavily shackled slaves as they were marched to the Angolan coast. Reproduced from *Leslie's Illustrated Weekly*, December 16, 1909.

Plate 4. Charles Swan found this recently dead slave with shackles and staff in Angola in October 1908. Swan laid blame for this "inhuman traffic" on the white man, who made "tempting offers of gain." Reproduced from Charles A. Swan, *The Slavery of To-day or, The Present Position of the Open Sore of Africa* (Glasgow, UK: Pickering & Inglis, 1909).

Plate 5. Removal of a shackle from a slave. Reproduced courtesy of Anti-Slavery International.

Plate 6. Cocoa pods grow directly from the tree trunk or larger branches. When ripe, the pods are broken open and the seeds set out to ferment and then to dry. From a São Tomé plantation, 2000. Reproduced courtesy of Ellen Satre.

Plate 7. Henry Nevinson's *A Modern Slavery* helped to make public Portugal's use of slaves in West Africa. The journalist, who was obsessed by what he had witnessed in Angola and São Tomé, could never understand why the major English chocolate firms failed to act decisively for such a long time. Reproduced from Henry W. Nevinson, *More Changes More Chances* (New York: Harcourt, Brace and Company, [1925]).

Plate 8. George Cadbury, a devout Quaker and philanthropist, was a director of Cadbury Bros. and the owner of the Liberal *Daily News*. He was proud of his nephew William Cadbury's leadership in pressuring Portuguese plantation owners to change their labor practices. Reproduced courtesy of Cadbury Trebor Bassett.

Plate 9. Henry Richard Fox Bourne was secretary of the Aborigines' Protection Society. Businesspeople and Foreign Office officials could not disregard the advice proffered by this knowledgeable and persistent defender of native laborers. Reproduced courtesy of Anti-Slavery International.

Plate 10. Joseph Burtt, who twice visited Portugal's West African colonies for Cadbury Bros., toured the United States on behalf of the British Anti-Slavery Society to warn Americans of the slave-produced São Tomé cocoa. Reproduced from *Leslie's Illustrated Weekly*, December 16, 1909.

Plate 11. E. D. Morel, the leader of the Congo Reform Association, was a confidant of William Cadbury and a critic of Henry Nevinson. Reproduced courtesy of Anti-Slavery International.

Plate 12. Foreign Secretary Edward Grey, shown here in a 1910 photograph, deplored Portuguese colonial labor practices, but chose for diplomatic and economic reasons not to express his concerns publicly. Copyright © Corbis.

Plate 13. The Victoria Law Courts on Corporation Street in Birmingham, completed in 1891, was considered one of the finest Victorian office buildings in Britain. The site of the 1909 trial of *Cadbury Bros., Ltd. v. the Standard Newspaper, Ltd.*, it is still in use today. Reproduced courtesy of Ellen Satre.

Plate 14. Edward Carson, a leading Conservative politician and a brilliant attorney, used his dramatic courtroom demeanor to defend the *Standard* in the 1909 trial and to cast doubts on the actions of Cadbury Bros.

Plate 15. Edward Carson, cartoon by "Matt." Reproduced from Earl of Birkenhead, *Contemporary Personalities* (London: Cassell and Company, Ltd., 1924).

Plate 16. The Liberal barrister Rufus Isaacs represented the Cadbury company in the 1909 trial. He was one of few who could match Carson in the courtroom. Though often on opposing sides at the bar, the two were friends.

Plate 17. Rufus Isaacs, cartoon by "Spy." Reproduced from *Vanity Fair*, February 14, 1904.

Plate 18. J. A. Wyllie, a British citizen and an army officer, was a fierce public defender of Portuguese labor practices on the islands of São Tomé and Príncipe. Reproduced from Francis Mantero, *Manual Labour in S. Thomé and Principe*, translated from Portuguese (Lisbon: Printing office of the Annuario Commercial, 1910; reprint, New York: Negro Universities Press, 1969).

Plate 19. John Harris led the British Anti-Slavery and Aborigines' Protection Society's campaign after 1909 against Portuguese abuse of labor in West Africa. British Foreign Office officials distrusted this former missionary to the Congo. This photograph is from the 1930s, when Harris was knighted for his humanitarian efforts. Reproduced courtesy of Anti-Slavery International.

Plate 20. This photograph, from a book published in 1910, shows serviçais on the Água Izé plantation, island of São Tomé, awaiting "payment of their wages" in front of the manager's dwelling. William Cadbury visited the plantations of Água Izé and Boa Entrada in 1908–9. Reproduced from Francis Mantero, *Manual Labour in S. Thomé and Principe*, translated from Portuguese (Lisbon: Printing office of the Annuario Commercial, 1910; reprint, New York: Negro Universities Press, 1969).

Plate 21. The same building on the Água Izé plantation in the year 2000. Little cocoa is exported from São Tomé plantations today. Reproduced courtesy of Ellen Satre.

Plate 22. Children of serviçais playing at the Boa Entrada plantation, island of São Tomé, in a 1910 photograph. Regarded as a model plantation, it still had a high mortality rate among its serviçais. Reproduced from Francis Mantero, *Manual Labour in S. Thomé and Principe*, translated from Portuguese (Lisbon: Printing office of the Annuario Commercial, 1910; reprint, New York: Negro Universities Press, 1969).

Plate 23. The same buildings on the Boa Entrada plantation in the year 2000. Many of the buildings today still house workers. Reproduced courtesy of Ellen Satre.

Plate 24. Workers in front of the manager's residence at the Boa Entrada plantation on the island of São Tomé in 1910. Reproduced from Francis Mantero, *Manual Labour in S. Thomé and Principe*, translated from Portuguese (Lisbon: Printing office of the Annuario commercial, 1910; reprint, New York: Negro Universities Press, 1969).

8 *Cadbury Bros., Ltd. v. The Standard Newspaper, Ltd.*

Knowing that it [slavery] was atrocious, you took the main portion of your supply of cocoa for the profit of your business from the islands conducted under this system?—Yes, for a period of some years.

You do not look upon that as anything immoral?—Not under the circumstances.

Have you formed any estimate of the number of slaves who lost their lives in preparing your cocoa during those eight years?—No, no.

William Cadbury, responding to Edward Carson at the trial

AFTER THE BOYCOTT of São Tomé cocoa, some might have expected that the slavery issue, at least in England, would gradually dissipate, but such was not the case. There is some evidence that Cadbury Bros. considered dropping the libel charges against the *Standard.* On February 17, 1909, about one month before William Cadbury returned from his trip to West Africa, John Harris of the Congo Reform Association reported his understanding that the chocolate companies had agreed to drop the suit: "The withdrawal of the libel action against the Standard is an eloquent testimony to the fact that the Cocoa firms are prepared to act decisively in opposition to William Cadbury upon any given time." Harris believed that to pursue the suit would be particularly damaging to the *Daily News,* for he added, "George Cadbury cannot afford—even if he desired to do so—to ruin the Daily News any more than Joseph Rowntree could wreck the Nation." Harris also understood that William Cadbury's relatives were concerned with public criticism of the Cadbury firm's activities in regard to São Tomé cocoa.[1] Later, in January 1909, Gardiner, the editor of the *Daily News,* told Nevinson that Cadbury's directors had decided to stop buying São Tomé cocoa "& agreed how stupidly they had mismanaged the whole thing."[2] Harris and Gardiner both implied that officials at Cadbury, Fry, and Rowntree expressed dissatisfaction with William Cadbury's leadership over the issue. In early June, Nevinson reported that the *Standard*'s editor, H. A. Gwynne, thought the Cadbury company might not proceed with the case.[3]

The suit was not dropped, but there is no doubt that many people, especially Nevinson, did not want Cadbury Bros. to carry on.[4] While there was admiration for the company regarding its lengthy effort to compel São Tomé planters to halt the use of slaves and move to a free labor system, many also believed that the endeavor had dragged on too long. The firm's decision to boycott was correct but much too late. To take action against a clearly partisan newspaper might be justified on legal grounds, but it appeared senseless to pursue the action once the chocolate firms refused to purchase Portuguese cocoa. William and George Cadbury, however, were determined to clear the company of the allegations of hypocrisy. What they got was a great deal of publicity, much of it negative.

The two parties to the suit prepared their respective cases. The preliminaries were long, complex, and costly. Attorneys for the *Standard* compiled two lists of "particulars" (details to be used by the defense) amounting to sixty pages, including descriptions of the atrocities of the Portuguese slave trade as contained in the writings of Nevinson and Burtt and in government reports. The particulars also quoted extensively from *Daily News* articles condemning the Conservative government for the use of Chinese coolies as "slaves" in rebuilding the South African economy after the war. The Cadbury attorneys did not wish the case to be centered around details regarding slavery, which they readily agreed existed in Portuguese West Africa; rather, they wanted to focus on their complaint that the *Standard* "called us hypocrites." In an appeal on the particulars, Cadbury Bros. gained a restriction on the need to respond to them, as the judge acknowledged that extraordinarily detailed particulars might hinder the goal of seeking justice.[5]

Wragge & Co., the solicitors for Cadbury Bros., arranged for testimony, most notably that of Foreign Secretary Edward Grey and Travers Buxton of the Anti-Slavery Society. William Cadbury wrote to Buxton in April 1909 that one of the *Standard*'s charges "is that we stated that we were in communication and had the support of the Anti-Slavery Society up to the time of the Liverpool meeting, and that this was not the case . . . we are most anxious that we shall not mis-represent you in this matter." He wanted confirmation that the society had never "suggested that we should cease buying S. Thome cocoa" before October 1907.[6] After this initial correspondence, Buxton confirmed that the society had not advised the firm to stop purchasing São Tomé cocoa, and he had found no indication in the correspondence "of any dispute between our Society and your firm in connection with the subject."[7] But Buxton was none too pleased about the "proposed proof" of his testimony, "as I think it unduly commits our Society." He reported to the society's president that Edmund Brooks, one of its board members and a Quaker, "dissents from 'every word' of the proof, and strongly opposes my appearance in support of it. Mr. Brooks thinks our Committee was too much 'led by the nose' by the Firms, and regrets its want of protest."[8] Ultimately, Buxton reluctantly agreed to a statement recognizing that William Cadbury had acted solely to facilitate reform.[9] Ironically, Buxton was not called as a witness at the trial, and Wragge forgot to inform him that he would not be summoned.[10] The Cadbury company's attempt to gain a similar confirmation about the Aborigines' Protection Society's relationship with the firm was unsuccessful; the society no longer existed after its merger with the Anti-Slavery Society, and no one from the latter was willing to testify on behalf of the now defunct organization.[11]

Baron Carl de Merck, who had been approached in November 1908 by representatives of the *Standard* seeking information on the firm of Cadbury, agreed to appear as a witness for Cadbury Bros. at the trial. William Cadbury thanked his broker friend in Lisbon for the offer: "I know that your presence would add much strength, as the main and serious charge is that my visits to Lisbon were of a purely humbug nature to blind the people at home, and to enable us to go on buying cocoa. However foolish this may appear it is a little difficult for me to prove my sincerity."[12] The Cadbury company was particularly concerned over Nevinson's possible testimony for the *Standard* at the trial, but Wragge, after assessing applicable correspondence, concluded that Nevinson "would admit in cross-examination that all that was done was for the best."[13]

The company's justification for continuing to purchase cocoa from the islands rested heavily on its statement that the Foreign Office had advised company officials to carry on with such acquisitions, thereby giving the Foreign Office the opportunity to use its diplomatic power to wrest reform from the Portuguese. Because the *Standard* disputed Cadbury's claim, the Cadbury solicitors sought confirmation of their stance from the Foreign Office, based primarily on George and William Cadbury's meeting with Grey on October 26, 1906. This meeting had been arranged to apprise the foreign secretary of the firm's concern with the islands' labor and to report that Cadbury's commissioner was presently investigating; his subsequent report would be available in the near future. Cadbury Bros. summarized that 1906 meeting in a letter to Grey of March 31, 1909: "At this meeting both Mr. George Cadbury and Mr. William A. Cadbury stated clearly that we were willing either then, or at any time, to cease purchasing San Thomé cocoa, if you said that you considered that by doing so we could best assist you in bringing about a better state of things in Portuguese West Africa. They understood your reply distinctly to be that you consider that, for the moment, the fact that cocoa was being largely bought by English cocoa manufacturers gave much greater weight to your representations in Portugal than if these representations were based purely on humanitarian grounds."[14] Unfortunately for the company, there proved to be no clear evidence for this claim. The absence of any summary of the twenty-minute meeting by Grey—in a Foreign Office that normally left a paper trail of any consultations—makes one wonder if the government was deliberately attempting to avoid assuming any real responsibility for putting pressure on the Portuguese.

The only record of the meeting in Foreign Office files was the memorandum submitted by Cadbury Bros. to Grey a few days thereafter. The company was preparing to notify cooperating chocolate firms of the results of the interview, and it wanted Grey's confirmation of the summary statement. Cadbury's memorandum, to be sent to the other companies, read in part: "Sir E. Grey asked us to refrain from calling public attention to the subject [contract labor] until he had seen the report of our commissioner [Mr. Burtt], and has had an opportunity of speaking to the Portuguese Minister on the subject."[15] There was no mention in the memorandum about continuing the purchase of cocoa beans.[16]

In a letter to Grey dated October 15, 1909, the company expressed the hope that the trial could be avoided by a "proper apology in open court, which is what we have all along insisted upon." Should the trial take place as scheduled in November, however, the Cadbury firm advised Grey that he would be asked to testify about the 1906 meeting. Solicitors promised that Grey's evidence could be presented as soon as he arrived at court. Cadbury justified its legal action partly on political grounds: "We felt that unless a stop was put to such slanderous statements they would be used all over the country, and especially at election times, to discredit supporters of the Liberal party."[17]

Grey and a Foreign Office law adviser met with a senior partner of Wragge & Co. on October 21 to discuss the foreign secretary's deposition. Grey suggested that it "would be a very unusual, inconvenient, and . . . unprecedented course for the Secretary of State for Foreign Affairs to attend and give evidence in a case, the principal subject matter of which involved and was still involving negotiations with a foreign Power." He emphasized that he could not testify under oath that he advised Cadbury Bros. to continue purchasing cocoa from the islands, as documents did not indicate this and he could not recollect such a statement as part of the discussion that took place three years earlier. Grey was willing to furnish whatever testimony he could for the company, for he thought it had been unfairly attacked.[18] Meanwhile, the Foreign Office worked hard to provide the many documents required for the trial, striking some entirely and deleting portions of others for reasons of national security.[19]

A week after speaking with Grey about his testimony, Wragge & Co. reminded the Foreign Office of a meeting on June 27, 1907, in which two officials had urged representatives of the three chocolate companies not to boycott São Tomé cocoa beans, as it "would distinctly prejudice the probability of obtaining reforms." However, C. H. Lyell, Grey's parliamentary secretary, could not recollect in 1909 that he and the senior clerk had connected a boycott with reform. Assistant Undersecretary Walter Langley wrote to Wragge & Co., "The opinions expressed by those two gentlemen were, of course, purely personal and informal, and did not purport in any way to represent the views of the Secretary of State."[20] With only a few weeks remaining before the trial, Cadbury Bros.'s case had one weak link: Foreign Office testimony would not support the contention that the British government had discouraged the use of a boycott.[21]

Meanwhile, in July 1909, attorneys for the *Standard* complained that the Cadbury company was extensively distributing a pamphlet favorable to the firm, titled "Thirty Years of Progress," as a means of influencing potential jury members. The eight-page pamphlet, issued in 1909 to celebrate the firm's thirty years at Bournville, commented under the "Conditions of Labour" section that Cadbury had stopped buying São Tomé cocoa because of the laboring conditions on the island.[22]

Interest in the trial dramatically increased because of the presence of the two outstanding advocates of the period—Edward Carson representing the *Standard* and Rufus Isaacs for Cadbury Bros.[23] From 1906 to 1909, members of the legal profession, as well as much of the general public, followed a series of celebrated cases in which the two attorneys faced one another. *Cadbury Bros., Ltd. v. The Standard Newspaper, Ltd.* was no exception. Though equally successful as barristers, the learned counselors came from different backgrounds and possessed dissimilar personalities and styles.

Edward Carson, born in 1854 in Dublin and educated at Trinity College, was called to the Irish bar in 1877. He gained recognition for powerful criminal prosecutions in Ireland in the late 1880s, when he enforced Arthur James Balfour's Crimes Act and often operated under threats to his life. Balfour appointed him solicitor general for Ireland in 1892. A few months later, Carson was elected to Parliament as a Conservative for Trinity College, Dublin, and he became "almost at once a commanding Parliamentary figure."[24] In 1893, Carson took silk in England—that is, he became a Queen's Counselor, or trial lawyer.[25] He gained notoriety in 1895 when he exposed Oscar Wilde, who had brought libel charges against the Marquis of Queensbury, as a homosexual. When Carson was named solicitor general of England in 1900, he took a considerable pay cut, the office offering but £6,000 per annum.

Rufus Isaacs was born in 1860 in London into a large Jewish family. He was a handsome young man with a good singing voice but also restless and prone to getting into scuffles. After attending various educational institutions, Isaacs was apprenticed to go to sea in 1876, where he remained for about a year. He then worked at the stock exchange, but he was forced to leave when he could not cover debts of about £8,000, a disgraceful outcome for an ambitious young man. In the 1880s, he boxed and danced, rode a thoroughbred, and "was still inclined to acts of self-advertisement like standing on his head in a box at the Empire Music Hall and applauding with his feet."[26] After the disastrous experience at the stock exchange, Isaacs studied for the bar, to which he was admitted in 1887. He established a legal practice and quickly repaid his debts. His practice was so successful that he became a Queen's Counselor in 1898 at the extraordinarily young age of thirty-seven. Isaacs entered politics rather late, unsuccessfully contesting North Kensington as a Liberal Imperialist in 1900 and finally gaining a seat at Reading in a 1904 by-election at age forty-three. Unlike Carson, Isaacs made no great impression on the Commons, partly because of his matter-of-fact manner of speaking, which was more effective in a courtroom than in Parliament.

The physical presence of the two attorneys differed strikingly. The tall, gaunt Edward Carson, with a prominent jaw and sheepish eyes, had a countenance that struck one as indifferent to the court proceedings. Yet while he might have seemed sickly at times, the proceedings quickly rejuvenated him. Carson put so much energy into his presentations that he would be drained at the end. Isaacs, though five feet, ten inches tall, looked short compared to Carson. The ever alert Isaacs was properly dressed compared to the slovenly appearance of his frequent opposite, whose wig and gown were often in disarray.

Carson was at his strongest in cross-examination. According to Isaacs's son, Carson could be singularly intimidating: "With sweeping arm and flashing eye he would hurl one deadly question after another, his Irish brogue gaining richness as the duel neared its climax. He had wit and he used it often with devastating effect, for his wit was apt to be barbed."[27] One biographer commented that Carson "had the most flexible voice imaginable, and could pass at will from thunder-tones to a not less menacing calm, or from a cynical drawl to a deadly hiss. Once he even burst into tears as the result of his own eloquence."[28] Carson believed intensely in the innocence of his clients, and he used his eloquence and gestures to persuade juries to identify with that conviction. He often ignored complexities in favor of simplifying the case at hand, concentrating his presentation and questions on a few key points. Isaacs, by contrast, commanded all the details of a case, which he could recall at a moment. He would lay out complex matters in a long speech—his eloquent voice projecting even in large halls—without recourse to notes. He was especially renowned for his understanding of financial matters. According to a contemporary attorney, "He seemed, indeed, almost to think in terms of double entry."[29] Isaacs was also a "deadly cross-examiner," tactful, pleasant, unruffled, and "firm without arrogance."[30] Unlike the theatrical Carson, he made a minimum of gestures in court: "He habitually stood in the characteristic attitude in which he is shown in 'Spy's' cartoon from *Vanity Fair,* with both hands raised almost to shoulder height and grasping the edges of his gown."[31] Neither of these two great advocates was a literary master. Their success at court was due not so much to the choice of words but to their arguments and presentations. The two attorneys operated out of the same Inn of Court, and throughout all of their legal encounters, they remained close friends.

Carson and Isaacs provided counsel in many important cases in the first decade of the twentieth century. Several were libel suits—occasionally involving newspapers—and the two advocates frequently represented opposing parties. In 1901, Isaacs defended the *Star* (a London newspaper) against libel charges brought by Arthur Chamberlain, Joseph Chamberlain's brother, over the sale of cordite to the government. While the *Star* was found guilty and had to pay a penalty of £200, Isaacs had performed ably against Sir Edward Clarke, "at that time the most famous and formidable advocate at the Bar in cases of this kind."[32] At Old Bailey in January 1902, Isaacs defended a South African on charges of incitement to murder, with Edward Carson, then solicitor general, the leading counsel for the Crown. The defendant was found guilty on a lesser charge and was sentenced to two years of imprisonment. The following year, Isaacs counseled Lord Suffield, a friend of King Edward, in a libel suit against the owner and the editor of *Truth* magazine; the parties reached a settlement without damages. In 1907, Carson was the advocate for the Lever soap-making company, which brought libel charges against the *Daily Mail* and other newspapers owned by the magnate Lord Northcliffe for publishing defamatory articles. By the second day of the trial, Isaacs, defending Northcliffe, recognized the strength of Lever's case and offered to settle for a tidy sum. Eventually, the court granted Lever £91,000 plus damages of £50,000, the largest sum "ever awarded until then to a litigant by a jury in the English courts."[33] In March 1909, Isaacs successfully represented Chancellor of the Exchequer David Lloyd George in a high-profile libel suit against the *People* newspaper, defended by Edward Carson. The plaintiff won £1,000 and an unqualified apology from the defendants.

In many of these legal cases, the leading counselor was supported by other attorneys. In *Cadbury Bros., Ltd. v. The Standard Newspaper, Ltd.*, both Carson and Isaacs formed strong teams; most notable in courtroom action was John Simon, who aided Isaacs. Simon, who had "deviled"[34] for Carson in the Alaska boundary dispute case of 1903, entered Parliament in 1906 as a Liberal. Born in Manchester in 1873, he enjoyed success at Wadham College, Oxford. Simon was called to the bar in 1899, where he quickly proved to be successful, gaining silk in 1908. He possessed a "smooth, even voice" that he used to quietly but "lucidly" marshal logical arguments.[35]

The trial was held in Birmingham at the Victoria Law Courts, a splendid, red terra-cotta structure on Corporation Street. The architect of the courthouse also designed the imposing buildings at the Birmingham University campus. Regarded as the "finest modern building in the country," the interior of the Victoria Law Courts was of yellow terra-cotta and included stained-glass windows celebrating the industrial workers of the town—for example, the penmaker, glassblower, ironworker, screwmaker, and gunsmith—and historical figures of the area, including William Shakespeare, Samuel Johnson, Joseph Priestley, Matthew Boulton, and James Watt.[36] George Cadbury had requested that the case be heard in Birmingham and not in London, home of the *Standard*, since the company's main witness, his nephew William Cadbury, was not well and did not wish to travel far.[37]

Through the entrance of this exceptional structure—its front doors were beneath statues of Queen Victoria and Saint George and the Dragon—passed the advocates, the interested parties, the curious, and the reporters on the morning of Monday, November 29, 1909, for the opening session of *Cadbury Bros., Ltd. v. The Standard Newspaper, Ltd.* Women from the Cadbury family and law students were part of the crowd, which began gathering up to one and a half hours before the judge appeared to witness a case that generated intense interest in the Midlands and throughout the country. The mountain of legal materials crowding the tables of the attorneys "promised a lengthy dispute."[38]

The trial was more than a disagreement between two powerful companies. Indeed, the proceedings symbolized the political crisis facing Britain at that very moment. Chancellor of the Exchequer David Lloyd George had just submitted a budget that dramatically increased the death duties and the income tax and also levied a tax on the unearned increment on land when it was sold. A general election loomed as the Conservative Party, using its overwhelming majority in the unelected House of Lords, threatened to exercise an effective veto over the spending proposal. Before entering the courtroom on November 29, a visitor might have read that morning's papers and noticed the bold headlines—"FINANCIAL CHAOS / AMAZING ATTACK ON BUDGET" in the *Daily News* and "THE FINANCIAL BILL / CRISIS" in the *Standard*.

According to a biographer of Carson, "it seemed almost as if the General Election was being fought at Birmingham in miniature." There, "the greatest Conservative leader of the day [Carson] was engaged for a Conservative organ [the *Standard*] against the most brilliant advocate in the Liberal Party [Isaacs], who was in turn attacking on behalf of the honour of a great Liberal family [the Cadburys], not unconnected with the most powerful Liberal organ [the *Daily News*]." Chinese slavery, which had played a prominent role in the resounding defeat of the Conservatives at the 1906 election, was clearly on the court docket. Moreover, Sir Edward Grey, foreign secretary and scion of a great northern Whig/Liberal family, was slated to testify. "Rufus Isaacs and Edward Carson," the biographer concluded, "seemed almost like knights chosen to fight at a tournament by their respective factions, as in mediæval days."[39]

How different the setting of this trial was—with its magnificent court, powerful business leaders, watchful journalists, and well-attired women—compared to one held just two months earlier in the Congo town of Leopoldville. There, in September 1909 in a broken-down courtroom, Compagnie de Kasai, a firm that held a monopoly on the rubber trade in Leopold's Congo, had brought libel charges against a black American missionary, William Sheppard, who had dared to describe the physical and human devastation caused by the firm's practices in the Kasai region. In a trial that gained a measure of international coverage, the judge found Sheppard innocent and slapped the hand of the company.[40] But while the settings of the two trials were so different, they both dealt with a common factor: the exploitation of raw materials through ruthless measures.

William Pickford, a judge of the High Court, King's Bench since 1907, presided over the proceedings of the Birmingham Assizes (a superior court), which began at 10:45 AM.[41] The case was presented to a "special jury" of citizens who were certainly well acquainted with the progressive labor practices and philanthropic contributions of the chocolate company. Such a jury, which could be requested by either party, included citizens who could legally be called esquires or who enjoyed substantial professional standing in the community, for example, merchants or bankers.[42]

In his opening remarks, Rufus Isaacs attempted immediately to counter the *Standard*'s claim that Cadbury Bros. had ignored the plight of the plantation workers in Portuguese West Africa. The company, he emphasized, was a model employer deeply concerned about its own employees and about those who produced cocoa beans. Its efforts had gained praise from many, including the *Standard* and its companion *Evening Standard*, yet the *Standard*, for reasons quite unknown, had reversed its judgment and claimed that Cadbury's efforts were a sham. According to Isaacs, Cadbury Bros. had brought suit because the *Standard*'s charges had "inflicted very great pain upon the plaintiffs, which reflected very seriously upon their character, and which were intended to convey grave imputations upon them."[43] The Cadbury company was highly respected, not only for its manufacture of chocolate but also for the care it provided to its employees. He acknowledged that the firm purchased cocoa from the Portuguese islands of São Tomé and Príncipe (as did many other manufacturers), and the cocoa was indeed produced by slave labor, as Cadbury's own inquiries had helped to prove. "There is no issue in this case about that," Isaacs stressed, "and never has been."[44] Having heard about the conditions of labor, the company told the humanitarian societies about the problem in the islands, spent a good deal of effort and money in sending a commissioner to investigate, and kept the Foreign Office under both Lansdowne and Grey informed. The Cadbury firm had been advised by many, including the Foreign Office, that it should not give up the immediate purchase of São Tomé cocoa. Isaacs detailed the work that had occurred even before Nevinson's articles appeared. He praised the "boundless energy" of William Cadbury, whose efforts in the matter "would be rather difficult to find certainly equalled, and more difficult, if not impossible to find excelled."[45] He noted that the *Evening Standard*—which, like the *Standard* itself, was owned by C. Arthur Pearson—had spoken a few months before the alleged libelous statement of the "good work" done by the chocolate firms. The *Standard*, however, had claimed in its September editorial that nothing had been accomplished by the company. The paper subsequently modified its argument, professing: "You [Cadbury] have done a great deal, but you are a set of canting hypocrites—you are liars—you are frauds. You have been pretending to do things [in order to continue your profitable trade]."[46] The gallery cheered Isaacs at the conclusion of his opening presentation, which lasted a full five hours and twenty minutes. He had carefully delineated the exemplary efforts of the firm, particularly those of William Cadbury, in attempting to reform the evil slavery of the cocoa islands.

On the morning of the second day of the trial, the *Times* carried sixteen full columns of the Finance Bill debate in the House of Lords, and the local *Birmingham Daily Post* wrote of "THE POLITICAL CRISIS / LORDS AND THE BUDGET." Meanwhile, in the stately chambers of the Victoria Law Courts, women from the Cadbury family and their friends sat in the ladies' gallery, while Nevinson and Burtt were at the solicitors' benches. John Simon, representing Cadbury Bros., began to question the first witness, William Cadbury.

Shortly after Cadbury began testifying, the foreign secretary appeared, and by prior agreement, he immediately went to the witness box. Grey had arrived by rail at New Street Station and was met with heavy security. The chief constable and several detectives accompanied his motorcade to the Victoria Law Courts. Extra police had carefully scrutinized women entering the court that day, fearing that militant suffragettes might gain admission and create a disturbance.[47]

Rufus Isaacs led Grey in the testimony, which centered on his meeting with George and William Cadbury on October 26, 1906. At that interview, Grey had recommended that once Burtt's report was received, the firm should send it to the Foreign Office, where it would be reviewed and, if appropriate, presented to the Portuguese government. He had advised them not to publicize the report but to give diplomacy a chance. Portugal might be more receptive to a report that came through government channels rather than one that might "look like a public attack upon their own conduct and their own affairs."[48] Grey was unable to confirm that the advisability of continuing to purchase São Tomé cocoa was raised at the meeting, as he could not recall all the details after three years. In cross-examination, Carson tried unsuccessfully to draw from Grey a statement that the Cadbury directors had suggested that Burtt's report not be publicized. Grey's testimony was brief and of little substance; the foreign secretary, who clearly put diplomatic relations before humanitarian concerns, was no more informative in the courtroom than he was in Parliament. He left the New Street Station by 2:45 PM.

John Simon then resumed his examination of William Cadbury. Under Simon's guidance, Cadbury described the steps he and the firm had taken since

1901 to bring about reform, filling in the details outlined in Isaacs's opening remarks. Cadbury Bros. had taken "the initiative in investigating the matter themselves, without any communication from the Aborigines Society or the Anti-Slavery Society"; had expressed its concerns to other chocolate firms (English, German, and American); and had asked the advice of several knowledgeable individuals, including John Holt, E. D. Morel, and Sir Martin Gosselin, the British minister to Lisbon who in 1903 had encouraged the firm not to stop purchases from the islands.[49] William Cadbury estimated that he had devoted one-fourth of his time since April 1903 to the labor issue: "I made it my first appointment, and allowed nothing else to stand in the way at any time."[50] Before employing Burtt to visit Portuguese West Africa, the company had considered appointing Nevinson, who wanted to combine the trip with his commission from *Harper's*. Nevinson, however, was unwilling to learn Portuguese or to agree to a long-term commitment, both deemed essential by the company. "I am quite sure," Cadbury testified, "the interview ended in a perfectly friendly way. . . . I gave him an introduction to the place where he stayed for a few days in Sao Thomé, and did all I could to forward the interest of his visit."[51]

Cadbury described the October 1906 conference with the foreign secretary. In the "formal interview," he and his uncle had been representing all the chocolate firms. When the meeting was over, they had told Grey in passing that if he "at any time felt that our buying cocoa stood in the way of his action, he had only to write us a line, or send us word, and we would follow his directions in the matter at once and stop buying cocoa. I cannot remember exactly his reply, but the effect of it was that for the moment at least we must . . . just do nothing in the matter, and he would undertake to do the best he could for us."[52]

Cadbury also explained the disagreement between the chocolate companies and Fox Bourne in June and July 1907. The secretary of the Aborigines' Protection Society had given up all hope of seeing action from Grey, with "some justification, because one knows sometimes these letters from the departments are somewhat trying in their politeness, and the way they say all this shall have attention and so on." (This statement must have drawn smiles from those in the audience who had received letters from Cadbury himself, for his were almost invariably polite and qualified to the extreme.) Six directors from the three English chocolate firms had met Fox Bourne on June 27, 1907: "I remember distinctly we made no impression at all upon Mr. Fox Bourne. He was not very well that day, and I remember saying that he was a courageous man to argue for two hours against six of us and stick to his guns at the end."[53] As to the contention that the Cadbury company would have suffered financially if it had given up the purchase of São Tomé cocoa, William Cadbury had told the Aborigines' Protection Society that although doing so might have posed a supply problem for a few months and cut into the profits, the problem would have been short-lived.

On Wednesday morning, December 1, the trial shared newspaper headlines once again with the ongoing confrontation in Parliament. The *Times* devoted two and a half pages to the debate in the House of Lords, which culminated in a 350-to-75 vote in favor of Lord Lansdowne's amendment rejecting the government's budget, and the *Daily News* trumpeted a three-column headline: "REVOLUTION BEGINS." Spectators crowded into the courtroom in Birmingham, where, later in the morning, Judge Pickford stopped a Manchester reporter from taking a photograph: "Put that away; we don't want any of those things in court."[54]

William Cadbury continued on the witness stand, questioned by Simon. Cadbury had been optimistic after his visit to Lisbon in late 1907, when he and Joseph Burtt discussed Burtt's report with the planters and met with the minister of the colonies, who promised that reform would be forthcoming shortly. But Cadbury had become discouraged during the course of 1908, particularly after the assassination of Portugal's king, the change in government, and Lisbon's decision to send Cid to study the labor situation. Cadbury resolved to visit Portuguese West Africa himself, along with Burtt, and to sponsor a trip by the missionary Charles Swan to Angola to determine finally the progress of reform. Cadbury found that repatriation remained a dead letter and that slave trade was still used to recruit labor. Thus, the three cooperating English companies decided to stop all purchases of São Tomé cocoa on March 15, 1909. In his closing questions, Simon concentrated on the company's sincere effort to help right a terrible wrong: "And in your judgment then and in your judgment now were the steps which you took the best steps to take if you were going to have any influence at all?" Cadbury answered, "Yes. Looking back over the past I honestly cannot see any other steps we could have wisely taken."[55] William Cadbury proved to be a very strong witness. His testimony clearly spelled out the company's long and costly efforts, driven by a humanitarian concern, to expose and to alter the heinous system of slavery.

Yet "a feeling of suppressed excitement" swept through the court when Carson rose to begin his cross-examination.[56] The formal but friendly atmosphere created by John Simon gave way to the aggressive scrutiny of Edward Carson. William

Cadbury's answers to the hostile barrister were terse. Near the beginning, when Cadbury responded emphatically to a question, Carson reacted: "Don't call out at me at this early stage. If you tell me I am wrong I shall sit corrected, and we shall get on very well, because we have a very long time to go through yet."[57] His remark drew laughter.

The purpose of Carson's rigorous cross-examination of Cadbury was to point out that his very profitable company early on understood the awful nature of the labor system providing it with cocoa beans yet took a remarkably long time to do anything about the situation. Carson's biographer points out that questions on the Cadbury firm's purchase of this slave-grown cocoa, which helped to set the tone of the day, "admitted of answers only in the affirmative. They were all derived from information contained in Messrs. Cadbury's own report. The questions, simple in themselves, but backed by Carson's masterful personality and melancholy dignity, grew in gravity, starting from an admission of mere slavery, and passing from cruelty to atrocity, and from atrocity to licensed murder on a large scale, until the plaintiff seemed to stand there as defendant in all but name, and sharing responsibility for the sorrows of the backward world."[58] Many of the questions were repetitious, worded only slightly differently but designed to belabor a point:

> Is it a fact that San Thomé cocoa has been slave-grown to your own knowledge for eight years?—As far as the report from Angola and the island of San Thomé is concerned, I am quite satisfied that slave-grown cocoa describes the conditions, generally speaking.
>
> Was it slavery of a very atrocious character?—In Angola itself the reports that have come to my knowledge give me every reason to suppose that in many cases, at least, it has been exceedingly bad.
>
> Would you say that it was slavery of an atrocious character?—Generally speaking, as far as the collecting of labour in Angola goes, that is true.
>
> The cocoa you were buying was procured by atrocious methods of slavery?—Yes.
>
> Men, women, and children taken forcibly away from their homes against their will?—Yes.
>
> Were they marched on the road like cattle?—I cannot answer that question. They were marched in forced marches down to the coast.
>
> Were they labelled when they went on board ship?—Yes.

How far had they to march?—Various distances. Some came from more than a thousand miles, some from quite near the coast.

Never to return again?—Never to return.

From the information which you procured, did they go down in shackles?—It is the usual custom, I believe, to shackle them at night on the march.

Those who could not keep up with the march were murdered?—I have seen statements to that effect.

You do not doubt it?—I do not doubt that it has been so in some cases.

Carson also raised the emotional issue of children inheriting the status of slave:

The children born to the women who are taken out as slaves become the property of the owners of the slaves?—I believe that the children born on the estates do. I have never been able to find any regulation that gives a child any freedom. I have been told a child is free, but I cannot substantiate it, and I do not believe that he is.

Carson read extensive extracts from Burtt's report, and then asked:

If it was an absolutely cruel and atrocious form of slavery that existed?—I am not justified in distinguishing between slavery and slavery. All slavery must necessarily be atrocious.

Knowing that it was atrocious, you took the main portion of your supply of cocoa for the profit of your business from the islands conducted under this system?—Yes, for a period of some years.

You do not look upon that as anything immoral?—Not under the circumstances.[59]

Another biographer explains that Carson, after getting Cadbury to paint a picture exhibiting the cruelty of the slave system, used short, dramatic questions to drive home his point. Answers were immaterial:

The wretched creatures were whipped if they tried to escape. *Ye knew that?*—Yes, but—

Never mind the buts. They never did escape. *Ye knew that?*[60]

Forty years after the trial, John Simon remarked that Carson's initial cross-examination of Cadbury was "the most devastating thing he had ever heard."[61] Cadbury's responses, however, had been proper and correct; he had remained cool under enormous fire. It was the nature of the attorney's questioning that cast doubt on the sincerity of the company's endeavors.

Carson hammered away at a company that prospered by way of a product supplied by slave labor. Cadbury admitted that the company purchased about half of its cocoa from São Tomé from 1901 through 1908, for which it paid £1,336,632 and with which it made a considerable profit. Carson asked,

> Then I take it that it was not against the principles of Messrs. Cadbury & Co. to make a considerable profit out of slave-produced cocoa?—The answer is, as I said before, "under certain circumstances."
>
> For eight years?—Yes.[62]

Cadbury, however, resolutely refused to admit that the company had attempted to hide the issue from the public. The company had always told anyone who inquired about the iniquitous nature of São Tomé's labor. Only in the case of Burtt's report had the company, deferring to the wishes of the Foreign Office, postponed publication.

At the beginning of the questioning, Carson tried to associate William Cadbury with the *Daily News*, but the witness would have none of it. Cadbury emphatically insisted that he knew nothing of the newspaper, which his uncle George Cadbury controlled. This assertion was misleading, for he did know that his uncle helped shape the newspaper's stories and used his influence to limit the *Daily News* coverage of slave-produced cocoa in São Tomé. Carson pointed out inconsistencies between the newspaper's columns and the actions of Cadbury Bros.: the Cadbury-owned *Daily News* crusaded against contract labor in South Africa between 1903 and 1905 at the same time that Cadbury Bros. was "spending thousands of pounds in buying raw material produced by slave labour."[63] Carson displayed example after example of Cadbury's advertisements showing the idyllic setting of Bournville while making no mention of São Tomé. Throughout the cross-examination, Carson's clever questions and statements drew repeated laughter from the spectators. At one point in the day's proceedings, he let his own infirmities (he suffered a good bit from indigestion) shape one of his questions. Did the repetitive frustrations with the Portuguese cause Cadbury "great heart-burnings"? Cadbury replied, "I don't think I am subject to heart-burn."[64]

On Thursday, December 2, the second day of his cross-examination of William Cadbury, Carson focused on three interconnected lines of thought directed toward one question: first, the Cadbury company had early on gathered material indicating there was slave labor on the islands, second, it had acted very slowly on that information, and third, it had deliberately discouraged the dissemination of that knowledge. What was the explanation for this activity on the firm's part? Carson maintained that the company wished to continue purchasing the cocoa because it made a profit for the business.

Carson drew from Cadbury how his company had gained knowledge of the slave trade in Angola and the slavery on the islands. Matthew Stober, a missionary in Angola who was highly recommended by Gosselin, visited Bournville in 1902 and confirmed the slave trade through his personal contacts with the natives. Ceffala, who ran the telegraph station in São Tomé, relayed reports about slavery and the farce of repatriation on the islands. Nevinson published his articles beginning in 1905, and on August 29, 1905, Burtt reported directly to Cadbury Bros. that there was slavery. Yet the company did not act. Carson addressed his witness:

> As far as I can see in the year 1905 there was nothing else done?—Probably not.
>
> Nor anything up to October, 1906, when you saw Sir Edward Grey?—No, probably not.[65]

After Carson and an associate read long sections of Nevinson's book, Rufus Isaacs stated that the plaintiff accepted as correct what the journalist "had seen, and verified," obviously a move on the part of Cadbury's legal team to claim that Nevinson's testimony supported the prosecution's own case.[66] It is ironic that Cadbury's attorney would sing the praises of Nevinson after William Cadbury had so frequently questioned the man's journalism. Carson then asked Cadbury:

> You read that book?—Yes.
>
> You have given me your estimate of Mr. Nevinson?—Yes.
>
> As a thoroughly honest man?—Yes.
>
> Did you not think the time had come for action then?—No, I thought it right to go on as we had been going on with the policy we already had in hand.[67]

Cadbury believed that Nevinson's judgment was clouded by his fear of being poisoned, which was partly explained by the fact that the journalist did not speak Portuguese: "When you are in a foreign country, particularly when you think everybody is your enemy, and you see them speaking to each other, you naturally feel suspicious."[68] Cadbury doubted Nevinson's story about managers in Príncipe hunting escaped slaves and then shooting them. He explained, "I have been entertained in the house of some of the people in Principe, and they are men of honour and respect." This left an opening for Carson:

> What are they?—Managers on the cocoa estates.
> You mean to say you honour and respect them?—Yes.[69]

In regard to George and William Cadbury's October 1906 meeting with Grey, Carson attempted to show that the firm of Cadbury tried to draw from the foreign secretary a statement that Burtt's report should not be published, a contention that William Cadbury denied. *Standard*'s counsel mocked him for assuming that an exceptionally busy foreign secretary, without benefit of a written notice, would ask the company, whenever it became appropriate, to stop purchasing cocoa from the islands:

> Did you expect the Foreign Secretary was going to keep that in mind?—Yes, I think probably he would.
> You never took any pains to put that down on paper for him?—No.
> How many interviews do you think the Foreign Secretary has in a day?—I don't know.
> And you expected him to retain the matter in his mind and drop you a card when he wanted you to give up buying?—Yes.[70]

Carson insinuated that the attempt by Cadbury officials to discourage publicity about Burtt's journey to West Africa was part of a plot to protect the business while appearing to be concerned humanitarians. Carson noted that William Cadbury, in a letter of February 9, 1904, had written to Fox Bourne that Burtt's "visit will not be hurried." He had added, "Under the circumstances I venture to hope that your society will not press the subject before public notice during the time of his visit, as we fear it might prejudice the planters and might lessen the value of his visit." Later in the questioning, Cadbury defended his request not to publicize Burtt's investigation: "You must remember that when you get to Portugal and West Africa people don't differentiate, and Cadbury Bros., the Anti-Slavery Society, and the Liverpool Chamber of Commerce are all hashed up in an extraordinary way into 'the English people.'" He admitted to the court that he had not wanted people to "agitate when Burtt was undertaking this delicate mission."[71]

Carson's questioning unveiled the nasty conflict between William Cadbury and Fox Bourne over the latter's intention to publish an article in 1907 about the cocoa industry and the slave trade. Carson read virtually all of Cadbury's letter of December 3, 1908, at the end of which Cadbury cut off his association with the Aborigines' Protection Society and wrote that the society should "give all the credit to the British Government and give them every encouragement to follow up the good work they have begun and have brought to such a successful point with the Portuguese Ministry." Carson then asked:

> Brought to such a successful point?—Yes, I think it was a great point gained.

Carson exclaimed, "A great point to get a promise from the Portuguese Government!"[72]

Cadbury admitted that he attempted to stop Nevinson's publication of an article in the *Fortnightly Review* about Portuguese West Africa "because condemning the British cocoa-makers meant condemning the British Government, who were working together."[73]

As he had done from the beginning of the cross-examination, Carson suggested that the company's actions over many years were hypocritical, designed to cover for a firm that wished to continue purchasing São Tomé cocoa, its essential raw material. Carson used as evidence a letter from Rowntree of November 2, 1904, warning Cadbury Bros. that a boycott "would involve a serious pecuniary loss to those who entered upon it."[74]

Throughout this grueling third day on the stand, William Cadbury continued to argue that the firm's actions were consistent with the policy decision taken very early in the century—to work with the government to attempt to force reform. According to one account, however, even Cadbury appeared disheartened at Carson's final question:

> Have you formed any estimate of the number of slaves who lost their lives in preparing your cocoa during those eight years?—No, no.[75]

A scholar who studied Rufus Isaacs's legal career has observed, "The last answer was half a cry, half a protest, and Mr. Cadbury winced visibly as it was put."[76]

The adjournment that day came early, as both Carson and Isaacs wished to attend a House of Commons debate in the evening.[77] They likely sat in the same coach on their way to London.

On Friday, December 3, the *Times* editorial headline read "THE END OF THE PARLIAMENT." The entire front page of the *Daily Mail* was a Cadbury advertisement with "Six *excellent* reasons why Cadbury's Cocoa is the best," including the fact that "it is manufactured under ideal conditions," and a half-page advertisement in the *Daily Mirror* noted, "Cadbury's Cocoa is nourishing and sustaining, made at Bournville under ideal conditions." Apparently, Cadbury's competitors or opponents had paid for these advertisements as an ironic commentary on a company that prided itself on the "ideal conditions" of its employees in Birmingham while purchasing cocoa from plantations that depended on slave labor. The court proceedings opened with a "large and interested attendance."[78]

Isaacs reexamined William Cadbury, restoring the plaintiff's case by reiterating certain points—specifically, that the firm worked consistently throughout the years toward the end of bringing about reform and that both Sir Martin Gosselin and Sir Edward Grey advised the Cadbury firm to continue the purchase of cocoa. Isaacs captured the thoroughness of the company's commitment in a closing question:

> Looking back now, is there any step which you could have taken which you have not taken?—No. I am sure there is not.[79]

Edward Thackray, the principal buyer of cocoa beans for Cadbury Bros., then took the witness stand. Under cross-examination by Carson, he admitted that the years 1908 and 1909 had seen a dramatic increase in the world's output of cocoa beans, so that it was easier by that date for the firm to find a new source of beans. He emphasized, however, that switching earlier would have been "awkward" but not "difficult."[80] For eight years, the company had considered finding a new source of cocoa because of concern over São Tomé; the issue of cost had never entered into discussions.

Joseph Burtt, who returned from his mission to the United States in order to give evidence at the trial, stressed that his instructions had called for him to undertake a fair and thorough study of conditions in West Africa and that he had never at any time believed William Cadbury wanted his report delayed. Burtt proved to be a very strong witness for William Cadbury; Carson gained nothing through questioning.

George Cadbury, seventy years old and the veteran head of the firm, testified proudly of his company's quest to alter labor practices on the islands and of the trust he had placed in his nephew William in directing the investigation. Both Isaacs and Carson, however, found it necessary to repeat questions to gain the desired answers. After several variations on a query, Isaacs said: "You have not quite answered my question," to which George Cadbury responded, "I have never been in the witness-box before, so far as I remember." Isaacs, eliciting a bit of humor, said, "It is a little late in life to start." Then he rephrased his question: "I want to know if there is any truth in the suggestion that you have not been acting honestly in the matter?" George Cadbury answered, with a glare at Carson, "I can say that there is no truth whatever, and look any man in the face."[81]

George Cadbury's responses to the questions, if not as focused as the advocates wished, did reflect his strong personal feelings and philosophy on slave labor. Isaacs also took the opportunity to neutralize potential testimony by Henry Nevinson by cleverly showing the journalist's close ties to the defendant. At one point, he asked George Cadbury to identify Nevinson:

> He is this gentleman [pointing] who has been handing slips to my learned friend [Carson]?—Yes.

Isaacs later read parts of a letter from Nevinson to George Cadbury of November 27, 1908, announcing the meeting of December 4 on Angola: "But I am sending you the letter myself because, in your conversation with Mr. Brailsford and me at the 'Daily News' office, you said that you hoped public opinion would be aroused as much as possible upon the subject of the Angola slavery, and you will be pleased to see that some steps are being taken with this subject. . . . We all recognize how much your firm has already done to bring the slave traffic to light."[82]

In one part of his cross-examination, Carson focused on how George Cadbury could possibly have accepted making a profit from the products of slaves. Cadbury struggled, trying to explain that "sentiment" encouraged him to stop the purchase of the São Tomé beans, while "common sense" indicated that continued purchase was the best way to influence the Portuguese. Finally, he justified the profits by saying, "I believe I can say nearly the whole of the profits since that time have gone to a benevolent fund."[83] Nevinson, in his autobiography written nearly twenty years later, commented, "I well remember the painful sense of derision with which I and others heard the worthy old man make that wretched and irrelevant excuse. Sir Edward Carson paused for a moment, and I think a touch of pity for his victim passed through a mind not given to pity."[84] Carson directed much of his attention to the *Daily News*, of which George Cadbury was the principal owner. Cadbury claimed that he gave the managing director complete control over running the company, although it "was to be on Liberal lines; that was all. I did not interfere with anything else." On this issue, Carson certainly gained favor with the jury, as he showed that George Cadbury obviously restricted what the *Daily News* carried about Portuguese West Africa. Cadbury admitted that although the newspaper conducted a campaign against Chinese labor in South Africa, it ran no articles about São Tomé. Moreover, he acknowledged that Brailsford had threatened to resign if the newspaper remained silent on the islands' slavery. George Cadbury testified that he disagreed with Brailsford: "I thought it was injudicious, because my nephew at that time was nobly risking his life, and I did not want to make it more difficult for him by causing antipathy on the part of the planters."[85]

By Saturday, December 4, the sixth day of the trial, the nation was engaged in a bitterly fought election campaign. Nonetheless, many spectators sat in the Birmingham Assizes to witness a "good show" put on by the brilliant barristers. According to an observer, the audience could expect Isaacs to draw on his vast knowledge, physically evident by the piles of documents that filled his table, to explain immediately and with eloquence a point overlooked or a mistake to be rectified. While Isaacs was noticeably attentive, Carson sat with eyes closed. Given the opportunity, however, Carson "employed all his powers of satire and irony; of mock sympathy and quiet but effective incredulity, though at times he was very bitter in his callous scepticism." He made effective use of humor, however, which helped the jury identify with him. His rich voice, with a "cultured Hibernian brogue," could also be as "quiet and gentle as a woman's." Carson could wiggle his ears, and when he wore a pince-nez, his eyes had a "Mephistophelean" quality.[86]

Carson completely surprised everyone by not calling any witnesses for the *Standard*. The defense had hurled many accusations against the Cadbury company, specifically on the charge of hypocrisy, and these charges required substantiation. But Carson, as in an earlier case, decided to present no witnesses, instead depending on his own closing statement. He did not wish to subject potential witnesses to Isaacs's cross-examination. It was a bold strategy that only someone with Carson's ability would dare undertake.

Carson's summary was long but simple in design, intended to show that by the ideals of the journalistic profession, the *Standard* was required to reveal the heinous nature of slavery that had been tolerated by the Cadbury company in order to continue profiting. If the *Standard* had erred in its article on Cadbury Bros., Carson pleaded, it would have apologized. But the newspaper's editors had made no mistake, and it was "one of their highest functions" to bring the matter to the attention of the public. Isaacs immediately interrupted Carson: "My friend is making a statement which is not supported. He is not going to call any witnesses, and yet says the 'Standard' had performed their functions in doing their duty. He is not entitled to say what he believes unless he calls evidence to establish that belief. It does not lie in counsel's mouth to say so except by way of argument." When the judge remarked that it "would not be admissible to say that the gentleman who wrote the article firmly believed in everything," Carson responded, "No. What I say is that the 'Standard' wrote the article and say it is true, and stand by it, and I have the right to say so."

Carson contended that Cadbury was no ordinary company. The plaintiffs had presented themselves as humanitarians. Some members of the firm owned a newspaper, the *Daily News*, that campaigned against the use of indentured labor in South Africa. Carson continued: "Therefore, as regards the plaintiff, it is not the case of an ordinary individual attacked by a newspaper, brought into prominence by a newspaper over questions of this kind. They are men in a peculiar position owing to the action which they had thought right from time to time to take in asserting themselves as the champions of labour, whether at home, in the Colonies, or in foreign countries."[87] Hence, slavery on the islands was a vital issue in this case, contrary to the contention of the plaintiffs.

Carson painted a grim picture of obtaining slaves in Angola and of their lot after arriving at the islands. In effect, he dramatically summarized the dark picture he had drawn during his cross-examinations:

> Slavery! Have you ever heard at any time of the world's history (and that is a broad statement) of worse conditions more revolting, more cruel, more tyrannous and more horrible than what has been deposed to as regards the slavery in Sao Thomé? Men recruited in Angola, women recruited in Angola, children recruited in Angola, torn away against their will from their homes in the interior, marched like droves

> of beasts through the Hungry Country, and when they are unable to walk along for a thousand miles to the coast shot down like useless dogs or useless animals and the others brought down to be labelled like cattle and brought over to Sao Thomé and Principé never again to return to their homes . . . when their children are born just as the calves of a cow or the lambs of the sheep they become the property, not of their parents but of the owners.[88]

For eight years, he said, Cadbury Bros. had supported this human exploitation by buying £1.3 million worth of cocoa beans. Why had it continued this purchase for such a long time? Carson asked rhetorically. The firm claimed it had done so for "humanitarian purposes," to retain a weapon or a "lever" that could be used to apply pressure to the Portuguese plantation owners and government officials. Yet nothing had improved for the slaves over the eight long years of Cadbury's activities. Carson charged that this painfully slow process was deliberate on the part of the company, which feared that profits would have suffered if it had switched its source of cocoa. Hence, the firm could not abide anyone, even the brave Fox Bourne, who dared propose a boycott of São Tomé cocoa.[89]

Carson, however, could be caught out. At the very end of his closing statement, he waxed eloquent about the *Standard*'s willingness to have the case heard in Birmingham, even though the newspaper was based in London. Isaacs objected to Carson's claim, as the *Standard* had fought the requested move "tooth and nail"; the judge agreed with Isaacs.[90]

Following Carson's powerful statement, which lasted two hours and thirty-five minutes, Isaacs began his summing up. His presentation was not as dramatic as his opponent's, but he articulated clearly the purpose of the trial, and he poked holes in several of Carson's arguments for which there was no proof. Carson and the defendants had failed to prove, as was required in this instance, that Cadbury Bros. had "been guilty of the acts of deceit and hypocrisy." Instead of calling witnesses, who would have been subject to cross-examination, Carson had relied on his own assertions. Isaacs stressed that Carson dared not call to the witness stand Nevinson, who was conspicuously absent on that day, for the defense attorney knew full well that the journalist would have acknowledged William Cadbury's integrity, as would Fox Bourne had he still been alive. The same would be true for all people who had contact with William Cadbury on the slavery issue. Carson, however, dismissed the testimony on the integrity of William Cadbury with "scoffing and sneering," an "art" in which he "[is] a master, whom no one can excel, certainly in our profession."[91] The company had taken the honorable course over slavery—to help to improve the life of the workers on the islands and the continent.

After a Sunday off, Isaacs wrapped up his summation on Monday morning, December 6, before a full house with a notably large number of women. His remarks were directed at Carson's accusation that the Cadbury firm used the Foreign Office to delay action on the labor issue. By 1906, Isaacs contended, the Foreign Office had told Cadbury Bros. and Fox Bourne that the government wanted to make diplomatic representations to the Portuguese government. Both the chocolate manufacturers and Fox Bourne put a time limit on British governmental action, with Fox Bourne insisting on an earlier deadline. Other than that disagreement, the Cadbury company and the former secretary of the Aborigines' Protection Society were in agreement. When Cadbury Bros. wanted to release the Burtt report to the planters in 1907, the Foreign Office asked for a delay, contending that it would be a breach of courtesy if the Portuguese government were not first informed.

After a summary lasting some five hours, Isaacs told the jury that his clients had "suffered the greatest injury" and that the jury could rectify that disservice to Cadbury Bros. by imposing significant damages against the *Standard*. Such a verdict, he claimed, would make it possible for his clients "to leave this court with the proud conscientiousness that they have substantiated to you that they are an honour and a credit to any community to which they may belong."[92]

Some members of the gallery applauded Isaacs as he sat down; the judge ordered the applause stopped and began his own summing up, which lasted three and a half hours. Brevity was not in order at this trial. Justice Pickford's summary was widely regarded as favorable to the Cadbury company. The core of his charge to the jury read that the defendants were required to prove that the company officials had been "throughout this matter acting in a dishonest way, making, or purporting to make, efforts which they knew could have no good effect in order that they might continue to make a profit out of the slave-grown cocoa." The judge warned members of the jury that much of the *Standard*'s presentation had no bearing on the case. The stance of the *Daily News* on Chinese coolie labor or Cadbury's use of its philanthropic activities in its advertisements, for instance, should not be treated as a factor. Pickford also stated that he believed the *Standard* must have had more than one editor in 1908, as the newspaper offered so many different opinions on conditions in São Tomé in that year. In addition, the judge warned the jury that the defendants had failed to offer any proof for several of the allegations contained in the particulars. The *Standard* charged that the chocolate firm had repeatedly taken steps to delay any action against the planters, yet Fox Bourne, who was so respected and trusted by the defendants and was cited as one who disagreed with the plaintiffs' actions, had counseled Cadbury Bros. to postpone sending out a commissioner until after hearing the results of Nightingale's visit to the islands. Moreover, all of those people who had knowledge of Cadbury's efforts, and there were many, "were absolutely convinced of the good faith of Messrs. Cadbury, nay, that the 'Standard' themselves only three months before they published this article were equally convinced of the good faith of Messrs. Cadbury and the other persons." Pickford closed his summary by stressing that if the jurors believed Cadbury had been libeled in the *Standard*'s article, they should award the chocolate firm "sufficiently substantial damages" to indicate such was the case.[93]

The jury retired to deliberate at 5:10 PM on Monday, December 6, the seventh day of the trial. The proceedings had been shorter than anticipated because Carson called no witnesses. Nevinson, who had been present for much of the first week's presentation, was no longer at court. His diary indicates that he was not especially pleased with the direction of the litigation. He judged Grey "quite useless for either side" and found Carson's initial cross-examination of William Cadbury "very slow & without much grasp." At one point, Nevinson exchanged pleasantries with William Cadbury. But he was mainly concerned with how he and his own ideas were presented, and in this, he was generally disappointed. His original report was not contradicted, but William Cadbury refused to accept his "story of hunted slaves" and still questioned his account of being poisoned. Long extracts from Nevinson's book were read in court, but they were "not at all well chosen." Although Nevinson was often praised in court, he believed that his reputation suffered; yet because he was not called as a witness, he could not defend himself or correct misstatements. He recorded in his diary, "Unhappy & irritable about the lies I couldn't give evidence against."[94]

At 6:05, fifty-five minutes after they retired to consider their verdict, the members of the jury returned to the courtroom. The deliberations were the only short part of the trial. The foreman reported that the jurors had found in favor of Cadbury Bros. When the court asked him the amount of damages against the *Standard*, he responded with the word for the smallest coin in the realm:

"One farthing."

9 The Verdict

> The jury were disgusted with the plaintiffs for dealing so long in slave-made cocoa.
>
> *Edward Carson*

> Messrs. Cadbury have always been known to be honourable men, and they will continue so to be known.
>
> *Birmingham Daily Post*

THE JURY'S AWARD of one farthing (one-fourth of a penny) in damages must have stunned all who followed the trial. Small awards like this are referred to as "contemptuous damages," and they can be granted when a jury believes that the "libel or slander complained of, though technically actionable, was nevertheless utterly trivial" or because the jury, "while finding that the words were defamatory and that the defendant has no defence, does not feel that the reputation of the plaintiff has been damaged by the libel."[1] The judge has discretion in awarding costs of the trial. In this instance, Judge Pickford decided that the guilty party, the *Standard*, would absorb the costs of both parties.

Although losing the verdict, Carson was pleased with the overall outcome. He wrote a friend that it was "a very big case and everyone seemed delighted . . . the jury were disgusted with the plaintiffs for dealing so long in slave-made cocoa."[2] Carson's admirers asserted that by deciding not to call any witnesses and depending entirely on his own rhetorical abilities, he avoided having to defend a weak legal case. Instead, he played on a very real feeling that the firm of Cadbury had purchased the slave-grown cocoa beans for too long.[3]

Nevinson, who learned of the verdict after dinner, wrote in his diary, "One farthing damages! It is a crushing blow: almost annihilating both for the firm and the D.N. [*Daily News*]. How they will wish to-night they had listened to me from the first & boycotted!"[4] But Nevinson was mistaken; it was not a "crushing blow" to the firm, to William Cadbury, or to the *Daily News*. In the immediate aftermath of the trial, the nation was preoccupied with the budget crisis and the election campaign. Ironically, just as the trial concluded with neither side a clear victor, the election ended with the Liberals and Conservatives winning nearly the same number of seats, so that the Liberal government thereafter depended on votes of Irish Nationalist and Labour MPs to remain in office. In a few instances, Conservatives invoked the name of Cadbury during the campaign as an example of the hypocrisy that permeated the Liberal and Radical world of politics.[5] Criticism of the role played by Cadbury Bros. and the *Daily News* in the story of São Tomé cocoa largely disappeared by the end of 1910. While the affair apparently preoccupied William Cadbury for much of his life, there is no indication that the company's sales or profits suffered unduly.

Almost all of the local Birmingham newspapers, even though they were supporters of Chamberlain and the Conservative Party and not the Liberal Party favored by the Cadburys, were critical of the jury for awarding contemptuous damages. Most other publications believed that Cadbury Bros. had been cleared of the charge of hypocrisy, but a few disagreed—vehemently. Grey was regarded as a less than impressive witness for the Cadbury firm, and it was often noted that Cadbury's close connections to the *Daily News* politicized the court proceedings. Many newspapers that followed the trial did not print editorials on the outcome, probably because of the national political crisis.[6]

The *Birmingham Daily Mail* found that the defense utterly failed to prove that the Cadburys had been hypocrites who tolerated the slave trade to benefit financially. Carson, however, had managed to introduce politics into the trial by examining the relationship between the Cadbury company and the *Daily News*.[7] The *Birmingham Daily Post* could "not pretend to understand the verdict." The newspaper was "glad to feel that the jury . . . have at least exonerated Messrs. Cadbury" from the charge of hypocrisy. The Cadburys, it added, "have always been known to be honourable men, and they will continue so to be known."[8] The *Birmingham Pictorial and Dart* stressed that "the unfortunate decision," which was "principally based on political motives," had "given rise to much strong criticism and even anger, not only locally, but all over the country." According to the newspaper, there was an appearance that the jury, made up of men with political opinions contrary to those of the Cadburys, "gave their verdict accordingly."[9] The *Birmingham Weekly Post* assessed the verdict a "feeble and unsatisfactory compromise." While Cadbury's directors may very well not have made the best decisions over the issue, all who knew them realized that they "did their honest best to mitigate a system of gross slavery." Cadbury Bros., the newspaper concluded, had placed too much trust in Grey; the company instead should have depended on its own efforts and quickly organized a boycott.[10]

Indeed, several individuals were very critical of Grey's remarks at the trial. A surgeon general thought that Grey's halfhearted testimony "certainly did not assist [Cadbury], and I warned Cadbury of this three years before the trial."[11] Morel, writing in his *African Mail,* heaped blame on an indecisive Foreign Office that appeared "incapable of anything but compromises and posing" and failed to make use of the powerful information provided by the Cadbury company. According to Morel (who had become increasingly disillusioned with a foreign office that refused to take a strong public stand against King Leopold's actions in the Congo), the foreign policy of Britain had "ceased to represent the moral force of the nation in external questions." The one person deserving of highest praise, he asserted, was William Cadbury: "If this slave traffic is eventually stopped, its unhappy victims will owe it primarily to the man who courageously, consistently, patiently, with complete self-sacrifice, and with an aversion amounting almost to quixotry to let the world know what he was doing, has battled and striven for the right, and who, in so doing, has worthily upheld the highest traditions of national honor."[12]

A letter to Cadbury Bros. from A. M. Tracey of Manchester, written after the first day of testimony and before Grey took the stand, illustrates why Grey's testimony was a key for the company—or could have been. Tracey had visited Angola between 1896 and 1897 on business, and while there, he witnessed the slave trade abetted by the Portuguese officials and "winked at by the British representative." He learned that W. Clayton Pickersgill, the British consul in Luanda and a former missionary in the Congo, had reported the trade to London, where Lord Salisbury served as both prime minister and foreign secretary, but "had received a very strong hint from head-quarters to leave such matters alone." Tracey closed with good advice, which Cadbury's counsel did not follow: "It appears to me that unless Sir. E. Grey is prepared to state clearly that the home government were perfectly aware of what was going on but did not think it advisable to press the matter, your advocates may have some difficulty in convincing an English jury that your earnest and sincere endeavors were really entirely nullified by the official desire to keep the real state of things from the general public."[13]

Rufus Isaacs, a Liberal MP, never attempted to draw from Grey, a Liberal foreign minister, the government's motives for its relations with Portugal or the extent to which the Foreign Office put pressure on Lisbon. Such a line of questioning at the trial would certainly have been refused by Grey as involving sensitive diplomatic negotiations. Neither Isaacs nor the Cadburys, as far as we know, ever indicated any misgivings about the sincerity of the Foreign Office's effort to push for reform or about Grey's lackluster testimony in court.

For several years, the government had refused to act on the information gathered by its own consuls or by Nevinson, Burtt, and other observers. The Liberal Party, heir to the great antislavery movement of the nineteenth century, put diplomatic and economic interests to the fore. The Liberal Imperialist Grey did little more than continue to implement policies of previous British administrations, which amounted to a benign tolerance of Portuguese endeavors.

The *British Weekly*, a Christian-oriented journal, believed that the proceedings had left "Messrs Cadbury's high and well-earned character absolutely unimpaired, not to say enhanced."[14] The *Morning Post* noted that had Cadbury's purchasing policies improved the lot of the slaves, "no question of the wisdom of the course adopted would have arisen."[15] The *Nation* ran a powerful editorial that focused on how a well-meaning company or individual, with exceptionally high standards, was subject to unfair and unreal expectations in all aspects of its actions and that anything short of perfection was regarded as unacceptable.[16]

A large number of newspapers believed that the Cadbury company's close connection with the *Daily News* had hurt the firm at the trial. The *Spectator*, the paper edited by John St. Loe Strachey, who had helped to coordinate the antislavery conference of December 1908, found the jury's decision unacceptable and admitted that Cadbury's weakest link was its "refusal to restrain the *Daily News* from fulminating against Chinese labour at a time when [its] own attitude was so vulnerable."[17] The *Globe*, owned by the brother of newspaper magnate Lord Northcliffe, laid responsibility for the unusual decision—an outcome pleasing neither party—squarely on Cadbury's connection to the *Daily News*, a fact that clearly influenced the jurors.[18] The Unionist *Saturday Review*, launching one of the most bitter attacks on Cadbury Bros., accused the company of condemning slavery, especially through the *Daily News*, while "parleying with it and tolerating it" for years in São Tomé.[19] The *Times* also admonished the *Daily News* for decrying the use of Chinese coolie labor while remaining virtually silent on São Tomé slavery.[20] Travers Buxton was apparently correct when he surmised that, in spite of the judge's warning, "the Jury treated the matter as a case of the 'Daily News' versus 'Standard.'"[21]

William and George Cadbury expressed relief that the trial was over, and they thanked Rufus Isaacs and John Simon for their efforts. George Cadbury was satisfied with the verdict, given the nature of the jury. Isaacs welcomed the outcome of what had always been seen as a very difficult case.[22] Edward Cadbury, a son of George Cadbury and a member of Cadbury's board, admitted to Buxton that the trial, whose verdict "might have been worse," had caused anxiety among company officials.[23] George Cadbury thanked Cadbury's staff members for their support during the trial. In his printed message to them, he pointed out that in summing up, the judge had "absolutely endorsed the action we had taken," and he praised the thoughtful and courageous efforts of William Cadbury over many years.[24]

Following the trial, the Cadbury company received many personal letters, most of them supportive but a few expressing displeasure. E. D. Morel wrote that he experienced "amazement, disgust and anger" over the verdict. He lauded William Cadbury for having pursued reform far beyond what any other business leader would have done and for having been, if anything, "too fair, too just." Morel was upset with Grey, whom he described as a "weak-kneed and not over scrupulous politician," offering evidence that was simple and feeble.[25] A Quaker complimented William Cadbury on his actions and remarked that other importers of commodities should attempt to secure better working conditions in the production of their raw materials. Another correspondent was certain that William Cadbury would long be pleased with "possessing in Mr. Isaacs a champion more than a match for the swashbuckler, Sir Edward Carson."[26] A number of the letters were religiously oriented, quoting biblical verses and promising prayers or enclosing religious tracts; some messages of support included original poems. Several correspondents expressed their approval of William Cadbury's comportment when under pressure from Carson.[27] A relative wrote to William Cadbury, "I hope no one in the family will ever name their child *Carson*."[28] Some writers believed that political considerations were foremost in the minds of the jurors: William Albright, a Quaker, perceptively noted that the election atmosphere had affected the jurors, who proved unwilling to "acquiesce in any verdict that gave substantial damages to their opponents."[29] A few thought that the trial and the Cadbury company's exemplary action would help improve the lot of laborers in the Portuguese colonies.[30]

Some of the letters were spiteful. A resident of Stoke Newington wrote: "It is a great shame that your work on behalf of the Radical Party about the Chinese Slavery question at the last General Election should have only been valued at one farthing. I therefore have the pleasure to enclose this small offering [an imitation farthing coin from Edward VII's 1902 coronation] which you will observe is as genuine as the Chinese Slavery Statements were."[31] The most hateful communication, written in pencil and replete with spelling and grammatical errors, read in part:

> Sirs
>
> What a mess. You fornicating sneaking hypocrites . . .
>
> You have proved yourselves the greatest sneaks every known.
>
> You ought to be in your modal village some time all together & an earthuate come & swallow you up & the village. You fornicating bad wretches . . .
>
> Dont show your faces any more. You scamping set of thieves.
>
> Poor Slaves
>
> Chained together at the bidding of Cadburys and driven like dogs.[32]

The firm apparently answered every communication, some with a "stock" letter, others with more personal attention. One client, a cakemaker, asked how she should respond to customers who refused to accept Cadbury's "Slave grown Cocoa." Cadbury Bros. replied, "We have pleasure in informing you that we have not purchased any of the Cocoa to which you refer for more than a year, & when we did so it was in order to enable us to have some influence in getting the conditions in the Portuguese Colony improved."[33] One response from Cadbury Bros. explained at some length the company's policy on São Tomé cocoa and concluded that if the company gained the cooperation of foreign firms in the boycott, "there is little doubt that the great object we have all along had in view would soon be accomplished."[34] The company also mailed a copy of the judge's summary to several people who had sent negative letters, with a note saying that he had obviously accepted "our absolute sincerity" and had required that the *Standard* pay the costs.[35]

The award of contemptuous damages was an embarrassment to Cadbury Bros. Both Isaacs and the judge, in their summations, stressed that if the *Standard* was guilty, the jury should award substantial damages. Instead, the jury expressed major reservations about the company's good reputation and integrity by awarding contemptuous damages. Carson had been dealt a weak hand, but he had played his cards with consummate skill, concentrating on Cadbury's vulnerable points: the *Daily News* and its inconsistent responses to the abuse of labor, a company that advertised the nearly idyllic conditions of its employees at Bournville but seemingly cared little for exploited natives, the extraordinarily slow process of pressing for reform while continuing to purchase the cocoa beans, and the naive trust in the capacity of Edward Grey and the Foreign Office to alter Portuguese labor practices. In the process, Carson created doubt in the jurors' minds about Cadbury's humanitarian interests.

Newspapers played up the parallel of the battle between the Liberals and Conservatives over the budget in Parliament to that of the trial, in which parties to the suit were clearly aligned to Britain's two dominant political affiliations. The implication was that the jurors' award reflected the influence of Birmingham's powerful Chamberlain family, leading lights of the Conservative Party. That implication, however, suggests that all of the jurors sympathized with the Chamberlain faction of Birmingham politics and opposed the Liberal-oriented Cadburys. This appraisal makes little sense, as the firm of Cadbury also enjoyed substantial support in the community; nor is there any reason to assume that all of the jurors had come from the Conservative camp. Moreover, Joseph Chamberlain, who earned his fortune as a screw manufacturer and founded the family political dynasty in about 1870, was initially on the Radical side of the Liberal Party, and Birmingham was an industrial town inclined to electing leftist politicians.

Whatever their individual political perspectives, the jurors were of one mind in regard to the case at hand. It took them less than one hour to decide on what was, in effect, two matters: the *Standard* was guilty of libel, but Cadbury fell far short of defending its humanitarian image, which had been key to its case against the *Standard*. William Cadbury, who was assigned by company directors to handle the São Tomé issue, used some poor judgment in handling the whole matter. In 1901, he was charged with determining if slave labor was used. Evidence confirming such slavery flowed in, not least of all from the company's own agent, Joseph Burtt. Many of the people whom William Cadbury consulted, including Merck and Gosselin in Lisbon, had warned him that the Portuguese would not listen to pleas of humanity to mend their ways. Many also stressed that the British government, the Foreign Office specifically, could not be relied on to bring about change. Yet William Cadbury refused to follow that advice. While he testified in court that he was satisfied with all of his actions in attempting to foster reform, it is hard to understand why he did not call for a boycott earlier, especially after receiving Burtt's report. His stubbornness apparently clouded his judgment, and he did not want his decisions questioned, especially by the likes of Nevinson and Fox Bourne or by the *Standard*.

Cadbury Bros. could at least be pleased with the actions of Judge Pickford, who summed up jury instructions in the company's favor and then insisted that the *Standard* pay the costs of the trial. The press speculated on the amount of those costs. The *Birmingham Pictorial and Dart* understood that the trial had been "one of the most costly civil actions ever" in Birmingham courts.[36] It is not known how much the *Standard* had to pay Carson and his assistants, but Isaacs charged £1,365 for his brief and £210 for each day in court.[37] The Cadbury firm paid him a total of approximately £2,700, Simon £1,735, and a third attorney £1,000.[38] Later reports indicate that Cadbury spent £8,239 on the trial. The *Standard* paid £2,978 of that amount, so Cadbury's net cost was £5,261.[39] The *Standard*'s legal expenses amounted to about £11,000, including the nearly £3,000 paid to Cadbury Bros.[40] Hence, the total for the two companies was a bit over £16,000. These monetary costs, however, were minor compared to the time and effort expended by both parties to the dispute, and they paled into insignificance when set against the suffering of the slaves in West Africa.

10 Humanitarians, the Foreign Office, and Portugal, 1910–1914

If the workers of the whole world, white or negroes, could only have one-half of the liberty, treatment, and care that the negro workers enjoy in the Portuguese Islands of San Thomé and Principe, the whole of humanity would have attained a degree of happiness from which it is still far away.

Portuguese legation, London, 1912

You have great wealth gained by means of the cocoa-seed, worked by the poor natives of San Thomé and natives in other parts of this wide world, and you exploit them and the Europeans who are helping in the amassing of your fortune.

Alfredo Augusto Freire de Andrade, former Portuguese colonial official, on Cadbury Bros., 1912

It is true that it would be shameful to throw over the Portuguese alliance in order to facilitate a division of her African colonies between Germany and ourselves.

It is also true that it would be morally indefensible to protect the scandalous state of things that exists in the Portuguese colonies, but the alliance gives us no discretion in this matter.

Sir Edward Grey, 1912

SHIPMENTS OF ANGOLANS to the cocoa islands ended in 1909 and did not recommence until 1913. Meanwhile, planters on São Tomé recruited laborers from other Portuguese colonies, primarily Mozambique, and began repatriating a few of the Angolans. Although the labor situation on the islands improved somewhat after 1909, significant issues remained. How plantation owners recruited and retained laborers remained controversial. Portuguese labor laws, reassuring as usual, were still not effectively enforced, and abuse of workers continued, especially the failure to ensure repatriation.

Reflecting the nature of their professions, humanitarians remained skeptical and journalists continued to be inquisitive about Portuguese endeavors.[1] John Harris, the effective head of the Anti-Slavery Society by 1912, became the primary spokesman for the humanitarians, while St. Loe Strachey, editor of the *Spectator*, was the most involved journalist. Nevinson, often away from England covering conflicts, occasionally gave his attention to the Portuguese labor system. In the period from 1910 to the outbreak of World War I in 1914, Parliament increasingly became the focal point for scrutinizing Portugal's treatment of its serviçais. Meanwhile, the Foreign Office, continually criticized for its inability to compel Portugal to mend its ways, responded in two manners. First, beginning in 1912, it issued a series of reports containing extensive correspondence between London and its representatives overseas. Designed to explain and defend the government's action, these papers more often led the Foreign Office to quarrel with MPs and humanitarians. Second, Grey, who grew increasingly disillusioned with Britain's old ally, negotiated an agreement with Germany that, had it been finalized, could have divided up Portugal's African empire.

With the conclusion of the trial, William Cadbury was free to publish the book he had written on his trip to West Africa: *Labour in Portuguese West Africa* appeared in January 1910.[2] The volume was straightforward and matter-of-fact, much as one would expect from a cautious and observant businessman. He reported that the hours of labor for serviçais were much too long and that their diet was a monotonous one, composed of rice and dried meat with few fresh vegetables. Their death rate remained far too high and the birth rate dramatically low. He was most critical of the failure of repatriation efforts.

Cadbury recalled a time some six years earlier during his first trip to Lisbon when he met an old priest, Father Rooney, who testified to the miserable life of the enslaved in Angola and São Tomé. Cadbury continued: "I shall not forget the remark of the priest, that in his despair he sometimes wished that the islands might be swallowed in the depths of the seas and all their trouble ended."[3] This passage raises a significant concern about Cadbury's actions after 1903. A few years after this memorable meeting, Nevinson and Burtt echoed the priest's lament that the islands lay at the heart of the suffering of the Angolan natives. Cadbury, however, along with many humanitarians and Foreign Office officials, insisted that the problem was centered not in the islands but in Angola. As a result, before 1909, he and others who believed that the main difficulty lay elsewhere had not forcefully demanded that the "friendly" owners of productive São Tomé roças enact immediate and effective reform measures.

William Cadbury's recommendations to Portugal entailed a total revamping of the recruiting system, correct application of contracting laws, reduction in the hours of labor, and effective repatriation.[4] There was little new in his report; Burtt had written about many of the same issues—albeit in fewer words.[5] Nevinson was upset that he was never mentioned in the text, and he told this to Cadbury, who apologized for the omission.[6] The book was also published as a "cheap edition," available to the public for three pence. Buxton was perturbed and surprised that Cadbury, who had recently criticized the Anti-Slavery Society, expected the organization to purchase many copies.[7] On the whole, the book generated relatively little notice in the press.[8]

Cadbury Bros. and the other chocolate firms remained in the spotlight in 1910. The *World*, in a series of vituperative articles from December 1909 to May 1910, ran lengthy excerpts from Nevinson's book, Burtt's report, and the trial, as well as information from the Anti-Slavery Society's *Reporter*. The articles were part of a sensational and sustained attack on Cadbury Bros.; on Liberals, Radicals, and Socialists; and on humanitarian societies and newspapers. The *World*, a "gossipy" weekly under the editorship of Lord Winterton, claimed to have coined the phrase *Cocoa Press*.[9] When the weekly asked Nevinson to submit a "series of sketches on S. Thomé slavery in the style of Uncle Tom's Cabin," he declined, "for fear of confounding fiction with my liberal report."[10] In 1910, the *World* published the articles as a pamphlet, entitled "*Modern Slavery:* An Exposure of 'Red Cocoa' and the Chinese Slavery Lie, to which is added the Financial History of the 'Daily News.'" The weekly claimed that seventy-five thousand copies of this work were either sold or given away.[11] The *World* ridiculed other newspapers for failing to censure the Cadbury company and pointed out the extraordinary power wielded by the chocolate firms through the cocoa press.[12]

Rowntree, who controlled the *Nation* through a trust, and George Cadbury, the primary owner of the *Daily News*, together bought the *Morning Leader* and the *Star* in 1909. In May and July 1910, the *National Review*, a monthly journal under the editorship of Leo Maxse, an imperialist and a supporter of Joseph Chamberlain and tariff reform, carried two long articles echoing many of the *World*'s complaints and elaborating on the cocoa press, which it accused of impeding the publication of information on Portuguese slavery while thundering against Chinese coolie labor and abuses in the Congo Free State.[13] The *National Review*, the *Pall Mall Gazette*, and Strachey's *Spectator* all charged the cocoa press with hypocrisy, notably for George Cadbury owning a paper, the *Daily News*, that was critical of gambling while raking in money from his *Morning Leader* and *Star*, popular publications that benefited from betting and racing coverage.[14] The Cadburys had left themselves open to charges of hypocrisy: they had attempted to limit coverage of laboring conditions in São Tomé, they had delayed boycotting

São Tomé cocoa beans for a long period, and their newspapers had played both ends of the gambling spectrum. Although the attacks by the *National Review* were primarily politically motivated, the Cadburys and Rowntrees were fair game, as they also "played politics," purchasing newspapers to espouse their Liberal/Radical philosophy.

The chocolate companies and their associated Liberal newspapers found themselves under assault in 1910 for embracing free trade while benefiting from a protective tariff. This issue had been raised before, in 1907.[15] Governments had been levying a tariff on imported cocoa since 1853, the charge depending on whether the cocoa was raw or processed. Originally designed to provide British chocolate manufacturers some protection from established European companies, the modest duty helped to discredit the Liberal government, which advocated free trade. The tariff cost ultimately fell mostly on members of the working class, who were heavy consumers of chocolate. In 1910, Cadbury Bros. asked Chancellor of the Exchequer David Lloyd George to remove the duty on cocoa, thereby reducing the cost of cocoa products and increasing company sales.[16] Should the duty remain, the company requested that the British chocolate firms be granted a "drawback" or rebate of the duty on the cocoa used in their extensive export trade, to make them more competitive in foreign markets.[17] In his maiden speech in July 1910, Arnold Rowntree, recently elected to Parliament as a Liberal for York and speaking for his firm as well as Cadbury Bros., called for an end to the cocoa tariff.[18] Though no changes occurred in 1910, the government's 1911 budget made adjustments in the cocoa duty and permitted a drawback on exported chocolate.[19] Charges by Conservatives that the chocolate firms benefited unfairly from protection seemed to diminish by 1911.

By the second decade of the century, the Gold Coast became Cadbury's chief source for cocoa. The firm claimed that the quality of the colony's beans had improved through the efforts of the peasant farmers and the colonial administration, and especially through instruction offered by Cadbury Bros. When arranging for the purchase of a model plantation in the colony, George Cadbury referred to the ideal of "uplifting the natives."[20] But according to an economist, the migrant farmers of the Gold Coast colony were themselves primarily responsible for the industry's development and were highly skilled in farming and adept at acquiring capital.[21] According to a historian, if the Cadbury company contributed in any way to the improved quality of the bean, it was by offering higher prices for a better product. William Cadbury acknowledged as much in 1913.[22] By 1911, the Gold Coast was the leading producer of cocoa beans in the world.[23] Cadbury Bros., which had purchased 41 tons of beans from British West Africa (this would have included both the Gold Coast and Ashanti) in the 1908–1909 period, bought 696 tons between 1909 and 1910, 1,222 tons between 1910 and 1911, and 2,768 tons between 1914 and 1915.[24]

The Cadbury firm gained a dependable source for cocoa beans in this changeover and faced little criticism of its cocoa-purchasing policy after 1910. One exception was a satirical article in the March 1912 *John Bull,* in which a phrenologist analyzed George Cadbury's brain only to discover a "*secretiveness*" lobe that "prompted" him not to disclose how his firm had gained cocoa from the "hideous slavery in San Thomé."[25]

Portuguese labor practices remained under the watchful eye of humanitarians. John Harris, the organizing secretary of the amalgamated Anti-Slavery and Aborigines' Protection Society (hereafter still referred to as the Anti-Slavery Society), took the lead in scrutinizing Portuguese affairs. Shortly after the conclusion of the trial, Harris spelled out his plan of action, which to a great extent dictated the endeavors of the humanitarians for the next four years: to force the Portuguese to carry on with reform by pressure from Great Britain brought about through parliamentary debates, by expanding the boycott and increasing propaganda, and by demanding a commitment on Grey's part for Foreign Office action. Harris was determined to devote his energies to the cause, and he expected to win no matter how hostile the resistance he encountered.[26] He had contacts with government officials, journalists, humanitarians, missionaries, and Africans. With a flair for publicity, the self-assured and determined Harris, whose wife, Alice, worked closely with him in the society, was, if anything, disliked even more than Fox Bourne.[27] Given its limited financial resources, the Anti-Slavery Society's endeavors in regard to Portuguese labor practices were extensive and included sponsoring Burtt's tour to the United States, coordinating its efforts with MPs, and supplying the Foreign Office with information on West Africa. The society's aggressive manner in Portuguese affairs after 1910 contrasted sharply with its acquiescence to the Cadbury firm's leadership up to 1909.

Joseph Burtt returned to the United States following his testimony at the trial. He again took up his tour, sponsored by the Anti-Slavery Society, to explain to Americans why they should not purchase São Tomé cocoa. While he met with members of congress, senators, and President William Howard Taft, all of whom expressed sympathy with his mission, São Tomé beans continued to find a ready market, particularly in New York City, Hamburg, and Holland.[28] Some brokers, especially those in Hamburg, would "bulk" or mix their beans, so that there was no way to determine their origin.[29] Following the completion of his tour, Burtt occasionally spoke and wrote about São Tomé. He feared that meaningful reform of Portuguese labor would be difficult to achieve because the slave trading centers were so remote from the Portuguese colonial administration, which remained weak and corrupt.[30] He wrote *Voice of the Forest* (1911), a novel set in the Congo and Angola, and dedicated it to William Cadbury for "his enduring work for freedom in West Africa." The hero of the book attempts to thwart the slave trade, which violates the Brussels Act.[31]

In March 1910, several MPs formed a committee, with close ties to the Anti-Slavery Society, to bring the issue of slavery to the attention of Parliament. Although instances of slavery in Peru, Nigeria, and Rhodesia were raised at the initial meeting, the subject of Portuguese labor in West Africa dominated the proceedings. Burtt and Nevinson both testified at the first meeting.[32] Partly because of the efforts of this committee, the government faced a substantial number of questions and debates about slavery in Parliament.[33] The questions seldom broke new ground, but they did keep the issue before the government and the public.

After 1910, Harris and Travers Buxton inundated the Foreign Office with correspondence about slave trade and labor conditions in Angola and the islands and about the inability or unwillingness of Portuguese authorities to enforce labor regulations and provide repatriation.[34] Foreign Office officials thought that Portugal's failure to require repatriation was a major mistake, and on June 27, 1910, Grey told the Marques de Soveral, the Portuguese minister to London, that Portugal had to show more success in the repatriation of workers. When Soveral responded that "it was unreasonable to demand compulsory repatriation, for the labourers in San Thomé were so well treated and the conditions there were so much better than those in the places from which the labourers came that the latter often did not wish to go back," Grey insisted that the laborers should have an unquestioned ability to return to their native lands.[35]

Grey readily agreed to receive a deputation from the Anti-Slavery Society in early July 1910. He welcomed the opportunity to express his views on Portuguese labor to a delegation rather than to the House of Commons, probably because he would not be subjected to sharp public questioning. The group included a long list of dignified humanitarians and politicians, as well as Strachey and Nevinson. Though Nevinson thought that he himself did not speak well at the meeting, his observations on the nature of slavery were both thoughtful and appropriate. No one, he argued, had charged the plantation owners with being "really cruel." Rather, the central issues were "the purchase of men and women for money and the compulsion to work without consent" and the granting of extraordinary authority to the plantation proprietor. He asked for true freedom for the natives, and he firmly opposed the compulsory labor that was common not only in Portuguese West Africa but also in many other European colonies.[36]

Grey replied at length, taking the opportunity to explain the British government's policy in regard to Portugal's labor practices. While Britain had carefully spelled out to Portuguese officials what appeared to be unacceptable labor practices, it had been careful not to challenge "the sovereign rights of the Portuguese." Portugal had responded in July 1909 by suspending recruitment from Angola and switching to sources of labor in Mozambique. Any subsequent recruitment from Angola would occur under much tighter regulations, as only licensed agents would be permitted to participate, and the numbers recruited would be restricted. Reengagement of laborers who had fulfilled their original contracts would take place only as a public event, with safeguards built in, including the presence of several impartial witnesses. Repatriation for those who wished it was to be assured, and natives would receive a substantial bonus equal to half of their wages (the money was to be withheld monthly from their pay) when they returned to the mainland. Grey emphasized that these new regulations per se could not guarantee improved conditions; the government awaited positive results. Most important, the foreign secretary announced that the British government would appoint and pay a British subject as vice-consul on the islands to help ensure that the new regulations were correctly implemented. This was a measure for which the humanitarian societies had been pressing for quite some time. Grey indicated that the British consul in Angola and the vice-consul in São Tomé had been instructed to regularly surveil labor practices. The consul to Luanda was specifically required to visit interior areas where recruiting took place. Finally, Grey underscored that he trusted the consuls' reports, which the Foreign Office planned to publish. Shortly after this meeting, many of the same issues were addressed in Parliament, including Britain's obligation to take action in regard to the mistreatment of natives because it was the preponderant power in Africa and had the right to interfere in Portuguese practices due to a series of treaties.[37] Clearly, Grey took a harder line with Portugal after 1909, perhaps because the agreement to contract Mozambique natives for the South African mines had been finalized.

Over the previous decade, political turmoil in Portugal had made it all but impossible for the government in Lisbon to carry out policies in the colonies. The assassination of the king and his heir in 1908 delayed the implementation of new labor regulations. In early October 1910, long-standing political discontent exploded into a full-scale political insurrection, as junior officers in the army and navy were joined by the urban classes in Lisbon to overthrow the unloved and inefficient monarch and to install a republic. The young King Manuel fled with his family on a ship, eventually going to England. As many as one hundred people lost their lives in the revolution, which was centered in the cities of Lisbon and Oporto. The British government made no attempt to restore the monarchy, instead sending two naval ships to protect British subjects and property. Order was quickly restored, but British authorities were reluctant to recognize the new government immediately.

Some members of the British government disliked the republicans, whom they identified as regicides who killed King Carlos in 1908, while others were sympathetic to the Portuguese monarchy, which had maintained close ties and friendship with the English royal family. Winston Churchill, president of the Board of Trade, wanted Portugal to hold elections to validate its new form of government, and Grey was increasingly disconcerted with the instability of the government in Lisbon.[38] Although relations between the two countries remained proper, as the new government informed Britain that it would honor all of its treaty obligations, Grey was in no rush to recognize the republican regime.[39] On April 13, 1911, he told Bernardino Machado, the Portuguese foreign minister, that the upcoming elections in Portugal were essential to confirm constitutionally the new government. He also warned Machado that "British public opinion would recognise the Portuguese government most willingly if the labour recruiting was entirely free."[40] Britain officially recognized the republican government on September 3, 1911, almost one year after the revolution.

The *Daily News* reported that the new government promised to initiate dramatic change by dismissing its freeloading overseas ministers (including Soveral in London), reorganizing government departments, reducing bloated staffs, and abolishing the "virtual slavery" of natives in the colonies. The paper also announced that the president of the new government believed in free trade.[41] The Cadbury firm, by contrast, was circumspect about the Republic. In a series of letters exchanged with Portuguese officials in October 1910, Cadbury Bros. emphasized that labor laws must be strengthened and enforced before the chocolate firm would again consider purchasing any cocoa beans from the islands.[42] William Cadbury called on Grey publicly to demand that the new Portuguese government take effective measures on specific problems.[43] In March 1911, while William Cadbury vacationed in Portugal with his wife, he and William Albright, an Anti-Slavery Society officer, met with the minister of marine and colonies. At this conference, Cadbury expressed the hope that the new Republic would take steps to ensure free labor in the islands, so that the chocolate firm could once again purchase the islands' cocoa.[44]

The Portuguese government, anxious to gain support in Britain, approached the Anti-Slavery Society in October 1910 and indicated that it wished to assure the British of its intentions to institute reform. The society quickly took steps to send to Lisbon a delegation consisting of Harris; Burtt; Nevinson; MP Joseph King; Georgina King Lewis, an influential Quaker; and Brooks, the society's treasurer. The series of meetings, however, nearly collapsed from the moment of the group's arrival in Lisbon. William Cadbury had recommended his friend Alfredo da Silva as the society's contact in Lisbon. Silva made arrangements in Lisbon and informed members of the new Portuguese Anti-Slavery Society as well as government ministers that the purpose of the British deputation's visit was to applaud the excellent effort on the part of the Portuguese to bring about reform.[45] Because the London delegation had no intention of engaging simply in a salutary celebration, there were negotiations for the first two days just to resolve differences over the purpose of the conference and to set up new meetings. The rescheduled sessions ended up being relatively cordial and correct, but Silva's actions, which were considered little less than sabotage, spoiled the entire journey, and the trip was regarded as futile.[46]

This visit to Lisbon by representatives of the Anti-Slavery Society, which began with such high hopes but ended in a feeling of despair, may have permanently soured these British humanitarians' perception of the new Portuguese government. For the next three years, the society, under the leadership of the aggressive Harris, would treat any actions taken by the Portuguese authorities in regard to native labor with great suspicion. The visit also led to a severing of relations between Harris and William Cadbury.

On December 13, 1910, Harris penned a long letter to Cadbury, referring to Silva's unacceptable actions in Lisbon. One excerpt from this message read: "The members of the deputation condemn as disloyal, to say the least, incontrovertible and definite acts of Mr. Da Silva; I fear we must say secret double-dealing. Tactlessness we could have forgotten, but deliberate, well tested, and ultimately acknowledged acts, can, unfortunately, never be effaced from our memories."[47] It was not only Harris who felt this way; Nevinson was also terribly upset with Silva, and Charles Swan, the more polite facilitator of some of the meetings, was sorry that Silva had "shown up so badly."[48]

William Cadbury replied to Harris three weeks later, after receiving another letter of January 6 in which Harris thanked Cadbury for his advice and announced that Harris and his wife were undertaking a tour of Africa to study the conditions of the natives. Cadbury's response reflected his ill will toward Harris. It also showed how loyal he could be to his friend Silva, who had telegraphed William Cadbury immediately following the overthrow of the monarchy and stated that the new republican government would "settle the San Thomé labour question with absolute justice and freedom to all natives."[49] Cadbury's letter to Harris of January 9, 1911, read in part:

> You recently have been to Lisbon—as usual you asked my "valuable advice." In a flying visit of two days you sow seeds of discord, and check the friendship of a local Anti-Slavery Society in its infancy, and you have the assurance to come home and tell that . . . [Silva]—a man who more than any other has spent himself in the Anti-Slavery Cause—a man I have known and worked with for five years, is a villain. If you are correct I am a most unsuitable person to advise you or any member of your Society, for I consider myself honoured by the friendship and confidence of Alfred da Silva—his son is at present on a visit to us.
>
> I wish you and your wife every success in your African tour, but it must be clear to you that our work in future will be best done apart. You have many and influential friends, and will get on excellently without me. In S. Thome I am somewhat of a "black number." The Vice-Consul will readily introduce you to all the big people: my few friends are of humbler standing, and I will on no account (after Lisbon) risk their reputation in your hands.[50]

Harris adamantly responded to Cadbury's letter on the following day. He denied that the British delegation was at fault and concluded his letter with an admonishment: "I wish you could have seen your way clear to have written a letter, if not in a more Christian spirit, at least with a closer relation to truth and justice."[51]

Foreign Office officials remained frustrated with Portugal's inaction. Portuguese officials could not provide reliable statistics on the numbers of serviçais exported from Angola and Mozambique to the islands for the period after 1900.[52] Reports of ongoing slave trade in Angola continued to surface, and planters on the islands resisted the new labor regulations.[53] Moreover, the consul in Lourenço Marques regarded the recruiting of natives from Mozambique for work on the cocoa islands as little more than coerced labor, often caused by corrupt, underpaid Portuguese officials.[54] F. E. Drummond-Hay, who succeeded Mackie as consul in Luanda, witnessed 430 natives from Mozambique on board a steamship bound to São Tomé in 1910. He considered them "well-cared for," although he noted that several died from exposure to the cold while rounding the cape and four more died while being landed on the island.[55]

British officials were bewildered by the inability of Portuguese officials to carry through on repatriation.[56] On too many occasions, the Portuguese, who contended that it was difficult to determine where serviçais came from, did little more than dump them on the shores of Angola. The Portuguese claimed that many of the serviçais had been captured while very young and had no knowledge of their origins; others were born on the islands and thus had no home villages.[57] Lisbon often frustrated attempts by the local governors to enforce repatriation, and planters demanded that the repatriation of eligible workers be held up until they could be replaced.[58] Remarkably few were repatriated, considering how many serviçais were qualified—at least 30,000—and desirous of returning to the mainland. The total number of Angolans repatriated in 1910 was a mere 388; for 1912, it was just 385.[59] What little information the British consuls provided painted a miserable picture.[60]

The British Anti-Slavery Society frequently advised the Foreign Office and the public on the state of the serviçais in the Portuguese colonies, offering reports from the field, particularly after John and Alice Harris returned in March 1912 from their trip to Portuguese West Africa.[61] In the press, at various gatherings, and in his book *Dawn in Darkest Africa* (1912), Harris highlighted the essential points: the importation of serviçais from Angola had stopped; repatriation, for which there were great expectations under the republican regime, was unacceptably slow and inadequate; and on the islands, corporal punishment of the serviçais with either the chicotte or the palmatória was far too commonplace.[62] Foreign Office officials and consuls were exceptionally critical of Harris, who, among many things, was charged with spending little time on the islands.[63] A. C. Cumming, who had worked on São Tomé at the telegraph station and as vice-consul, contended that Harris obtained evidence of cruelty from repatriated serviçais. Since Harris gained this testimony through an interpreter, Cumming argued, it could never be trusted: "The Angola native or any other nigger never tells the truth. He simply says what he thinks will please the listener." Cumming admitted that repatriation was proceeding slowly because of inefficient Portuguese government; however, to force the serviçais to be returned to Angola would mean "sending some thousands of natives, who at the present moment are well fed, well clothed, well cared for, and not by any means overworked, back to a state of savagery and starvation. . . . The life of the native on the Roças is ideal, and I do not think, there is a parallel to it in the world."[64]

While humanitarians focused attention on the continuation of the slave labor system and the lack of repatriation, defenders of the Portuguese planters—especially Francisco Mantero and J. A. Wyllie—sought to project the planters on São Tomé as operating in the best interests of the laborers. Mantero, a planter himself, published *Manual Labour in S. Thomé and Principe* in 1910, a handsome volume containing maps and photographs and a ringing defense of the plantation owners. Mantero charged that the English—he lumped Nevinson, Pienaar, and Burtt together as particular evildoers—had waged a half-century campaign that "impeded the progress of the Colony." The planters were all concerned with the welfare of the laborers who had been rescued from the filthy, unhealthy, and socially depraved area of Angola, and the owners provided them with shelter, clothing, food, medical care, and pay in an idyllic setting: "[The laborers] pay no costs and have free legal advice . . . ; they are not subject to military service, nor do they pay taxes; they receive good conduct rewards from the planters, instruction in agriculture and trades, a home in old age . . . ; they are encouraged by the advice and example of their employers to give up heathenism, and, with their families, are prepared for baptism . . . ; the planters suppress polygamy and encourage the formation of family ties." Mantero dismissed repatriation as too costly, a disservice to the serviçais, and an impediment to the continued development of a colony vital to the economic well-being of Portugal.[65] The Anti-Slavery Society's *Reporter*, Morel, and Nevinson all roundly castigated this book, which was translated by Wyllie. Morel stressed that Mantero failed entirely to address the issue of high mortality rates on the island or the means by which the laborers were procured, while Nevinson attacked Mantero's supposition that the natives were grateful for having been saved from a life of depravity in Angola.[66]

Mantero gave a major speech in Portugal on February 13, 1911, defending planters as law-abiding individuals and condemning the British for calling for forced repatriation of the workers, which would simply be returning them to a state of slavery from which they had been rescued. Wyllie, who wrote the introduction to a book containing Mantero's speech, blamed the difficulties on the Africans, who enslaved and traded natives on the continent: "The root of the evil is African—pure African. . . . What he has done with impunity and by instinct for hundreds of years he still does, and will be found doing hundreds of years hence."[67] Wyllie corresponded frequently with English newspapers in defense of the São Tomé planters, although he did not deny the appalling conditions in Angola. In January 1911, he complained that the Cadbury firm's estimate of the death rate in São Tomé was much too high and added that, even then, it compared "very favorably indeed with the officially recorded negro mortality in the Rand Mines."[68] He also showered Morel's *African Mail* with letters and engaged Nevinson in a dispute in the pages of the *Yorkshire Observer*.[69] One of the most implausible claims came from the Portuguese legation in London in response to criticisms expressed at an Anti-Slavery Society meeting in June 1912: "It would be flagrant injustice not to recognize that Portugal, after the revolution of October 5th, 1910, did more in favour of the natives of its colonies than any other civilized country in the last twenty-five years . . . if the workers of the whole world, white or negroes, could only have one-half of the liberty, treatment, and care that the negro workers enjoy in the Portuguese Islands of San Thomé and Principe, the whole of humanity would have attained a degree of happiness from which it unfortunately is still far away."[70]

A number of Portuguese leaders continued to find fault with their own colonial labor system. Their criticisms appeared both before and after the republican revolution of October 1910. Henrique de Paiva Couceiro, former governor of Angola, published a book in 1910 in which he called for required repatriation and for employers to pay high enough wages to attract laborers for any industry or project.[71] In September of the same year, the *African Mail* ran a series of quotations from D. Simões Raposa, a former magistrate and judge on the island of Príncipe, describing the brutal treatment and corporal punishment of the serviçais, their attempted flight, and the failure of repatriation.[72] The *Economista* of Lisbon appealed to the new republican government for reforms leading to truly free labor on the islands.[73] The *Voz de San Thome* of March 2, 1911, reported major physical abuse and torture of serviçais on two plantations and told of a curator who seemed more concerned about which workers had divulged the information than about whether a wrong had occurred.[74] In 1911, Major Viera, the new republican-appointed governor of Príncipe, found the "negroes not badly treated on the cocoa plantations," but he believed that repatriation of the laborers (over fifty thousand were eligible) had to be "strictly enforced," even though doing so would harm the plantation owners financially, because "the Government cannot sacrifice the interests of humanity for the sake of mere private interests."[75] Unfortunately, the new republican government that seized control in Lisbon in 1910 required, like its predecessor, that natives in the colonies be involved in gainful employment.[76] As a result, the abusive treatment of laborers continued.

Repatriation often went awry, according to Portuguese witnesses. The writer of a June 8, 1912, letter related that a few days after being repatriated, 50 of 269 former serviçais died of starvation in Benguela.[77] The most powerful condemnation of repatriation came in an article in the Luanda *Reforma* in August 1911. The serviçais on the islands, the newspaper charged, had been used and abused and worn out, and when no longer valuable, they were returned to Angola without any resources. Angola, a poor colony, was then forced to provide for these physically ruined natives: "They eat the meat and send us the bones."[78] Col. Manuel Maria Coelho, who earlier lived in Angola, was the first governor of that colony under the Republic. He used strong measures to end forced labor but resigned for lack of support in March 1912.[79]

While the owners of the roças found alternative markets for their cocoa beans following the boycott, they obviously had difficulties maintaining their expensive labor force. These problems may have been the reason that, between 1911 and 1912, some owners considered selling their plantations to international companies, reportedly British and Anglo-French concerns.[80] Nothing apparently came of these negotiations due to the high prices demanded by the Portuguese planters, whose most profitable plantations returned 12 to 15 percent per annum before World War I.[81] Because these transactions were not finalized, they sustained the Portuguese belief that the boycott was part of a scheme to decrease the net worth of the plantations, making it easier for foreigners to purchase them.

Sleeping sickness ravaged Príncipe and threatened the very continuation of the roças there, although abandonment of the island was deemed politically impossible.[82] By 1911, passengers on board ships that sailed into the island's port did not disembark, and the two clerks staffing the office of the cable company seldom left their "fly-proof" house.[83] A report by the commander of the British ship *Dwarf* in 1911 stated that several people died daily from sleeping sickness.[84] Drainage, clearing of forests, and better housing conditions may have reduced the prevalence of sleeping sickness, but it was not until the 1920s that the government contained the tsetse fly.[85]

In 1912, the Foreign Office found itself under increasing pressure to confront the Portuguese on the labor issue. The Anti-Slavery Society appointed a new committee, including Strachey and Nevinson, to focus on Portuguese colonial labor, and it arranged for questions to be raised in Parliament.[86] Grey had no easy task defending the government's policy on West African labor. In early 1913, the government admitted that some British subjects had been illegally recruited for the Spanish colony of Fernando Po, and it had to deal with reports that natives from British colonies were among the slaves in Angola.[87] MPs and humanitarians attempted to show that treaties with Portugal offered Britain the opportunity to insist that the natives be freed and properly treated. Grey normally responded that while Britain followed through on inquiries, the ultimate responsibility rested squarely on the Portuguese and not on the British.

On June 25, 1912, the Anti-Slavery Society held a meeting on "Portuguese Slavery and British Responsibility" at the Westminster Palace Hotel; the audience included several MPs. The focus of the meeting was to generate publicity for the society's conviction that if slavery and slave trading continued in Portuguese West Africa and if Portugal failed to take steps to abolish these practices, Great Britain should drop its alliance with Portugal. William Cadbury, who was unable to attend, submitted a letter that called on the British government to publish its consuls' reports on Angola and the islands. He suggested that if no solution to the labor problem was forthcoming, Britain should not block the "transfer" of Portuguese territory to a "more vital and not less humane colonising Power." Cadbury's letter, which was published in the *African Mail* on July 5, also called on the British government to appoint a special commission of inquiry to investigate Portugal's actions in Angola.[88]

The Anti-Slavery Society followed its June meeting with a lengthy statement to Grey on July 15—it was also published as a pamphlet—summarizing its concerns over Portuguese labor: the slave trade violated international treaties; many of the slaves on the islands were Belgian and British colonial subjects; the Portuguese often did not repatriate slave families as a unit; there was massive fraud in the repatriation fund, from which the princely sum of at least £100,000 had mysteriously disappeared; and slavery continued as a practice in Angola.[89] Members of Parliament also broached the issue of Portuguese slavery in a July debate in the House of Commons. Noel Buxton, MP, after bemoaning the ill treatment of Portuguese native laborers, suggested that a possible answer to the problem was for Germany to purchase the colonies of Portuguese southwest Africa; he hoped that Britain would facilitate that process. At the conclusion of the debate, Grey admitted that certain issues raised had to be addressed and that he would consider publishing pertinent papers.[90]

One month later, in August 1912, the Foreign Office published a white paper (a government report) on contract labor in Portuguese West Africa. The document, mainly a selection of letters from consuls in Luanda, suggested that repatriation was failing, partly because the standard of living for natives was considerably higher on the islands than in Angola and because the latter colony had little or nothing to offer returning serviçais. Indeed, Drummond-Hay's letter of June 8, 1912, gave an almost glowing account of conditions in São Tomé.[91]

Strachey's *Spectator* concluded that the government's correspondence printed in the white paper confirmed that Portugal still could not govern its colonies effectively. The weekly newspaper cited an admission made by a leading Portuguese official in March 1912 that governors sent out by Lisbon to halt abuses were unable to overcome the "power of the vested interests, European and native, which . . . they found arrayed against them."[92] The Anti-Slavery Society, in its *Reporter*, asserted that the Foreign Office had finally delivered a "clear verdict" on Portuguese labor policy—"Slavery—'Beyond Doubt'." The society then issued a warning in a resolution to Grey stating that it would call on the government to end its alliance with Portugal if that country did not "abolish slavery in her dominions effectively and without delay."[93] Harris congratulated Walter Langley on the "splendid White Book," which demolished "the Portuguese case."[94]

The Foreign Office was not pleased with these responses, as officials there thought that the abuses referred to were based on old information or on Harris's accounts, which they did not trust, and failed to take into account the more positive reports of British consuls.[95] When Foreign Office officials Eyre A. Crowe and J. W. Tilley met with Harris and Buxton on October 22, they were not impressed with either of the Anti-Slavery Society leaders. Tilley deemed Harris naive for having accepted testimony from serviçais. Crowe thought Buxton "dumb," whereas he believed Harris spoke without thinking and could not understand that for

Britain to abrogate the Portuguese alliance due to slavery required evidence far beyond that found in the white paper. Grey's note on the interview was much more realistic: he feared that laborers would not be repatriated.[96] In a follow-up letter to the interview, the brash Harris warned Tilley that if the Anti-Slavery Society were to accept the Foreign Office conviction that the Portuguese system of labor was simply "ordinary contract labour, with abuses," the society could very well turn its attention to contract labor in the British colonies, where conditions were often worse than in the Portuguese colonies.[97] In another letter, Harris and Buxton appropriately emphasized that the white paper itself had identified one of the major problems in the Portuguese administration of São Tomé—the twenty-five governors appointed in the "short space of ten years" were powerless against "vested interests" on the island.[98]

William Cadbury and E. D. Morel joined the controversy over the white paper with an article in the October 1912 issue of *The Nineteenth Century and After*. The authors asserted that administration over such a large colony as Angola required a "trained body of public servants" that Portugal, a country acutely short of resources, did not possess. Cadbury and Morel stressed that while the Portuguese were, in "some respects," more sympathetic to natives than were the British, Lisbon failed "to ensure protection for her subjects or respect for her laws; and nowhere in the world, perhaps, does a weak hand at the helm facilitate abuses to the extent which is the case in tropical Africa." Consular reports about the inability to return the serviçais to a meaningful life on the mainland provided dramatic evidence of Portuguese failure. While admitting that Britain had earlier participated in the slave trade, Cadbury and Morel asserted that Portugal had not taken steps to halt a slavery in Angola that was comparable to that of the fifteenth and sixteenth centuries.[99] In all of this, Cadbury and Morel reflected the common assumptions of their period: there was no questioning the right of suitable Europeans to exercise control over colonial Africa, and natives were perceived as people with minimal needs.[100]

The article by Cadbury and Morel drew a long and vehement response from Alfredo Augusto Freire de Andrade, the former governor-general of Mozambique. Portugal, he admitted, was no different from other colonizing nations in requiring that natives be engaged in labor; it was one of the means of civilizing them. He had seen natives work under armed guards in Kimberley (British Cape Colony), and compulsory labor was still utilized in many other European colonies in Africa. He was particularly disturbed that Cadbury equated the slavery of fifteenth-century Angola with the conditions of 1910. Meaningful attempts by the Portuguese to bring about reform, including repatriation that was fraught with major problems, were conveniently ignored by Cadbury. The author's resentment of William Cadbury's wealth and power boiled over: "You have great wealth gained by means of the cocoa-seed, worked by the poor natives of San Thomé and natives in other parts of this wide world, and you exploit them and the Europeans who are helping in the amassing of your fortune. You have, therefore, ample means at your disposal—money, publicity, and, in fact, everything that money can buy, and you are using these means to slander our administration. I, on the contrary, have nothing of the kind, having all my life been working for my country and her good name, and this is not a sure means of accumulating riches."[101]

The differences between the Anti-Slavery Society and the Foreign Office grew more heated. Foreign Office officials believed that they had to defend themselves against what they regarded as the incorrect assumptions set forth by the Anti-Slavery Society in its letter of July 15, 1912.[102] A flurry of letters between the society and the Foreign Office ensued, and reports from British consuls in West Africa, reacting to the society's charges, flowed into London. Officials at the Foreign Office found themselves in a difficult position. They believed that the accounts by Harris and the detailed testimony by others were often taken out of context or were dated, that repatriation was extraordinarily difficult to implement and might not truly aid the serviçais, and that the Anti-Slavery Society's estimate that there were over thirty thousand serviçais awaiting repatriation was inflated. Nevertheless, the facts remained that Portuguese efforts were falling far short and that conditions for the natives were often appalling, most notably in Angola.[103] Acting Consul Robert Smallbones wrote from Luanda in September 1912 that there were large areas of Angola not yet under Portuguese rule and "whole regions in which a Portuguese soldier or officer cannot show his face." He visited a plantation in Angola in which labor conditions were unsatisfactory. In spite of promises, the Portuguese government had not provided land for repatriated serviçais.[104] Moreover, plantation owners had discontinued repatriation until replacement workers could be contracted.[105] The repatriation fund, as the Anti-Slavery Society charged, was extraordinarily short on revenue, partly because plantation owners were behind on their payments but also because administrators of the fund had failed to invest in interest-bearing accounts. As one staff member noted, "The charge of criminal slackness in the administration of a trust is, I think, established."[106] Foreign Office officials were frustrated, for they believed that they had done their best, given diplomatic constraints, to make known to the Portuguese the many problems.[107] Although Grey thought that there had been "real improvement as regards Angola & Principe labour," he had "no confidence in Portuguese administration."[108]

On February 28, 1913, the Foreign Office published another white paper on Portuguese West Africa—a series of correspondence replying to the Anti-Slavery Society letter of July 15, 1912.[109] Several MPs cited documents in the white paper that testified to a lack of reliable statistics and the failure of repatriation.[110] The *Spectator* found that the Foreign Office's defense of its actions and of Portugal rang hollow, as "Grey and his officials are at heart much too honest and too sensible to make good apologists for slavery. . . . They are trying to bury the body of Slavery in a very shallow grave and with an altogether insufficient quantity of earth. Do what they will, a toe or an elbow or the tip of the victim's nose will keep pushing through and betraying them."[111] In reviewing the white paper for the *British Friend*, a liberal monthly Quaker journal, Joseph Burtt charged that there was little foundation to the argument made by some British officials that the serviçal preferred life on the island to that on the mainland. The Angolan, he emphasized, signified that he "preferred, shamelessly, to remain a squalid savage in Angola. And the conclusive proof of this decision is to be found in the shackles, big shackles, little shackles, heaps of shackles, that have been used to force him from Angola against his will."[112]

Lord Cromer, a member of the Baring banking family who had been the British proconsul and effective ruler of Egypt from 1883 to 1907, weighed in with three lengthy and argumentative articles concerning the white paper in the *Spectator* in August 1913. Cromer was mildly critical of the Foreign Office for focusing on generally minor differences with the antislavery advocates rather than concentrating on the larger issue of the slave trade. To solve the problem of providing workers for the islands, he advocated a move to free labor, much as Wyllie had proposed in a December 8, 1912, memorandum submitted to the Foreign Office.[113]

In June 1913, John Harris penned his passionate book *Portuguese Slavery: Britain's Dilemma.* Citing government reports, missionary accounts, testimony at the libel trial, and excerpts from the writings of Nevinson and Burtt, Harris indicted the Portuguese for their abhorrent labor practices. He praised the chocolate firms for their efforts to expose the practice of slavery on the islands. Harris found dramatic differences between Africans on the islands and on the mainland. Workers on island plantations acted like slaves, with a "downcast and sullen expression" and an "absence of the merry laugh," whereas the free African was "full of jolly quips and sallies; lightheartedly he wields his axe, paddle, or machete, to the rhythm of his song." At the end of the book, which was widely distributed by the

Anti-Slavery Society, Harris called on Britons to do their duty and demand effective repatriation.[114]

William Cadbury was mainly responsible for the publication of a pamphlet that exposed the lot of serviçais on Príncipe plantations. In 1911, he agreed to pay for the printing of a report by Paiva De Carvalho, who was curator of the serviçais in Príncipe for five years up to 1907.[115] Cadbury's friend Alfredo da Silva published Carvalho's account in 1912 in Portugal under the title *Alma Negra*. Burtt translated selections from *Alma Negra* for the pamphlet issued by the British Anti-Slavery Society in 1913; these passages also appeared in the *Spectator*.[116] The excerpts described conditions in 1907: labor on Príncipe was slavery, the contracts for the laborers were "fiction," and it was all but impossible for a serviçal to lodge an appeal to the curator.[117] The publication of *Alma Negra* in Portugal and its excerpts in England created a storm of criticism directed at Silva by patriotic Portuguese. Students refused to attend his classes, and he feared that his house would be burned down. The rumor that Cadbury had helped Portuguese monarchists living in England in their struggle against the Republic caused at least part of the furor.[118]

The publication of the government's white paper in February 1913 spurred debate in the House of Lords on July 23, 1913. Discussion concentrated on the slow rate of repatriation of serviçais and the continuation of the slave trade in Angola. Lord Morley, lord president of the council, spoke for the government, having received from the Foreign Office a detailed, ten-page background document.[119] His response clearly spelled out how the Liberal government itself believed in a European mission to exploit and civilize so-called lesser beings in Africa. Morley admitted that there was a state of "bondage" in the labor involved, but, he added, "you cannot prevent the conditions of labour in the tropics under white management, and so forth, from being at present stage of human things unpleasantly akin to slavery." And certainly, he stated, there was slavery in Angola's interior, and he apologized for a Portuguese government that could not govern there: "This evil state of things goes on in regions so remote, so inaccessible." Although the Foreign Office could do little more than offer "counsel, advice, protest, and remonstrance," since Portugal was a sovereign nation, Britain had helped to gain the suspension of recruiting from Angola in 1909 and to secure new regulations. Moreover, repatriation was proceeding at a "proper and practicable rate, and every labourer who is entitled to repatriation shall be repatriated." While the repatriation fund had not been well handled, he noted, "we cannot administer that fund." He concluded by claiming that the Portuguese officials were "doing their best. Some of their local authorities are acting extraordinarily courageously."[120] Well might Morley downplay this entire issue of compulsory labor, for Great Britain and other colonial powers regularly utilized some version of it in their own possessions. In January 1913, Grey had rejected a call by a Portuguese official for an international conference on contract labor because "there would be great difficulty in arranging a conference of this kind."[121] Obviously, Grey did not want to be in a position of defending contract labor in British colonies.

Lord Cromer, responding to Morley, encouraged the cabinet to make the Portuguese government aware that Britain had no desire to defend the colonies of an ally that used slave labor, whereas Lord Lansdowne, who had served as the Conservative foreign secretary from 1900 to 1905, accepted that "the case is one where we must be content with a gradual improvement." At the same time, however, he warned of the danger of forceful public opinion being at odds with the government's international obligations.[122] Nevinson, who witnessed the debate, thought one of the peers gave a "good speech," but the "silly formalities" of the House of Lords offended him, and he derided the lord chancellor "walking to & fro from Woolsack to benches like a ferry boat. Certainly he earns his money by exercise." Nevinson, however, was amazed that the subject of slavery would actually be addressed: "Six years ago who c[oul]d have imagined such a debate on my old cause?"[123]

Plots against the Portuguese government once again pointed out the fragility of the new Republic. Although attempts to topple the government in April and July 1913 ended quickly in failure, old monarchists, workers in Lisbon and Oporto, and clergy all expressed their discontent with the government. This violence and unrest strengthened the doubts, expressed in the House of Lords debate and raised regularly by other critics, that the Portuguese government did not possess the power to implement reform in its empire.[124]

While many people openly questioned Britain's alliance with a country that used slave labor, the British government surreptitiously engaged in discussions with Germany to divide up Portugal's African colonies should Lisbon be unable to maintain them.[125] These negotiations relative to Portugal's empire were part of several attempts by Britain to improve relations with Germany in the years just before World War I.[126] Grey was at least partly motivated to provide for the possible dismantling of Portugal's colonies because of that country's inefficiency and of colonies that he described as "sinks of iniquity."[127] He often despaired of

Portugal's attitude toward native labor in West Africa and Mozambique.[128] He was caught in a difficult position, wishing to respect the Anglo-Portuguese alliance yet obviously chagrined by Lisbon's poor administration of its colonies. In a short memorandum submitted to the cabinet in July 1912, Grey wrote: "It is true that it would be shameful to throw over the Portuguese alliance in order to facilitate a division of her African colonies between Germany and ourselves. It is also true that it would be morally indefensible to protect the scandalous state of things that exists in the Portuguese colonies, but the alliance gives us no discretion in this matter."[129]

Lewis Harcourt, the colonial secretary and a Germanophile, took the lead in negotiations with Germany in 1911 in regard to Portugal's African colonies.[130] Modeled after the 1898 agreement between Germany and Britain, the proposed treaty provided that the two nations would aid Portugal financially, holding Portugal's colonies as collateral for loans extended. Should Portugal not be able to fulfill its financial obligations, Germany would gain authority over northern Mozambique, all of Angola except for an eastern slice that would be attached to Britain's northern Rhodesia, and the islands of São Tomé and Príncipe, while Britain would acquire control over much of Mozambique. Debate ensued within the British government, specifically in the Foreign Office, between Germanophiles and Francophiles. In the Foreign Office, Eyre Crowe and Arthur Nicolson feared that by failing to ensure the integrity of Portugal's colonies, Portuguese ports in the Azores might fall into the hands of a more powerful European nation, particularly Germany. Moreover, Britain's actions could alienate not only the Portuguese but also the French and the Belgians, who had important possessions in central Africa.

The treaty was initialed in 1913 but did not go into effect, as Grey insisted that this agreement as well as the earlier Anglo-German Convention of 1898 and the Anglo-Portuguese declaration of 1899 all had to be published before the treaty being negotiated went into effect. He argued that Britain's treaties should be made public; it was his way of assuring Portugal that Britain wanted to maintain the integrity of Portugal's colonies. Although this demand on Grey's part halted implementation of the treaty, it did not scuttle the agreement, as negotiations to activate the treaty were still taking place when war erupted in August 1914.[131]

Arthur Nicolson, a Foreign Office official, viewed this whole episode as "one of the most cynical diplomatic acts in my memory."[132] Government officials and many others, including Strachey, Morel, and William Cadbury, looked with favor on Germany as a colonial administrator, whereas Harris and Cromer would agree to German control only as a last resort.[133] These proponents of German rule overlooked or tolerated Germany's shameful record on native rights; it had carried out a massacre of Hereroes and other natives in its own West African possession between 1904 and 1907, an affair that was known to the British government.[134]

Reports from British consuls in West Africa throughout 1913 became more pessimistic about the effectiveness of Portuguese authorities protecting the serviçais on the islands and arranging for their return to Angola. These consuls, H. Hall Hall and Robert T. Smallbones, were far more critical of the Portuguese than their predecessors had been. According to these later consuls, natives welcomed repatriation, even under the most trying conditions. Smallbones offered two moving examples: "Even a woman who had had both her legs amputated below the knee insisted on wobbling on her hideous stumps to her native country, and a man whom also an accident on the plantation had deprived of both legs faced cheerfully the perils of the journey clinging to the back of a sturdy friend." Smallbones believed that of all the serviçais from Angola with whom he was acquainted, none had ever voluntarily entered the contracts, which were "deliberate untruths," and their recontracting was a "farce."[135] On one of Marquez de Valle Flôr's plantations, the serviçais "recontracted against their will," as they were "obviously intimidated," while Smallbones found those reengaging at Bela Vista "behaving like cattle driven by their taskmaster."[136] Smallbones believed that recontracting was so coerced that the only solution was to require compulsory repatriation of all of the serviçais; those who wished to sign on again should do so only after they returned to the mainland.[137] The British vice-consul in Fernando Po argued that while physical abuse was not prevalent among the Portuguese planters, "I believe I am right in stating that the planters are unable to understand or forgive a boy for wishing to return to his home, and that the general feeling among them is that 'he has no business to wish to leave at all.' This feeling is so strong that I can quite believe many planters do not realise the hardship they impose in preventing a boy's repatriation."[138]

The consuls maintained that repatriation was unnecessarily slow. Portuguese authorities were wrong when they contended that the lack of space on ships restricted the number of serviçais they could return to Angola. From May to July 1913, ships carried 2,189 serviçais to the islands while returning only 956 to Angola, even though they were carrying less cargo when leaving São Tomé and Príncipe.[139] Some serviçais, so distraught over their retention after fulfilling their contracts, fled the plantations; others were forcibly retained on the estate. Grey, obviously exasperated at the Portuguese actions, ordered Lancelot Carnegie, the British minister in Lisbon, to inform the Portuguese government that "His Majesty's Government are forced to the conclusion that the local authorities are again allowed the use of illegal practices in connection with the labor supply of the islands."[140] These were strong words from Grey. In August 1913, according to Hall Hall, when the curator threatened to repatriate serviçais if the plantation owners did not pay them higher wages retrospectively from an earlier date as decreed by law, the proprietors lodged a protest with the governor, who overruled the curator.[141] Hall Hall related that while plantations set up in Angola for repatriated workers appeared to be a "complete failure," most of the workers received a bonus, albeit too small to be of much help.[142] Smallbones found that measures to stop slave trading in the Bihé district of Angola were generally successful and that some of the repatriated serviçais in the area were surviving.[143]

Meanwhile, brutal treatment of labor directly implicating the British emerged in South America. The Putumayo territory of the Amazon region of Peru and neighboring countries was the scene of exploitation similar to the atrocities of the Congo, although on a smaller scale. Laborers, including blacks from the Caribbean and Native Americans, were coerced, by debt bondage and beatings even to the point of death, to extract and deliver rubber to company officials. These officials, representing the Peruvian Amazon Company, operated in remote areas beyond government authority, not unlike slave traders in the interior of Angola and parts of the Congo. Since the blacks recruited were from British colonies in the Caribbean and because there were British investors in the company, which made huge profits, the British government, spurred by journalists and humanitarians, investigated the matter and issued a white paper in 1912. Roger Casement, who had exposed the brutal and deadly practices of Leopold's agents in the Congo, helped once again as a consul to uncover the odious practices in Peru.[144] As a result, the Foreign Office required that its consuls become acquainted with British companies using native labor and report any abuses immediately to the Foreign Office.[145] The Anti-Slavery Society pushed the government to make any British nationals, as individuals or as representatives of a company, responsible for such actions.[146]

In April 1914, the government issued another white paper on Portuguese labor in West Africa, its third in three years.[147] Grey also announced that he was appointing a consul general for Portuguese West Africa, whose assignment would be to monitor the recruiting and use of labor in the area.[148] The letters in this white paper included many of those by Smallbones and Hall Hall, and they reflected the problems persistent in Angola and the islands, as well as the serviçais' enormous desire for repatriation. William Cadbury believed this the most valuable of the three white papers, and Burtt judged it "an official vindication of ten long years of work for freedom in Portuguese West Africa."[149] Harris rejoiced that slaveholding had finally been "officially confirmed" and pressed the British Foreign Office to make repatriation a reality.[150]

Nevinson, in reviewing the white paper, took a moment to reflect on the "long and bitter controversy" surrounding those who exposed the conditions of the natives in West Africa. He personally had been derided for his comments both by those with vested interests and by British government officials. The late Fox Bourne was "the only public man" who had supported him. Eventually, Burtt, William Cadbury, Swan, and Harris had all provided evidence confirming Nevinson's original disclosures. The Foreign Office, Nevinson added, had been extraordinarily slow in recognizing the validity of his allegations. This was due partly to the environment in which the consuls operated and to diplomatic practice: "A Consul needs exceptional courage to expose a vast system of established iniquity among the people with whom he has to live. Every inducement is offered him to minimize it or to hold his tongue. Then there are the diplomatic difficulties, especially the difficulty of telling an allied Government that its excellent regulations have no influence whatever upon reality. I suppose all officials feel bound to believe that official decrees are of some value, and that when a Government decree declares the slave-trade illegal, and all slaves liberated, the trade ceases and slaves are free." Recent consuls—most notably Robert Smallbones, Nevinson stressed—had the courage to visit the plantations on the islands and to tell the truth. According to Nevinson, one major task remained to be done: the repatriation of an estimated thirty thousand serviçais on the islands.[151]

Interest in Portuguese labor remained high. On July 10, 1914, an MP pressed Grey to address the scandalous shortage of money in the Portuguese repatriation fund.[152] A few days later, on July 16, 1914, a conference on slavery in Portuguese territories was held in London. While many present spoke of the marked improvement of conditions in the colonies, Strachey, Morel, and others emphasized that much remained to be done, as the Portuguese officials and planters persisted in tolerating the use of forced labor and still came up markedly short in repatriation.[153] Within two weeks, however, Britain and Europe's attention would be focused on World War I.

11 The Aftermath

The contest is not over; the cause is not won; and perpetual vigilance is still required to vindicate freedom against the perpetual encroachments of a lucrative and callous exploitation.

Henry W. Nevinson on labor in Portuguese West Africa in 1925

It is probable, on the evidence I collected, that there are now more slaves in Angola than there were fifty years ago.

Basil Davidson, 1954

Last week was a bad one for some very big corporate names. The problem was not about their results, but about their public images. Chocolate manufacturers such as Nestlé and Cadbury were accused of turning a blind eye to child slavery in the cocoa industry.

Financial Times, April 23, 2001

ALTHOUGH CADBURY BROS. expressed an interest in purchasing cocoa beans from São Tomé after the boycott of 1909, it never did. Instead, the Gold Coast became the primary source of the firm's raw material. As for the Portuguese, plantation owners were unable to satisfy the Quaker chocolate firms and the humanitarians that labor on the islands was truly voluntary or that the workers were properly treated. Eventually, São Tomé stepped out of the spotlight as one of the great cocoa producers in the world. Tragically, the islands and Angola continued to use coerced labor into the second half of the twentieth century. Not until São Tomé gained independence in 1975 did that practice disappear.

After 1914, most of those in Great Britain who had been involved in the controversy over Portuguese West African labor turned their attention to other matters. For William Cadbury and Henry Nevinson, however, the issue would remain in their minds for many years. The Anti-Slavery Society persevered in its mission to rid the world of slave labor, but even at the turn of the twenty-first century, use of coerced labor in West African cocoa farms persisted.

With the outbreak of World War I in 1914, the Anti-Slavery Society dropped its focus on Portuguese West Africa, although the society's *Reporter* ran missionaries' letters in 1915 testifying to a notable reduction of the slave trade in Angola.[1] The society concentrated its efforts on exposing abuses in Germany's colonies, and the Harrises became, in effect, spokespersons of the British government in the war against Germany.[2] The Foreign Office continued to receive reports from its consuls in West Africa and to publish white papers on labor in Portuguese West Africa in 1915 and 1917.[3] By 1915, William Cadbury was pleased to learn that workers were in every sense free and were not signing labor contracts under compulsion. There were still, however, far too many delays in repatriating laborers to Angola.[4] Consul Hall Hall reported in October 1916 that the mortality rate on the islands had dropped to 5 percent, and therefore, he suggested that the British chocolate firms should consider purchasing cocoa from the Portuguese colonies once again.[5] On February 27, 1917, Foreign Secretary Arthur James Balfour told the British minister to Lisbon that he should inform the Portuguese authorities that the boycott would most likely end, as the British government believed that labor on the islands was free and that repatriation was effective.[6] As a result of this report, the Cadbury firm wrote to Balfour on April 19, 1917, stating that the company would drop the boycott, although it would continue to purchase its cocoa beans from the Gold Coast colony where native landownership was so successful.[7] A week later, Joseph Burtt congratulated William Cadbury on what appeared to be "a culminating point of success in your African work." He added, "Your efforts have probably saved the lives of from 20 to 40 thousand natives. . . . Today there must be thousands of men and women in Africa who but for you would be toiling hopelessly in slavery, or lying dead in the grass by the route."[8] Unfortunately, the information about São Tomé was misleading. The Anti-Slavery Society pointed out that the annual mortality rate for the islands had been miscalculated: the correct figure was 10 percent, not 5 percent. The death rate was particularly high among children, although sleeping sickness on Príncipe had been reduced. In response, Cadbury Bros. promised that the company would continue its boycott until the death rate dropped to 5 percent.[9]

Burtt, Nevinson, and William Cadbury, along with the *Spectator* and the Anti-Slavery Society, occasionally criticized the treatment of laborers, but the Foreign Office turned a deaf ear to these comments and discontinued its consul in São Tomé after 1920.[10] In the postwar period, the Harrises pressed the League of

Nations to eradicate slavery throughout the colonial world. The British government, still distrusting the Anti-Slavery Society, outmaneuvered the Harrises and brought about a "slavery convention" in 1926 that was sadly limited in scope, giving colonial administrators a great deal of latitude in dealing with the conditions of colonial native labor.[11]

Slave trade in the interior of Angola ended shortly after World War I, when the Portuguese government finally gained control over that area. By 1921, the Republic abolished the practice of recontracting the laborers in São Tomé, so that repatriation became automatic.[12] There were exceptions, however, and the use of coerced labor remained common on the islands and in Angola.[13] In 1924, Edward Ross, an American sociology professor, and one of his colleagues spent several weeks in Angola, visiting villages without warning officials. They found repeated instances of forced labor, or, as they termed it, "state serfdom."[14] Ross submitted his *Report on Employment of Native Labor in Portuguese Africa* to the Temporary Slavery Commission of the League of Nations in 1925. Defenders of Portugal attacked the study and dismissed it as inaccurate; Portuguese colonial officers prosecuted Protestant missionaries who had provided evidence to Ross.[15]

In the second volume of his autobiography, written in 1925, Nevinson acknowledged that instances of enslavement in Angola and slave labor on the island continued: "The contest is not over; the cause is not won; and perpetual vigilance is still required to vindicate freedom against the perpetual encroachments of a lucrative and callous exploitation." He still believed that much good had been done since the time of his travel to Angola and São Tomé in 1905, when no serviçais had ever been released or repatriated. He hoped that on his deathbed he might have "a vision of 10,000 little black men and women dancing around my bed . . . and crying in grateful ecstasy: 'He sent us home! He sent us home!'"[16]

The Portuguese Republic fell in a 1926 coup due partly to international repercussions of the Ross report; it was shortly thereafter replaced by the dictatorial regime of António Salazar, who governed from the late 1920s until leaving office in 1968.[17] Salazar's government retained the Portuguese labor code of 1899, which required natives to be engaged in productive labor. Although the law pledged to protect natives, the reality was that the labor force suffered abuse from both the state and private owners.[18] As production of cocoa beans became less efficient and declined in the face of increasing competition from other West African colonies (the Gold Coast produced over 40 percent of the world's cocoa beans by 1925), the amount of labor required in São Tomé decreased. The labor force on the islands dropped from 38,000 in 1921 to 17,000 in 1954.[19] Laborers were primarily people contracted from Mozambique, Angola, and the Cape Verde Islands, and convicts sentenced to work in the colonies for "political" crimes. In the 1950s, Angolan mothers still lamented the loss of their sons who were seized and sent to São Tomé.[20]

Forced labor on European-owned plantations, however, was always relatively costly, be it in the flagrant slaving period at the turn of the twentieth century or the more tightly regulated coercion in the mid-1900s. Recruiting and transportation charges for laborers bound for São Tomé were always expensive, and mortality rates were high, so that replacements remained a constant necessity. With their high cost of inefficient labor and limited land, these plantations were, for much of the twentieth century, at a disadvantage compared to the more efficient, peasant-owned farms of West Africa that constantly cleared and opened fertile lands suitable for cocoa-bean trees.[21]

The economies of Portuguese West Africa and Mozambique were directly tied to their huge contingents of forced laborers who toiled in the Portuguese territories or in neighboring European colonies.[22] Basil Davidson, who became one of the leading Africanists of the twentieth century, helped to focus attention on Portuguese West Africa in the mid-1900s, much as Nevinson had in the early twentieth century. In his *African Awakening* (1955), he asserted that 379,000 Angolans were under forced-labor contracts in 1954.[23] Interestingly, Davidson was commissioned that year by *Harper's* to report on Angola, exactly fifty years following a similar commission given to Henry Nevinson. Davidson entered Angola via the Belgian Congo on the Benguela railway heading to Lobito on the coast. He found 2,018 *contradados*, akin to the serviçais of the early twentieth century, working on the railroad owned mainly by British investors. Davidson noted, "There is much less cruelty than in Nevinson's day. Otherwise the system is unchanged; and it is probable, on the evidence I collected, that there are now more slaves in Angola than there were fifty years ago." These slaves no longer walked to their destinations but arrived via truck or train.[24] Physical punishments were still meted out, in the form of the chicotte and the palmatória.[25] In 1952, the Portuguese government imprisoned an official who dared to berate the regime publicly for its labor practices in Angola.[26] In 1953, Portugal brutally suppressed an uprising by the local Creoles in São Tomé. The workers involved in this uprising, known as the Batepá Massacre, were not contract laborers from the continent but natives on the island who feared that the Portuguese intended to force them to work in the manner of contracted laborers.[27] Old Fort São Sebastian, which overlooks São Tomé's harbor, today serves as a museum displaying photographs depicting the horrendous reprisals carried out by authorities.

George Cadbury, patriarch of the family and the firm, remained convinced that the company took the correct path in pressing the Portuguese to transform their labor practices. He was inordinately proud of the leadership displayed by his nephew William Cadbury in this effort, and he was pleased that the Cadbury company was victorious over the *Standard* before what he considered to be an unfriendly Birmingham jury. Married twice, George Cadbury had eleven children. In World War I, his son Laurence John and daughter Molly served with ambulance units, while son Bertie enlisted in the Royal Naval Air Service and received medals for helping to shoot down two zeppelins. Following the war, George Cadbury arranged for the care of eighteen children from Vienna in Bournville, and he also contributed three tons of chocolate for children in Vienna. The Viennese referred to him as "Der Schokoladen Onkel" (the chocolate uncle), and grateful Viennese children sent two wreaths for his funeral. Although George Cadbury was forced to curtail his activities following a stroke in 1913, he continued to visit the factory regularly. On his death on October 24, 1922, at the age of eighty-three, he left an estate valued at £1,071,099. His ashes were buried in the Bournville village green, and a modest bust of him is located in a recessed area of the Friends Meeting House in Bournville.[28]

The *Daily News*, still under the ownership of members of the Cadbury family, merged with the *Daily Chronicle* in 1930 and lived on as the *News Chronicle*. The owner of the *Daily Mail* purchased the *News Chronicle* in 1960 and closed it immediately.[29] John St. Loe Strachey, who opened the columns of the *Spectator* to the comments of Nevinson, Harris, and other humanitarians, remained editor and owner of the influential Unionist weekly until 1925. He died at age sixty-seven in 1927.[30]

Edward Carson, the attorney for the *Standard* who so ruthlessly cross-examined George and William Cadbury in the trial, played a controversial role in British politics until his death in 1935. Shortly after the 1909 trial, he led Ulster's opposition to the Liberal government's Irish home rule bill, even to the point of organizing armed resistance. But this unlawful activity did not keep him from joining Herbert Asquith's coalition government in 1915, in which he served as attorney general for nearly eighteen months. He was part of David Lloyd George's government, initially as first lord of the Admiralty and then as a member of the war cabinet. He resigned from the cabinet in 1918 in protest to Lloyd George's plans for Irish home rule. A. J. P. Taylor judged Carson as "dangerous in opposition . . . ineffective in office."[31] Carson continued to defend Ulster interests after the war. In 1921, he entered the House of Lords as Baron Carson of Duncairn. He was regarded as one of the most powerful advocates at the bar and "a great orator—perhaps the greatest of his time, if the test of oratory is its power to move men to the very depth of their souls."[32] Carson was twice married and had five children.

Rufus Isaacs, Carson's opponent in the trial, enjoyed an exceptional public career. He represented Reading in the House of Commons from 1904 to 1913. Though never a notable speaker in Parliament, he served Asquith's Liberal government in the offices of solicitor general, attorney general, and lord chief justice. His record was blemished temporarily by the Marconi scandal, in which his purchase of stock was questionable at best. On being appointed lord chief justice, he was raised to the peerage as Baron Reading. While holding the office of lord chief justice from 1913 to 1921, he negotiated several agreements with the United States during World War I and served as ambassador to Washington, D.C., between 1918 and 1919. As viceroy of India from 1921 to 1926, he attempted to accommodate the increasing demands of the Indian National Congress and the Moslem League. He was briefly foreign secretary in Ramsay MacDonald's first National government in 1931. John Simon, Isaacs's legal associate in the 1909 trial, wrote that Isaacs was a "man of impressive personality and a winning charm" who exercised considerable "courtesy and tact." Isaacs had one son, and following the death of his first wife, he remarried in 1931. He died in 1935, the same year as Carson.[33]

John Simon was also an extraordinarily successful lawyer. A. G. Gardiner, editor of the *Daily News*, reported that Simon had "that rare gift of making difficult things seem simple and crooked things seem straight"; another author contended that no other barrister "could present a case more logically and more lucidly."[34] First elected to Parliament in 1906, Simon sat in the House of Commons until 1940, with a brief respite from 1918 to 1922. A Liberal, he held at various times the offices of home secretary, chancellor of the exchequer, solicitor general, attorney general, and lord chancellor. From 1931 to 1935, he had an unsuccessful term as foreign secretary. Powerful and respected, he was not loved. He was, if anything, too reserved and private to be an inspirational leader. Twice married, he died in 1954 at age eighty.[35]

The presiding judge at the trial in Birmingham, William Pickford, was promoted to the court of appeal in 1914. He was a member and chair of the

1916–1917 Dardanelles Committee, which inquired into the failed British effort in the Gallipoli campaign. He was raised to the peerage as Baron Sterndale in 1918. In his younger days, he was an avid bicyclist, cricketer, and climber and later was "as good a judge of port as he was of men and things."[36] He died in 1923 at the age of seventy-four.

Edward Grey served as foreign secretary for eleven very long and crisis-ridden years until December 1916. A biographer's description of Grey's life stresses that he much preferred the outdoors but found himself occupied for long hours in his London office.[37] He loved bird-watching and fly-fishing, on which he wrote a book in 1899; it has since become a classic. He was regarded as knowledgeable and of good judgment in foreign affairs, although he traveled little outside Britain. According to a contemporary observer, Grey's "habitual calmness," even in the midst of strife, sometimes "proved an irritant."[38] He is often judged as having been much too secretive as a foreign minister. Grey's basic policy was not to side with any one group in Europe but to walk a delicate middle line to help ensure peace. He proved willing to negotiate with Germany, even though there was often friction between the two nations. As foreign secretary when World War I erupted in 1914, he has been severely criticized by scholars and politicians for failing to spell out clearly to other powers, particularly to Germany, how Britain would respond in the event of a conflict.[39] He entered the House of Lords in 1916 as Lord Grey of Falloden, taking the title of his beloved home in Northumberland. He carried out government tasks after leaving the Foreign Office, but his increasing blindness limited such activities. He wrote extensively even as he lost his sight and published an account of his public life in *Twenty-Five Years, 1892–1916* (1925). He died in 1933. Twice married, he had no children.[40]

One of Grey's fiercest critics was E. D. Morel. His Congo Reform Association met for the last time in June 1913, its mission on the whole achieved. In the process of exposing Leopold II, Morel had become, according to one scholar, "the greatest British investigative journalist of his time." Earlier, in 1912, Morel was adopted as a Liberal candidate for Parliament by Birkenhead. A handsome offer of financial support from William Cadbury made this career move possible.[41] Morel was forced to resign as a Liberal candidate during World War I because of his criticism of Britain's participation in that conflict. During the war, he helped to establish the Union of Democratic Control, the main voice of dissent, and, for his efforts, he was criticized by friend and foe. He was imprisoned in 1917 and 1918 for violating war regulations, and his six months in the harsh Pentonville prison environment weakened him mentally and physically and may have led to his death on November 12, 1924, at the age of fifty-one. He was survived by his wife and four children. Following the war, Morel had continued to censure European colonial administrations and to defend the right of natives to landownership. He dedicated his book *The Black Man's Burden* (1920) to William Cadbury and his wife, Emmeline Hannah; it contains a substantial chapter on Angola and São Tomé. In the volume, he praised William Cadbury for recognizing manufacturers' obligation to assure that the materials they purchased were produced under humane conditions.[42] Abandoning the Liberal Party for the Labour Party, Morel was elected to Parliament for Dundee, Scotland, defeating Winston Churchill in the 1922 election. Although recognized as knowledgeable on foreign affairs and a formidable critic of the Treaty of Versailles, Morel was passed over by Ramsay MacDonald for foreign secretary in 1924.[43]

John Holt, the successful Liverpool-based shipper who generously backed Morel's Congo Reform Association and respected Cadbury's efforts in Portuguese West Africa, suffered an incapacitating stroke in 1910. His admiration for William Cadbury and Morel was evident in a letter he wrote to Cadbury in August 1910: "It is . . . a source of great satisfaction to me that I . . . know that there are such men as yourself and Morel, who are striving to help the helpless ones of the earth."[44] When Holt died in 1915 at age seventy-three, he left an annuity of £100 to Morel and his wife.[45]

John and Alice Harris jointly filled the office of organizing secretary of the Anti-Slavery and Aborigines' Protection Society from 1910 to 1934; from 1934 to 1940, John Harris alone was the organization's parliamentary secretary. His "flair for publicity" strengthened the society and increased its membership.[46] Harris represented North Hackney as a Liberal MP between 1923 and 1924 and worked tirelessly for the League of Nations Union. He was knighted for his humanitarian endeavors in 1933. John Simon remarked that Harris "possessed three attributes essential in a great crusade—'boundless enthusiasm and optimism, detailed knowledge, and courage!'"[47] He died in 1940 at age sixty-five, survived by his widow and four children. Alice Harris, who utilized photographs as evidence of slavery and was a very effective public speaker, retained close ties to the Anti-Slavery Society until her death in 1970.[48]

Travers Buxton, who helped the Harrises run the Anti-Slavery Society, edited the *Anti-Slavery Reporter and Aborigines' Friend* until his death in January 1945. An officer in the Marylebone Presbyterian Church, he devoted his life to working with various volunteer societies. According to the *Manchester Guardian*, Buxton "probably served on more of them than any other Londoner of his generation."[49] The

British Anti-Slavery and Aborigines' Protection Society lives on into the twenty-first century as Anti-Slavery International, with offices at the Thomas Clarkson House in South London. It still publishes the *Reporter* and fights against slavery as it did in the early twentieth century.

The thoughtful and hardworking Joseph Burtt involved himself in several humanitarian causes. He organized the Friends' relief for Russia in 1916 and investigated the plight of Armenian exiles in Greece and Smyrna in 1925, from which emerged his study *The People of Ararat* (1926). In this work, Burtt eloquently examined the Turkish massacres of the Armenians in the 1890s and in World War I, and he strongly questioned Britain's subsequent inaction. Several of his poems, published in 1929, relate to his African experience. He was a Fellow of the Royal Geographical Society. According to the *Friend*, he was "blessed with a gay, affectionate disposition, a handsome appearance which lasted throughout life, unbounded energy and a lively sense of humour. He loved the earth and enjoyed outdoor activities. He had a wide knowledge of poetry [and] was a gifted reciter and an impressive speaker."[50] Burtt and his wife had two sons. He died in 1939 at the age of seventy-six.

William A. Cadbury, like Burtt, involved himself in Friends' projects overseas, and he was for a long time clerk of his Friends' Monthly Meeting. Active in Birmingham politics, he served on the city council and as an alderman. He was lord mayor from 1919 to 1921 and was made a freeman of the city in 1938. His community interests included the Birmingham hospitals, public health and housing, the public library, and the art gallery. In 1930, he was awarded an honorary doctor of laws degree by the University of Birmingham. While active on committees, he was, according to one commentator, naturally shy. He and his wife, Emmeline, had six children. Cadbury was athletic early in life and enjoyed playing cricket and football. In 1950, he had a leg amputated. Cadbury died at age ninety in 1957.[51]

The *Birmingham Mail* headed its obituary of Cadbury "Birmingham Freeman Who Fought Slavery."[52] In many ways, Cadbury's campaign of the early twentieth century was the defining moment of his life. On his death, the *Friend* wrote: "His greatest contribution to public and business life was his strict integrity, and in more than one capacity he has been described as 'a rock.' If he believed in a cause or a person, however unpopular, he stood by them against all criticism. Nothing was too much trouble."[53]

William Cadbury long remained defensive in regard to São Tomé, believing that he and his firm had been unfairly treated, mainly by Nevinson. In October 1949, the *Friend* carried a brief article that included this statement: "Nor must we forget H. W. Nevinson's difficulties in persuading Quaker cocoa firms to boycott the importation of slave-grown cocoa from Angola [*sic*], a boycott which was not imposed till 1909."[54] Later in 1949, Cadbury wrote a very short work on the affair entitled *Inside History*, perturbed because the article in the *Friend* illustrated that "the old fable that the half-hearted Cocoa Firms had to be whipped into action by an original disclosure of fact by H. W. Nevinson" was still alive after forty years. There was virtually no new information in this short document. Cadbury stressed that he turned to Morel "for *consultation and advice*. He remained all through my confidant, and we agreed on every point of the campaign," which was to gather information on the Portuguese mainland and island colonies (emphasis in original).

One American historian contends that this statement supports a conclusion that William Cadbury had, from the beginning of the affair, cooperated with Morel to delay action by the Cadbury company until an alternative source of cocoa beans had been secured.[55] Cadbury, however, did not begin his contact with Morel until 1903, so for at least the first two years of the controversy, Morel was not a factor. In *Inside History*, Cadbury wrote that he had turned down Nevinson's offer "to go out and investigate on our behalf." He added, "I have no doubt that Nevinson left, confirmed in his opinion that I was playing for 'delay and safety,' and from that time on he became the open opponent of our programme." He continued: "We have never at any time replied directly or in print to any of his attacks, and neither his demand for immediate boycott, or his subsequent articles from Harper's Magazine 1905–6, reprinted in a book, had the slightest effect on a policy which was decided upon long before he appeared on the scene, and followed out step by step in consultation with E. D. Morel, who gave us never failing support in the African Mail—the paper of which he was Editor." Cadbury denied the accusation "that we were only spurred to action by Nevinson's articles: this is untrue, and no one knew better than H. W. Nevinson, and the knowledge added bitterness to all his subsequent attacks. . . . I add to the credit of H.W.N. that he never dared to question the integrity of Joseph Burtt." After praising Burtt, Cadbury closed with this comment: "The Trial made me many friends, and two years after I entered the City Council as Councillor for Kings Norton Ward."[56]

William Cadbury was chairman of the board of Cadbury Bros. from 1922 to 1937. The Cadbury signature on many of the firm's chocolate products and on the storefronts of buildings familiar from the post–World War II period until today is that of William Cadbury. In 1919, Fry, the Bristol chocolate firm, merged with Cadbury Bros. under the name British Cocoa and Chocolate Company, and later, in 1935, Cadbury completely absorbed Fry. The firm of Cadbury merged with

Schweppes in 1969 to create a giant international confectionery and drinks corporation.[57] Cadbury World, an entertainment center highlighting the history and development of chocolate and of Cadbury Bros. and offering a tour of part of the Cadbury factory, was opened at the Bournville plant in 1990. There is no mention of the trial in its displays.[58] A member of the Cadbury family remained on the board of the corporation until 2000, when Dominic Cadbury retired as chairman. The family continues to maintain its leadership presence in the Birmingham community, including involvement in the Bournville Trust, the housing estate founded by George Cadbury.[59]

Henry W. Nevinson covered conflicts and engaged in movements to enhance human life for much of the rest of his long career. He contributed to the *Nation* until 1923, while also writing for other newspapers, including stints with the *Daily News*.[60] He was that newspaper's Berlin correspondent when World War I erupted in 1914. He covered various fronts of the war, among them the Dardanelles, about which he published a book and where he suffered a head injury. Toward the end of the war, he and a press officer accepted the surrender of a few German soldiers in the Somme area; one of the Germans thought that Nevinson was an army officer, which must have pleased him. Journalist Philip Gibbs remarked that as a war correspondent, Nevinson "received salutes from all the army, because he looked as a 'field marshal' would like to look."[61] Nevinson wrote sympathetically of the brutal conflict in Ireland that followed World War I. His classic, three-volume autobiography appeared in the 1920s. A scholar in his own right, he penned a study of Goethe, published in 1931.[62] One of his admirers wrote in 1932 that "in between his many campaigns the man has written—Lord knows how—sheaves of exquisite impressions, sheaves of fine essays, sheaves of Knightly leaders, and a shelf-full of great books."[63] Following the death of his long-estranged wife, Margaret, who was a justice of the peace and a Poor Law guardian (one who helped administer relief to the poor), Nevinson married Evelyn Sharp, a leader in the women's suffrage movement. From his first marriage, he had a daughter and a son, the painter C. R. W. Nevinson.[64] When Nevinson died at age eighty-five in 1941, a writer remarked that at Nevinson's request "[Beethoven's] Allegretto to the Seventh Symphony was played at his funeral. . . . It is not surprising that Nevinson loved the great musician for he loved beauty in all its forms—prose and poetry, music and art, mountain and river. His life was a great piece of music, for it was devoted to noble causes and he sought ever to bring to the forgotten and the unknown, to the poor and the oppressed, not only liberty and justice, but human sympathy, fellowship and affection."[65] Henry Brailsford, who met Nevinson in Greece in 1897 and remained close to him for the rest of his life, believed that of all Nevinson's many crusades, "his struggle to end the slave trade in Portuguese Angola was the most difficult and prolonged," but he "made us understand at what price we drank cocoa in England." Brailsford pointed out that the slaves never thanked him, for they "have never heard his name."[66]

The *Friend* acknowledged that he could make people uncomfortable but always for a good purpose: "Friends found themselves side by side with him in many causes. Perhaps we sometimes winced at his criticisms or irony. But there was piercing truth and not malice in them."[67] The hypersensitive and brilliant Nevinson was no easy colleague. A. G. Gardiner, his editor at the *Daily News*, remarked on Nevinson's death that Saint Peter "will find him something of a handful, for I can't imagine him comfortable in heaven with no heroics to indulge in & nothing to do but twang a harp."[68]

Opposition to Portugal's rule in Africa mounted in the post–World War II era. Armed resistance broke out in Angola in 1961 and led to fifteen years of increasing violence there and in Mozambique. The revolution of April 25, 1974, overthrew the dictatorial regime in Lisbon and introduced political change in Portugal. In 1975, the Portuguese government recognized the independence of Angola, Mozambique, and São Tomé. In the postindependence period, Angola suffered through one of the bloodiest civil wars in Africa, fed for many years by the Cold War's prime competitors, the United States and the Soviet Union. Fighting broke out among three factions, the Popular Movement for the Liberation of Angola (MPLA) supported by the Soviet Union and Cuba, the National Front for the Liberation of Angola (FNLA) aided by the United States, and the National Union for Total Independence of Angola (UNITA) under the leadership of Jonas Savimbi. The MPLA gained control, and the United States switched its support to Savimbi and the UNITA. With these two factions drawing on the mineral resources of the nation, including oil and diamonds, the civil war raged for the rest of the century. The conflict cost between one-half to two million lives, with many dying from malnutrition. By 2000, Angola's life expectancy was forty-two years, and the death rate among children was notoriously high.[69] The death of Savimbi in 2002 and the collapse of UNITA brought an uneasy end to the fighting, leaving some room for hope of a lasting peace. Stories of family reunions after separations of many years are reminders of similar gatherings that would have occurred in the repatriation of serviçais earlier in the twentieth century.[70]

The micronation of São Tomé and Príncipe did not suffer from bitter factional fighting. The country has, however, struggled to establish political stability and a viable economy. Efforts by São Tomé's government to expand the production of cocoa beans and to diversify the one-crop economy failed after 1975. In the colonial era, the Portuguese had provided all the expertise and leadership, so when they fled São Tomé following independence, only inexperienced workers remained. The government took over control of the large plantations, but, caught in an extraordinarily competitive market and in a Cold War era in which the United States was unwilling to purchase basic goods from a leftist-governed nation; it was unable to restore lasting prosperity to the cocoa fields or any other part of the economy.[71] São Tomé revised its constitution and moved from a one-party state to a multiparty democracy, with its first free elections in 1991. Subsequent elections have brought a relatively stable, if inefficient, government, which has been able to tap financial resources from abroad, including investments by several European countries, Taiwan, and the United Nations. Although the government is heavily indebted, there is no apparent malnutrition in the population, and basic education is available for all children; sadly, there is a marked absence of reading material for the people.

In 2000, I traveled to the island of São Tomé with my wife, Ellen. The primary purpose of the trip was to view the cocoa plantations for ourselves. We saw three of the plantations that William Cadbury visited between 1908 and 1909—Boa Entrada, Monte Café, and Água Izé—and went to a fourth, Agostino Neto. Most of the buildings and the Decauville narrow-gauge rails on these plantations date from the early twentieth century. Several structures on the roça Boa Entrada shown in photographs in Francisco Mantero's *Manual Labour in S. Thomé and Principe* (1910) are still standing, although they are considerably more shabby. Monte Café is a functioning plantation, but depressing poverty hangs over Água Izé. The fourth plantation, originally Rio Do Ouro, was renamed Agostino Neto following São Tomé's independence, in honor of the president of the MPLA who led Angola to independence and served as its first president.

The town of São Tomé, with a population estimated at 67,000, is by far the largest urban center in São Tomé and Príncipe, which has a total of about 161,000 people. Although the main roads in the town and throughout the northern part of the island are hard surfaced and well maintained, there is remarkably little traffic. Open-bed trucks hauling people and goods, plus a few conspicuous sport utility vehicles, share the road with a taxi fleet of old, yellow-painted Toyotas driven by entrepreneurial locals. Many of the buildings in São Tomé, mostly from the early twentieth century, are in disrepair. The old Fort São Sebastian still protects the harbor, which is too shallow to accommodate large ships. Efforts to promote tourism on these islands, billed as a "Paradise on Earth," have proven difficult.[72] The islands have few transportation ties to either Europe or nearby Africa, and facilities for tourists, such as restaurants and hotels, are lacking. There is also a rainy season from October to May. Idyllic beaches and friendly people are not, in themselves, sufficient to attract many visitors.

Life in São Tomé could change dramatically in the near future. As the United States seeks a dependable alternative source of oil to that of the Middle East, Americans have looked increasingly to the Gulf of Guinea as well as to Angola. São Tomé stands to benefit from the drilling, as bidding for licenses to develop the oil fields could bring untold wealth to the tiny nation, now the most heavily indebted in the world. The United States has also made inquiries about placing a military facility on the island. The impact of additional revenue—by no means all positive—and the presence of a sizable foreign contingent on a tiny, sleepy, out-of-the-way nation would be considerable.[73] The most immediate repercussion of the potential oil bonanza was a military coup in July 2003. The leaders of the rebellion claimed that they wanted to provide a more equitable distribution of São Tomé's wealth. After a week of negotiations, led by officials from neighboring nations, the rebels relinquished control after being promised that they would have a role in deciding the allocation of future oil income.[74]

Nearly one hundred years after *Cadbury Bros., Ltd. v. The Standard Newspaper, Ltd.*, the purchase of cocoa beans from plantations utilizing slave labor still troubles the giant chocolate company. On April 23, 2001, the *Financial Times* ran an editorial stating: "Last week was a bad one for some very big corporate names. The problem was not about their results, but about their public images. Chocolate manufacturers such as Nestlé and Cadbury were accused of turning a blind eye to child slavery in the cocoa industry."[75] The newspaper's remarks were made in response to an international incident followed closely by humanitarians and the media. In April 2001, a crippled ship, the *M. V. Etireno*, limped into the port city of Cotonou, in the West African nation of Benin. On board were twenty-three children, most of them under the age of ten, destined to serve as domestic servants or to work on small cocoa farms.[76] This incident was simply the most dramatic in a series of reports asserting that child labor remains a problem in West Africa, caused by the desperate poverty of countries such as Mali, Burkina Faso, and Benin, from which children are sent out or sometimes kidnapped to work in the more prosperous countries of Ivory Coast and Gabon.[77] The number of child laborers and of those actually in slavery is difficult to determine, just as it was a century ago; it is no easy task to visit the farms, many of them in remote areas. Anti-Slavery International cited a 2002 study estimating that 284,000 children work in West Africa's cocoa industry, up to 2,500 of them in slavery, and another source suggests that there may be 15,000 child slaves in the Ivory Coast alone.[78]

One of the reasons for the increased use of inexpensive child laborers in recent years has been the sharp drop in the price of cocoa beans.[79] In late 2000, Channel 4 in the United Kingdom televised a program showing in grim detail evidence of slave labor in the cocoa fields of the Ivory Coast. The Cadbury company, in response to a letter from a concerned citizen, remarked: "We were completely unaware of the allegations concerning cocoa growing in the Cote d'Ivoire. . . . Of course we share your concern and are deeply shocked and horrified at the scenes we witnessed." The firm pointed out that most of its cocoa was purchased from Ghana, where there was "absolutely no evidence to suggest that slavery is a feature of cocoa cultivation." Nevertheless, the company, as a "part of the international chocolate industry," was working with others "to ensure that such practices do not occur." The letter included this pledge: "Our business is firmly based on the principles of honesty and integrity in all of our dealings and we will do everything in our power to ensure that these principles are not compromised."[80]

Several studies, some of them commissioned by the cocoa industry, have been published recently about child labor on cocoa farms in West Africa.[81] Chocolate manufacturers fear that humanitarians in the Western world will call for a boycott of chocolate products to protest the child and slave labor used by farmers who produce cocoa beans.[82] And they are right to be concerned. Chocolate is big business. In 2002, Americans spent $8.5 billion on chocolate products, Britons £4.1 billion (about $6 billion). In 1998, each person in the United States consumed, on the average, 12.2 pounds of chocolate a year, in Britain, 19.07 pounds. The *Economist* reported in 1989 that the British spent one-third more money on chocolate than on bread.[83]

If Henry Nevinson were writing in the early twenty-first century, he would demand that the huge international chocolate conglomerates use some of their enormous resources to ensure that the cocoa farmers earn a decent price for their products and that the farmers never use slave laborers, whether children or adults. As he did in the opening years of the twentieth century, Nevinson would expect humanitarian organizations, including the United Nations Children's Fund (UNICEF) and Anti-Slavery International, to keep the issue forcefully before the public, lest interest dissipate in "modern slavery."[84]

ACKNOWLEDGMENTS

Many people made this book possible, and to all of them I extend my thanks. Three of my colleagues in the history department at Youngstown State University read all or part of the manuscript: Martin Berger pointed out many inconsistencies, Daniel Ayana corrected several aspects of European involvement in Africa, and I enjoyed and benefited from my new colleague David Simonelli's enthusiasm for the project, his extraordinary knowledge of modern British history, and his pointed and often satirical remarks on several drafts of the book. Pres Crews, my friend of over forty years and a devotee of British history, offered his sage advice on the manuscript. My brother-in-law George Ohlson, an astute copy editor, managed to simplify what appeared to him to be hopelessly confusing sentences. Michael Rowlinson not only read the manuscript, encouraging me to clarify the text and more sharply define British institutions and events, but also shared with me information about Cadbury Bros. Tom Kennedy, a fellow historian and a friend dating back to graduate school days, offered insight into personalities of the period and broadened my understanding of the Society of Friends. Gerhard Seibert saved me from errors in Portuguese terms and in São Tomé history. William Gervais Clarence-Smith directed me to valuable studies on colonialism and responded to my queries on Portuguese history. Thanks also to Judith Filkin and Tony Hunt for their hospitality in London, and to Sir Martin Gilbert for his support of my project. I enjoyed meeting Sir Adrian Cadbury, former CEO and president of Cadbury Schweppes, who is deeply interested in the history of Cadbury Bros. He responded kindly to my requests for information.

I appreciated the support of my department colleagues at Youngstown State University, particularly Martha Pallante, chair, and of the deans of the College of Arts and Sciences, Barbara Brothers and Robert Bolla. A sabbatical and a research professorship from the university enabled me to complete this book. My graduate assistants Elizabeth Glasgow and Raymond Krohn cheerfully trooped to the library to follow up on a succession of queries. Thanks also go to Carl Leet, university photographer, who reworked the many photographs; to Craig Campbell, of the geography department, who introduced me to the world of mapmaking and encouraged me to draw two of the maps; and to Maureen Wilson and her staff at the university's Media and Academic Computing Services, for helping to prepare the maps.

As anyone involved in historical research knows, librarians are the lifeblood of the profession. We simply can't do our jobs without them. Jean Romeo and her librarians at Youngstown State University's Maag Library enthusiastically responded to my many requests for information, while Amy Kyte facilitated the acquisition of material through OhioLINK. Louisa Berger at the Public Library of Youngstown and Mahoning County proved to be a goldmine of information. Special thanks to the librarians and staff members of various British libraries and archives: British Library, National Archives (Public Record Office and Historical Manuscripts Commission), House of Lords Record Office, British Library of Political and Economic Science, Friends House Library (London), Anti-Slavery International, Public Record Office of Northern Ireland, Birmingham University Library Special Collections, Birmingham Central Library, Woodbrooke, Cadbury Schweppes Information and Library Service, Bodleian Library, and Rhodes House Library. I extend special recognition to Cadbury Schweppes Ltd., which presented the extensive Cadbury Papers associated with the trial of 1909 to the University of Birmingham Library Special Collections in 1972. These papers are indispensable to anyone studying the trial. Thanks also to the institutions who responded to my inquiries about photographs.

I am grateful to Gillian Berchowitz, senior editor, and her staff at Ohio University Press/Swallow Press for the care and thoroughness they put forth in publishing my book. I also thank the friendly people of São Tomé for making our visit to their fascinating and beautiful island so rewarding and enjoyable.

My family was also involved in this project. Our grandchildren never quite figured out why I would so willingly spend hours in my study working on the manuscript. My daughter-in-law Maria, in the midst of running a busy household, read the entire manuscript over a couple of days and raised valuable questions about the contexts. Our children, Lorie, Ruth, Peter, and Jody, were consistently interested in and proud of the project. This book is at least as much my wife Ellen's book as it is mine. Ellen served as my research assistant, traveling many miles within Great Britain and to Portugal, most of it by bicycle, and to São Tomé. Throughout it all, she continued to feed me, encourage me, and love me. She read the manuscript many times, and I know that she sometimes feared that her criticisms were too harsh. Our joint work, however, not only improved the fruit of our labor, but deepened our relationship.

Any errors which remain in this book are mine, and not those of the many readers and editors who tried their hardest to set me straight.

Appendix

The Standard EDITORIAL OF SEPTEMBER 26, 1908

We learn with profound interest from Lisbon that Mr. Cadbury, the head of the famous firm of cocoa manufacturers, is about to go to Angola, where he will investigate for himself the manner in which labourers are "recruited" for the plantations of the islands which supply Messrs. Cadbury with the raw material of their justly celebrated products. Mr. Cadbury then proposes to go to Sao Thomé itself to inquire into the allegation that "conditions of slavery" prevail in that profitable possession of our ancient allies the Portuguese. We congratulate Mr. Cadbury upon his journey, which does not come too soon. As a philanthropist and friend of humanity Mr. Cadbury's reputation stands as high as his renown for the sale of cocoa. In his model village and factories of Bournville the welfare of the workpeople is studied as closely as the quality of the goods manufactured. There are lecture-rooms and gymnasia, and no public-houses; the young ladies in the firm's employ visit the swimming bath weekly, and they have prayers every morning before beginning their honourable task of supplying the British public with wholesome food. But in this latter useful process they are not the only agents. The white hands of the Bournville chocolate makers are helped by other unseen hands some thousands of miles away, black and brown hands, toiling in plantations, or hauling loads through swamp and forest. In the plenitude of his solicitude for his fellow-creatures Mr. Cadbury might have been expected to take some interest in the owners of those same grimed African hands, whose toil also is so essential to the beneficent and lucrative operations of Bournville. His sympathies are wide and readily aroused, nor are they limited by race and colour, especially where the Government of his own country is concerned. He is understood to be largely interested in a newspaper which is the champion of the down-trodden coloured person groaning under the oppressions of British justice. To his alert conscience the thought of Chinese labour imported into South Africa was a loathing and an offence. What though the astute Celestial was under no compulsion to go, though he was only too delighted to have the chance of earning wages beyond his dreams, though the nicest precautions of the British and the Chinese Governments were taken to secure him against wrong or maltreatment, though it was proved indeed that he was better off than nearly all his countrymen and a good many of our own? All this was nothing. The hint, the suspicion, the remote possibility of slavery is enough to stir the anger of such a sensitive soul, and Mr. Cadbury's journal denounced the accursed thing without stint or measure.

Such being the case, we can only express our respectful surprise that Mr. Cadbury's voyage of discovery has been deferred so long. One might have supposed that Messrs. Cadbury would themselves have long ago ascertained the condition and circumstances of those labourers on the West Coast of Africa and the islands adjacent who provide them with raw material. That precaution does not seem to have been taken. It was left to others to throw light on those favoured portions of the earth's surface which enjoy the rule of Portugal in Africa. Other observers have anticipated Mr. Cadbury and have described the state of affairs in certain of these districts. In order to secure definite information the proprietors of an American magazine, nearly four years ago, commissioned Mr. H. W. Nevinson to investigate that part of Africa. No person could be better qualified. Mr. Nevinson has travelled widely, studied many lands and peoples, and brought to bear on all he has seen a penetrating observation and a trained judgment; he writes very brilliantly, but very moderately; and though he has strong political opinions his honesty can no more be questioned than his competence. His journey was undertaken four years ago; the record of its results appeared soon afterwards. It is a book of great power, transparent sincerity, and the most painful interest. No Englishman can read it without a certain sense of shame; for it shows that the negro slavery, which it is one of the glories of our history to have assailed so often, still flourishes in its wickedness and its cruelty in those Portuguese colonies. It is not called slavery; "contract labour" they name it now; but in most of its essentials it is that monstrous trade in human flesh and blood against which the Quaker and Radical ancestors of Mr. Cadbury thundered in the better days of England. At much personal risk to himself Mr. Nevinson visited the Angola towns, and explored the Hinterland of the interior. He saw many of the deeds and scenes which were the nightmare of a past generation; he tells us that men and women, boys and girls are still purchased from the chiefs, or kidnapped, or decoyed; they are still brought down in gangs, manacled and shackled, to the coast; they are still flogged and driven like cattle; and still, as in the past, they are left to die in the forest or slaughtered when their strength gives out on the march. He declares that the so-called contract is a farce; the stolen negro, brought before a Portuguese official hundreds of miles from his home, is no more a free agent than his forefathers sent under the hatches of the Guinea slaver to America two hundred years ago. And once on the plantations he is a slave for life. He does not seem to be tortured, and he is not starved; but he has no freedom; he is herded into compounds (think of that, Mr. Cadbury; compounds!); he works from sunrise to sunset, year in, year out; the children born to him are the property of his owner; he is beaten if he does not work hard enough, and nearly whipped to death if he tries to escape. Portuguese law requires that he shall be "repatriated" (it is another term Mr. Cadbury should appreciate!) in five years; but he is never repatriated, for he either dies before the five years are out or is kept to his servitude till his death: about one of these free and independent labourers in every five dies in the first year. And the worst of all this slavery and slave-driving and slave-dealing is brought about by the necessity of providing a sufficient number of hands to grow and pick cocoa on the islands of Principe and Sao Thomé, the islands which feed the mills and presses of Bournville! Such is the terrible indictment, made, as we have said, by a writer of high character and reputation on the evidence of his own eyesight. There is only one thing more amazing than his statements: and that is the strange tranquillity with which they were received by those virtuous people in England whom they intimately concerned.

ABBREVIATIONS

APS	Aborigines' Protection Society
BFASS	British and Foreign Anti-Slavery Society
CBBM	Cadbury Brothers' Board Minutes
CP	Cadbury Papers
CRA	Congo Reform Association
DNB	*Dictionary of National Biography*
FO	Foreign Office
MP	Member of Parliament

NOTES

Chapter 1

1. All references in this chapter, including quotations, come from Henry W. Nevinson, *A Modern Slavery*, with an introduction by Basil Davidson (New York: Schocken, 1968; first published 1906).

2. That Brussels Conference also restricted the sale of arms to Africans, thus eliminating any opportunity they might have to defend themselves from the likes of the slave traders. Suzanne Miers, "The Brussels Conference of 1889–1890: The Place of the Slave Trade in the Policies of Great Britain and Germany," in Prosser Gifford and Wm. Roger Louis, eds., *Britain and Germany in Africa* (New Haven, Conn.: Yale University Press, 1967), 83–118; Suzanne Miers, *Britain and the Ending of the Slave Trade* (New York: Africana Publishing, 1975), 261–70.

3. For a sample labor contract, see William A. Cadbury, *Labour in Portuguese West Africa*, 2nd ed. (London: George Routledge & Sons, 1910; reprint, New York: Negro Universities Press, 1969), appendix E.

4. Three chapters in the book *A Modern Slavery*—chapter 4, "On the Route to the Slave Centre"; chapter 5, "The Agents of the Slave-Trade"; and chapter 8, "Savages and Missions"—were not published in *Harper's*. *Harper's* articles included more photographs than did the book.

5. For a recent study of labor conditions on the islands during the period of Nevinson's trip, see William Gervase Clarence-Smith, "Labour Conditions in the Plantations of São Tomé and Príncipe, 1875–1914," *Slavery and Abolition* 4 (April 1993): 149–67.

Chapter 2

1. William Gervase Clarence-Smith, *Cocoa and Chocolate, 1765–1914* (London: Routledge, 2000), 2.

2. Sophie D. Coe and Michael D. Coe, *The True History of Chocolate* (London: Thames & Hudson, 1996); Arthur W. Knapp, *The Cocoa and Chocolate Industry: The Tree, the Bean, the Beverage* (London: Sir Isaac Pitman & Sons, [1923]); Tim Richardson, *Sweets* (London: Bloomsbury, 2002), 217–44.

3. Ian Campbell Bradley, *Enlightened Entrepreneurs* (London: Weidenfeld and Nicolson, 1987), 120–21; J. Othick, "The Cocoa and Chocolate Industry in the Nineteenth Century,"

in Derik Oddy and Derik Miller, eds., *The Making of the Modern Diet* (London: Croom Helm, 1976), 77–90.

4. James Walvin, *The Quakers: Money and Morals* (North Pomfret, Vt.: John Murray, 1997).

5. For background material on Cadbury Bros., see Chris Smith, John Child, and Michael Rowlinson, *Reshaping Work: The Cadbury Experience* (Cambridge: Cambridge University Press, 1990), which has a short summary of the company, 50–57; Charles Dellheim, "The Creation of a Company Culture: *Cadburys*, 1861–1931," *American Historical Review* 92 (February 1987): 13–44; Coe and Coe, *True History of Chocolate*, 242–48; Carl Chinn, *The Cadbury Story: A Short History* (Studley, Warwickshire, UK: Brewin Books, 1998); Iolo A. Williams, *The Firm of Cadbury, 1831–1931* (New York: Richard R. Smith, 1931).

6. Standish Meacham, *Regaining Paradise: Englishness and the Early Garden City Movement* (New Haven, Conn.: Yale University Press, 1999), 11–43.

7. Smith, Child, and Rowlinson, *Reshaping Work*, 54–57, 60–61.

8. Dellheim, "Creation of a Company Culture," 22.

9. Chinn, *Cadbury Story*, 27; *Parliamentary Debates*, 4th ser., vol. 56 (April 21, 1898), 672.

10. Smith, Child, and Rowlinson, *Reshaping Work*, 71; Chinn, *Cadbury Story*, 35.

11. *Daily News*, March 1904, see headlines and stories; A. K. Russell, *Liberal Landslide: The General Election of 1906* (Hamden, Conn.: Archon Books, 1973), 196–200.

12. David Owen, *English Philanthropy, 1660–1960* (Cambridge, Mass.: Belknap Press of Harvard University Press, 1964), 434–42; Stephen Koss, *Rise and Fall of the Political Press*, vol. 2, *The Twentieth Century* (Chapel Hill: University of North Carolina Press, 1984), 44–45; A. G. Gardiner, *Life of George Cadbury* (London: Cassell, 1923), 210–37; Alan J. Lee, "The Radical Press," in A. J. A. Morris, ed., *Edwardian Radicalism, 1900–1914* (London: Routledge & Kegan Paul, 1974), 48–50.

13. Cadbury Papers [hereafter cited as CP], 180/183, W. Cadbury, "A Private *Inside History* of the Connection of Cadbury Bros. Ltd. with African Slavery . . . "; Kevin Patrick Grant, "'A Civilised Savagery': British Humanitarian Politics and European Imperialism in Africa, 1884–1926" (Ph.D. diss., University of California, Berkeley, 1997), 186, points out that William Cadbury over the years provided "inconsistent accounts about how he and his company became aware of labor problems" on the islands.

14. Cadbury Brothers Board Minutes [hereafter cited as CBBM], April 30, 1901. Excerpts of some of the board minutes relating to slave labor in São Tomé are also available in CP 133.

15. Dellheim, "Creation of a Company Culture," 21.

16. *Bournville Works Magazine* (August 1957): 271–72; *William A. Cadbury, 1867–1957* (Printed for private circulation, 1958); Dellheim, "Creation of a Company Culture," 21; Carol Kennedy, *The Merchant Princes: Family, Fortune and Philanthropy—Cadbury, Sainsbury and John Lewis* (London: Hutchinson, 2000), 34–35.

17. CBBM, March 15, 1910, Cocoa Cleared; Roger J. Southall, "Cadbury on the Gold Coast, 1907–1938: The Dilemma of the 'Model Firm' in a Colonial Economy" (Ph.D. diss., University of Birmingham, 1975), 39, indicates that by 1900, Cadbury was buying over 50 percent of its cocoa beans from the islands.

18. CP 4/2, copy of letter Cadbury Bros. to H. M. Consul, Luanda, December 7, 1900; CP 4/3, copy of letter Arthur Nightingale to Cadbury Bros., March 7, 1901.

19. CP 4/5, copy of letter Cadbury to Sturge, April 27, 1901; CP 4/6, copy of letter Cadbury to Sturge, May 1, 1901.

20. CP 4/4, copy of letter W. Cadbury to Albright, May 2, 1901.

21. CP 180/126, copy of letter Albright to Buxton, May 23, 1901.

22. *Times*, October 29, 1915, 11c; *Anti-Slavery Reporter*, January 1916, 77–84; *Dictionary of National Biography* [hereafter cited as *DNB*].

23. *Manchester Guardian*, January 31, 1945, 4d.

24. *Anti-Slavery Reporter*, May 1884, 93–96, includes a citation of Earl of Mayo, *De Rebus Africanus* (London: W. H. Allen, 1883), 25–26, a short book that was often cited by humanitarians as evidence of African slavery.

25. *Anti-Slavery Reporter*, November 1884, 204–7.

26. Ibid., January–February 1891, 34–35.

27. Ibid., November–December 1900, 161–63.

28. Ibid., January–February 1901, 17–19.

29. Ibid., June–July 1902, 83.

30. CP 143, list of subscriptions to humanitarian societies; Grant, "'Civilised Savagery,'" 166; *World*, February 15, 1910, 269–70.

31. [H. R. Fox Bourne], *The Aborigines Protection Society: Chapters in Its History* (London: P. S. King & Son, 1899); *Times*, February 6, 1909, 13d.

32. Charles Swaisland, "The Aborigines Protection Society, 1837–1909," in Harold Temperley, ed., *After Slavery: Emancipation and Its Discontents* (London: Frank Cass, 2000), 265–66.

33. *Anti-Slavery Reporter*, March–May 1903, 60–61; reference to the letter is in CP 180/130, Buxton to W. Cadbury, March 2, 1903.

34. CP 4/9, copy of letter Buxton to Cadbury, June 9, 1902; CP 4/10, copy of letter Cadbury to Buxton, June 10, 1902.

35. BFASS Papers, MSS Brit. Emp. S 18, C 79/5, Cadbury to Buxton, March 6, 1903.

36. *Anti-Slavery Reporter*, November–December 1902, 153.

37. CBBM, February 17, 1903.

38. CP 4/12, copy of letter W. Cadbury to Joseph Storrs Fry, February 17, 1903.

39. Foreign Office [hereafter cited as FO] 63/1447, Cadbury Bros. to Secretary of State, February 24, 1903; CP 180/959, summary file on M. Z. Stober; CP 180/946, notes on meeting between W. Cadbury and Stober, February 1903; CP 4/12, copy of letter W. Cadbury to J. Fry, February 17, 1903.

40. CP 180/336 and 4/20, report of Cadbury to Cadbury Bros., March 17, 1903.

41. CP 180/339, report of Cadbury to Cadbury Bros., March 19, 1903.

42. CP 180/341, report of Cadbury to Cadbury Bros., March 20, 1903.

43. CP 180/339, report of Cadbury to Cadbury Bros., March 19, 1903.

44. Williams, *Firm of Cadbury*, 193.

45. James Duffy, *A Question of Slavery: Labour Politics in Portuguese Africa and the British Protest, 1850–1920* (Cambridge, Mass.: Harvard University Press, 1967), 147, 160, 182; Grant, "'Civilised Savagery,'" 189. The Foreign Office correspondence that Duffy cites is from June 1903, which was three months following Cadbury's visit to Lisbon, but chances are that Gosselin had also been given verbal instructions on the issue. See chapter 4 for a discussion of the recruitment of labor for the South African mines.

46. CP 180/343, report of Cadbury to Cadbury Bros., March 24, 1903; *Evening Despatch*, December 1, 1909, 5c; Clarence-Smith, *Cocoa and Chocolate*, 239.

47. FO 63/1447, Gosselin to Lansdowne, May 3, 1903.

48. CP 180/341, report of Cadbury to Cadbury Bros., March 20, 1903.

49. CP 180/343, report of Cadbury to Cadbury Bros., March 24, 1903.

50. CP 180/336, report of Cadbury to Cadbury Bros., March 17, 1903.

51. *Anti-Slavery Reporter*, March–May 1903, 61.

52. CBBM, April 7, 1903.

53. CP 180/4, copy of letter Cadbury Bros. to Fox Bourne, May 12, 1903, document incorrectly dated May 12, 1902.

54. CP 4/41, copy of letter W. Cadbury to Fox Bourne, May 20, 1903; CP 4/43, copy of letter W. Cadbury to Cadbury Bros., June 4, 1903; CP 180, copies of several letters between William Cadbury and Fox Bourne and Buxton, in 1903 and 1904; BFASS Papers, MSS Brit. Emp. S 18, C 79, several letters between Cadbury Bros. and Buxton, 1903 and 1904.

55. CP 180/654, Gosselin to W. Cadbury, June 18, 1903.

56. CBBM, July 7, 1903, and June 7, 1904.

57. CP 4/49, Fox Bourne to W. Cadbury, July 23, 1903 [A copy of the same letter in CP 180/13 incorrectly lists a May 23, 1903, date. See CP 4/52, J. S. Fry to Cadbury Bros., July 27, 1903.]

58. Grant, "'Civilised Savagery,'" 187–88, 191.

59. CP 4/49, Fox Bourne to Cadbury, July 23, 1903.

60. *Aborigines' Friend*, April 1903, 365–66.

61. CP 180/35, copy of letter W. Cadbury to Fox Bourne, February 10, 1906; CP 5/18, Burtt to W. Cadbury, February 12, 1906; FO 367/46, Cadbury Bros. to Langley, December 27, 1907.

62. Henry W. Nevinson, *More Changes More Chances* (New York: Harcourt, Brace, [1925]), 46.

63. CP 180/655, copy of letter Cadbury to Gosselin, September 15, 1903.

64. CP 4/53, 55, 57, copies of letters Ceffala to Cadbury Bros., 1903 and 1904.

65. FO 367/141, no. 17972, copy of letter Gosselin to W. Cadbury, April 2, 1904; this letter is in CP 180/663, less the final paragraph, which was blocked out, "cancelled by desire of the F. O." as part of the papers provided for the 1909 libel trial; CP 180/348, copy of memorandum, W. Cadbury to Cadbury Bros., April 13, 1904.

66. CP 180/349, memorandum from W. Cadbury to Cadbury Bros., July 5, 1904.

67. CP 180/343, report of Cadbury to Cadbury Bros., March 24, 1903; BFASS Papers, MSS Brit. Emp. S 19, D 1/2, p. 172, copy of letter Buxton to Gosselin, April 24, 1904.

68. CP 180/665, copy of letter Gosselin to W. Cadbury, May 1, 1904.

69. Grant, "'Civilised Savagery,'" 191–92.

70. BFASS Papers, MSS Brit. Emp. S 18, C 76/96, Fox Bourne to T. Buxton, October 4, 1904.

71. CP 180/662, copy of letter Cadbury to Gosselin, March 21, 1904.

72. CP 180/350, copy of letter Cadbury to George Cadbury, July 6, 1904.

73. CP 4/84, report of visit to Fry on labor conditions in S. Thome, July 4, 1904, by W. Cadbury; CP 180/960, Stollwerck file.

74. CP 4/122 and 123.

75. CP 4/124, J. B. Morrell of Rowntree & Co. to Cadbury Bros., November 2, 1904.
76. CP 4/134, copy of letter J. S. Fry & Sons to Cadbury Bros., November 5, 1904.
77. CP 4/131, copy of letter Walter Baker & Co. to Cadbury Bros., November 7, 1904.
78. MSS. Eng. Misc. e.613/1, Bodleian Library, Nevinson's Diary, September 18 and 25, October 5 and 6, 1904 [hereafter cited as Nevinson's Diary]; Nevinson, *More Changes*, 38–39.
79. Henry W. Nevinson, *Changes and Chances* (New York: Harcourt, Brace, 1924), and Nevinson, *More Changes*.
80. CP 180/845 and 846, Nevinson to W. Cadbury, October 10 and 12, 1904. Although scheduled to leave on October 28, he postponed the trip because of a possible war in Angola and did not depart until November 5, 1904; Nevinson's Diary, October 26 and November 7, 1904.
81. BFASS Papers, MSS Brit. Emp. S 18, C 79/16, Cadbury to Buxton, October 21, 1904.
82. CP 180/849, copy of letter W. Cadbury to Nevinson, October 21, 1904.
83. CP 180/352, copy of memorandum, unsigned but from W. Cadbury to George Cadbury, October 10, 1904, reviews Cadbury Bros. contacts with other chocolate companies and comments on Burtt and Nevinson as potential agents; BFASS Papers, MSS Brit. Emp. S 18, C 79/16, Cadbury to Buxton, October 21, 1904.
84. *Friend*, May 19, 1939, 408–10.
85. BFASS Papers, MSS Brit. Emp. S 19, D 1/2, p. 295, copy of letter Buxton to E. W. Brooks, November 3, 1903, and D 1/2, pp. 270, 279, 285, 297, copy of letters Buxton to Burtt, October 7, 17, and 20, and November 4, 1903.
86. Ibid., p. 510, copy of letter Buxton to Burtt, August 15, 1904.
87. CP 180/183, Cadbury, "A Private *Inside History*."
88. BFASS Papers, MSS Brit. Emp. S 18, C 150/121, Cadbury to Fox Bourne, February 9, 1905; CP 180/354, copy of letter W. Cadbury to G. Cadbury, January 20, 1905.
89. J. G. Lockhart and C. M. Woodhouse, *Cecil Rhodes, the Colossus of Southern Africa* (New York: Macmillan, 1963), 272–73.
90. CP 4/157, copy of letter Merck to Cadbury, April 11, 1905.
91. CP 4/158, copy of letter Cadbury to Merck, April 17, 1905.
92. CP 180/24, Fox Bourne to Cadbury, June 7, 1905.
93. CP 180/26, copy of letter Cadbury to Fox Bourne, June 8, 1905.
94. "Joseph Burtt and Dr. Horton's Report on the Conditions of Coloured Labour on the Cocoa Plantations, July, 1907," in Cadbury, *Labour*, 103–4; CP 180/950, introductory note to file on Ceffala.
95. Nevinson's Diary, June 19, 1905.
96. Ibid., June 26, 1905.
97. Ibid., June 29, 1905.

Chapter 3

1. Tony Hodges and Malyn Newitt, *São Tomé and Príncipe: From Plantation Economy to Microstate* (Boulder, Colo.: Westview Press, 1988), 18; Gerhard Seibert, *Comrades, Clients and Cousins: Colonialism, Socialism and Democratization in São Tomé and Príncipe* (Leiden, the

Netherlands: Leiden University, 1999), 17–25; David M. Abshire and Michael A. Samuels, eds., *Portuguese Africa: A Handbook* (London: Pall Mall Press, 1969), 94.

2. W. R. Aykroyd, *Sweet Malefactor: Sugar, Slavery and Human Society* (London: Heinemann, 1967), 19; Hugh Thomas, *The Slave Trade: The Story of the Atlantic Slave Trade, 1440–1870* (New York: Simon & Schuster, 1997), 107–8.

3. Joseph C. Miller, "A Marginal Institution on the Margin of the Atlantic System: The Portuguese Southern Atlantic Slave Trade in the Eighteenth Century," in Barbara L. Solow, ed., *Slavery and the Rise of the Atlantic System* (Cambridge: Cambridge University Press, 1991), 125; Philip D. Curtin, *The Rise and Fall of the Plantation Complex: Essays in Atlantic History* (Cambridge: Cambridge University Press, 1990), 23–28; Philip D. Curtin, "The External Trade of West Africa to 1800," in J. F. A. Ajayi and Michael Crowder, eds., *History of West Africa*, vol. 1, 2nd ed. (Harlow, UK: Longman Group, 1985), 632–33; Robert L. Paquette, "Revolts," in Seymour Drescher and Stanley L. Engerman, eds., *A Historical Guide to World Slavery* (New York: Oxford University Press, 1998), 336.

4. Luiz Ivens Ferraz, *The Creole of São Tomé* (Johannesburg: Witwatersrand University Press, 1979), 18–19; Robert Garfield, *A History of São Tomé Island, 1470–1655: The Key to Guinea* (San Francisco: Mellen Research University Press, 1992).

5. C. R. Boxer, *Race Relations in the Portuguese Colonial Empire: 1415–1825* (Oxford: Clarendon Press, 1963), 1–40.

6. Joseph C. Miller, *Way of Death: Merchant Capitalism and the Angolan Slave Trade, 1730–1830* (Madison: University of Wisconsin Press, 1988), 673; David Birmingham, *Portugal and Africa* (New York: St. Martin's Press, 1999), 20–21; Gerald J. Bender, *Angola under the Portuguese* (Berkeley: University of California Press, 1978), 60–61.

7. James Duffy, *Portugal in Africa* (Baltimore, Md.: Penguin Books, 1963), 47.

8. Hodges and Newitt, *São Tomé and Príncipe*, 26–27; Seibert, *Comrades, Clients and Cousins*, 32.

9. W. G. Clarence-Smith, *The Third Portuguese Empire, 1825–1975: A Study in Economic Imperialism* (Manchester, UK: Manchester University Press, 1975).

10. Daniel Headrick, *The Tools of Empire: Technology and European Imperialism in the Nineteenth Century* (New York: Oxford University Press, 1981); Jared Diamond, *Guns, Germs, and Steel: The Fates of Human Societies* (New York: W. W. Norton, 1997), 241–44, 397–401.

11. Roland Oliver and J. D. Fage, *A Short History of Africa* (Harmondsworth, UK: Penguin, 1962); Thomas Pakenham, *The Scramble for Africa: The White Man's Conquest of the Dark Continent from 1876 to 1912* (London: Weidenfeld and Nicolson, 1991).

12. H. V. Livermore, *A History of Portugal* (Cambridge: Cambridge University Press, 1947), 179.

13. Eduardo Brazão, *The Anglo-Portuguese Alliance* (London: Sylvan Press, 1957).

14. Harold Nicolson, *The Congress of Vienna* (New York: Harcourt Brace Jovanovich, 1946), 213–14; S. E. Crowe, *The Berlin West African Conference, 1884–1885* (London: Longmans, Green, 1942), 202–3; A. W. Ward and G. P. Gooch, eds., *The Cambridge History of British Foreign Policy, 1783–1919*, vol. 1, *1783–1815* (Cambridge: Cambridge University Press, 1922; reprint, New York: Octagon Books, 1970), 15, 16, 22, 166, 372–81, 497–98; vol. 2, *1815–1866* (Cambridge: Cambridge University Press, 1923; reprint, New York: Octagon Books, 1970), 78–83, 187, 189, 296.

15. Clarence-Smith, *Third Portuguese Empire*, 63; Ronald Robinson and John Gallagher, *Africa and the Victorians: The Official Mind of Imperialism*, 2nd ed. paperback (London:

Macmillan, 1981), 170; Eric Axelson, *Portugal and the Scramble for Africa, 1875–1891* (Johannesburg: Witwatersrand University Press, 1967), 64; Crowe, *Berlin West African Conference,* 11–22; Pakenham, *Scramble for Africa,* 189–90; Suzanne Miers, "The Brussels Conference of 1889–1890," 86–87; Parliament, *General Act of the Conference of Berlin Signed February 26, 1885,* Africa No. 3, C. 4739, 1886.

16. Clarence-Smith, *Third Portuguese Empire,* 81.

17. William Gervase Clarence-Smith, "Capital Accumulation and Class Formation in Angola," in David Birmingham and Phyllis M. Martin, eds., *History of Central Africa,* vol. 2 (New York: Longman, 1983), 163–99.

18. Richard J. Hammond, "Some Economic Aspects of Portuguese Africa in the Nineteenth and Twentieth Centuries," in Peter Duignan and L. H. Gann, eds., *Colonialism in Africa, 1870–1960,* vol. 4, *The Economics of Colonialism* (Cambridge: Cambridge University Press, 1975), 256–65.

19. Clarence-Smith, *Cocoa and Chocolate,* 239. For this six-year period, São Tomé slightly outproduced Brazil and Ecuador.

20. Cabinet Papers for 1889 and 1890 contain several documents (see especially 37/25/46 and 49, and 37/26, 2 and 6) on Britain's response to Portugal; Axelson, *Portugal and the Scramble for Africa,* 186–297; Birmingham, *Portugal and Africa,* 110–21; Leroy Vail and Landeg White, *Capitalism and Colonialism in Mozambique: A Study of Quelimane District* (London: Heinemann, 1980), 106.

21. J. A. S. Grenville, *Lord Salisbury and Foreign Policy: The Close of the Nineteenth Century* (London: Athlone Press, 1964), 177–98; C. J. Lowe, *The Reluctant Imperialists: British Foreign Policy, 1878–1902,* 1st American ed. (New York: Macmillan, 1969), 218–24; G. P. Gooch and Harold Temperley, eds., *British Documents on the Origins of the War, 1898–1914,* vol. 1 (London: His Majesty's Stationery Office, 1927; reprint, New York: Johnson Reprint, 1967), 42–87, contains correspondence over the Anglo-German negotiations.

22. Jacques Willequet, "Anglo-German Rivalry in Belgian and Portuguese Africa?" in Prosser Gifford and Wm. Roger Louis, eds., *Britain and Germany in Africa* (New Haven, Conn.: Yale University Press, 1967), 265; Robinson and Gallagher, *Africa and the Victorians,* 446–49; Livermore, *History of Portugal,* 445–47; Cabinet Papers 37/47 contain extensive correspondence on the division of Portugal's colonies; Gooch and Temperley, *British Documents,* vol. 1, 88–99.

23. Joseph Chamberlain Papers, JC7/3/2A/59, Arthur Balfour, "Suggestions about Delagoa Bay," December 25, 1899, and JC7/3/2A/61, Lord Salisbury, "Occupation of Delagoa Bay," December 27, 1899; Wm. Roger Louis, "Great Britain and German Expansion in Africa, 1884–1919," in Prosser Gifford and Wm. Roger Louis, eds., *Britain and Germany in Africa* (New Haven, Conn.: Yale University Press, 1967), 24–27.

24. Miers, *Britain and the Ending of the Slave Trade,* 24–25.

25. Duffy, *Question of Slavery,* 9.

26. Duffy, *Portugal in Africa,* 130.

27. Ibid., 130–31.

28. Linda M. Heywood, "Slavery and Forced Labor in the Changing Political Economy of Central Angola, 1850–1949," in Suzanne Miers and Richard Roberts, eds., *The End of Slavery in Africa* (Madison: University of Wisconsin Press, 1988), 417–19.

29. Seibert, *Comrades, Clients and Cousins,* 33.

30. Hodges and Newitt, *São Tomé and Príncipe,* 28–33.

31. *Evening Despatch*, December 1, 1909, 5c.

32. R. J. Hammond, *Portugal and Africa, 1815–1910* (Stanford, Calif.: Stanford University Press, 1966), 314–20.

33. Seibert, *Comrades, Clients and Cousins*, 34.

34. Duffy, *Portugal in Africa*, 132.

35. Ibid.

36. H. H. Johnston, "The Portuguese Colonies of West Africa," *Journal of the Society of the Arts* 32 (February 15, 1884): 240.

37. Hugh Tinker, *A New System of Slavery: The Export of Indian Labour Overseas, 1830–1920* (London: Oxford University Press, 1974); David Northrup, *Indentured Labor in the Age of Imperialism, 1834–1922* (New York: Cambridge University Press, 1995), 6; Kay Saunders, ed., *Indentured Labour in the British Empire, 1834–1920* (London: Croom Helm, 1984); *Spectator*, June 19, 1909, 969–70.

38. Roland Oliver and G. N. Sanderson, eds., *The Cambridge History of Africa*, vol. 6, 1870 to 1905 (Cambridge: Cambridge University Press, 1985), 310–12, 330, 456–57, 527, 534; Patrick Harries, *Work, Culture, and Identity: Migrant Laborers in Mozambique and South Africa, c. 1860–1910* (Portsmouth, N.H.: Heinemann, 1994), 170–71; Grant, "'Civilised Savagery,'" 21–22; Roger Thomas, "Forced Labour in British West Africa: The Case of the Northern Territories of the Gold Coast, 1906–1927," *Journal of African History* 14 (1973): 79–103; Robert I. Rotberg, *The Rise of Nationalism in Central Africa* (Cambridge, Mass.: Harvard University Press, 1965), 24, 40.

39. Roland Oliver, *Sir Harry Johnston and the Scramble for Africa* (London: Chatto & Windus, 1957), 197–271; Rotberg, *Rise of Nationalism*, 13–19.

40. Adam Hochschild, *King Leopold's Ghost* (New York: Houghton Mifflin, 1998); Oliver, *Sir Harry Johnston*, 48, indicates that Johnston was aware of the abuse of natives in the Congo in the 1880s. Johnston, in his introduction to E. D. Morel's *Red Rubber: The Story of the Rubber Slave Trade Flourishing on the Congo in the Year of Grace 1906* (1906; reprint, New York: Negro Universities Press [1969]), says that he was unaware of the scale of the problem until after 1905, which is hard to believe for someone so knowledgeable.

41. *Times*, December 22, 1902, 12.

42. William Gervase Clarence-Smith, "Cocoa Plantations and Coerced Labour in the Gulf of Guinea, 1870–1914," in Martin A. Klein, ed., *Breaking the Chains: Slavery, Bondage, and Emancipation in Modern Africa and Asia* (Madison: University of Wisconsin Press, 1993), 150–70.

43. Heywood, "Slavery and Forced Labor," 420–21.

44. Verney Lovett Cameron, *Across Africa*, new ed. (London: George Philip & Son, 1885; first published 1877). Nevinson cited this book in *A Modern Slavery*.

45. See chapter 2.

46. Duffy, *Question of Slavery*, 117–26. For the treaty, see the discussion earlier in this chapter.

47. Johnston, "The Portuguese Colonies of West Africa," 234–35, 240.

48. Duffy, *Question of Slavery*, 75–78.

49. FO 63/1447, Cohen to Granville, July 16, 1882.

50. Duffy, *Question of Slavery*, 98.

51. Parliamentary Debates, 4th ser., vol. 25 (June 4, 1894), 285–86.

52. *DNB*.

53. FO 63/1447, Pease to Grey, June 5, 1894, and correspondence; draft of letter FO to Luanda, June 16, 1894; Brock to FO, August 28, 1894.

54. FO 63/1447, Pickersgill to Kimberley, December 15, 1894, and minutes.

55. FO 63/1314, no. 22, draft of letter FO to Pickersgill, December 28, 1896, and 63/1447, no. 8, Pickersgill to Salisbury, March 16, 1897, and minutes; Duffy, *Question of Slavery*, 101.

56. Parliament, Foreign Office, *Diplomatic and Consular Reports. Trade of Province of Angola for the Year 1899*, No. 2555, Cd. 429–13, February 1901, pp. 6–7.

57. FO 2/640, Nightingale to Lansdowne, June 20, 1902.

58. Ibid., Nightingale to Lansdowne, July 8, 1902.

59. FO 63/1447, no. 25, Casement to Lansdowne, September 17, 1902.

60. Ibid., Gosselin to Lansdowne, February 4 and 7, 1903, and Nightingale to Lansdowne, April 3, 1903.

61. Ibid., no. 90, minutes regarding Gosselin's letter of May 6, 1903, to FO.

62. Ibid., no. 102, draft of letter Lansdowne to Gosselin, June 24, 1903, and draft of letter FO to Nightingale, June 12, 1903.

63. Grant, "'Civilised Savagery,'" 191.

64. FO 63/1447, no. 20, Nightingale to Lansdowne, May 5, 1904.

65. Ibid., Gosselin to Lansdowne, October 28, 1904.

66. Ibid., minutes on October 10, 1904, letter BFASS to FO.

67. FO 2/883, Brock to Lansdowne, November 28, 1904, and minute; FO 63/1447, Gosselin to FO, December 16, 1904, December 28, 1904, January 1, 1905, and minutes.

68. FO 63/1427, no. 4, Nightingale to FO, March 13, 1905, and minutes; FO 63/1447, Brock to FO, June 30, 1905.

69. Colin Harding, *In Remotest Barotseland* (London: Hurst and Blackett, 1905), 207, 211, 221.

70. FO 63/1447, Gosselin to Lansdowne, November 4, 1904; Douglas C. Wheeler and C. Diane Christensen, "To Rise with One Mind: The Bailundu War of 1902," in Franz-Wilhelm Heimer, ed., *Social Change in Angola* (Munich, Germany: Weltforum Verlag, 1973), 53–93; Heywood, "Slavery and Forced Labor," 417–22.

71. FO 63/1447, Gosselin to Lansdowne, February 16, 1905; H. H. Johnston, *A History of Colonization of Africa by Alien Races* (1913; New York: Cooper Square Publishers, 1966), 97; Basil Davidson, *In the Eye of the Storm: Angola's People* (Garden City, N.Y.: Doubleday, 1971), 133; J. B. Thornhill, *Adventures in Africa under the British, Belgian and Portuguese Flags* (London: John Murray, 1915), 180; *Times*, October 1907, several articles; *West African Mail*, September 6, 1907, 572, and September 27, 1907, 641; *African Mail*, September 24, 1909, 507.

Chapter 4

1. *Daily Chronicle*, March 30, 1906, 4d.

2. *Clarion*, August 4, 1905, 2d–e.

3. *Tribune*, June 7, 1906, 2c.

4. *Daily Chronicle*, June 9, 1906, 3c.

5. CP 305, p. 75, contains clipping of *British Friend,* October 1906, 269–70.

6. *Daily Mail,* July 26, 1906, cited in Grant, "'Civilised Savagery,'" 167.

7. FO 367/18, no. 7265, minutes on letter William Tallack to Edward Grey, February 26, 1906.

8. FO 367/18, no. 9864, memo by Barrington on meeting with Fox Bourne and Nevinson, March 14, 1906.

9. FO 63/1447, Clarke to Campbell, October 4, 1905.

10. FO 367/18, no. 7265, William Tallack to Edward Grey, February 26, 1906, and minutes.

11. FO 63/1447, Fox Bourne to Lansdowne, July 25, 1905, draft of letter FO to APS, August 9, 1905, Fox Bourne to Lansdowne, August 19, 1905, and Buxton to Lansdowne, October 10, 1904; *Aborigines' Friend,* December 1904, 242–45, Fox Bourne to Lansdowne, October 17, 1904.

12. *Anti-Slavery Reporter,* August 1905–February 1906, summarized Nevinson's articles; BFASS Papers, MSS Brit. Emp. S 18, C 76/108, Fox Bourne to Buxton, September 2, 1905.

13. *Aborigines' Friend,* March 1906, 504.

14. CP 180/31, Fox Bourne to W. Cadbury, February 3, 1906.

15. H. G. C. Matthew, *The Liberal Imperialists* (Oxford: Oxford University Press, 1973), 139, 195–97; G. R. Searle, *The Quest for National Efficiency: A Study in British Politics and Political Thought, 1899–1924* (Berkeley: University of California Press, 1971).

16. FO 367/18, no. 23071, Memorandum Respecting Contract Labour ("Serviçaes") for San Thomé and Principe, by E. F. Gye, December 30, 1905. This ten-page summary covering 1876 to 1905, with references to various FO documents, indicates the FO recognized that serviçais were a very old problem, to which the Portuguese were exceptionally sensitive. The memorandum also mentions the several times that the APS raised the issue with the FO.

17. FO 367/18, no. 7402, Fox Bourne to Lord Fitzmaurice, February 27, 1906, and no. 9864, memorandum by Barrington on meeting with Fox Bourne and Nevinson, March 14, 1906.

18. Nevinson, *More Changes,* 93 n; Nevinson's Diary, March 14, 1906.

19. *Aborigines' Friend,* May 1906, 569–72, Fox Bourne to Grey, April 3, 1906.

20. CP 180/855, Nevinson to Cadbury, July 25, 1905.

21. CP 180/858, Nevinson to Cadbury, October 5, 1905.

22. CP 180/715, Merck to Cadbury, October 5, 1905.

23. Philip R. Warhurst, *Anglo-Portuguese Relations in South-Central Africa, 1890–1900* (London: Longmans, 1962), 119–27; Lockhart and Woodhouse, *Cecil Rhodes,* 272–73; CP 180/716, Merck to Cadbury, December 10, 1905.

24. *Anti-Slavery Reporter,* March–May 1906, 29.

25. CP 180/32–3, copy of letter Cadbury to Fox Bourne, February 6, 1906.

26. CP 5/1, copy of letter Burtt to Cadbury, January 3, 1906.

27. CP 5/18, copy of letter Burtt to Cadbury, February 12, 1906.

28. CP 180/948, digest of correspondence, Burtt to Cadbury Bros., 1904–1908, and 180/947, digest of W. Cadbury's letters to Burtt.

29. CP 5/28, copy of letter W. Claude Horton to W. Cadbury, July 28, 1906.

30. CP 5/29, copy of letter W. Claude Horton to W. Cadbury, September 17, 1906.

31. BFASS Papers, MSS Brit. Emp. S 18, C 150/123, Cadbury to Fox Bourne, June 6, 1905.

32. Ibid., S 18, C 79/18, Cadbury to Buxton, February 23, 1906.

33. CP 5/1, copy of letter Burtt to Cadbury, January 3, 1906.

34. CP 180/357, copy of letter W. Cadbury to George Cadbury, April 6, 1906.

35. FO 367/18, no. 41656, Cadbury to Grey, December 10, 1906.

36. BFASS Papers, MSS Brit. Emp. S 22, G 268/A, copy of letter Mathias to Cadbury, November 22, 1906.

37. CP 5/18, copy of letter Burtt to Cadbury, February 12, 1906.

38. Ibid.

39. CP 5/19, copy of letter Burtt to Cadbury, March 19, 1906.

40. FO 63/1447, draft of letter, FO to Nightingale, October 18, 1905.

41. FO 367/18, no. 5276, Nightingale to Clarke, January 17, 1906.

42. CP 180/34, Fox Bourne to Cadbury, February 9, 1906.

43. *Aborigines' Friend*, May 1906, 569–72, Fox Bourne to Grey, April 3, 1906, and November 1906, 657–58, copy of letter, Fox Bourne to Grey, July 30, 1906. FO 367/18 has correspondence on requests for the report, including communication between the FO and Nightingale, and letters from Fox Bourne to FO.

44. *Parliamentary Debates*, 4th ser., vol. 160 (July 5, 1906), 229–30; FO 367/18, no. 23071, FO minutes on Parker's question of the Board of Trade.

45. FO 367/18, no. 8806, Report on the Treatment of the "Serviçaes," or Contract Labourers, in the Portuguese Islands Known as the Province of São Thomé and Principe, *Confidential*.

46. Ibid., no. 28370, minutes on Nightingale's report.

47. Duffy, *Question of Slavery*, 193.

48. Ibid., 141.

49. Simon E. Katzenellenbogen, *South Africa and Southern Mozambique: Labour, Railways and Trade in the Making of a Relationship* (Manchester, UK: Manchester University Press, 1982), 49–100; Harries, *Work, Culture, and Identity*, 129–40, 170; Duffy, *Question of Slavery*, 141–59; Alan H. Jeeves, *Migrant Labour in South Africa's Mining Economy: The Struggle for the Gold Mines' Labour Supply, 1890–1920* (Kingston, Canada: McGill-Queen's University Press, 1985).

50. FO 367/18, no. 28370, copy of letter, F. A. Campbell to Fox Bourne, September 12, 1906, indicates that the report enclosed was "those portions of Consul Nightingale's report which deal with the present state of the Serviçaes and the regulations concerning them now in force . . . this extract from Consul Nightingale's report is communicated to you on the distinct understanding that no portion of it is to be published." *Aborigines' Friend*, November 1906, 659; BFASS Papers, MSS Brit. Emp. S 18, C 76/117, Fox Bourne to Travers Buxton, October 1, 1906.

51. FO 367/18, no. 32379, Fox Bourne to FO, September 24, 1906, and minutes.

52. Ibid., draft of letter Barrington to Fox Bourne, October 10, 1906. Fox Bourne sent a copy of this letter to Cadbury, CP 180/42, Fox Bourne to W. Cadbury, October 19, 1906.

53. CP 180/42, Fox Bourne to W. Cadbury, October 19, 1906.

54. FO 367/18, no. 37074, questions about Nightingale's report, October 29, 1906.

55. FO 367/46, no. 69, January 1907.

56. FO 367/18, no. 37074, questions about Nightingale's report, October 29, 1906.

57. *Parliamentary Debates*, 4th ser., vol. 163 (October 29, 1906), 675.

58. FO 367/18, no. 38021, Villiers to FO, November 7, 1906.

59. *Times*, September 22, 1906, 13b.

60. Villiers later indicated that Soveral was upset because Portuguese officials had not been notified of Nightingale's visit to the islands; FO 367/47, no. 5640, minute by Clarke on Mackie's mission, February 18, 1907.

61. FO 367/46, no. 157, minutes dated January 2, 1907, on the Nightingale report.

62. FO 63/1423, Arthur Peel to Lansdowne, February 26 and March 12, 1905.

63. FO 367/18, no. 41793, Villiers to FO, December 7, 1906, and Barrington to Villiers, December 29, 1906.

64. FO 367/46, no. 157, minutes dated January 2, 1907, on the Nightingale report. It is not known if the report submitted to the Portuguese was the abbreviated one sent to the APS or the full report.

65. CP 180/487, copy of letter George Cadbury to Grey, October 19, 1906 [original in FO 367/18, no. 35394], and 180/488, copy of accompanying statement by Cadbury Bros. on labor on the cocoa plantations.

66. FO 367/18, no. 36737, George Cadbury to Grey, October 27, 1906.

67. CP 180/491, FO to George Cadbury, November 6, 1906.

68. FO 367/18, no. 37618, Cadbury Bros. to the undersecretary of state, November 7, 1906, and memorandum.

69. CP 180/497, Barrington to Cadbury Bros., November 13, 1906.

70. Morel Papers, Morel F8/12/41, Cadbury to Morel, October 27, 1906.

71. FO 367/18, no. 27074, letter from Harvey, July 6, 1906, sent by Admiralty to FO.

72. FO 367/18, no. 37123, Cadbury to Grey, November 2, 1906, and no. 38182, Cadbury to FO, November 12, 1906. The article by Prister, "The Slave Trade in Angola in the 20th Century," was included with the November 2 letter. The APS also received a copy, BFASS Papers, MSS Brit. Emp. S 22, G 268/A. *Anti-Slavery Reporter*, November–December 1906, 117–21, included long excerpts from the article.

73. Morel Papers, Morel F8/11/1, W. Cadbury to Morel, September 2, 1903.

74. CP 180/183, Cadbury, "A Private *Inside History.*"

75. Hochschild, *King Leopold's Ghost;* Catherine Ann Cline, *E. D. Morel, 1873–1924: The Strategies of Protest* (Belfast, UK: Blackstaff Press, 1980); Alice Stopford Green, "A Founder of the Society" [appreciation of John Holt], *Journal of the African Society* 15 (October 1915): 11–16.

76. Hochschild, *King Leopold's Ghost,* 195–208.

77. For a discussion of the differences between the BFASS, the APS, and the CRA, see Andrew Porter, "Trusteeship, Anti-Slavery, and Humanitarianism," in Andrew Porter, ed., *The Oxford History of the British Empire,* vol. 3, *The Nineteenth Century* (Oxford: Oxford University Press, 1999), 215–20; and Grant, "'Civilised Savagery.'"

78. Holt Papers, MSS Afr., S.1525/18, File 2, Morel to Holt, February 27, 1904.

79. Morel Papers, Morel F8/11/22, Cadbury to Morel, June 15, 1905; Morel F8/11/24, Cadbury to Morel, [June 1905]; Morel F8/11/25, Morel to Cadbury, June 26, 1908.

80. Ibid., Morel F8/12/14, Morel to Cadbury, December 5, 1905.

81. Wm. Roger Louis and Jean Stenger, *E. D. Morel's History of the Congo Reform Movement* (Oxford: Clarendon Press, 1968), 258–60; Cline, *Morel,* 49; Grant, "'Civilised Savagery,'" 194–95.

82. Morel Papers, Morel F8/11/47, Morel to Cadbury, August 4, 1905.

83. Nevinson, *More Changes*, 85.

84. Grant, "'Civilised Savagery,'" 75–121; Hochschild, *King Leopold's Ghost*, 216–17; *Anti-Slavery Reporter*, October 2001, 13; Morel Papers, Morel F8/11/49, Morel to W. Cadbury, August 8, 1905, and F8/11/56, W. Cadbury to Morel, October 14, 1905.

85. Cline, *Morel*, 41–42, including letter Fox Bourne to Morel, February 1, 1904; Grant, "'Civilised Savagery,'" 87–88; Swaisland, "Aborigines Protection Society," 275–76.

86. Morel Papers, Morel F8/11/98–9, Morel to Cadbury, October 31, 1905.

87. Ibid., F8/11/96, Cadbury to Morel, October 30, 1905.

88. Ibid., F8/12/16, W. Cadbury to Lord Beauchamp, December 12, 1905, and F8/12/45, W. Cadbury to Morel, November 12, 1906.

89. Cline, *Morel*, 7; Hochschild, *King Leopold's Ghost*, 210–11.

90. CP 180/32–3, copy of letter Cadbury to Fox Bourne, February 6, 1906.

91. BFASS Papers, MSS Brit. Emp. S 18, C 79/21, Cadbury to Buxton, February 20, 1907.

92. CP 305, 91, copy of daily schedule, W. Cadbury, October 1907.

Chapter 5

1. FO 367/46, no. 8897, Cadbury Bros. to Grey, March 15, 1907.

2. CP 180/888, memorandum from Joseph Rowntree on the interview between Joseph Burtt and the Rowntree board, May 2, 1907.

3. FO 367/46, no. 8897, FO minutes regarding letter Cadbury to FO, March 15, 1907.

4. CP 180/508, Barrington to Cadbury Bros., May 2, 1907.

5. CP 180/49, Fox Bourne to Cadbury, April 29, 1907.

6. CP 180/50, copy of letter Cadbury to Fox Bourne, April 30, 1907.

7. CP 180/510, suggested letter Cadbury Bros. to FO, n.d., but May 3, 1907, penciled in. A note on the draft says, "This letter was apparently not sent—but the purport of it was given in conversation at interview with F. O., of June 27, 1907."

8. CBBM, May 14, 1907, and July 30, 1907.

9. FO 367/46 contains correspondence regarding Burtt's report; for examples, see Cadbury Bros. to FO, May 16, 1907, and June 10, 1907.

10. FO 367/46, no. 29406, draft of letter Lyell to Beaumont, September 2, 1907; also CP 118, Notes of an Interview at the FO, July 11, 1907.

11. FO 367/46, no. 28725, Cadbury Bros. to Lyell, August 22, 1907.

12. Ibid., no. 8897, minutes regarding letter Cadbury to FO, March 15, 1907, included Lyell's comments.

13. CP 180/510, suggested letter Cadbury Bros. to FO, n.d., but May 3, 1907, penciled in.

14. CP 180/860 and 862, copy of letters Cadbury to Nevinson, May 15 and 31, 1907.

15. CP 180/863, Nevinson to W. Cadbury, June 1, 1907.

16. CP 180/121, unpublished statement by Fox Bourne.

17. CP 180/52, Fox Bourne to Cadbury Bros., June 21, 1907.

18. CP 180/55, Fox Bourne to W. Cadbury, June 26, 1907.

19. Robert Fitzgerald, *Rowntree and the Marketing Revolution, 1862–1969* (Cambridge:

Cambridge University Press, 1995), 38, 51, 97, 228; Dellheim, "Creation of a Company Culture," 21.

20. Seebohm Rowntree, *Poverty: A Study of Town Life* (London: Macmillan, 1901); Edward Cadbury, M. Cecile Matheson, and George Shann, *Women's Work and Wages* (London: T. Fisher Unwin, 1906); Edward Cadbury and George Shann, *Sweating* (London: Headley Bros., 1907); J. H. Viet-Wilson, "Paradigms of Poverty: A Rehabilitation of B. S. Rowntree," in David Englander and Rosemary O'Day, eds., *Retrieved Riches: Social Investigation in Britain, 1840–1914* (Aldershot, UK: Scholar Press, [1995]), 201–37.

21. CP 180/944, notes of meeting with Fox Bourne, June 27, 1907.

22. This discussion at the two meetings is reconstructed from the following: CP 180/53, 4-page typescript copy of a draft reply to APS by Cadbury Bros., June 23, 1907, with note "not sent" on it; 180/3, notes by W. Cadbury for his statement to the Committee of APS; 180/944, notes on conference of July 4, 1907, APS file, 17–18.

23. CP 180/61, Fox Bourne to Cadbury Bros., July 5, 1907.

24. CP 180/60, Fox Bourne to W. Cadbury, July 5, 1907.

25. CP 180/63, copy of letter Cadbury to Fox Bourne, July 8, 1907.

26. CP 180/65, Fox Bourne to Cadbury, July 10, 1907.

27. CP 180/66, copy of letter, Cadbury to APS, July 11, 1907; CP 180/67, copy of letter, Cadbury to Fox Bourne, July 11, 1907; CP 180/68, Fox Bourne to Cadbury, July 12, 1907.

28. Nevinson's Diary, April 29, 1907. Figure of 13 percent is based on information in Clarence-Smith, *Cocoa and Chocolate*, 239, and *Evening Despatch*, December 1, 1909, 5c. Fry may have imported a greater quantity from São Tomé.

29. Nevinson's Diary, May 28, 1907.

30. Nevinson, *More Changes*, 215; Elfrida Vipont, *Arnold Rowntree* (London: Bannisdale, 1955), 52–53.

31. Koss, *Political Press*, 42.

32. FO 367/46, no. 25330, Cross to Clarke, July 26, 1907.

33. CP 5/174, copy of letter Cadbury Bros. to Rowntree, July 26, 1907.

34. Vipont, *Rowntree*, 52; Thomas C. Kennedy, *British Quakerism, 1860–1929: The Transformation of a Religious Community* (Oxford: Oxford University Press, 2001), 324.

35. CP 5/178, copy of letter Cross to Cadbury, July 29, 1907.

36. Nevinson's Diary, August 1, 1907.

37. CP 5/188, copy of memorandum Nevinson to Massingham, August 2, 1907.

38. CP 5/187, copy of letter Nevinson to Cross, n.d., but obviously August 1907; Nevinson's Diary, August 13, 1907.

39. CP 5/186, copy of letter Cross to Cadbury, August 20, 1907.

40. Henry W. Nevinson, "The Angola Slave Trade," *Fortnightly Review* 82 (September 1907): 488–97.

41. CP 177, newspaper cutting of *Review of Reviews*, September 1907, 266; see numerous entries in Nevinson's Diary, February 12 to August 13, 1907.

42. CP 6/9, copy of letter Liverpool Chamber of Commerce to Cadbury Bros., September 30, 1907; FO 367/46, no. 32662, telegram, Liverpool Chamber of Commerce to FO, September 30, 1907.

43. FO 367/46, no. 32836, minutes regarding Liverpool Chamber of Commerce meeting, following telegram from them of September 30, 1907; *Birmingham Daily Post*, October 2, 1907, 5b; *Manchester Guardian*, October 2, 1907, 8e; *Times*, October 4, 1907, 16d.

44. BFASS Papers, MSS Brit. Emp. S 22, G 268A, Statement Made by Mr. William Cadbury . . . to the Council of the Liverpool Chamber of Commerce, October 21, 1907.

45. *Manchester Guardian*, October 22, 1907, 9a–b.

46. *Times*, October 22, 1907, 11c; *Liverpool Daily Post*, October 24, 1907, 11e.

47. Green, "Founder of the Society," 11–12.

48. *Liverpool Daily Post*, October 4, 1907, 9e–f.

49. CP 180/682, Holt to Cadbury Bros., October 11, 1907; Holt Papers, MSS. Afr. S. 1525, Box 18/10, copy of letter Holt to Morel, October 23, 1907.

50. For an extensive discussion of the Liverpool School, see Bernard Porter, *Critics of Empire: British Radical Attitudes to Colonialism in Africa, 1895–1914* (New York: St. Martin's Press, 1968), 239–90, and Kingsley Kenneth Dike Nworah, "Humanitarian Pressure-Groups and British Attitudes to West Africa, 1895–1915" (Ph.D. diss., London University, 1966), 20–111; for Holt and his merchant activities, see Cherry Gertzel, "John Holt: A British Merchant in West Africa in the Era of Imperialism" (Ph.D. diss., Oxford University, 1959), and John Holt and Co. (Liverpool), Ltd., *Merchant Adventure* (Liverpool: John Holt and Company (Liverpool), Limited, [1951]).

51. Grant, "'Civilised Savagery,'" 29–30.

52. CP 305, p. 90, press cutting, *West Indian Committee Circular*, October 29, 1907; CP 177, press cutting, *British and Foreign Confectioner, Baker and Restaurateur*, November 1907, 692.

53. CP 180/764, copy of letter Cadbury to Morel, November 2, 1907.

54. *Liverpool Daily Post*, October 25, 1907, 11h.

55. *Birmingham Daily Post*, October 3, 1907, 11d.

56. CP 180/76, Fox Bourne to Cadbury Bros., October 25, 1907.

57. *Anti-Slavery Reporter*, November–December 1907, 125–26; *Manchester Guardian*, November 11, 1907, 4d.

58. *Parliamentary Debates*, 4th ser., vol. 178 (July 18, 1907), 916, vol. 177 (July 9, 1907), 1436–37, vol. 179 (July 25, 1907), 130, vol. 179 (July 30, 1907), 740–41.

59. Ibid., vol. 178 (July 22, 1907), 1189–90.

60. Ibid., vol. 174 (May 14, 1907), 898–99. For a discussion of this duty, see chapter 10.

61. Jane Lacey, "Cadbury's, Sao Tomé and the Gold Coast: A Study of Industrial Involvement in Imperial Problems" (Ph.D. diss., University of Sussex, 1970), 3–5; Gardiner, *Cadbury*, 239, claimed that *World* invented the phrase *Cocoa Press*; Koss, *Political Press*, 42.

62. *Daily Graphic*, September 3, 1907, 9d. Nonconformists were Protestants, often of a puritanical "conscience," who were separate from the established Church of England. Nonconformists, also referred to as dissenters, generally supported the Liberal Party.

63. CP 180/477, copy of letter Cadbury Bros. to the editor, *Daily Graphic*, October 22, 1907; *Daily Graphic*, October 24, 1907, 4d.

64. James Duffy's books on Portuguese Africa are especially useful on the treatment of native laborers. On the Angolan response, see his *Question of Slavery*, 175–78, and *Portugal in Africa*, 134–35; Bender, *Angola under the Portuguese*, 140; Douglas L. Wheeler and René Pélissier, *Angola* (New York: Praeger, 1971), 104–8.

65. FO 63/1447, Brock to Lansdowne, June 10, 1904, included a translation of the May 19, 1904, article in *A Defeza de Angola*.

66. Bender, *Angola under the Portuguese*, 140.

67. FO 367/46, Mackie to Grey, April 20, 1907; 367/48, no. 8896, minutes regarding

coolie labor, March 1907, no. 12591, M. C. Seton to Barrington and minutes, April 18, 1907, no. 24829, Mackie to Grey, June 28, 1907, and no. 33466, Beaumont to Grey, October 3, 1907; Parliament, Foreign Office, *Diplomatic and Consular Reports. Trade of Angola for the Year 1906*, No. 3928, Cd. 3727–11, September 1907, p. 5.

68. Duffy, *Portugal in Africa*, 134–35.

69. Duffy, *Question of Slavery*, 178.

70. FO 63/1447, copy of letter Soveral to BFASS, February 26, 1903.

71. *Anti-Slavery Reporter*, June–July 1907, 78–80, reviews and quotes from annual publication, *Documents relatifs à la traite des esclaves* [Documents Relating to the Slave Trade], Brussels, year 1907.

72. Henrique José Monteiro de Mendonça, *The Boa Entrada Plantations*, trans. J. A. Wyllie (Edinburgh: Oliphant Anderson & Ferrier, 1907); for comments on Mendonça and his book, see FO 367/46, no. 36616; *Anti-Slavery Reporter*, November–December 1907, 126–27; *African Mail*, December 6, 1907, 83.

73. *Times*, October 4, 1907, 7b.

74. Sidney Lee, *King Edward VII*, vol. 2 (New York: Macmillan, 1927), 222–26.

75. FO 367/47, no. 3184, draft of letter Barrington to Mackie, February 8, 1907; no. 5640, minute by Clarke on Mackie's mission, and draft of letter, Barrington to Villiers, February 22, 1907.

76. FO 367/46, no. 34257, Mackie to Grey, September 18, 1907.

77. Ibid., no. 38843, Villiers to Grey, November 18, 1907.

78. Ibid., no. 39656, Chatelain to Clarke, November 28, 1907, and minute by Clarke, December 5, 1907.

79. CP 180/686, *The Good Templars Watchword*, October 12, 1907, 481–82.

80. FO 367/18 includes extensive correspondence between Villiers and the FO over Pienaar.

81. FO 367/47, minute by Clarke, October 14, 1907, and by Langley.

82. *Anti-Slavery Reporter*, November–December 1906, 115–16; *Aborigines' Friend*, March 1907, 12–19; *West African Mail*, March 15, 1907, 1218; *Throne*, November 2, 9, and 16, 1907.

83. FO 367/46, no. 69, Beaumont to Tyrrell, October 9, 1907.

84. BFASS Papers, MSS Brit. Emp. S 18, C 79/53–56, Cadbury to Buxton, October 17, 18, 23, and 24, 1907; S 19, D 1/3, 711–13, copy of letter Buxton to Brooks, October 25, 1907; Morel Papers, Morel F8/12/67, Cadbury to Harris, October 22, 1907; CP 180/175, Buxton to Cadbury, October 22, 1907, and 180/177, Buxton to Cadbury, October 25, 1907.

85. *Daily Telegraph*, April 30, 1908, 11d.

86. CP 177, newspaper cuttings of *Evening Standard*, April 30 and May 16, 1908.

87. CP 197, Joseph Burtt, "Report on the Conditions of Coloured Labour in the Cocoa Plantations of S. Thomé and Principe, and the Method of Procuring It in Angola, Luanda, December 24th, 1906" [hereafter cited as Burtt Report 1906], 4, 6–8.

88. Burtt Report 1906, 9; Cadbury, *Labour in Portuguese West Africa*, appendix A, 103–31, contains "Joseph Burtt and Dr. Horton's Report on the Conditions of Coloured Labour on the Cocoa Plantations, July, 1907" [hereafter cited as Burtt Report 1907], quotation on 115. The several "final" reports contained in CP vary from each other slightly.

89. Burtt Report 1906, 9–10; Burtt Report 1907, 116.

90. Burtt Report 1906, 24.

91. Burtt Report 1907, 130–31.

92. CP 5/192, copy of letter Burtt to Cadbury, August 21, 1907.

93. CP 5/192, copy of letter Burtt to W. Cadbury, August 26, 1907, 5/193, Burtt to W. Cadbury, August 21, 1907, 180/361, copy of cover letter [unsigned but most likely by W. Cadbury] on copy of final draft of Burtt report to Cadbury's directors, August 28, 1907.

94. FO 367/46, no. 29406, draft of letter Lyell to Beaumont, September 2, 1907.

95. FO 367/46, Villiers to Langley, October 5, 1907.

96. CP 180/325, copy of letter Baldwin to Burtt, October 18, 1907.

97. FO 367/46, no. 33573, Cadbury Bros. to Grey, October 8, 1907.

98. Ibid., minutes; CP 180/537, Langley to Cadbury Bros., October 15, 1907.

99. FO 367/46, no. 36396, Villiers to Grey, October 26, 1907; CP 180/549, Clarke to W. Cadbury, October 31, 1907.

100. CP 180/365, copy of letter W. Cadbury to Cadbury Bros., November 19, 1907.

101. CP 180/370, W. Cadbury to Cadbury Bros., November 22, 1907.

102. CP 180/365, copy of letter W. Cadbury to Cadbury Bros., November 19, 1907.

103. CBBM, November 26, 1907.

104. CP 180/371, Cadbury to Cadbury Bros., November 23, 1907.

105. CP 180/375, Cadbury to Cadbury Bros., November 25, 1907.

106. FO 367/46, no. 39565, Villiers to Grey, November 26, 1907.

107. CP 6/73, copy of letter Merck to W. Cadbury, November 26, 1907, 180/365, copy of letter W. Cadbury to Cadbury Bros., November 19, 1907.

108. BFASS Papers, MSS Brit. Emp. S 22, G 268A, Statement Made by William Cadbury on Behalf of the English Cocoa Makers, to a Committee of the Proprietors of the Cocoa Estates of S. Thomé and Principé, Lisbon, Nov. 28th, 1907; also in Cadbury, *Labour in Portuguese West Africa,* appendix C.

109. CP 180/388, W. Cadbury to Cadbury Bros., November 28, 1907.

110. CP 180/383, poem by [W. Cadbury].

111. FO 367/46, no. 40348, Villiers to Grey, November 30, 1907; CP 180/552, Langley to Cadbury Bros., December 2, 1907.

112. Cadbury, *Labour in Portuguese West Africa,* 147–48.

113. FO 367/46, no. 40348, Villiers to Grey, November 30, 1907, no. 38843, Cadbury Bros. to FO, December 3, 1907, no. 40616, Cadbury Bros. to FO, December 10, 1907; FO 367/46, for a summary of the conference and proprietors' response dated December 4, 1907; CP 180/552, Langley to Cadbury Bros., December 2, 1907; CP 119, 8-page summary of the conference; BFASS Papers, MSS Brit. Emp. S 18, C 79/27, W. Cadbury to Buxton, December 10, 1907.

114. CP 180/870, copy of letter Cadbury Bros. to Ornellas, December 16, 1907; *Birmingham Daily Mail,* December 16, 1907, 2a, 5c; *Daily News,* December 16, 1907, 6d, 8d; *Daily Chronicle,* December 16, 1907, 6b; *Manchester Guardian,* December 16, 1907, 6d; *African Mail,* December 27, 1907, 114; *Times,* December 16, 1907, 10f; *Anti-Slavery Reporter,* November–December 1907, 127–28.

115. *Birmingham Daily Post,* December 17, 1907, 4b.

116. CP 180/185, Buxton to Cadbury, December 18, 1907; BFASS Papers, MSS Brit. Emp. S 18, C 79/87, Cadbury Bros. (obviously written by W. Cadbury) to Buxton, December 19, 1907.

117. CBBM, December 17, 1907.

118. CP 180/4, copy of letter Cadbury Bros. to Fox Bourne, May 12, 1903, document incorrectly dated May 12, 1902.

119. Burtt Report 1907, 127.

120. CP 180/26, copy of letter W. Cadbury to Fox Bourne, June 8, 1905.

121. CP 180/63, Cadbury to Fox Bourne, July 8, 1907.

122. CBBM, December 17, 1907.

Chapter 6

1. CP 180/93, Fox Bourne to Cadbury Bros., December 17, 1907.

2. CP 180/94, copy of letter W. Cadbury to Fox Bourne, December 18, 1907.

3. *Aborigines' Friend,* January 1908, 102–8, quotations from 107–8.

4. BFASS Papers, MSS Brit. Emp. S 18, C 79/89, Cadbury Bros. to APS, February 3, 1908; CP 180/99, copy of same letter with indication of copy to others.

5. CP 180/775, copy of letter W. Cadbury to Morel, February 5, 1908; BFASS Papers, MSS Brit. Emp. S 18, C 79/30a, W. Cadbury to Buxton, February 3, 1908.

6. CP 180/100, Fox Bourne to Cadbury Bros., February 5, 1908.

7. BFASS Papers, MSS Brit. Emp. S 18, C 150/125, copy of letter W. Cadbury to the APS, February 8, 1908.

8. CP 6/167, copy of letter W. Cadbury to Burtt, February 10, 1908.

9. J. D. Vincent-Smith, "The Portuguese Republic and Britain, 1910–14," *Journal of Contemporary History* 10 (October 1975): 709; Charles Hardinge, *Old Diplomacy: The Reminiscences of Lord Hardinge of Penshurst* (London: John Murray, 1947), 149–50.

10. FO 800/24, Charles Hardinge to Villiers, April 2, 1908; Gooch and Temperley, *British Documents,* vol. 8, 59–61, contains correspondence between Lisbon and London over the British naval forces.

11. FO 367/46, no. 40616, Cadbury Bros. to Langley, December 10, 1907, and accompanying documents.

12. *Anti-Slavery Reporter,* January–February 1908, 11–12, Buxton to the Secretary of the Portuguese Legation, early January 1908; FO 367/86, no. 1366, Buxton to Grey, January 11, 1908.

13. FO 367/86, no. 5978, Fox Bourne to FO, February 19, 1908.

14. *Parliamentary Debates,* 4th ser., vol. 183 (February 10, 1908), 1408, statement made by Churchill for Grey.

15. FO 367/86, no. 9054, Villiers to FO, March 7, 1908, and minutes, no. 12693, Villiers to Langley, April 8, 1908, and minutes, no. 15049, Fox Bourne to FO, May 1, 1908, no. 20248, Buxton to FO, June 11, 1908.

16. *Aborigines' Friend,* April 1908, 131, Langley to Fox Bourne, March 2, 1908; *Anti-Slavery Reporter,* June–July 1908, 76, Langley to Buxton, May 21, 1908.

17. FO 367/86, no. 15049, minutes regarding Fox Bourne's recently published pamphlet, "Slave Trade in Portuguese Africa," and his letter to FO, May 1, 1908, and copy of letter FO to Villiers, May 20, 1908, no. 20538, Villiers to Grey, June 8, 1908.

18. FO 367/86, nos. 20137 and 22820, Cadbury Bros. to Langley, June 10, 1908, and July 1, 1908.

19. BFASS Papers, MSS Brit. Emp. S 18, C 79/40, W. Cadbury to Buxton, July 2, 1908.

20. *Daily Chronicle*, March 30, 1908, 4d.

21. Nevinson's Diary, April 3, 1908; *Anti-Slavery Reporter*, March–May 1908, 45–46; *Times*, April 4, 1908, 9a; BFASS Papers, MSS Brit. Emp. S 19, D 1/4, p. 7, copy of letter Buxton to Nevinson, April 8, 1908.

22. *Aborigines' Friend*, May 1908, 146–47.

23. CP 305, 104, press cuttings give the date of the *Manchester Guardian* article as April 4, 1908, but it should read April 8; this letter does not appear in some April 8 editions of the newspaper.

24. Nevinson's Diary, April 13 and 15, 1908; *Manchester Guardian*, April 14, 1908, 7d, April 15, 1908, 7e; CP 177 and 305, p. 104.

25. Nevinson's Diary, April 18, 1908.

26. CP 6/172, copy of letter Cadbury to Burtt, April 7, 1908.

27. CP 180/805, Morel to Cadbury, July 27, 1908.

28. H. R. Fox Bourne, *Slave Traffic in Portuguese Africa* (London: P. S. King & Son, [1908]).

29. *Aborigines' Friend*, July 1908, 170; *Nation*, May 30, 1908, 301–2; *Manchester Guardian*, May 5, 1908, 6d.

30. *Daily News*, May 6, 1908, 4b–c; Nevinson's Diary, May 2, 5, and 8, 1908.

31. CP 180/107, copy of letter Cadbury to Fox Bourne, April 25, 1908, 180/104, copy of letter, Cadbury to Fox Bourne, April 8, 1908, 180/781, copy of letter Cadbury to Morel, April 27, 1908; Williams, *Firm of Cadbury*, 199.

32. CP 180/782, Morel to Cadbury, May 4, 1908, 180/783, copy of letter Cadbury to Morel, May 5, 1908.

33. See especially FO 367/86 for correspondence between the FO and the two societies in 1908 and also the *Anti-Slavery Reporter* and the *Aborigines' Friend*, which contain much of this correspondence verbatim.

34. FO 367/86, no. 5978, minute, August 18, 1908; *Aborigines' Friend*, July 1908, 171–74, November 1908, 208–23.

35. BFASS Papers, MSS Brit. Emp. S 18, C166/40, FO to BFASS, May 21, 1908, C166/43, FO to BFASS, June 27, 1908, C166/46, FO to BFASS, August 8, 1908, C 166/47, notes of interview held August 17, 1908, recorded on back of letter FO to BFASS, August 15, 1908.

36. *Parliamentary Debates*, 4th ser., vol. 183 (February 10, 1908), 1408, vol. 185 (March 12, 1908), 1748, vol. 190 (June 18, 1908), 1033–35, vol. 198 (December 11, 1908), 938.

37. Ibid., vol. 193 (July 27, 1908), 961, 975–76.

38. Ibid., 878. Charles Dilke, who asked the question, had been encouraged to do so by Morel; Dilke Papers, Add. Ms. 43897, fol. 227, copy of letter H. K. Hudson [for Dilke] to Morel, July 23, 1908.

39. FO 367/86, no. 597, correspondence with the English and Scottish Co-operative Wholesale Societies, January 6 and 13, 1908, and minutes.

40. Society of Friends, *Extracts from the Minutes and Proceedings of London Yearly Meeting of Friends, Held in Birmingham* (London: Society of Friends, 1908), 157.

41. *Chronicle of the London Missionary Society*, April 1908, 62.

42. Nevinson's Diary, April 14, 1908.

43. *Chronicle of the London Missionary Society*, June 1908, 102–3.

44. BFASS Papers, MSS Brit. Emp. S 18, C 79/126, Chatelain to Travers Buxton, July 5, 1908.

45. *Manchester Guardian*, May 5, 1908, 6d.

46. BFASS Papers, MSS Brit. Emp. S 18, C 89/52, Stober to Buxton, June 20, 1908.

47. Ibid., S 22, G 268A, "A Few Facts of the Continued Blot & Curse of the Slave Trade" by M. Z. Stober, undated [1908 or early 1909].

48. FO 367/86, no. 24110, Villiers to Grey, July 4, 1908.

49. FO 367/87, no. 33499, Villiers to Grey, September 19, 1908, and minutes, September 28, 1908.

50. CP 180/411, W. Cadbury to Cadbury Bros., June 22, 1908; FO 367/86, no. 23581, Cadbury Bros. to FO, July 6 and 20, 1908; CP 308, West Africa trip book, a list of issues, drawn up by Richard Cross, September 24, 1908, that Cadbury should pursue, including interviewing serviçais.

51. CP 180/411, W. Cadbury to Cadbury Bros., June 22, 1908; BFASS Papers, MSS Brit. Emp. S 18, C 79/41, W. Cadbury to Buxton, July 6, 1908.

52. CP 180/879, copy of letter W. Cadbury to Augusto Vidal de Castilho, August 17, 1908; CP 308, Augusto Castilho [to W. Cadbury], October 5, 1908.

53. CP 180/731, copy of letter W. Cadbury to Merck, June 17, 1908; CP 180/743, copy of letter W. Cadbury to Monkswell, September 25, 1908.

54. Clarence-Smith, *Cocoa and Chocolate*, 121–22. Francis Mantero, *Manual Labour in S. Thomé and Principe*, translated from Portuguese (1910; reprint, New York: Negro Universities Press, 1969), appendix, "Agricultural Companies in S. Thomé and Principe," lists Henry Burnay & Co. as directors for three agricultural estates in São Tomé in 1910.

55. CP 180/811, Morel to Cadbury, September 28, 1908; CP 180/786, Morel to Cadbury, July 4, 1908.

56. CP 180/732, Merck to Cadbury, July 23, 1908.

57. *Daily Chronicle*, October 1, 1908, 3c; *Standard*, September 26, 1908, 7e; *John Bull*, October 10, 1908, 339–40; *Daily News*, September 28, 1908, 6f; *African Mail*, July 17, 1908, 406; *Bournville Works Magazine*, November 1908, 4–5; CP 308, West Africa trip book, 1908–9.

58. CP 180/408, Cadbury Bros. to Thackray, April 7, 1908; CP 180/731, copy of letter W. Cadbury to Merck, June 17, 1908.

59. See chapter 5.

60. Geoffrey I. Nwaka, "Cadburys and the Dilemma of Colonial Trade in Africa, 1901–1910," *Bulletin de l'Institut Fondamental d'Afrique Noire* 42 (October 1980): 790; CP 186/138, William Leslie to Cadbury Bros., July 9, 1907; Williams, *Firm of Cadbury*, 147–48.

61. CP 180/776, copy of letter Cadbury to Morel, March 26, 1908, and 6/172, copy of letter Cadbury to Burtt, April 7, 1908.

62. CP 186/147, W. Cadbury to Leslie, May 30, 1908; Nwaka, "Cadburys and the Dilemma of Colonial Trade," 790–92.

63. *Anti-Slavery Reporter*, June–July 1908, 78.

64. CP 180/196, Buxton to Cadbury, June 13, 1908; BFASS Papers, MSS Brit. Emp. S 19, D 1/4, 205–6, copy of letter T. Buxton to Fowell Buxton, July 28, 1908.

65. Ibid., S 18, C 79/37, Cadbury to Buxton, June 17, 1908.

66. Ibid., S 18, C 79/44, Cadbury to Buxton, July 20, 1908.

67. Ibid., S 19, D 1/4, 219, copy of letter Buxton to Swan, August 10, 1908.

68. CP 180/201, Buxton to Cadbury, June 19, 1908.

69. BFASS Papers, MSS Brit. Emp. S 18, C 79/43, W. Cadbury to Buxton, July 11, 1908, and C 79/91, Cadbury Bros. to the BFASS, August 6, 1908; FO 367/86, no. 23813, Cadbury Bros. to FO, July 9, 1908; CP 180/593, Langley to Cadbury Bros., July 24, 1908.

70. *Daily News,* October 9, 1908, 8a; CP 177, press cutting, *Western Morning News,* October 10, 1908; *Manchester Guardian,* October 9, 1908, 6d.

71. *African Mail,* October 9, 1908.

72. FO 367/87, no. 37273, copy of letter Brooks to Morel, October 11, 1908.

73. Ibid., which contains the copies of several letters from or to Morel about the Conference; BFASS Papers, MSS Brit. Emp. S 18, C 85/126, Morel to Buxton, October 13, 1908, and S 19, D 1/4, 358–59, copy of letter Buxton to Morel, October 15, 1908.

74. CP 180/324, copy of letter [Morel] to Brooks, October 13, 1908.

75. CP 180/789, 791, 792, 796, 799, 800, and 801 contain this correspondence between Morel and Cadbury.

76. BFASS Papers, MSS Brit. Emp. S 18, C 86/40, Nevinson to Buxton, October 8, 1908, and C 86/41, Nevinson to Buxton, October 21, 1908.

77. Nevinson's Diary, October 22, 1908.

78. *Anti-Slavery Reporter,* November–December 1908, 124–38, gives a reasonably detailed summary of the meeting; Nevinson's quotation, 130.

79. Fox Bourne's long statement was reproduced in the *Aborigines' Friend,* November 1908, 208–23, and forwarded to Grey; Fox Bourne's quotation, 223.

80. Nevinson's Diary, October 22, 1908; FO 367/87, no. 39068, Clarke's comments, November 10, 1908.

81. CBBM, August 25, 1908, the company asked Barrow to representative the firm.

82. *Anti-Slavery Reporter,* November–December 1908, 135, 137; information on Spender, *Times,* April 16, 1926, 16d.

83. *Manchester Guardian,* October 23, 1908, 6d.

84. Ibid., November 3, 1908, 6f, and see also October 29, 1908, 4c–d.

85. Ibid., November 4, 1908, 3b, and see also the response by Walter Barrow, Cadbury's solicitor, November 3, 1908, 6f, and an editorial, November 24, 1908, 6d.

86. Stephen Koss, *Fleet Street Radical: A. G. Gardiner and the Daily News* (London: Allen Lane, 1973), 112; Koss, *Political Press,* 104–5.

87. Koss, *Fleet Street Radical,* 112–13; F. M. Leventhal, *The Last Dissenter: H. N. Brailsford and His World* (Oxford: Clarendon Press, 1985), 64.

88. Nevinson's Diary, June 19, 1908.

89. Ibid., August 11, 1908.

90. CP 180/822, Morel to Mrs. W. Cadbury, November 7, 1908.

91. Nevinson's Diary, November 1, 1908.

92. CP 180/824, Morel to Mrs. W. Cadbury, [November 9, 1908].

93. BFASS Papers, MSS Brit. Emp. S 18, C 89/13, Spender to Buxton, November 8, 1908.

94. Nevinson's Diary, November 5, 1908.

95. A. G. Gardiner, *Pillars of Society* (London: James Nisbet, 1913), 187, 190; E. T. Raymond, *Portraits of the New Century (The First Ten Years)* (London: Ernest Benn, 1928), 237.

96. BFASS Papers, MSS Brit. Emp. S 18, C 89/13, Spender to Buxton, November 8, 1908.

97. Ibid., S 19, D 1/4, 430–31, copy of letter Buxton to Spender, November 11, 1908.

98. Ibid., S 18, C 86/43, Nevinson to Buxton, November 12, 1908.

99. *Times*, November 21, 1908, 10c; Galsworthy wrote a letter on slavery to the *Times*, January 14, 1909, 4f.

100. Nevinson's Diary, November 19, 1908; BFASS Papers, MSS Brit. Emp. S 19, D 1/4, 454, 458, copy of letter Travers Buxton to Fowell Buxton, November 23, 1908.

101. Strachey Papers, S/25/3/1, copy of letter Strachey to George Cadbury, November 18, 1908; CP 180/866, Nevinson to George Cadbury, November 20, 1908.

102. Strachey Papers, S/25/3/2, Cadbury to Strachey, November 23, 1908.

103. Nevinson's Diary, November 18, 1908.

104. Ibid., December 3, 1908.

105. Ibid., December 4, 1908; Nevinson, *More Changes*, 87.

106. Strachey Papers, S/25/3/2, George Cadbury to Strachey, November 23, 1908; FO 367/87, no. 41209, minutes in response to the *Times*'s announcement of the meeting.

107. Nevinson's Diary, December 4, 1908.

108. *Daily Chronicle*, December 5, 1908, 6b.

109. *Anti-Slavery Reporter*, November–December 1908, 141–42.

110. Nevinson's Diary, December 11, 1908; *Spectator*, December 12, 1908, 984–85; *Anti-Slavery Reporter*, November–December 1908, 141–42; *Aborigines' Friend*, January 1909, 240–42; *Manchester Guardian*, December 5, 1908, 11e; *Daily Chronicle*, December 5, 1908, 6b. *Times*, December 5, 1908, 9e, incorrectly included the term *immediately* in the second resolution—"unless strong measures are immediately taken to abolish the slave traffic"; Morel's letter to the *Times*, December 15, 1908, 18c, pointed out the mistake.

111. BFASS Papers, MSS Brit. Emp. S 18, C 86/47, Nevinson to Buxton, December 7, 1908; C 86/46, Nevinson to Buxton, December 11, 1908; C 89/57, Strachey to Buxton, December 9, 1908; C 89/58, Strachey to Buxton, December 16, 1908.

112. Nevinson's Diary, December 10, 1908.

113. BFASS Papers, MSS Brit. Emp. S 18, C 86/49, Nevinson to Buxton, December 17, 1908.

114. FO 367/87, no. 44211, memorandum of deputation's meeting with Grey, December 10, 1908.

115. FO 367/140, no. 1282, Villiers to Grey, January 2, 1909.

Chapter 7

1. CP 305, newspaper cuttings, *John Bull*, June 13, 1908, 558, June 20, 1908, 594.

2. CBBM, June 10, 1908.

3. CP 305, *John Bull*, June 27, 1908, 615.

4. *Chronicle of the London Missionary Society*, January 1909, 3, February 1909, 32.

5. *Standard*, September 26, 1908, 6e–f.

6. *DNB*; see also Sydney Dark, *The Life of Sir Arthur Pearson* (London: Hodder and Stoughton, [1922]).

7. *DNB*; Nevinson, *More Changes*, 5.

8. Nevinson's Diary, October 1, 1908.

9. *Standard*, October 6, 1908, 8e.

10. CBBM, September 29, 1908.

11. CP 1/1, 1908.—C.—No. 3211. In the High Court of Justice. King's Bench Division, Fos. 23. Writ issued October 5, 1908. Statement of Claim [by Plaintiffs].

12. CP 180/421, copy of letter W. Cadbury to Mrs. Cadbury, October 29, 1908.

13. FO 367/18, no. 8806, Report on the Treatment of the "Serviçaes," or Contract Labourers, in the Portuguese Islands Known as the Province of São Thomé and Principe, *Confidential*.

14. Williams, *Firm of Cadbury*, 200.

15. CP 308, copy of letter W. Cadbury to Governor of San Thomé, November 12, 1908.

16. CP 308, West Africa trip book, 1908–1909.

17. CP 180/435, copy of letter W. Cadbury to Mrs. Cadbury, November 24, 1908.

18. CP 180/447, copy of letter W. Cadbury to Cadbury Bros., December 24, 1908.

19. FO 367/140, no. 3840, Mackie to Grey, December 26, 1908, and no. 5727, Mackie to Grey, January 6, 1909.

20. Ibid., no. 2747, Mackie to Grey, December 15, 1908.

21. CP 180/439, W. Cadbury to Cadbury Bros., December 6, 1908.

22. C. Norman Edwards, *Cadburys on the Gold Coast and Ghana* (Privately printed, Birmingham, UK, 1958) 5–6, book available in CP 247; CP 308, copies of letters W. Cadbury to [?Mrs. Cadbury], February 2 and 3, 1909.

23. CP 186/128, Cadbury to Mate Kole, April 7, 1909; "Cocoa in West Africa," *Bournville Works Magazine*, February 1945, 22–25.

24. CBBM, January 5 and 12, 1909.

25. *Bournville Works Magazine*, April 1909, 165–67.

26. CP 180/896, copy of letter Arnold Rowntree to Walter [Barrow], March 16, 1909; BFASS Papers, MSS Brit. Emp. S 18, C 82/109, Harris to Buxton, March 13, 1909.

27. *Spectator*, March 20, 1909, 453, listed Cadbury, Epps, Fry, Rowntree, Stollwerck, Suchard, and Van Houten as participating in the boycott; for examples of announcements or letters, see *Manchester Guardian*, March 19, 1909, 5e, March 22, 1909, 5e, March 29, 1909, 5b; *Spectator*, March 13, 1909, 416–17, March 27, 1909, 496.

28. *Birmingham Daily Mail*, March 17, 1909, 4d; *Daily Chronicle*, March 17, 1909, 1e; *Daily Telegraph*, March 17, 1909, 6g; *Morning Leader*, March 17, 1909, 5e; *Times*, March 17, 1909, 8d; *Baker and Confectioner*, March 19, 1909, 274.

29. CP 177, newspaper cutting, *Daily News*, March 17, 1909; *Spectator*, March 20, 1909, 453.

30. *Manchester Guardian*, March 17, 1909, 5d.

31. *Nation*, March 20, 1909, 915.

32. *John Bull*, March 27, 1909, 347.

33. CP 305, p. 118, newspaper cutting, *Yorkshire Herald*, April 5, 1909.

34. *Friend*, March 26, 1909, 193–94.

35. BFASS Papers, MSS Brit. Emp. S 19, D 1/4, 676–77, copy of letter Buxton to Harris, March 19, 1909.

36. *Daily News*, March 17, 1909, 6.

37. *Nation*, March 20, 1909, 925–26.

38. CP 180/867, Nevinson to W. Cadbury, April 9, 1909.

39. CP 180/672, Grundler to Cadbury, May 23, 1909.

40. CP 180/329, copy of letter Cadbury to Burtt, March 17, 1909.

41. CP 180/838, copy of letter Cadbury to Morel, March 13, 1909, and 180/839, copy of letter Cadbury to Morel, March 17, 1909.

42. CP 180/844, copy of letter Cadbury to Morel, April 22, 1909; FO 367/140, no. 17035, Cadbury Bros. to FO, May 4, 1909; BFASS Papers, MSS Brit. Emp. S 18, C 79/66, 68, and 69, Cadbury Bros. or W. Cadbury to Buxton, May 4, 21, and 24, 1909.

43. Duffy, *Question of Slavery*, 201.

44. *Aborigines' Friend*, November 1908, 218–19, copy of letter Fox Bourne to Grey, November 4, 1908.

45. *Times*, February 6, 1909, 13d; see also *Aborigines' Friend*, May 1909, 250–54.

46. *Manchester Guardian*, February 6, 1909, 8g.

47. Ibid., June 28, 1909, 3e.

48. Nevinson's Diary, June 11, 1909.

49. CP 177, press cutting, *Financial News*, April 24, 1909; Strachey Papers, S/25/3/12, Cadbury Bros. to Strachey, October 19, 1909, with copy of letter Baker to Cadbury Bros., October 11, 1909, and copy of letter Cadbury Bros. to Baker, October 19, 1909.

50. BFASS Papers, MSS Brit. Emp. S 19, D 1/4, 970, copy of letter Buxton to W. Cadbury, May 14, 1909, and D 1/5, 180–81, copy of letter Buxton to Burtt, August 23, 1909.

51. BFASS Papers, MSS Brit. Emp. S 24, J 26, 380, newspaper cuttings.

52. Strachey Papers, S/25/3/10, W. Cadbury to Strachey, October 8, 1909.

53. BFASS Papers, MSS Brit. Emp. S 19, D 1/5, 63, copy of letter Buxton to Burtt, July 21, 1909.

54. FO 367/141, no. 38694, Bryce to FO, October 9, 1909, and draft of letter FO to Bryce, October 18, 1909.

55. Joseph Burtt, "How America Can Free the Portuguese Cocoa Slave," *Leslie's Illustrated Weekly*, October 14, 1909, 368–69, and "My Success in America," *Leslie's Illustrated Weekly*, December 16, 1909, 608; BFASS Papers, MSS Brit. Emp. S 22, G 267, interim report by Burtt, December 30, 1909; *Anti-Slavery Reporter and Aborigines' Friend*, April 1910, 81–85, includes Burtt's report at the conclusion of the trip, February 1910.

56. FO 367/141, no. 38694, Tilly to Langley, October 18, 1909.

57. *Anti-Slavery Reporter*, November–December 1908, 138–40.

58. FO 367/87, no. 19894, Mackie to Grey, March 15, 1908, and minutes.

59. Ibid., no. 39906, Villiers to Langley, November 9, 1908, and enclosure.

60. FO 367/140, no. 2747, copy of letter Mackie to Cid, December 15, 1908.

61. *Parliamentary Debates*, 5th ser., vol. 1 (February 22, 1909), 428–29, and (March 3, 1909), 1415, 1423, vol. 2 (March 8, 1909), 25.

62. Ibid., vol. 2 (March 11, 1909), 492–94.

63. BFASS Papers, MSS Brit. Emp. S 18, C 166/49, FO to BFASS, January 28, 1909.

64. FO 367/140, no. 14817, Mackie to Grey, March 18, 1909, and no. 17232, Mackie to Grey, April 5, 1909.

65. Ibid., no. 16609, Villiers to Grey, April 27, 1909. The missionary was Wesley Maier Stover.

66. Ibid., no. 13721, Villiers to Grey, April 7, 1909; CP 180/625, FO to Cadbury Bros., April 29, 1909; identical letter sent to BFASS, April 29, 1909, BFASS Papers, MSS Brit. Emp. S 18, C 166/56.

67. *Anti-Slavery Reporter and Aborigines' Friend*, October 1909, 3–5.

68. FO 367/141, no. 29535, Villiers to FO, July 31, 1909.

69. CP 180/616, translated copy of terms of engagement of natives from the Province of Mozambique, issued December 15, 1908, sent to FO by R. C. F. Maugham, British consul at Lourenço Marques; copy also included as an appendix in Cadbury, *Labour in Portuguese West Africa*, 158–60.

70. FO 367/141, no. 32730, W. Cadbury to Langley, August 28, 1909, containing a translation of article in *O Século* dated August 9, 1909, no. 38481, Villiers to FO, October 14, 1909.

71. Ibid., no. 38502, Mackie to FO, September 21, 1909, no. 40146, transcription of telegram, Mackie to FO, November 1, 1909, and minutes.

72. Parliament, *Correspondence Respecting Contract Labour in Portuguese West Africa*, Africa No. 2, Cd. 6322, 1912, pp. 29–31, Mackie to Grey, November 30, 1909; available also in CP 250/1.

73. FO 367/46, no. 41309, Cadbury Bros. to FO, December 16, 1909, draft of letter Langley to Cadbury Bros., December 24, 1909, and minutes.

74. *Daily Graphic*, November 23–29, 1909; *Manchester Guardian*, November 19, 1909, 7d.

75. CP 180/738, Merck to W. Cadbury, March 23, 1909.

76. *Times*, March 27, 1909, 9e–f.

77. FO 367/140, no. 11906, Villiers to FO, March 23, 1909.

78. *Times*, June 4, 1909, 3c.

79. *Financial Times*, April 24, 1909, 4c–d.

80. *Times*, March 19, 1909, 5f; *Globe*, March 17, 1909, 8c.

81. CP 180/698, translation of letter Francisco Mantero to W. Cadbury, March 22, 1909.

82. BFASS Papers, MSS Brit. Emp. S 22, G 268/A, copy of Negreiros's article.

83. Ibid., G 268B, Nevinson to Mr. Bryant, March 24, 1909, and S 18, C 86/55, Nevinson to Buxton, September 28, 1909.

84. *African Mail*, April 2, 1909, 252.

85. CP 305, 161, newspaper cutting, *Tropical Life*, December 1911, 242, 247.

86. *Times*, June 4, 1909, 3c–d.

87. *Times*, June 5, 1909, 3c.

88. *Times*, September 28, 1909, 16d–e.

89. *Times*, September 30, 1909, 10f.

90. *Spectator*, October 2, 1909, 498, and October 16, 1909, 603.

91. BFASS Papers, MSS Brit. Emp. S 22, G 267, copy of letter Wyllie to M. Teixeira de Mattos, c/o Morel, December 10, 1909.

92. Annie E. Coombes, *Reinventing Africa: Museums, Material Culture and Popular Imagination in Late Victorian and Edwardian England* (New Haven, Conn.: Yale University Press, 1994); John M. MacKenzie, "Empire and Metropolitan Cultures," in Andrew Porter, ed., *The Oxford History of the British Empire*, vol. 3, *The Nineteenth Century* (Oxford: Oxford University Press, 1999), 270–93; Douglas A. Lorimer, "Race, Science and Culture: Historical Continuities and Discontinuities, 1850–1914," in Shearer West, ed., *The Victorians and Race* (Aldershot, UK: Ashgate, 1996), 18–19.

93. Patrick Brantlinger, *Rule of Darkness: British Literature and Imperialism, 1830–1914* (Ithaca, N.Y.: Cornell University Press, 1988), 173–97, quotation on 184.

94. Ronald Hyam, *Britain's Imperial Century, 1815–1914* (New York: Barnes and Noble,

1976), 134, 158; Nicholas Thomas, *Colonialism's Culture: Anthropology, Travel and Government* (Princeton, N.J.: Princeton University Press, 1994), 143–57.

95. Taking advantage of his contacts, Nevinson throughout 1909 continued to contribute letters and articles on slavery to many newspapers, e.g., *Spectator*, July 10, 1909, 54; *Economist*, November 27, 1909, 1102–3.

96. BLPES Archives, Coll Misc 851, Cadbury Bros. [most likely W. Cadbury] to R. Mudie Smith, London Missionary Society, April 27, 1908.

97. *Spectator*, March 27, 1909, 491–92.

98. CP 180/911, copy of letter Cadbury to Strachey, March 30, 1909; Strachey Papers, S/25/3/6, Cadbury to Strachey, April 2, 1909, and S/25/3/8, Cadbury to Strachey, April 7, 1909.

99. Ibid., S/25/3/5, copy of letter Strachey to Cadbury, April 1, 1909, and S/25/3/7, copy of letter Strachey to Cadbury, April 5, 1909.

100. Nevinson's Diary, April 16, 1909.

101. Ibid., April 21, 1909.

102. CP 180/332, copy of letter Cadbury to Burtt, April 16, 1909.

103. Nevinson's Diary, June 3, 1909.

104. Ibid., September 17, 1909.

105. Ibid., July 20, 1909.

106. Koss, *Fleet Street Radical*, 112.

107. Ibid., 118–20; Nevinson, *More Changes*, 323–25; *Times*, October 5, 1909, 8c–d.

108. *Times*, September 2, 1909, 3d–e. "Also a Spectator," an acquaintance of Nevinson, contributed one lengthy and several short letters on the slave trade to the *Spectator* during 1909, January 9, 1909, 50–51, April 3, 1909, 536.

109. CP 1/8, Assizes's records, December 6, 1909; BFASS Papers, MSS Brit. Emp. S 18, C 79/43, W. Cadbury to Buxton, July 11, 1908, and C 79/48, Cadbury to Buxton, August 11, 1908.

110. *Times*, June 22, 1909, 8d; FO 367/141, no. 20881, Swan's report, submitted June 2, 1909.

111. CP 180/920, Swan to Cadbury, May 10, 1909.

112. CP 180/924, copy of letter Cadbury to Swan, May 21, 1909.

113. CP 180/926, copy of letter Swan to Cadbury, July 5, 1909.

114. CBBM, October 9, 1906; Michael C. Rowlinson, "Cadburys' New Factory System, 1879–1919" (Ph.D. diss., University of Aston, Birmingham, 1987), 76–78.

115. Many historians have commented on the response of Cadbury Bros. to the use of slave labor in the production of cocoa in São Tomé. Several historians stress or assume that the Cadbury firm's response was based exclusively or primarily on humanitarian reasons. These include Iola Williams, *The Firm of Cadbury, 1831–1931* (1931), Gillian Wagner, *The Chocolate Conscience* (1979), and Carol Kennedy, *The Merchant Princes. Family, Fortune and Philanthropy: Cadbury, Sainsbury and John Lewis* (2000). James Walvin, who has written extensively about slavery, does not mention the São Tomé cocoa controversy in *The Quakers: Money and Morals* (1997). James Duffy, in his excellent *A Question of Slavery* (1967), believes that Cadbury's directors were unaware that the Foreign Office was reluctant to pursue the issue because of the need for Mozambique labor in British South Africa. In 1980, Geoffrey I. Nwaka, a Nigerian historian, implied in an article titled "Cadburys and the Dilemma of

Colonial Trade in Africa, 1901–1910" that Cadbury Bros., fearing an adverse impact on company profits, postponed boycotting São Tomé cocoa beans until after an alternative supply was identified. According to Nwaka, it was no accident that the Cadbury firm announced the boycott only after the company had concluded that suitable beans could be grown and processed in the Gold Coast area. Kevin Grant, in his 1997 doctoral dissertation, "'A Civilised Savagery': British Humanitarian Politics and European Imperialism in Africa, 1884–1926," takes this argument even further, charging that as soon as the issue of slavery emerged in 1901, William Cadbury took deliberate steps to safeguard the company's primary source of cocoa beans in São Tomé and to discourage humanitarians from publicly drawing attention to the issue. Grant contends that Cadbury worked to counter Nevinson's report, even before it began to appear in *Harper's* in August 1905. Cadbury found a friend and a talented supporter in his attempt to downplay Portuguese abuses in E. D. Morel, who feared that public exposure of the cocoa scandal would detract from much worse conditions in the Congo, which he was determined to abolish. Grant says that Cadbury's directors did not cut themselves off from their primary source of beans until they had helped to develop cocoa production in the Gold Coast. Roger Southall, in his doctoral dissertation of 1975, "Cadbury on the Gold Coast, 1907–1938," argues that the Cadbury firm was well aware of the possible negative impact that an early boycott could have on its business. Charles Dellheim, in a 1987 article, "The Creation of a Company Culture: *Cadburys*, 1861–1931," p. 36, expresses the belief that economic concerns played an important role in the company's response to the slavery controversy: "Given the Quaker abhorrence of slavery, one would have expected the Cadburys to have acted quickly and unequivocally. But, although their will was good, their judgment was dubious and their actions were slow. They relied on the advice of the Foreign Office—rarely a wise idea—but even when we take this into account, it is difficult to avoid the conclusion that commercial interests constrained their actions."

116. In June 1910, when Nevinson visited two cocoa dealers, Oldendorff and Bond, the latter expressed his belief that the Cadbury company "didn't declare boycott till the Accra [Gold Coast] plantations were ready" and that Fry bought a huge contract of São Tomé beans "the very day before boycott was declared, & continued drawing [on] it for many months." Nevinson's Diary, June 3, 1910.

117. CP 1/8, Assizes's record, December 3, 1909.

118. Nevinson's Diary, October 6, 1909.

119. George Cadbury contributed to the BFASS beginning in 1892 and the APS from 1901 to 1908, and William Cadbury contributed to the BFASS from 1900 to 1908 and the APS in 1905; CP 143, list of subscriptions, prepared for court, trial proceedings; Grant, "'Civilised Savagery,'" 166; *World*, February 15, 1910, 269–70.

Chapter 8

1. BFASS Papers, MSS Brit. Emp. S 18, C 82/106, Harris to Buxton, February 17, 1909.
2. Nevinson's Diary, January 28, 1909.
3. Ibid., June 3, 1909.
4. Ibid., July 20, 1909.
5. CP 115, Supreme Court of Judicature, Court of Appeal (July 28, 1909), Cadbury

Brothers v. the Standard Newspapers Limited, Judgment; *Birmingham Daily Post,* July 29, 1909, 12f.

6. CP 180/230, copy of letter Cadbury to Buxton, April 18, 1909, 180/232, copy of letter Cadbury to Buxton, April 20, 1909.

7. CP 180/233, Buxton to Cadbury, April 24, 1909.

8. BFASS Papers, MSS Brit. Emp. S 19, D 1/5, 426, copy of letter T. Buxton to Fowell Buxton, October 28, 1909.

9. Ibid., 410–11, Buxton to Albright, October 27, 1909, and 416, comments on the proof, S 19, D 2/1, Proof of Mr. Travers Buxton, in the High Court of Justice, 1908 C. No. 3211, and Writ of Subpoena, S 18, C 91/54, Wragge to Buxton, November 2, 1909; CP 180/241, Buxton to Wragge, November 6, 1909.

10. BFASS Papers, MSS Brit. Emp. S 18, C 91/61, Wragge to Buxton, December 6, 1909.

11. Ibid., S 19, D 1/5, 428, copy of letter Buxton to W. Cadbury, October 20, 1909; CP 180/109, copy of letter W. Cadbury to A. J. Bryant, April 20, 1909, and 180/117, Bryant to W. Cadbury, June 8, 1909.

12. CP 180/733, Merck to Mrs. W. Cadbury, November 30, 1908; CP 180/741, Merck to W. Cadbury, April 22, 1909; CP 180/742, copy of letter Cadbury to Merck, April 26, 1909.

13. CP 121, Notes for the Cross-Examination of Mr. Nevinson.

14. FO 367/140, no. 12543, Cadbury Bros. to Grey, March 31, 1909. The date of the meeting, listed in this printed letter as October 26, 1907, is incorrect. It should read October 26, 1906.

15. FO 367/18, no. 37618, Cadbury Bros. to FO, November 7, 1906, and memorandum, November 7, 1906; FO 367/141, no. 39798, Memorandum Respecting Messrs. Cadbury's Action against the "Standard" Respecting Contract Labour in Portuguese West Africa—communicated to Lord Chancellor, October 27, 1909.

16. See chapter 4 for a discussion of this meeting.

17. FO 367/141, no. 38554, Cadbury Bros. to Grey, October 15, 1909.

18. Ibid., no. 39798, Memorandum Respecting Messrs. Cadbury's Action.

19. CP 180/629 through 640 and FO 367/140 and 141 contain extensive correspondence on documents to be provided by the FO for the trial.

20. FO 367/141, no. 40667, Wragge & Co. to FO, November 4, 1909, and Langley to Wragge & Co., November 6, 1909; FO 367/46, no. 21143, FO minutes of meeting of deputation from three chocolate firms with Clarke and Lyell at the FO, June 27, 1907.

21. FO 367/140, nos. 12543 and 14717 cover questions raised in Parliament by Levering Lewis, MP, of Grey, about the October 26, 1906, meeting.

22. CP 180/696, Messrs. Mackrell & Co. to Cadbury Bros., July 21, 1909; CP 202, "Thirty Years of Progress."

23. Among the many studies of these two attorneys and their cases, see H. Montgomery Hyde, *Carson* (1953; reprint, New York: Octagon Books, 1974); A. T. Q. Stewart, *Edward Carson* (Dublin: Gill and Macmillan, 1981); Edward Marjoriebanks, *Carson the Advocate* (New York: Macmillan, 1932); Derek Walker-Smith, *Lord Reading and His Cases: The Study of a Great Career* (London: Chapman & Hall, 1934); Gardiner, *Pillars of Society;* Lewis Broad, *Advocates of the Golden Age* (London: John Long, 1958); and others cited in this chapter.

24. Earl of Birkenhead, *Contemporary Personalities* (London: Cassell, 1924), 196.

25. William Allen Jowitt, ed., *The Dictionary of English Law*, also known as *Jowitt's Dictionary of English Law*, vol. 2, 2nd ed. (London: Sweet & Maxwell, 1977), 1482: "Queen's Counsel, barristers who have obtained the appointment of counsel to the Crown by reason, as old writers put it, of their learning and talent. They wear silk gowns, sit within the bar and take precedence in court over utter barristers, that is to say, the ordinary barristers, who sit outside the bar." They become a King's or a Queen's Counsel automatically, as appropriate.

26. Denis Judd, *Lord Reading* (London: Weidenfeld and Nicolson, 1982), 21.

27. Marquess of Reading, *Rufus Isaacs, First Marquess of Reading* (New York: G. P. Putnam's Sons, 1940), 185.

28. Raymond, *Portraits of the New Century*, 305.

29. Birkenhead, *Contemporary Personalities*, 107.

30. Raymond, *Portraits of the New Century*, 307–8.

31. Reading, *Rufus Isaacs*, 81.

32. Ibid., 85.

33. H. Montgomery Hyde, *Their Good Names: Twelve Cases of Libel and Slander* (London: Hamish Hamilton, 1970), 195. Hyde gives the total figure of £220,000; Charles Wilson, *A History of Unilever: A Study in Economic Growth and Social Change*, vol. 1 (London: Cassell, 1954), 82–88, reports £91,000.

34. According to the *Oxford English Dictionary*, a "devil" is "a junior legal counsel who does professional work for his leader, usually without fee."

35. James Johnston, *Westminster Voices: Studies in Parliamentary Speech* (London: Hodder and Stoughton, 1928), 146–47; H. Montgomery Hyde, *United in Crime* (London: William Heinemann, 1955), 60–61; Gardiner, *Pillars of Society*, 132–39; David Dutton, *Simon: A Political Biography of Sir John Simon* (London: Aurum Press, 1992).

36. Birmingham Magistrates' Court, "Victoria Law Courts Visitor Guide," n.d.; *Birmingham Evening Mail*, March 31, 1987, 7a–e, from newspaper file on Victoria Law Courts, Birmingham Central Library.

37. Kennedy, *Merchant Princes*, 57.

38. *Birmingham Daily Mail*, November 29, 1909, 2g–3a.

39. Edward Marjoriebanks, *Carson the Advocate* (New York: Macmillan, 1932), 393.

40. Hochschild, *King Leopold's Ghost*, 260–65; Pagan Kennedy, *Black Livingstone: A True Tale of Adventure in the Nineteenth-Century Congo* (New York: Viking, 2002), 177–87; The *Times* gave minor coverage to the 1909 trial on April 11, 3e, May 18, 5d, October 2, 5b, October 7, 3b, and October 8, 3b.

41. The account of this trial is drawn from the records of the Assizes, found in CP 1/8, as well as several newspapers, including the *Evening Despatch* and the *Times*.

42. William Allen Jowitt, ed., *The Dictionary of English Law*, vol. 2, 1st ed. (London: Sweet & Maxwell, 1959), 1660.

43. *Evening Despatch*, November 29, 1909, 5.

44. CP 1/8, Assizes, November 29, 1909.

45. Ibid.

46. Ibid.

47. *Birmingham Gazette and Express*, December 1, 1909, 6f.

48. CP 1/8, Assizes, November 30, 1909.

49. *Times*, December 1, 1909, 4a.

50. CP 1/8, Assizes, November 30, 1909.
51. Ibid.
52. Ibid.
53. Ibid.
54. *Evening Despatch*, December 1, 1909, 5d.
55. CP 1/8, Assizes, December 1, 1909.
56. *Evening Despatch*, December 1, 1909, 5b.
57. Ibid.
58. Marjoriebanks, *Carson the Advocate*, 395.
59. *Times*, December 2, 1909, 4.
60. Hyde, *Carson*, 252.
61. Ibid., 250.
62. CP 1/8, Assizes, December 1, 1909.
63. *Evening Despatch*, December 1, 1909, 5d.
64. Ibid.
65. CP 1/8, Assizes, December 2, 1909.
66. *Manchester Guardian*, December 3, 1909, 10a.
67. CP 1/8, Assizes, December 2, 1909.
68. Ibid.
69. *Evening Despatch*, December 2, 1909, 5c.
70. Ibid., 5d.
71. Ibid., 5c.
72. CP 1/8, Assizes, December 2, 1909.
73. Ibid.
74. *Evening Despatch*, December 2, 1909, 5c.
75. *Times*, December 3, 1909, 4.
76. Walker-Smith, *Lord Reading and His Cases*, 231.
77. *Daily News*, December 3, 1909, 9e.
78. *Evening Despatch*, December 3, 1909, 5a.
79. Ibid.
80. CP 1/8, Assizes, December 3, 1909.
81. Ibid.; Marjoriebanks, *Carson the Advocate*, 397.
82. CP 1/8, Assizes, December 3, 1909.
83. Ibid.
84. Nevinson, *More Changes*, 91.
85. CP 1/8, Assizes, December 3, 1909.
86. *Birmingham Daily Mail*, December 7, 1909.
87. *Evening Despatch*, December 4, 1909, 5a.
88. CP 1/8, Assizes, December 4, 1909.
89. Ibid.
90. Ibid.
91. Ibid.
92. *Evening Despatch*, December 6, 1909, 5b.
93. CP 1/8, Assizes, December 6, 1909.
94. Nevinson's Diary, November 30–December 4, 1909.

Chapter 9

1. Peter F. Carter-Ruck, *Carter-Ruck on Libel and Slander*, 3rd ed. (London: Butterworths, 1985), 153–54; Julie A. Scott-Bayfield, *Defamation: Law and Practice* (London: FT Law & Tax, 1996), 120.

2. Hyde, *Carson*, 255.

3. Ibid., 253; Marjoriebanks, *Carson the Advocate*, 400–401.

4. Nevinson's Diary, December 6, 1909.

5. CP 178/207, clipping from the *North Essex Conservative and Unionist Monthly Magazine*, December 1909; CP 180/887, H. Moray to W. Cadbury, December 12, 1909.

6. Among newspapers without editorials were the *Manchester Guardian*, *Daily Telegraph*, *Daily News*, *Daily Chronicle*, *Northern Echo*, *Financial News*, *Newcastle Daily Chronicle*, *Daily Mirror*, and *Pall Mall Gazette*.

7. *Birmingham Daily Mail*, December 7, 1909, 4b.

8. *Birmingham Daily Post*, December 7, 1909, 6d–e.

9. *Birmingham Pictorial and Dart*, December 17, 1909, 11.

10. *Birmingham Weekly Post*, December 11, 1909, 8b.

11. BFASS Papers, MSS Brit. Emp. S 18, C 90/98, Whitla to T. Buxton, January 19, 1910.

12. *African Mail*, December 10, 1909, 92.

13. CP 180/927, A. M. Tracey to Cadbury Bros., November 30, 1909.

14. CP 305, 133, newspaper cutting, *British Weekly*, December 16, 1909; Koss, *Political Press*, 101.

15. *Morning Post*, December 7, 1909, 6e.

16. *Nation*, December 11, 1909, 450.

17. *Spectator*, December 11, 1909, 983.

18. *Globe*, December 7, 1909, 1b.

19. *Saturday Review*, December 11, 1909, 716, 721–22.

20. *Times*, December 7, 1909, 9f–10a.

21. BFASS Papers, MSS Brit. Emp. S 19, D 1/6, p. 65, copy of letter Buxton to Burtt, December 8, 1909.

22. Simon Papers, MS Simon 48, fol. 8, G. Cadbury to J. Simon, December 8, 1909; CP 305, Isaacs to W. Cadbury, December 7, 1909.

23. BFASS Papers, MSS Brit. Emp. S 18, C 91/62, Edward Cadbury to Buxton, December 7, 1909.

24. CBBM, file no. 10, December 7, 1909, resolution from employees, and minutes, December 14, 1909, George Cadbury's statement to employees.

25. CP 178/128 [misnumbered 178/28, it follows 178/127], Morel to Cadbury, December 7, 1909.

26. CP 178/200, Sturge to Cadbury, December 8, 1909; CP 178/168, Read to Cadbury, December 8, 1909.

27. See especially letters in CP 178 and CP 180/470–474, letters to Mrs. Cadbury.

28. CP 178/34, J. Cadbury to W. Cadbury, December 6, 1909.

29. CP178/2, Albright to Cadbury, December 7, 1909; 178/8, Sir Barclay to W. Cadbury, December 7, 1909; 178/53, William Darby to W. Cadbury, December 7, 1909.

30. CP 178/86, Hilda Grundler to W. Cadbury, December 9, 1909.

31. CP 179/38, S. S. Massey to Cadbury Bros., December 8, 1909.

32. CP 180/42, unsigned letter to Cadbury Bros., n.d.

33. CP 178/14, Miss Benson, Bride Cake Maker, to Cadbury Bros., December 22, 1909, 178/16, copy of letter Cadbury Bros. to Benson, December 23, 1909.

34. CP 179/19, copy of letter Cadbury Bros. to Mrs. Davis, December 21, 1909.

35. CP 179/4, copy of letter Cadbury Bros. to A. Bakewell, December 8, 1909, and others.

36. *Birmingham Pictorial and Dart*, December 10, 1909, 3.

37. Rufus Isaacs (Reading) Papers, MSS Eur. F. 118/143, a list of fees in the case.

38. CP 176. For each of these three counsels, two figures are listed. For example, Isaacs is printed as £2759–8–0, with £2698–15–6 penciled in. There are similar calculations for Simon and Craig. According to the *Birmingham Daily Mail*, December 7, 1909, 6c, the taxing master in London had the power to reduce costs, and this may be reflected in the two sums in the Cadbury Papers.

39. CBBM, March 22, 1910.

40. CBBM, April 25, 1910, clipping from *Financial Times*, April 12, 1910.

Chapter 10

1. Duffy, *Questions of Slavery*, 211–29, regards the humanitarians as much too critical of the Portuguese labor system after 1910.

2. This was the second edition. The 1909 first edition was little more than a private printing sent to a few friends and the Foreign Office; for the second edition, Cadbury added a chapter recounting Portugal's newly issued labor code. The book contains several useful appendixes, including Burtt's report, William Cadbury's statements in 1907 to the Liverpool Chamber of Commerce and to the Lisbon planters, and sample Angolan labor contracts.

3. Cadbury, *Labour in Portuguese West Africa*, 71.

4. Ibid., 99.

5. Historians differ as to the value of Cadbury's book. Duffy, in a *Question of Slavery*, 209, regards Cadbury's account as "the most meticulously proper and restrained statement to be written by an English philanthropist during the whole controversy," while at the other extreme, Grant, in "'Civilised Savagery,'" 207, regards it as a "brilliant piece of propaganda, rendering Cadbury an author of protest, rather than an ambiguous victim of libel."

6. Nevinson's Diary, February 1 and 5, 1910.

7. BFASS Papers, MSS Brit. Emp. S 18, C 79/74 and 75, Cadbury to Buxton, April 2 and 5, 1910, S 19, D 1/7, 155, copy of letter T. Buxton to Fowell Buxton, May 24, 1910.

8. Reviews or notices appeared in Morel's *African Mail*, January 28, 1910, 163; Cadbury's *Daily News*, February 11, 1910, 3c; and *Bournville Works Magazine*, March 1910, 131–34.

9. Koss, *Political Press*, 97–98; Earl Winterton, *Pre-war* (London: Macmillan, 1932), 148–54; *World*, May 17, 1910, 846.

10. Nevinson's Diary, December 29, 1909.

11. Copy located in Birmingham Central Library, Local History; *World*, May 17, 1910, 846.

12. *World*, April 19, 1910, 668, and May 17, 1910, 846.

13. *DNB*; *National Review*, May 1910, 402–16, July 1910, 761–75.

14. Joseph Rowntree purchased the Darlington *Northern Echo* and two associated newspapers in 1903 and transferred the holdings to the Rowntree Trust, which also bought the *Sheffield Independent* in 1909; Koss, *Political Press*, 42–43. *National Review*, July 1910, 761–64; *Pall Mall Gazette*, May 9, 1910, 7; Gardiner, *Cadbury*, 220–21, 230–33; Nevinson's Diary, July 1, 1910.

15. See chapter 5.

16. CBBM, June 7, 1910; Cadbury Bros. made plans to reduce the price of its products immediately if the government eliminated the cocoa duty.

17. CBBM, copy of letter Cadbury Bros. to David Lloyd George, June 4, 1910.

18. Vipont, *Rowntree*, 54–55; Gardiner, *Cadbury*, 241–42; *Parliamentary Debates*, 5th ser., vol. 18 (July 6, 1910), 1679–83, and see also June 30, 1910, 1214–18, July 4, 1910, 1393, and July 6, 1910, 1743, for the debate on cocoa duty.

19. CBBM, May 16 and 18, 1911.

20. CP 180/467A, George Cadbury to W. Cadbury, n.d., but marked 1909; *Bournville Works Magazine*, March 1914, 78–79, speech by William Cadbury; *William A. Cadbury, 1867–1957*, 15–20; Williams, *Firm of Cadbury*, 146–52.

21. Polly Hill, *The Gold Coast Farmer: A Preliminary Survey* (London: Oxford University Press, 1956); Hill, *The Migrant Cocoa-Farmers of Southern Ghana* (Cambridge: Cambridge University Press, 1963); Hill, *Studies in Rural Capitalism in West Africa* (Cambridge: Cambridge University Press, 1970).

22. Southall, "Cadbury on the Gold Coast," I, 71–72; Gold Coast, Miscellaneous Official Publication. *Correspondence Relating to the Gift of £3,000 by Cadbury Brothers, Limited for the Purpose of Assisting the Government of the Gold Coast in the Training of Practical Cacao Farmers: "Hunter Hostels"* (Accra, Gold Coast: Government Printing, 1931), indicates that as late as 1926 and 1930, Cadbury Bros. gave a total of £8,000 for scholarships and housing for students being trained in cocoa farming.

23. Allister Macmillan, ed., *The Redbook of West Africa* (London: W. H. & L. Collingridge, 1920), 158.

24. CP 291/10, memorandum on Cadbury's purchases in British West Africa.

25. *John Bull*, March 9, 1912, from Library of Religious Society of Friends, book of press cuttings, 115.

26. BFASS Papers, MSS Brit. Emp. S 18, C 82/120, copy of letter Harris to Edm. Brooks, December 23, 1909.

27. Suzanne Miers, *Slavery in the Twentieth Century: The Evolution of a Global Problem* (New York: AltaMira Press, 2003), 63–65.

28. *Spectator*, February 12, 1910, 251–52; *Times*, March 5, 1910, 6a; BFASS Papers, MSS Brit. Emp. S 19, D 1/6, 255–56, copy of letter Buxton to Harris, February 14, 1910.

29. *African Mail*, October 21, 1910, 23, article by W. Cadbury; FO 367/186, no. 1507, Mackie to Grey, January 14, 1910; *Spectator*, May 7, 1910, 767.

30. *Friend*, July 22, 1910, 485. For a list of some of Burtt's publications, see the Bibliography.

31. Joseph Burtt, *The Voice of the Forest* (London: T. Fisher Unwin, 1911).

32. *Manchester Guardian*, March 17, 1910, 6e.

33. *Parliamentary Debates*, 5th ser., vol. 15 (March 22, 1910), 956–57, vol. 16 (April 5, 1910), 192–94, vol. 17 (April 28, 1910), 625–26.

34. See BFASS Papers, MSS Brit. Emp. S 18, C 166. After 1911, the society used its Portuguese West Africa brochures to recruit members.

35. FO 367/187, no. 23417, Buxton to Grey, June 28 and 29, 1910, and minutes, no. 23774, Grey to Gaisford, June 27, 1910.

36. Ibid.; Nevinson's Diary, July 1, 1910. The most detailed report of the deputation is found in the *Anti-Slavery Reporter and Aborigines' Friend*, October 1910, 154–63; *Times*, July 2, 1910, 8b, has a short version.

37. *Parliamentary Debates*, 5th ser., vol. 19 (July 21, 1910), 1569–74, 1588–92, (July 28, 1910), 2319–20.

38. David Birmingham, *A Concise History of Portugal* (Cambridge: Cambridge University Press, 1993), 147–48; Keith Robbins, *Sir Edward Grey: A Biography of Lord Grey of Fallodon* (London: Cassell, 1971), 223; Douglas L. Wheeler, "The Portuguese Revolution of 1910," *Journal of Modern History* 44 (June 1972): 172–94; Vincent-Smith, "The Portuguese Republic and Britain," 710–13; *Manchester Guardian*, October 6, 1910, 7b, and October 10, 1910, 6b–c; *Spectator*, October 8, 1910, 544–45, and October 15, 1910, 588–89.

39. Gooch and Temperley, *British Documents*, vol. 8, 72–73, Villiers to Grey, October 10, 1910, with enclosure Bernardino Machado to Villiers, October 9, 1910.

40. FO 367/234, no. 14370, copy of letter Grey to Villiers, April 13, 1911.

41. *Daily News*, October 13, 1910, 1g.

42. Ibid., November 16, 1910, 3c.

43. Ibid., October 13, 1910, 2b.

44. BFASS Papers, MSS Brit. Emp. S 22, G 267, translation of "Conference between the Colonial Minister and Messrs Cadbury and Albright" from *Século*, March 23, 1911; CP 180/677, translation of article, "Anti-Slavery," that appeared in *Diario de Noticias*, March 24, 1911.

45. FO 367/187, no. 42686, Langley's note on Villiers to FO, November 19, 1910.

46. The summary of the trip contained in the *Anti-Slavery Reporter and Aborigines' Friend*, January 1911, 185–91, gives no indication of the discord. For some indication of the friction, see FO 367/187, no. 42686, Villiers to Grey, November 19, 1910.

47. BFASS Papers, MSS Brit. Emp. S 22, G 267, copy of letter Harris to W. Cadbury, December 13, 1910.

48. Nevinson's Diary, November 14, 15, and 16, 1910; BFASS Papers, MSS Brit. Emp. S 19, D 2/2, Nevinson to T. Buxton, March 28, 1911, MSS Brit. Emp. S 22, G 269, Swan to Smith, December 2, 1910.

49. *Daily News*, October 13, 1910, 2b.

50. BFASS Papers, MSS Brit. Emp. S 22, G 267, copy of letter Cadbury to Harris, January 9, 1911. Morel Papers, Morel/F8/13/26–8, W. Cadbury to Morel, October 7, 1909. Cadbury had not thought highly of Harris for quite some time, and Morel also clashed with him when Harris worked for the Congo Reform Association.

51. BFASS Papers, MSS Brit. Emp. S 22, G 267, copy of letter Harris to Cadbury, January 10, 1911.

52. FO 367/186, no. 18250, Maugham to Grey, April 30, 1910, no. 11841, minutes, 1910.

53. FO 367/234, no. 2827, Buxton to Grey, January 23, 1911; FO 367/186, no. 17472, Mackie to Grey, April 12, 1910, no. 1505, Mackie to Grey, November 30, 1909.

54. FO 367/186, no. 21023, has several pieces of correspondence between the FO and Consul Reginald Maugham in 1910 over recruiting in Portuguese East Africa; FO 367/234, no. 6271, Maugham to Grey, January 23, 1911, and no. 37288, Maugham to Grey, August 28, 1911; Duffy, *Question of Slavery*, 162–64; Clarence-Smith, "Cocoa Plantations and Coerced Labour," 165–66; Vail and White, *Capitalism and Colonialism in Mozambique*, 184–85; Allen Isaacman and Barbara Isaacman, *Mozambique: From Colonialism to Revolution, 1900–1982* (Boulder, Colo.: Westview Press, 1983), 29–38.

55. FO 367/187, no. 41579, Drummond-Hay to Grey, October 20, 1910.

56. FO 367/234, no. 21812, Villiers to Grey, May 31, 1911, and minutes.

57. Ibid., Drummond-Hay to Grey, May 15, 1911, and no. 51833, Drummond-Hay to Grey, November 27, 1911.

58. Ibid., no. 9473, Drummond-Hay to Grey, February 13, 1911, no. 6391, Villiers to Grey, February 17, 1911, no. 10421, T. Buxton to Grey, March 20, 1911; *Times*, February 1, 1911, 7b.

59. FO 367/234, no. 7307, Drummond-Hay to Grey, February 1, 1911, and minutes, no. 31514, Langley to Buxton, August 16, 1911; FO 367/285, no. 10703, Drummond-Hay to Grey, February 6, 1912.

60. FO 367/234, no. 51833, Drummond-Hay to Grey, November 27, 1911; FO 367/285, no. 17210, Drummond-Hay to Grey, March 18, 1912.

61. FO 367/234, no. 31400, T. Buxton to Grey, August 8, 1911, no. 40204, interview with Buxton and other documents; *Anti-Slavery Reporter and Aborigines' Friend*, January 1912, 132–33.

62. *Spectator*, March 23, 1912, 473; *Anti-Slavery Reporter and Aborigines' Friend*, July 1912, 178–89; the *Reporter* carried Harris's letters from Africa starting in July 1911; John H. Harris, *Dawn in Darkest Africa*, with an introduction by the Earl of Cromer (London: Smith, Elder, 1912), 138, 161–62; John H. Harris, "Portuguese Slavery," *Contemporary Review* 101 (May 1912): 635–45.

63. FO 367/285, no. 28137, comments on *Times*'s letter of July 2, 1912, no. 19413, reaction to Harris's *Contemporary Review* article.

64. FO 367/285, no. 18241, Cumming to Tilley, April 28, 1912, no. 22018, Cumming to Tilley, May 19, 1912, no. 14381, Grey to Hardinge, April 11, 1912.

65. Mantero, *Manual Labour in S. Thomé and Principe*, quotations on 20, 32–33.

66. *Anti-Slavery Reporter and Aborigines' Friend*, October 1910, 164–65; *African Mail*, August 19, 1910, 451–52; *Spectator*, August 13, 1910, 234–35; *Liverpool Daily Post*, 1910, 9d–f.

67. Francisco Mantero, *Portuguese Planters and British Humanitarians: The Case for S. Thomé*, trans. J. A. Wyllie (Lisbon, 1911), 6.

68. *Times*, January 25, 1911, 17d.

69. *African Mail*, March 8 and 17, April 8 and 21, 1911; the *Yorkshire Observer*, June 1, 7, 14, 16, 20, 29, and July 3, 1911, contains correspondence between Wyllie, Nevinson, and Buxton; most of these letters are reprinted in Mantero, *Portuguese Planters and British Humanitarians*, 156–74.

70. BFASS Papers, MSS Brit. Emp. S 24, J 26, p. 79, newspaper clipping, *Spectator*, August 14, 1912; see also letter from José D'Almada, first secretary in the Colonial Office, Lisbon, extolling the virtues of working on São Tomé, in the *Times*, July 2, 1912, 5f.

71. *African Mail*, August 5, 1910, 433–34, translation of a chapter of the book, provided by W. Cadbury.

72. *African Mail*, September 30, 1910, 514, citing quotations carried in the *Economista* (Lisbon).

73. *African Mail*, November 11, 1910, 54, reprint of an article from the *Economista*.

74. CP 305, 150, translation of articles in *O Economista Portuguez* and containing article from *Voz de San Thome*.

75. *Times*, May 4, 1911, 5f.

76. Duffy, *Question of Slavery*, 218.

77. *A Pavement of Good Intentions or, S. Thomé Repatriation: Its Farce and Its Tragedy*, translation from *A Capital* (Lisbon: Redaccâo da Reforma, Praça de Camoens, [June 1912]), 6–7.

78. FO 367/234, no. 36362, translated excerpt from *Reforma*, August 19, 1911.

79. Wheeler and Pélissier, *Angola*, 109–10.

80. *Times*, December 15, 1911, 7f, December 23, 1911, 5b, December 28, 1911, 3b, March 26, 1912, 8b, April 16, 1912, 23f; *African Mail*, February 9, 1912, 181.

81. Great Britain, Foreign Office, *San Thomé and Príncipe* (London: His Majesty's Stationery Office, 1920), 28, 30. The less successful plantations still returned 5 to 6 percent.

82. FO 367/285, no. 433, Sleeping Sickness Bureau to FO, January 2, 1912; FO 367/334, no. 286, Hardinge to Grey, December 27, 1912.

83. FO 367/234, no. 49544, Drummond-Hay to Grey, November 7, 1911.

84. Ibid., no. 48238, Commander Strong to the Admiralty, November 5, 1911.

85. Bernard F. Bruto da Costa, *Sleeping Sickness in the Island of Principe*, trans. J. A. Wyllie (London: Baillière, Tindall & Cox, 1913); Jens Erik Torp, L. M. Denny, and Donald I. Ray, *Mozambique, São Tomé and Príncipe: Economics, Politics and Society* (London: Pinter, 1989), 134.

86. BFASS Papers, MSS Brit. Emp. S 19, D 6/1, 98, copy of letter Buxton to Drummond-Hay, April 29, 1912; *Anti-Slavery Reporter and Aborigines' Friend*, October 1912, 214; FO 367/285, no. 29638, minute of July 9, 1912, by Langley on a conversation with Harris.

87. FO 367/334, no. 2701, Crowe to BFASS, January 31, 1913, and FO 367/286 file; *Parliamentary Debates*, 5th ser., vol. 46 (January 14, 1913), 1855–56, vol. 47 (January 23, 1913), 584, vol. 48 (February 13, 1913), 1153–54.

88. *Anti-Slavery Reporter and Aborigines' Friend*, October 1912, 216–35, quotation from Cadbury, 217; *Spectator*, June 29, 1912, 1032–33; *African Mail*, July 5, 1912, 395.

89. The pamphlet, entitled "Portuguese Slavery and British Responsibility," is in BFASS Papers, MSS Brit. Emp. S 18, C 166/122; FO 367/285, no. 30248, BFASS to Grey, July 15, 1912.

90. *Parliamentary Debates*, 5th ser., vol. 40 (July 10, 1912), 2003, 2040.

91. Parliament, *Correspondence Respecting Contract Labour in Portuguese West Africa*, Africa No. 2, Cd. 6322, 1912, pp. 109–12, Drummond-Hay to Grey, June 8, 1912.

92. *Spectator*, August 17, 1912, 225–26.

93. *Anti-Slavery Reporter and Aborigines' Friend*, October 1912, 236–37; FO 367/286, no. 42326, Buxton to Grey, October 8, 1912.

94. FO 367/285, no. 33413, Harris to Langley, August 15, 1912.

95. Ibid., no. 35388, minutes on the *Spectator* article of August 17, 1912; FO 367/286, no. 42326, minutes on Buxton to Grey, October 8, 1912.

96. FO 367/286, no. 45083, minutes of October 22, 1912, meeting between officials of FO and BFASS; FO 367/285, no. 20621, minutes dated May 9, 1912. Crowe had agreed to talk to Harris earlier in the year, "so long as he doesn't stay long."

97. FO 367/286, no. 45083, Harris to Tilley, October 24, 1912; BFASS Papers, MSS Brit. Emp. S 18, C 166/115, Tilley to Harris, October 25, 1912.

98. FO 367/286, no. 47707, Buxton and Harris to Grey, November 8, 1912.

99. William A. Cadbury and E. D. Morel, "The West African Slave Traffic: Britain's Duty Towards Angola and San Thomé," *The Nineteenth Century and After* 72 (October 1912): 836–51, quotations on 836–37.

100. The Quaker John W. Graham, in *Evolution and Empire* (London: Headley Bros., 1912), 115–16, 124, expressed similar if stronger views, indicating the need for Western societies to regulate native labor to ensure that Europeans gained the benefits of Africa's raw materials. Cited in Kennedy, *British Quakerism*, 304–5.

101. FO 367/334, no. 5510, extract from "Revista Colonial" dated December 30, 1912; see another letter in the *Spectator*, April 5, 1913, 570–71, and a response by Cadbury, *Spectator*, April 19, 1913, 651–52.

102. See earlier in this chapter.

103. See especially FO 367/286 and 334 for pertinent correspondence.

104. Parliament, *Further Correspondence Respecting Contract Labour in Portuguese West Africa*, Africa No. 2, Cd. 6607, 1913, pp. 37–39, 41–43, Smallbones to Grey, September 23 and 25, 1912.

105. FO 367/286, no. 47664, Smallbones to Grey, October 4, 1912.

106. FO 367/285, no. 34337, several documents, August 1912; FO 367/286, no. 47663, Smallbones to Grey, October 3, 1912, and minutes.

107. FO 367/334, no. 2701, copy of letter, Crowe to BFASS, January 31, 1913; same letter available in BFASS Papers, MSS Brit. Emp. S 18, C 166/127; FO 367/334, no. 10318, minutes by Crowe.

108. FO 367/334, no. 2701, minutes by Grey on draft of a letter responding to letter from Buxton, January 17, 1913, no. 5510, minutes by Grey on a letter from D'Andrade, December 30, 1912.

109. Parliament, *Further Correspondence Respecting Contract Labour in Portuguese West Africa*, Africa No. 2, Cd. 6607, 1913.

110. *Parliamentary Debates*, 5th ser., vol. 50 (March 27, 1913), 1874–83, vol. 53 (May 29, 1913), 421–34, 458–59.

111. *Spectator*, March 8, 1913, 389–90; see also *Anti-Slavery Reporter and Aborigines' Friend*, July 1913, 64–67, for report on the society's annual meeting.

112. *British Friend*, August 1913, 214.

113. Evelyn Baring, 1st Earl of Cromer, *Political & Literary Essays, 1908–1913* (1913; reprint, Freeport, N.Y.: Books for Libraries Press, 1969), 372–406, Wyllie proposal, 398–403. Essays on "Portuguese Slavery" first published in *Spectator*, August 16, 23, and 30, 1913.

114. John H. Harris, *Portuguese Slavery: Britain's Dilemma* (London: Methuen, 1913), 46, 124–26; *Manchester Guardian*, June 9, 1913, 4e.

115. CP 309, 9, copy of letter W. Cadbury to Alfred da Silva, August 18, 1911, and other documents.

116. Strachey Papers, S/25/2/2, copy of letter Strachey to Harris, February 18, 1913.

Strachey indicates that he had been offered this document earlier, probably at the same time as Cadbury. This letter gives some of the history of the document and its translation for the BFASS. *Spectator,* March 15, 1913, 436–37.

117. Jeronimo Paiva de Carvalho, *Slavery in West Africa: Portuguese Revelations* (London: Anti-Slavery and Aborigines' Protection Society, [1912]), available in CP 305. Although the publication date is normally listed as 1912, it did not become available until early 1913.

118. CP 309, Silva to Cadbury, February 8, 1913, April 8, 15, 17 and 24, 1913, Cadbury to Silva, April 25, 1913; *Spectator,* April 5, 1913, 570–71, April 12, 1913, 613, April 19, 1913, 651–52.

119. FO 367/336, no. 35452.

120. *Parliamentary Debates,* Lords, 5th ser., vol. 14 (July 23, 1913), 1293–96.

121. FO 367/334, no. 3299, Grey to Hardinge, January 29, 1913.

122. *Parliamentary Debates,* Lords, 5th ser., vol. 14 (July 23, 1913), 1304–6.

123. Nevinson's Diary, July 23, 1913.

124. *Times,* July 30, 1913, 9d–e.

125. Rumors of these negotiations filled British newspapers by early 1912: *Manchester Guardian,* January 24, 9c–d, February 8, 7d; *Daily Express,* January 31, 1c; BFASS Papers, MSS Brit. Emp. S 24, J 26, 63, newspaper clippings include *Daily Chronicle,* January 23, *Morning Leader,* January 29.

126. Zara S. Steiner, *Britain and the Origins of the First World War* (New York: St. Martin's Press, 1977), 94–109.

127. FO 800/61, Grey to Goschen, private (copy), December 29, 1911, cited in Louis, "Great Britain and German Expansion," 36. In Gooch and Temperley, *British Documents,* vol. 10, pt. 2, 424, the term *sinks of iniquity* is omitted "for reasons of international courtesy." Documents in this volume, pp. 421–579, examine British negotiations with Germany over Portuguese colonies, 1911–1914, and point out the debate within the FO.

128. Vail and White, *Capitalism and Colonialism in Mozambique,* 185–86.

129. Cabinet Papers, 37/111, no. 91, Grey on Portugal in Africa, July 17, 1912.

130. C. J. Lowe and M. L. Dockrill, *The Mirage of Power,* vol. 1, *British Foreign Policy, 1902–14* (London: Routledge & Kegan Paul, 1972), 51–52.

131. Richard Langhorne, "Anglo-German Negotiations Concerning the Future of the Portuguese Colonies, 1911–1914," *Historical Journal* 16 (1973): 361–87; J. D. Vincent-Smith, "The Anglo-German Negotiations over the Portuguese Colonies in Africa, 1911–1914," *Historical Journal* 17 (1974): 620–29; Glyn A. Stone, "The Official British Attitude to the Anglo-Portuguese Alliance, 1910–1945," *Journal of Contemporary History* 10 (October 1975): 729–31; Willequet, "Anglo-German Rivalry," 265–70; Lowe and Dockrill, *Mirage of Power,* 51–52, 124–27; Louis, "Great Britain and German Expansion," 36–39; G. P. Gooch, "Triple Alliance and Triple Entente," in A. W. Ward and G. P. Gooch, eds., *The Cambridge History of British Foreign Policy, 1783–1919,* vol. 3, *1866–1919* (1923; reprint, New York: Octagon, 1970), 477–78; Robbins, *Edward Grey,* 270; Herbert Feis, *Europe: The World's Banker, 1870–1914* (New Haven, Conn.: Council on Foreign Relations, 1930), 243–57.

132. Lowe and Dockrill, *Mirage of Power,* 124.

133. *Manchester Guardian,* March 3, 1913, 16b, Morel favorably compares Germany to the Belgian- and French-controlled areas of the Congo; Louis, "Great Britain and German

Expansion in Africa, 1884–1919," 36–39; *Anti-Slavery Reporter and Aborigines' Friend*, October 1912, 217, in a letter to the BFASS meeting of June 25, 1912, W. Cadbury was probably referring to Germany when he wrote that should Portugal be unable to govern its colonies "as a civilised State should govern . . . we should at least not hinder any bargain that she may wish to make for the honourable transfer of such lands to a more vital and not less humane colonising power." Harris, *Dawn in Darkest Africa*, XXI–XXII, 293–304.

134. Helmut Bley, "Social Discord in South West Africa, 1894–1904," in Prosser Gifford and Wm. Roger Louis, eds., *Britain and Germany in Africa* (New Haven, Conn.: Yale University Press, 1967), 607–30; Mark Cocker, *Rivers of Blood, Rivers of Gold* (London: Jonathan Cape, 1998), 269–357.

135. Parliament, *Further Correspondence Respecting Contract Labour in Portuguese West Africa*, Africa No. 1, Cd. 7279, April 1914, pp. 28–31, Smallbones to Grey, April 29, 1913.

136. Ibid., 32, Smallbones to Durão, April 17, 1913.

137. FO 367/336, no. 47570, Smallbones to Hall Hall, September 26, 1913.

138. Parliament, *Further Correspondence Respecting Contract Labour in Portuguese West Africa*, Africa No. 1, Cd. 7279, April 1914, p. 85, Vice-Consul Bernays to Hall Hall, October 25, 1913.

139. FO 367/336, no. 46437, Hall Hall to Grey, September 5, 1913, no. 47570, Smallbones to Hall Hall, September 26, 1913.

140. Ibid., no. 47570, Grey to Carnegie, November 25, 1913.

141. Ibid., no. 42290, Hall Hall to Grey, August 15, 1913.

142. Ibid., no. 47569, Hall Hall to Grey, September 27, 1913.

143. FO 367/337, no. 58369, Smallbones to Grey, December 10, 1913.

144. W. E. Hardenburg, who helped expose the atrocities, published *Putumayo: The Devil's Paradise* (London: T. F. Unwin [1912]), which includes portions of Casement's report, Parliament, *Correspondence Respecting the Treatment of British Colonial Subjects and Native Indians Employed in the Collection of Rubber in the Putumayo District*, Cd. 6266, 1912; John Harris, *A Century of Emancipation* (London: J. M. Dent & Sons, 1933), 168–78; W. Kloosterboer, *Involuntary Labour since the Abolition of Slavery: A Survey of Compulsory Labour throughout the World* (Leiden, the Netherlands: E. J. Brill, 1960), 101–4; Roger Sawyer, *Casement, the Flawed Hero* (London: Routledge & Kegan Paul, 1984), 77–108.

145. *Manchester Guardian*, January 2, 1914, 7a.

146. Ibid., December 1, 1913, 7f–g, March 5, 1914, 10b, July 21, 1914, 8d.

147. Parliament, *Further Correspondence Respecting Contract Labour in Portuguese West Africa*, Africa No. 1, Cd. 7279, April 1914.

148. FO 367/336, no. 47570, Grey to Carnegie, November 25, 1913; *Nation*, May 2, 1914, 178, letter from Nevinson.

149. CP 305, 199, *Bournville Works Magazine*, May 1914, "Labour in Portuguese West Africa," by W. Cadbury; *Friend*, May 22, 1914, 356–57.

150. CP prior to 250/3, newspaper cutting of *Daily Chronicle*, April 30, 1914; BFASS Papers, MSS Brit. Emp. S 19, D 6/1, 400, copy of letter from officers of the BFASS to Grey, May 18, 1914.

151. *Nation*, May 2, 1914, 177–78.

152. *Parliamentary Debates*, 5th ser., vol. 64 (July 10, 1914), 1425.

153. *Anti-Slavery Reporter and Aborigines' Friend*, October 1914, 92–95.

Chapter 11

1. *Anti-Slavery Reporter and Aborigines' Friend*, April 1915, 14–17, January 1915, 126, Stober wrote of a new village in Angola named St. Thomé, where repatriated serviçais lived; Duffy, *Question of Slavery*, 226–27.

2. Grant, "'Civilised Savagery,'" 219–28, 232–34.

3. Parliament, *Further Correspondence Respecting Contract Labour in Portuguese West Africa*, Africa No. 1, Cd. 7960, 1915; Parliament, *Further Correspondence Respecting Contract Labour in Portuguese South-West Africa*, Africa No. 1, Cd. 8479, 1917–18.

4. CP 205/4, *Bournville Works Magazine*, September 1915, 232–34, "Labour in Portuguese West Africa," by W. Cadbury.

5. Parliament, *Further Correspondence Respecting Contract Labour in Portuguese South-West Africa*, Africa No. 1, Cd. 8479, 1917–18, pp. 66–69, Hall Hall to Grey, October 30, 1916.

6. Ibid., Balfour to Carnegie, February 27, 1917, 70.

7. CP 250/5, copy of letter Cadbury Bros. to A. J. Balfour, April 19, 1917.

8. Ibid., Burtt to Cadbury, April 29, 1917.

9. Ibid., copy of letter Cadbury Bros. to the *Daily News*, May 3, 1917, and W. Cadbury, "Labour in Portuguese West Africa," reprinted from the *Bournville Works Magazine*, June 1917, 150–54.

10. Duffy, *Question of Slavery*, 227; *Anti-Slavery Reporter and Aborigines' Friend*, October, 1920, 75–76.

11. Grant, "'Civilised Savagery,'" 242–46, 254–68.

12. Davidson, *In the Eye of the Storm*, 97; Hodges and Newitt, *São Tomé and Príncipe*, 39–40.

13. Clarence-Smith, "Labour Conditions in the Plantations of São Tomé and Príncipe, 1875–1914," 162.

14. Edward Alsworth Ross, *Report on Employment of Native Labor in Portuguese Africa* (New York: [Abbott Press], 1925); *Anti-Slavery Reporter and Aborigines' Friend*, October 1925, 103–7, carried excerpts of the report.

15. Oliveira Santos, "Reply to the Accusations Addressed to the League of Nations by Mr. Edward A. Ross against the Portuguese in Angola" (Lisbon, 1930); Robert Nii Nartey, "From Slave to Serviçal Labor in the Plantation Economy of São Tome and Principe, 1876–1932" (Ph.D. diss., University of Illinois, Chicago, 1986), 190–92; Basil Davidson, *The African Awakening* (New York: Macmillan, 1955), 191.

16. Nevinson, *More Changes*, 95.

17. Clarence-Smith, *Third Portuguese Empire*, 140.

18. Duffy, *Portugal in Africa*, 182–86; Bender, *Angola under the Portuguese*, 141–44; Nartey, "From Slave to Serviçal Labor in the Plantation Economy," 193–96.

19. Raymond W. Bixler, *The West African Cocoa Story* (New York: Vantage Press, 1972), 13; Hodges and Newitt, *São Tomé and Príncipe*, 40.

20. Davidson, *African Awakening*, 225–28.

21. William Gervase Clarence-Smith and François Ruf, "Cocoa Pioneer Fronts: The Historical Determinants," in William Gervase Clarence-Smith, ed., *Cocoa Pioneer Fronts since 1800* (London: Macmillan, 1996), 1–11; Clarence-Smith, "Cocoa Plantations and Coerced Labour," 166.

22. Peter Ritner, *The Death of Africa* (New York: Macmillan, 1960), 111–19.

23. Davidson, *African Awakening*, 203; Lawrence W. Henderson, *Angola: Five Centuries of Conflict* (Ithaca, N.Y.: Cornell University Press, 1979), 120–24.

24. Davidson, *African Awakening*, 191–96.

25. Ibid., 217–18.

26. Duffy, *Portugal in Africa*, 186.

27. The number killed is disputed, with estimates ranging from under 100 to as many as 1,032; Seibert, *Comrades, Clients and Cousins*, 55–75; Davidson, *In the Eye of the Storm*, 167–68; Davidson, *African Awakening*, 229–30.

28. Gardiner, *Cadbury*, 248–49; Kennedy, *Merchant Princes*, 59–65; Birmingham Central Library, newspaper cuttings, *Birmingham Gazette*, October 25 and 30, 1922, *Birmingham Mail*, February 8, 1923; Paul H. Emden, *Quakers in Commerce: A Record of Business Achievement* (London: Sampson Low, Marston, [1939]), 228–30.

29. Kennedy, *Merchant Princes*, 83, 96–100.

30. *Times*, August 27, 1927, 12b–c.

31. A. J. P. Taylor, *English History, 1914–1945* (Oxford: Oxford University Press, 1965), 31 n.

32. *DNB*.

33. *Times*, December 31, 1935, 6; *DNB*.

34. Hyde, *United in Crime*, 60–61; Gardiner, *Pillars of Society*, 137.

35. Dutton, *Simon; DNB*.

36. *DNB*.

37. Robbins, *Edward Grey*, 211.

38. Johnston, *Westminster Voices*, 95–96.

39. Keith Neilson, "'Control the Whirlwind': Sir Edward Grey as Foreign Secretary, 1906–16," in T. G. Otte, ed., *The Makers of British Foreign Policy: From Pitt to Thatcher* (New York: Palgrave, 2002), 128–49; Doreen Collins, *Aspects of British Politics, 1904–1919* (Oxford: Pergamom Press, 1965), 109–10. Niall Ferguson, *The Pity of War* (New York: Basic Books, 1999), 55–81, judges Grey's diplomacy leading up to World War I as a failure.

40. *DNB*.

41. Hochschild, *King Leopold's Ghost*, 187; Cline, *Morel*, 70–78, 92; Morel Papers, Morel/F8/13/54–5, Cadbury to Morel, April 12, 1912.

42. E. D. Morel, *The Black Man's Burden* (1920; reprint, New York: Modern Reader Paperbacks, 1969), 149–60.

43. Cline, *Morel*, 98–145; *Times*, November 14, 1924, 8e.

44. Holt Papers, MSS. Afr. S. 1525, Box 12/7, copy of letter Holt to Cadbury, August 20, 1910.

45. *Anti-Slavery Reporter and Aborigines' Friend*, October 1915, 68–72; Green, "Founder of the Society," 11–16; *Times*, September 21, 1915, 11e.

46. *Anti-Slavery Reporter and Aborigines' Friend*, July 1940, 43.

47. *Times*, May 2, 1940, 9f.

48. *Reporter* (Anti-Slavery International), October 2001, 12–13.

49. *Manchester Guardian*, January 31, 1945, 4d.

50. Joseph Burtt, *Sonnets and Other Poems* (London: Oliphants, [1929]); *Friend*, May 19, 1939, 408–10.

51. *William A. Cadbury*, 21–22; John F. Crosfield, *A History of the Cadbury Family*, vol. 2 ([London]: [J. F. Crosfield], 1985), 393.

52. Cited in *Bournville Works Magazine*, August 1957, 271–79.

53. *Friend*, July 26, 1957, 665–66.

54. *Friend*, October 14, 1949, 843.

55. Grant, "'Civilised Savagery,'" 210–11.

56. CP 180/183, Cadbury, "A Private *Inside History*."

57. Chinn, *Cadbury Story*, 55–56, 84, 97–98.

58. Michael Rowlinson, "Cadbury World," *Labour History Review* 67 (April 2002): 112.

59. *Guardian*, February 26, 2000.

60. Alfred F. Havighurst, *Radical Journalist: H. W. Massingham* (London: Cambridge University Press, 1974), 149–50; his "middles" were published in *Essays in Freedom* (1909) and *Essays in Rebellion* (1913).

61. Henry W. Nevinson, *Last Changes Last Chances* (London: Nisbet, 1928), 54–55, 144–45; Philip Gibbs, *More That Must Be Told* (New York: Harper and Brothers, 1921), 71.

62. Nevinson's three-volume autobiography, *Changes and Chances*, *More Changes More Chances*, and *Last Changes Last Chances*, was abridged by Ellis Roberts as *Fire of Life* (London: James Nisbet, 1935).

63. W. R. Titterton, *A Candle to the Stars* (London: Grayson & Grayson, 1932), 179.

64. Ronald Schuchard, "'An Attendant Lord': H. W. Nevinson's Friendship with W. B. Yeats," in Warwick Gould, ed., *Yeats Annual No. 7* (London: Macmillan, 1990), 129, n. 35; Becky W. Lewis, "Henry Woodd Nevinson," in William B. Thesing, ed., *Dictionary of Literary Biography*, vol. 135 (Detroit, Mich.: Gale Research, 1994), 255–61; *Times*, November 10, 1941, 6d.

65. J. Howard Whitehouse, "Henry Nevinson," *Contemporary Review* 161 (January 1942): 47.

66. Henry W. Nevinson, *Essays, Poems and Tales of Henry W. Nevinson*, edited and with an introduction by H. N. Brailsford (London: Victor Gollancz, 1948), 10–11.

67. *Friend*, November 14, 1941, 531. In a 2000 novel based on his diaries, Nevinson plays a key role as a humane correspondent in the siege of Ladysmith during the South African War; Giles Foden, *Ladysmith* (New York: Alfred A. Knopf, 2000).

68. Quoted in Koss, *Political Press*, 105.

69. Peter Schwab, *Africa: A Continent Self-Destructs* (New York: Palgrave, 2002), 84–87; "Angola Paradox: Awash in Oil, Mired in Poverty," *Washington Post*, washingtonpost.com, accessed on and byline September 18, 2000.

70. *New York Times*, September 18, 2002, A1.

71. Torp, Denny, and Ray, *Mozambique, São Tomé and Príncipe*, 170–72.

72. Official São Tomé and Príncipe Tourist site, www.saotome.st/, accessed on February 1, 2004.

73. Jon Lee Anderson, "Our New Best Friend," *New Yorker*, October 7, 2002, 74–83; *New York Times*, September 19, 2002, A1; *Vindicator*, September 20, 2002, A1.

74. "Sao Tome Coup Leaders Win Guarantees on Oil Wealth," by Reuters, *New York Times*, nytimes.com, accessed on and byline July 24, 2003.

75. Quoted in Rowlinson, "Cadbury World," 111.

76. "Mystery Surrounds Alleged Slave Ship," *Washington Post*, washingtonpost.com, ac-

cessed on and byline April 17, 2001; "U.N. Searches for Possible Slave Ship Amid Mystery," *U. S. A. Today*, usatoday.com, accessed on and byline April 17, 2001.

77. *New York Times*, July 29, 2001, A1; *Vindicator*, June 24, 2001, A1.

78. "284,000 Children Work in Hazardous Conditions on West Africa's Cocoa Farms," Anti-Slavery International, http://www.antislavery.org/homepage/news/cocoareport290702.htm, accessed on August 28, 2002, byline July 29, 2002; Tim Richardson, *Sweets* (London: Bloomsbury, 2002), 308.

79. Ivan Manokha, "Modern Slavery and Fair Trade Products: Buy One and Set Someone Free," in Christine van den Anker, ed., *The Political Economy of New Slavery* (Basingstoke, Hampshire, UK: Palgrave Macmillan, 2004), 227.

80. P. M. [?Lavell], Cadbury Ltd. to J. Filkin, October 17, 2000. Amanda Berlan, "Child Labour, Education and Child Rights Among Cocoa Producers in Ghana," in Christine van den Anker, ed., *The Political Economy of New Slavery* (Basingstoke, Hampshire, UK: Palgrave Macmillan, 2004), 158–78, finds little evidence of child slavery on cocoa farms in Ghana.

81. For example, International Institute of Tropical Agriculture, "Child Labour in the Cocoa Sector of West Africa," August 2002. Available at www/iita.org, this study was sponsored by the cocoa industry, the U. S. Department of Labor, and the U. S. Agency for International Development.

82. Charlotte Denny, "Child Slavery in West Africa Gives Chocolate a Bad Taste," *Manchester Guardian Weekly*, May 31–June 6, 2001.

83. See http://www.bccca.org.uk/, accessed on January 6, 2004, information from the Biscuit Cake Chocolate and Confectionery Alliance; http://infotract.galegroup.com/itw/infomark, accessed on January 6, 2004, *U.S. News & World Report*, November 13, 2000, 16; http://galenet.galegroup.com/servlet, accessed on January 6, 2004, *Economist* (U.S.), August 5, 1989, 58; http://www.census.gov/industry/1/ma311d02.pdf, accessed on January 6, 2004, Current Industrial Reports. Confectionery: 2002.

84. Olenka Frenkiel, "Lost Children," *Manchester Guardian Weekly*, October 25–31, 2001, 22; Kevin Bales, *Disposable People: New Slavery in the Global Economy* (Berkeley: University of California Press, 1999).

BIBLIOGRAPHY

Manuscripts

Asquith, H. H. Papers. Bodleian Library, Oxford.
British and Foreign Anti-Slavery and Aborigines' Protection Society Papers. Rhodes House Library, Oxford.
Cadbury Papers. University of Birmingham Library, Special Collections.
Cadbury Brothers Board Minutes. Cadbury Offices, Bournville, Birmingham.
Campbell-Bannerman, Henry Papers. British Library, London.
Carson, Edward Papers. Public Record Office of Northern Ireland, Belfast.
Chamberlain, Austin Papers. University of Birmingham Library, Special Collections.
Chamberlain, Joseph Papers. University of Birmingham Library, Special Collections.
Dilke, Charles Papers. British Library, London.
Gardiner, A. G. Papers. British Library of Political and Economic Science, London.
Grey, Edward Papers. Public Record Office, London.
Gwynn, H. A. Papers. Bodleian Library, Oxford.
Harris, John Papers. Rhodes House Library, Oxford.
Holt, John Papers. Rhodes House Library, Oxford.
Hyde, H. Montgomery Papers. Public Record Office of Northern Ireland, Belfast.
Isaacs [Lord Reading], Rufus Papers. Oriental & India Office Collections, British Library, London.
Morel, E. D. Papers. British Library of Political and Economic Science, London.
Nevinson, Henry Woodd Papers. Diaries. Bodleian Library, Oxford.
Simon, John Papers. Bodleian Library, Oxford.
Spender, J. A. Papers. British Library, London.
Strachey, J. St. Loe Papers. House of Lords Record Office, London.

Government Collections and Publications: United Kingdom

Cabinet Papers, available on microfilm at many libraries.
Foreign Office. *Foreign Office List*. Annual. London: Harrison.
Foreign Office. *San Thomé and Príncipe*. London: His Majesty's Stationery Office, 1920.
Foreign Office Papers, London.
Overseas Trade, Department of. *Economic Conditions in Angola (Portuguese West Africa)*. Report by R. T. Smallbones. London: His Majesty's Stationery Office, 1929.
Parliamentary Debates.

Parliamentary Papers in Chronological Order

Parliament. *General Act of the Conference of Berlin Signed February 26, 1885*. Africa. No. 3. C. 4739. 1886.

———. *Treaty between Her Majesty and His Majesty the King of Portugal Defining Their Respective Spheres of Influence in Africa*. Portugal No. 1. C. 6375. 1891.

———. Foreign Office. *Diplomatic and Consular Reports on Trade and Finance. Portugal. Report for the Year 1893 on the Trade, &c., of Angola*. No. 1333. C. 7293-3. March 1894.

———. Foreign Office. *Diplomatic and Consular Reports on Trade and Finance. Portugal. Report for the Year 1896 on the Trade of Angola*. C. 8277-167. June 1897.

———. Foreign Office. *Diplomatic and Consular Reports. Trade of Angola for the Years 1897 and 1898*. No. 2363. Cd. 1. November 1899.

———. Foreign Office. *Diplomatic and Consular Reports. Trade of Province of Angola for the Year 1899*. No. 2555. Cd. 429-13. February 1901.

———. Foreign Office. *Diplomatic and Consular Reports. Portugal. Report for the Year 1900 on the Trade and Commerce of Angola*. No. 2721. Cd. 786-25. October 1901.

———. Foreign Office. *Diplomatic and Consular Reports. Trade of the Province of St. Thomé and Principe for the Year 1901*. No. 2922. Cd. 786-226. December 1902.

———. Foreign Office. *Diplomatic and Consular Reports. Trade of Angola for the Year 1906*. No. 3928. Cd. 3727-11. September 1907.

———. *Correspondence Respecting Contract Labour in Portuguese West Africa*. Africa. No. 2. Cd. 6322. 1912.

———. *Further Correspondence Respecting Contract Labour in Portuguese West Africa*. Africa. No. 2. Cd. 6607. 1913.

———. *Further Correspondence Respecting Contract Labour in Portuguese West Africa*. Africa. No. 1. Cd. 7279. April 1914.

———. *Further Correspondence Respecting Contract Labour in Portuguese West Africa*. Africa. No. 1. Cd. 7960. 1915.

———. *Further Correspondence Respecting Contract Labour in Portuguese South-West Africa*. Africa. No. 1. Cd. 8479. 1917–18.

Newspapers and Journals

Aborigines' Friend

African Mail (originally the *West African Mail*)

African World

Anti-Slavery Reporter (the *Anti-Slavery Reporter and Aborigines' Friend* after 1909; today, it is the *Reporter*)

Baker and Confectioner

Birmingham Daily Mail

Birmingham Daily Post

Birmingham Evening Mail

Birmingham Gazette

Birmingham Gazette and Express

Birmingham Illustrated Weekly Mercury
Birmingham Pictorial and Dart
Birmingham Sunday Mail
Birmingham Weekly Post
Bournville Works Magazine
British Friend
British Weekly
Chronicle of the London Missionary Society
Clarion
Daily Chronicle
Daily Express
Daily Graphic
Daily Mail
Daily Mirror
Daily News
Daily Sketch
Daily Telegraph
Economist
Evening Despatch
Evening Standard & St. James's
Financial News
Friend
Glasgow Herald
Globe
Graphic
Illustrated London News
John Bull
Labour Leader
Leeds Mercury
Listener
Liverpool Daily Post and Liverpool Mercury
Liverpool Echo
Manchester Guardian (later the *Guardian*)
Manchester Guardian Weekly
Morning Leader
Morning Post
Municipal Journal
Nation (formerly *Speaker*)
National Review
Newcastle Daily Chronicle
New York Times
Northern Echo
Pall Mall Gazette
Punch
Reporter (Anti-Slavery International)

Reynolds's
Saturday Review
Spectator
Standard
Sunday at Home
Sunday Telegraph
Throne and Country
Times (London)
Tribune
Tropical Life
Truth
U.S. News & World Report
Vindicator (Youngstown, Ohio)
Washington Post
West African Mail (later the *African Mail*)
Westminster Gazette
World
Yorkshire Observer
Yorkshire Post

Contemporary Sources: Books, Articles, Collections of Letters, and Autobiographies

Allen, Charles H. "Slavery and the Slave Trade." *The Leisure Hour* (1884): 418–21.

Almada, José de. *Comparative Essay on Indentured Labour at St. Thomé and Principe.* Lisbon: National Printing Office, 1913.

[Andrade, A. Freire d', et al.]. *Nouveaux documents sur la main d'œuvre à St. Thomé et à l'Île du Prince: Réponse aux accusations contre le Portugal* [New Documents on the Labor Force on São Tomé and Príncipe: Response to the Accusations against Portugal]. Berne: Imprimerie Neukomm & Zimmermann, 1913.

Anti-Slavery and Aborigines Protection Society. "Memorandum on Portuguese Slavery Addressed to the Right Hon. Sir Edward Grey." London, May 1913.

———. "Portuguese Slavery: Britain's Responsibility." London, May 1914.

———. "Portuguese Slavery and British Responsibility: Memorandum Addressed to Sir Edward Grey." London, July 1912.

Arnot, F. S. *Garenganze or, Seven Years' Pioneer Mission Work in Central Africa.* 1889; new ed., London: Frank Cass, 1969.

———. *Missionary Travels in Central Africa.* London: Alfred Holness, 1914.

Baring, Evelyn [1st Earl of Cromer]. *Political & Literary Essays, 1908–1913*, 372–406. 1913; reprint, Freeport, N.Y.: Books for Libraries Press, 1969. Essays on "Portuguese Slavery" first published in *Spectator*, August 16, 23, and 30, 1913.

Bates, Jean Victor. *Sir Edward Carson: Ulster Leader.* London: John Murray, 1921.

Bell, Mackenzie. "Portugal, Old and New." *Fortnightly Review* n.s. 88 (November 1910): 783–95.

Birkenhead, Earl of. *Contemporary Personalities*. London: Cassell, 1924.

British and Foreign Anti-Slavery Society. *Sixty Years against Slavery: A Brief Record of the Work and Aims of the British and Foreign Anti-Slavery Society, 1839–1899*. London: British and Foreign Anti-Slavery Society, 1900.

Buell, Raymond Leslie. *The Native Problem in Africa*. Vol. 1. New York: Macmillan, 1928.

Burtt, Joseph. "How America Can Free the Portuguese Cocoa Slave." *Leslie's Illustrated Weekly*. October 14, 1909, 368–69.

———. "Indentured and Forced Labour." Presented to the First Universal Races Congress, 1911. In *Papers on Inter-racial Problems*, edited by G. Spiller, 323–24. London: P. S. King & Son, 1911.

———. "Joseph Burtt and Dr. Horton's Report on the Conditions of Coloured Labour on the Cocoa Plantations, July, 1907." In *Labour in Portuguese West Africa* by William Cadbury, 103–31. 2nd ed. London: George Routledge & Sons, 1910; reprint, New York: Negro Universities Press, 1969.

———. "My Success in America." *Leslie's Illustrated Weekly*. December 16, 1909, 608.

———. *The People of Ararat*. London: Leonard and Virginia Woolf at the Hogarth Press, 1926.

———. *San Thomé*. In *Misc. Pamphlets on the Portuguese in Africa* (bound pamphlets in Rhodes House Library). Reprinted from the *Bournville Works Magazine*, July 1917.

———. "The Slave and the Diplomat." *Friend* 54 (May 22, 1914): 356–57.

———. "Slave-Grown Cocoa." *Friend* 49 (September 17, 1909): 620–22.

———. "Slavery in S. Thome." *Friend* 50 (July 22, 1910): 485.

———. "Slave Labour on Cocoa Plantations." *Contemporary Review* 96 (October 1909): 468–73.

———. *Sonnets and Other Poems*. London: Oliphants, [1929].

———. "Still Portuguese Slavery." *Friend* 53 (June 27, 1913): 426–27.

———. *The Voice of the Forest*. London: T. Fisher Unwin, 1911.

Cadbury, Edward, M. Cecile Matheson, and George Shann. *Women's Work and Wages*. London: T. Fisher Unwin, 1906.

Cadbury, Edward, and George Shann. *Sweating*. London: Headley Bros., 1907.

[Cadbury, Richard]. *Cocoa: All about It*. London: Sampson Low, Marston, 1896.

Cadbury, William A. *Labour in Portuguese West Africa*. 2nd ed. London: George Routledge & Sons, 1910; reprint, New York: Negro Universities Press, 1969.

———. ed. *The Pumphrey Pedigree*. Birmingham, UK, 1909.

———. "Statement Made by Mr. William A. Cadbury on Behalf of Cadbury Bros., Bournville, *et al*, to the Council of the Liverpool Chamber of Commerce . . . " In *Labour in Portuguese West Africa* by William Cadbury, 134–40. 2nd ed. London: George Routledge & Sons, 1910; reprint, New York: Negro Universities Press, 1969.

Cadbury, William A., and E. D. Morel. "The West African Slave Traffic: Britain's Duty towards Angola and San Thomé." *The Nineteenth Century and After* 72 (October 1912): 836–51.

Cameron, Verney Lovett. *Across Africa*. 1877; new ed., London: George Philip & Son, 1885.

Carvalho, Jeronimo Paiva de. *Slavery in West Africa: Portuguese Revelations*. London: Anti-Slavery and Aborigines Protection Society, [1912].

Chatelain, Héli, coll. and ed. *Folk-Tales of Angola: Fifty Tales, with Ki-Mbundu Text, Literal English Translation, Introduction, and Notes*. Boston: Houghton Mifflin, 1894.
Cocks, F. Seymour. *E. D. Morel: The Man and His Work*. London: George Allen & Unwin, 1920.
Costa, Bernardo F. Bruto da. *Sleeping Sickness in the Island of Principe*. Translated by J. A. Wyllie. London: Baillière, Tindall & Cox, 1913.
Crawford, D. *Thinking Black: Twenty-two Years without a Break in the Long Grass of Central Africa*. London: Morgan and Scott, 1912.
Dark, Sydney. *The Life of Sir Arthur Pearson*. London: Hodder and Stoughton, [1922].
Debrett's House of Commons and the Judicial Bench. 43rd annual ed. London: Dean & Son, 1909.
Dilke, Charles W. "Forced and Indentured Labour in South America." In *Nationalities and Subject Races: Report of Conference Held in Caxton Hall, Westminster, June 28–30, 1910*. London: P. S. King & Son, [1910].
———. "Indentured and Forced Labour." In *Papers on Inter-racial Problems*, edited by G. Spiller, 312–22. London: P. S. King & Son, 1911.
Dillon, E. J. "Republican Portugal." *Contemporary Review* 98 (November 1910): 513–34.
Eckardstein, Baron von. *Ten Years at the Court of St. James: 1895–1905*. Translated and edited by George Young. London: Thornton Butterworth, 1921.
[Fox Bourne, H. R.]. *The Aborigines Protection Society: Chapters in Its History*. London: P. S. King & Son, 1899.
Fox Bourne, H. R. *Blacks and Whites in West Africa: An Account of the Past Treatment and Present Condition of West African Natives under European Influence or Control*. London: P. S. King & Son, [1901].
———. *Slave Traffic in Portuguese Africa*. London: P. S. King & Son, [1908].
Fyfe, Hamilton. *Sixty Years of Fleet Street*. London: W. H. Allen, 1949.
Gardiner, A. G. *Life of George Cadbury*. London: Cassell, 1923.
———. *Pillars of Society*. London: James Nisbet, 1913.
Gibbs, Philip. *More That Must Be Told*. New York: Harper and Brothers, 1921.
Gold Coast. Miscellaneous Official Publication. *Correspondence Relating to the Gift of £3,000 by Cadbury Brothers, Limited for the Purpose of Assisting the Government of the Gold Coast in the Training of Practical Cacao Farmers: "Hunter Hostels."* Accra, Gold Coast: Government Printing, 1931.
Gooch, G. P., and Harold Temperley, eds. *British Documents on the Origins of the War, 1898–1914*. Vols. 3, 6, 7, 8, and 10, pt. 2. London: His Majesty's Stationery Office, 1928–1938. Vol. 1, 1927; reprint, New York: Johnson Reprint Corporation, 1967.
Grey of Fallodon, Viscount. *Twenty-five Years, 1892–1916*. New York: Frederick A. Stokes, 1925.
Hardenburg, W. E. *Putumayo: The Devil's Paradise*. London: T. F. Unwin, [1912].
Harding, Colin. *In Remotest Barotseland*. London: Hurst and Blackett, 1905.
Harris, John. *Africa: Slave or Free?* London: Student Christian Movement, 1919.
———. *A Century of Emancipation*. London: J. M. Dent & Sons, 1933.
———. *Dawn in Darkest Africa*. With an introduction by the Earl of Cromer. London: Smith, Elder, 1912.
———. "Portuguese Slavery." *Contemporary Review* 101 (May 1912): 635–45.
———. *Portuguese Slavery: Britain's Dilemma*. London: Methuen, 1913.

Hatton, Joseph. *Cocoa.* London: Barclay & Fry, 1892.

Head, Brandon. *The Food of the Gods: A Popular Account of Cocoa.* London: R. Brimley Johnson, 1903.

Hobhouse, L. T. *Democracy and Reaction.* London: T. Fisher Unwin, 1904.

Hodgkin, J. E., ed. *Quakerism and Industry.* Darlington, UK: North of England Newspaper Co., [1918].

Johnson, W. H. *Cocoa: Its Cultivation and Preparation.* London: John Murray, 1912.

Johnston, H. H. *A History of Colonization of Africa by Alien Races.* 1913; new ed., New York: Cooper Square Publishers, 1966.

———. "The Portuguese Colonies." *The Nineteenth Century and After* 71 (March 1912): 497–510.

———. "The Portuguese Colonies of West Africa." *Journal of the Society of the Arts* 32 (February 15, 1884): 231–41.

Kingsley, Mary H. *Travels in West Africa.* 2nd ed. London: Macmillan, 1897.

Knapp, Arthur W. *The Cocoa and Chocolate Industry: The Tree, the Bean, the Beverage.* London: Sir Isaac Pitman & Sons, [1923].

———. *Cocoa and Chocolate: Their History from Plantation to Consumer.* London: Chapman & Hall, 1920.

Lewis, Georgina King. *Slavery in the 20th Century.* London: Headley Brothers, [1910].

Lichnowsky, Prince. *Heading for the Abyss.* London: Constable, 1928.

———. *My Mission to London: 1912–1914.* London: Cassell, 1918.

Lugard, Sir F. D. *Dual Mandate in British Tropical Africa.* Edinburgh: William Blackwood and Sons, 1922.

Macmillan, Allister, ed. *The Redbook of West Africa.* London: W. H. & L. Collingridge, 1920.

Malleson, George Bruce. *Delagoa Bay: The Key to South Africa.* London: Harrison & Sons, 1896.

Mantero, Francis. *Manual Labour in S. Thomé and Principe.* Translated from the Portuguese. Lisbon: Printing office of the Annuario Commercial, 1910; reprint, New York: Negro Universities Press, 1969.

———. *Portuguese Planters and British Humanitarians: The Case for S. Thomé.* Translated by J. A. Wyllie. Lisbon: Redacção da Reforma, 1911.

Mayo, Earl of. *De Rebus Africanus.* London: W. H. Allen, 1883.

Mendonça, Henrique José Monteiro de. *The Boa Entrada Plantations.* Translated by J. A. Wyllie. Edinburgh: Oliphant Anderson & Ferrier, 1907.

Möller, P. *Journey in Africa through Angola, Ovampoland and Damaraland.* Translated and annotated by Ione and Jalmar Rudner. Swedish ed., 1899; Cape Town, South Africa: C. Struik, 1974.

Morel, E. D. *The Black Man's Burden.* 1920; reprint, New York: Modern Reader Paperbacks, 1969.

———. *Red Rubber: The Story of the Rubber Slave Trade Flourishing on the Congo in the Year of Grace 1906.* With an introduction by Harry H. Johnston. 1906; reprint, New York: Negro Universities Press, 1969.

Mountmorres, Viscount. *Maize, Cocoa, Rubber: Hints on Their Production in West Africa.* Liverpool, UK: Liverpool University Institute of Commercial Research in the Tropics, 1907.

Murray, Gilbert. *The Foreign Policy of Sir Edward Grey, 1906–1915*. Oxford: Clarendon Press, 1915.

Nevinson, Henry W. "The Angola Slave Trade." *Fortnightly Review* n. s. 82 (September 1907): 488–97.

———. *Between the Acts*. New York: E. P. Dutton, 1904.

———. *Changes and Chances*. New York: Harcourt, Brace, 1924.

———. *Essays in Freedom*. London: Duckworth, 1909.

———. *Essays in Freedom and Rebellion*. New Haven, Conn.: Yale University Press, 1921.

———. *Essays, Poems and Tales of Henry W. Nevinson*. Edited and with an introduction by H. N. Brailsford. London: Victor Gollancz, 1948.

———. *Fire of Life*. [Abridgement of his three volumes of memoirs.] London: James Nisbet, 1935.

———. *Goethe: Man and Poet*. London: Nisbet, 1931.

———. *In the Dark Backward*. New York: Harcourt Brace, 1934.

———. *Last Changes Last Chances*. London: Nisbet, 1928.

———. *A Modern Slavery*. With an introduction by Basil Davidson. 1906; reprint, New York: Schocken, 1968.

———. *More Changes More Chances*. New York: Harcourt Brace, [1925].

———. "The New Slave Trade." *Harper's Monthly Magazine*, August 1905–February 1906.

———. *Visions and Memories*. London: Oxford University Press, 1944.

Olivier, Sidney. *White Capital and Coloured Labour*. London: Independent Labour Party, 1906.

A Pavement of Good Intentions or, S. Thomé Repatriation: Its Farce and Its Tragedy. Translations from *A Capital*, a Lisbon newspaper. Lisbon: Redaccâo da Reforma, Praça de Camoens, [June 1912].

Potter, Archdeacon Beresford. *Great Britain, Slavery, and Indentured Labour in the 20th Century*. London: Robert Banks & Son, [1911].

Raymond, E. T. *Portraits of the New Century (the First Ten Years)*. London: Ernest Benn, 1928.

Ross, Edward Alsworth. *Report on Employment of Native Labor in Portuguese Africa*. New York: [Abbott Press], 1925.

Rowntree, B. Seebohm. *Poverty: A Study of Town Life*. London: Macmillan, 1901.

Santos, Oliveira. "Reply to the Accusations Addressed to the League of Nations by Mr. Edward A. Ross against the Portuguese in Angola." Lisbon, 1930.

Satow, Ernest. *A Guide to Diplomatic Practice*. 2 vols. London: Longmans, Green, 1917.

Simon, John. *Retrospect: The Memoirs of the Rt. Hon. Viscount Simon*. London: Hutchinson, 1952.

Smith, Harold Hamel. *The Future of Cacao Planting*. London: "Tropical Life" Publishing Department, 1908.

Society of Friends. *Extracts from the Minutes and Proceedings of London Yearly Meeting of Friends, Held in Birmingham*. London: Office of the Society of Friends, 1908.

Stead, F. H. "Character Sketch: George Cadbury." *Review of Reviews* 25 (April 1902): 350–57.

Strachey, Amy. *St. Loe Strachey: His Life and His Paper*. London: Victor Gollancz, 1930.

Strachey, John St. Loe. *The Adventure of Living: A Subjective Autobiography*. London: Hodder and Stoughton, 1922.

———. *The River of Life*. London: Hodder and Stoughton, [1924].

Swan, Charles A. *The Slavery of To-day or, The Present Position of the Open Sore of Africa*. Glasgow, UK: Pickering & Inglis, 1909.
Taylor, Hannah H., coll. *John Cadbury, 1905–1985*. York, UK: William Sessions Limited, the Ebor Press, 1986.
Thornhill, J. B. *Adventures in Africa under the British, Belgian and Portuguese Flags*. London: John Murray, 1915.
Trevelyan, George Macaulay. *Fallodon: The Life and Letters of Sir Edward Grey*. Boston: Houghton Mifflin, 1937.
Van Hall, C. J. J. *Cocoa*. London: Macmillan, 1914.
Vasconcellos, Ernesto de. *As Nossas Colonia de Africa* [Our African Colonies]. Lisbon: Typ. Do Annuario Commercial, 1920.
Winterton, Earl. *Pre-war*. London: Macmillan, 1932.
World. "*Modern Slavery:* An Exposure of 'Red Cocoa' and the Chinese Slavery Lie, to which is added the Financial History of the 'Daily News.'" [1910].

Secondary Sources: Books and Articles

Abshire, David M., and Michael A. Samuels, eds. *Portuguese Africa: A Handbook*. London: Pall Mall Press, 1969.
Adams, W. S. *Edwardian Portraits*. London: Secker & Warburg, 1957.
Ajayi, J. F. A., and Michael Crowder, eds. *History of West Africa*. Harlow, UK: Longman Group. 3rd ed., Vol. 1, 1985. 2nd ed., Vol. 2, 1987.
Anderson, Jon Lee. "Our New Best Friend." *New Yorker*, October 7, 2002, 74–83.
Austen, Ralph A., and Rita Headrick. "Equatorial Africa under Colonial Rule." In *History of Central Africa*, edited by David Birmingham and Phyllis Martin. Vol. 2, 27–94. London: Longman, 1983.
Austin, Gareth. "Mode of Production or Mode of Cultivation: Explaining the Failure of European Cocoa Planters in Competition with African Farmers in Colonial Ghana." In *Cocoa Pioneer Fronts since 1800*, edited by William Gervase Clarence-Smith, 154–75. London: Macmillan, 1996.
Axelson, Eric. *Portugal and the Scramble for Africa, 1875–1891*. Johannesburg: Witwatersrand University Press, 1967.
Aykroyd, W. R. *Sweet Malefactor: Sugar, Slavery and Human Society*. London: Heinemann, 1967.
Bales, Kevin. *Disposable People: New Slavery in the Global Economy*. Berkeley: University of California Press, 1999.
Ballinger, Jeff. "Nike in Indonesia." *Dissent* 45 (Fall 1998): 18–21.
Barendt, Eric, Laurence Lustgarten, Kenneth Norrie, and Hugh Stephenson. *Libel and the Media: The Chilling Effect*. Oxford: Clarendon Press, 1997.
Beckett, J. C. *Confrontations: Studies in Irish History*. London: Faber & Faber, 1972.
Bender, Gerald J. *Angola under the Portuguese*. Berkeley: University of California Press, 1978.
Berlan, Amanda. "Child Labour, Education and Child Rights among Cocoa Producers in Ghana." In *The Political Economy of New Slavery*, edited by Christine van den Anker, 158–79. Basingstoke, Hampshire, UK: Palgrave Macmillan, 2004.

Bernstein, George L. *Liberalism and Liberal Politics in Edwardian England*. Boston: Allen & Unwin, 1986.

Birmingham, David. *A Concise History of Portugal*. Cambridge: Cambridge University Press, 1993.

———. *Portugal and Africa*. New York: St. Martin's Press, 1999.

Birmingham, David A., and Phyllis Martin, eds. *History of Central Africa*. 2 vols. London: Longmans, 1983.

———, eds. *History of Central Africa: The Contemporary Years since 1960*. London: Longman, 1998.

Birmingham Magistrates' Court. "Victoria Law Courts Visitor Guide," n.d.

Bixler, Raymond W. *The West African Cocoa Story*. New York: Vantage Press, 1972.

Bley, Helmut. "Social Discord in South West Africa, 1894–1904." In *Britain and Germany in Africa*, edited by Prosser Gifford and Wm. Roger Louis, 607–30. New Haven, Conn.: Yale University Press, 1967.

Boahen, A. Adu., ed. *General History of Africa*. Vol. 7, *Africa under Colonial Domination 1880–1935*. London: Heinemann, 1985.

Boxer, C. R. *The Portuguese Sea-Borne Empire: 1415–1825*. London: Hutchinson, 1969.

———. *Race Relations in the Portuguese Colonial Empire: 1415–1825*. Oxford: Clarendon Press, 1963.

Boyce, D. G. "Edward Carson (1845–1935) and Irish Unionism." In *Worsted in the Game: Losers in Irish History*, edited by Ciaran Brady, 145–57. Dublin: Lilliput Press, 1989.

Bradley, Ian Campbell. *Enlightened Entrepreneurs*. London: Weidenfeld and Nicolson, 1987.

Brantlinger, Patrick. *Rule of Darkness: British Literature and Imperialism, 1830–1914*. Ithaca, N.Y.: Cornell University Press, 1988.

Brazão, Eduardo. *The Anglo-Portuguese Alliance*. London: Sylvan Press, 1957.

Briggs, Asa. *History of Birmingham*. Vol. 2, *Borough and City, 1865–1938*. London: Oxford University Press, 1952.

Broad, Lewis. *Advocates of the Golden Age*. London: John Long, 1958.

Brooks, David. *The Age of Upheaval: Edwardian Politics, 1899–1914*. Manchester, UK: Manchester University Press, 1995.

Bury, J. P. T. "Diplomatic History, 1900–1912." In *The New Cambridge Modern History*. Vol. 12, *The Shifting Balance of World Forces, 1898–1945*, edited by C. L. Mowat, 112–39. 2nd ed. Cambridge: Cambridge University Press, 1968.

Busch, Briton Cooper. *Hardinge of Penshurst: A Study in the Old Diplomacy*. Hamden, Conn.: Archon Books, 1980.

Campbell, Alexander. *The Heart of Africa*. New York: Alfred A. Knopf, 1954.

Carreira, Antonio. *The People of the Cape Verde Islands: Exploitation and Emigration*. Hamden, Conn.: Archon Books, 1982.

Carter-Ruck, Peter F. *Carter-Ruck on Libel and Slander*. 3rd ed. London: Butterworths, 1985.

Cecil, Algernon. *British Foreign Secretaries, 1807–1916*. London: G. Bell and Sons, 1927.

Cherry, Gordon E. "Bournville, England, 1895–1995." *Journal of Urban History* 22 (May 1996): 493–508.

Chilcote, Ronald H. *Portuguese Africa*. Englewood Cliffs, N.J.: Prentice-Hall, 1967.

Child, John. "Quaker Employers and Industrial Relations." *Sociological Review* n.s. 12 (November 1964): 293–315.

Chinn, Carl. *The Cadbury Story: A Short History*. Studley, Warwickshire, UK: Brewin Books, 1998.

Clarence-Smith, William Gervase. "Capital Accumulation and Class Formation in Angola." In *History of Central Africa*, edited by David Birmingham and Phyllis Martin. Vol. 2, 164–99. London: Longmans, 1983.

———. *Cocoa and Chocolate, 1765–1914*. London: Routledge, 2000.

———, ed. *Cocoa Pioneer Fronts since 1800*. London: Macmillan, 1996.

———. "Cocoa Plantations and Coerced Labour in the Gulf of Guinea, 1870–1914." In *Breaking the Chains: Slavery, Bondage, and Emancipation in Modern Africa and Asia*, edited by Martin A. Klein, 150–70. Madison: University of Wisconsin Press, 1993.

———. "The Hidden Costs of Labour on the Cocoa Plantations of São Tomé and Príncipe, 1875–1914." *Portuguese Studies* 6 (1990): 152–72.

———. "Labour Conditions in the Plantations of São Tomé and Príncipe, 1875–1914." *Slavery and Abolition* 4 (April 1993): 149–67.

———. "The Myth of Uneconomic Imperialism: The Portuguese in Angola, 1836–1926." *Journal of Southern African Studies* 5 (April 1979): 165–80.

———. "Slavery in Coastal Southern Angola, 1875–1913." *Journal of Southern African Studies* 2 (1976): 214–23.

———. *Slaves, Peasants and Capitalists in Southern Angola, 1840–1926*. Cambridge: Cambridge University Press, 1979.

———. *The Third Portuguese Empire 1825–1975: A Study in Economic Imperialism*. Manchester, UK: Manchester University Press, 1975.

Clarence-Smith, William Gervase, and François Ruf. "Cocoa Pioneer Fronts: The Historical Determinants." In *Cocoa Pioneer Fronts since 1800*, edited by William Gervase Clarence-Smith, 1–22. London: Macmillan, 1996.

Cline, Catherine Ann. *E. D. Morel, 1873–1924: The Strategies of Protest*. Belfast, UK: Blackstaff Press, 1980.

Cocker, Mark. *Rivers of Blood, Rivers of Gold*. London: Jonathan Cape, 1998.

Coe, Sophie D., and Michael D. Coe. *The True History of Chocolate*. London: Thames & Hudson, 1996.

Collins, Doreen. *Aspects of British Politics, 1904–1919*. Oxford: Pergamom Press, 1965.

Committee for Freedom in Mozambique, Angola and Guine. *Partners in Crime: The Anglo-Portuguese Alliance Past and Present*. London: Committee for Freedom in Mozambique, Angola and Guine, 1973.

Cookey, S. J. S. *Britain and the Congo Question: 1885–1913*. London: Longmans, 1968.

Coombes, Annie E. *Reinventing Africa: Museums, Material Culture and Popular Imagination in Late Victorian and Edwardian England*. New Haven, Conn.: Yale University Press, 1994.

Coquery-Vidrovitch, C. "The Colonial Economy of the Former French, Belgian and Portuguese Zones, 1914–35." In *General History of Africa*. Vol. 7, *Africa under Colonial Domination, 1880–1935*, edited by A. Adu Boahen, 351–81. London: Heinemann, 1985.

Courtwright, David T. *Forces of Habit: Drugs and the Making of the Modern World*. Cambridge, Mass.: Harvard University Press, 2001.

Crewe-Milnes, Robert Offley. *Lord Rosebery*. 2 vols. London: John Murray, 1931.

Crosfield, John F. *A History of the Cadbury Family*. 2 vols. London: J. F. Crosfield, 1985.

Crowe, S. E. *The Berlin West African Conference, 1884–1885*. London: Longmans, Green, 1942.

Curtin, Philip D. *The Atlantic Slave Trade: A Census.* Madison: University of Wisconsin Press, 1969.

———. *Cross-Cultural Trade in World History.* New York: Cambridge University Press, 1984.

———. "The External Trade of West Africa to 1800." In *History of West Africa,* vol. 1, edited by J. F. A. Ajayi and Michael Crowder, 624–47. 3rd ed. Harlow, UK: Longman Group, 1985.

———. *The Rise and Fall of the Plantation Complex: Essays in Atlantic History.* Cambridge: Cambridge University Press, 1990.

Davidson, Basil. *The African Awakening.* New York: Macmillan, 1955.

———. *In the Eye of the Storm: Angola's People.* Garden City, N.Y.: Doubleday, 1971.

Delap, Mick. "In Search of São Tomé." *Focus on Africa* 1 (November–December 1990): 36–42.

Dellheim, Charles. "The Creation of a Company Culture: *Cadburys,* 1861–1931." *American Historical Review* 92 (February 1987): 13–44.

Derrick, Jonathan. *Africa's Slaves Today.* New York: Schocken Books, 1975.

Deva, Siddharth. "The Anti-slavery Movement from 1890 to 1934." M. Phil. thesis, Oxford University, 1993.

Diamond, Jared. *Guns, Germs, and Steel: The Fates of Human Societies.* New York: W. W. Norton, 1997.

Dictionary of National Biography. London: Oxford University Press. Various editions, including decennial supplements for the twentieth century.

Drescher, Seymour, and Stanley L. Engerman, eds. *A Historical Guide to World Slavery.* New York: Oxford University Press, 1998.

Duffy, James. *Portugal in Africa.* Baltimore, Md.: Penguin Books, 1963.

———. *Portuguese Africa.* Cambridge, Mass.: Harvard University Press, 1959.

———. *A Question of Slavery: Labour Politics in Portuguese Africa and the British Protest, 1850–1920.* Cambridge, Mass.: Harvard University Press, 1967.

Duncan, Colin, and Brian Neill. *Defamation.* London: Butterworth, 1978.

Duncan, T. Bentley. *Atlantic Islands.* Chicago: University of Chicago Press, 1972.

Dutton, David. *Simon: A Political Biography of Sir John Simon.* London: Aurum Press, 1992.

Edwards, C. Norman. *Cadburys on the Gold Coast and Ghana.* Birmingham, UK: Privately printed, 1958.

Eltis, David. *Economic Growth and the Ending of the Transatlantic Slave Trade.* New York: Oxford University Press, 1987.

Eltis, David, and James Walvin, eds. *The Abolition of the Atlantic Slave Trade: Origins and Effects in Europe, Africa and the Americas.* Madison: University of Wisconsin Press, 1981.

Emden, Paul H. *Quakers in Commerce: A Record of Business Achievement.* London: Sampson Low, Marston, [1939].

Evans, D. Wyn, comp. *Catalogue of the Cadbury Papers.* Birmingham, UK: University of Birmingham, 1973.

Ewald, Janet J. "Slavery in Africa and the Slave Trades from Africa." *American Historical Review* 97 (April 1992): 465–85.

Feis, Herbert. *Europe: The World's Banker, 1870–1914.* New Haven, Conn.: Council on Foreign Relations, 1930.

Ferguson, Niall. *The Pity of War*. New York: Basic Books, 1999.
Ferraz, Luiz Ivens. *The Creole of São Tomé*. Johannesburg: Witwatersrand University Press, 1979.
Fitzgerald, Robert. *Rowntree and the Marketing Revolution, 1862–1969*. Cambridge: Cambridge University Press, 1995.
Foden, Giles. *Ladysmith*. New York: Alfred A. Knopf, 2000.
Francis, A. D. *The Methuens and Portugal, 1691–1708*. Cambridge: Cambridge University Press, 1966.
Frankel, S. H. *Capital Investment in Africa*. London: Oxford University Press, 1938.
Furley, Oliver. "The Humanitarian Impact." In *Britain Pre-eminent: Studies of British World Influence in the Nineteenth Century*, edited by C. J. Bartlett, 128–51. London: Macmillan, 1969.
Gallagher, T. *Portugal: A Twentieth Century Interpretation*. Manchester, UK: Manchester University Press, 1983.
Garfield, Robert. *A History of São Tomé Island, 1470–1655: The Key to Guinea*. San Francisco: Mellen Research University Press, 1992.
Gertzel, Cherry. "John Holt: A British Merchant in West Africa in the Era of Imperialism." Ph.D. diss., Oxford University, 1959.
Gifford, Prosser, and Wm. Roger Louis, eds. *Britain and Germany in Africa*. New Haven, Conn.: Yale University Press, 1967.
Gooch, G. P. "Triple Alliance and Triple Entente." In *The Cambridge History of British Foreign Policy, 1783–1919*. Vol. 3, *1866–1919*, edited by A. W. Ward and G. P. Gooch, 385–508. 1923; reprint, New York: Octagon, 1970.
Gordon, James. "Cocoa: Its Nature, Habitat, and Cultivation." In *Cocoa Production: Economic and Botanical Perspectives*, edited by John Simmons, 3–29. New York: Praeger, 1976.
Gosses, F. *The Management of British Foreign Policy before the First World War*. Translated by E. C. van der Gaaf. Leiden, the Netherlands: A.W. Sijthoff's Uitgeversmaatschappij, 1948.
Gowan, Susan Jean. *Portuguese-Speaking Africa, 1900–1979: A Select Bibliography*. Vol. 3. Braamfontein, South Africa: South African Institute of International Affairs, 1983.
Grant, Kevin Patrick. "'A Civilised Savagery': British Humanitarian Politics and European Imperialism in Africa, 1884–1926." D. Phil. diss., University of California, Berkeley, 1997.
Green, Alice Stopford. "A Founder of the Society [John Holt]." *Journal of the African Society* 15 (October 1915): 11–16.
Grenville, J. A. S. *Lord Salisbury and Foreign Policy: The Close of the Nineteenth Century*. London: Athlone Press, 1964.
Gungwu, Wang, ed. *Global History and Migrations*. Boulder, Colo.: Westview Press, 1997.
Halstead, John P., and Sarafino Porcari, eds. *Modern European Imperialism: A Bibliography of Books and Articles, 1815–1972*. Vol. 2. Boston: G. K. Hall, 1974.
Hammond, Richard J. *Portugal and Africa, 1815–1910*. Stanford, Calif.: Stanford University Press, 1966.
———. "Some Economic Aspects of Portuguese Africa in the Nineteenth and Twentieth Centuries." In *Colonialism in Africa, 1870–1960*. Vol. 4, *The Economics of Colonialism*, edited by Peter Duignan and L. H. Gann, 256–80. Cambridge: Cambridge University Press, 1975.

———. "Uneconomic Imperialism: Portugal in Africa before 1910." In *Colonialism in Africa, 1870–1960*. Vol. 1, *The History and Politics of Colonialism, 1870–1914*, edited by L. H. Gann and Peter Duignan, 352–82. Cambridge: Cambridge University Press, 1969.

Hanbury, Harold Greville. *English Courts of Law*. London: Oxford University Press, 1944.

Hanna, A. J. *The Story of the Rhodesias and Nyasaland*. London: Faber and Faber, 1960.

Hardinge, Charles. *Old Diplomacy: The Reminiscences of Lord Hardinge of Penshurst*. London: John Murray, 1947.

Harries, Patrick. *Work, Culture, and Identity: Migrant Laborers in Mozambique and South Africa, c. 1860–1910*. Portsmouth, N.H.: Heinemann, 1994.

Havighurst, Alfred F. *Radical Journalist: H. W. Massingham*. London: Cambridge University Press, 1974.

Hayes, Paul. *The Twentieth Century, 1880–1939*. New York: St. Martin's Press, 1978.

Headrick, Daniel. *The Tentacles of Progress: Technology Transfer in the Age of Imperialism, 1850–1940*. New York: Oxford University Press, 1988.

———. *The Tools of Empire: Technology and European Imperialism in the Nineteenth Century*. New York: Oxford University Press, 1981.

Heimer, Franz-Wilhelm, ed. *Social Change in Angola*. Munich, Germany: Weltforum Verlag, 1973.

Henderson, Lawrence W. *Angola: Five Centuries of Conflict*. Ithaca, N.Y.: Cornell University Press, 1979.

Heuston, R. F. V. *Lives of the Lord Chancellors: 1885–1940*. Oxford: Clarendon Press, 1964.

Heywood, Linda M. "Slavery and Forced Labor in the Changing Political Economy of Central Angola, 1850–1949." In *The End of Slavery in Africa*, edited by Suzanne Miers and Richard Roberts, 415–36. Madison: University of Wisconsin Press, 1988.

Hickman, Douglas. *Birmingham*. London: Studio Vista, 1970.

Hill, Polly. *The Gold Coast Farmer: A Preliminary Survey*. London: Oxford University Press, 1956.

———. *The Migrant Cocoa-Farmers of Southern Ghana*. Cambridge: Cambridge University Press, 1963.

———. *Studies in Rural Capitalism in West Africa*. Cambridge: Cambridge University Press, 1970.

Hochschild, Adam. *King Leopold's Ghost*. New York: Houghton Mifflin, 1998.

Hodges, Tony, and Malyn Newitt. *São Tomé and Príncipe: From Plantation Economy to Microstate*. Boulder, Colo.: Westview Press, 1988.

Hogg, Peter C. *The Slave Trade and Its Suppression*. London: Frank Cass, 1973.

Holborn, Guy. *Sources of Biographical Information on Past Lawyers*. Warwick, UK: British and Irish Association of Law Librarians, 1999.

Holt, John, & Co. (Liverpool) Ltd. *Merchant Adventure*. Liverpool: John Holt (Liverpool), [1951].

Hopkins, A. G. *An Economic History of West Africa*. New York: Columbia University Press, 1973.

Hyam, Ronald. *Britain's Imperial Century, 1815–1914*. New York: Barnes and Noble, 1976.

Hyde, H. Montgomery. *Carson*. 1953; reprint, New York: Octagon Books, 1974.

———. *Lord Reading: The Life of Rufus Isaacs, First Marquess of Reading*. London: Heinemann, 1967.

———. *Their Good Names: Twelve Cases of Libel and Slander.* London: Hamish Hamilton, 1970.

———. *United in Crime.* London: William Heinemann, 1955.

International Institute of Tropical Agriculture. "Child Labour in the Cocoa Sector of West Africa." August 2002. Available at www/iita.org.

International Labor Organization. "Report of the Commission Appointed under Article 26 of the Constitution of the International Labour Organisation to Examine the Complaint Filed by the Government of Ghana Concerning the Observance by the Government of Portugal of the Abolition of Forced Labour Convention, 1957 (No. 105)." In *Official Bulletin* 45 (April 1962).

Isaacman, A., and J. Vansina. "African Initiatives and Resistance in Central Africa, 1880–1914." In *General History of Africa.* Vol. 7, *Africa under Colonial Domination, 1880–1935,* edited by A. Adu Boahen, 169–93. London: Heinemann, 1985.

Isaacman, Allen, and Barbara Isaacman. *Mozambique: From Colonialism to Revolution, 1900–1982.* Boulder, Colo.: Westview Press, 1983.

Isichei, Elizabeth. *Victorian Quakers.* London: Oxford University Press, 1970.

Jeeves, Alan H. *Migrant Labour in South Africa's Mining Economy: The Struggle for the Gold Mines' Labour Supply 1890–1920:* Kingston, Canada: McGill-Queen's University Press, 1985.

Jeremy, David J. *Capitalists and Christians: Business Leaders and the Churches of Britain, 1900–1960.* Oxford: Clarendon Press, 1990.

———, ed. *Dictionary of Business Biography.* Vol. 1. London: Butterworths, 1984.

John, Angela. "A New Slavery?" *History Today* 52, June 2002, 34–35.

Johnston, James. *Westminster Voices: Studies in Parliamentary Speech.* London: Hodder and Stoughton, 1928.

Jowitt, William Allen, ed. *The Dictionary of English Law.* [Also known as *Jowitt's Dictionary of English Law.*] London: Sweet & Maxwell, 1959, 1st ed., and 1977, 2nd ed.

Judd, Denis. *Lord Reading.* London: Weidenfeld and Nicolson, 1982.

Katzenellenbogen, Simon E. *South Africa and Southern Mozambique: Labour, Railways and Trade in the Making of a Relationship.* Manchester, UK: Manchester University Press, 1982.

Keating, P. J. *The Working Classes in Victorian Fiction.* London: Routledge & Kegan Paul, 1971.

Kennedy, Carol. *The Merchant Princes: Family, Fortune and Philanthropy—Cadbury, Sainsbury and John Lewis.* London: Hutchinson, 2000.

Kennedy, Pagan. *Black Livingstone: A True Tale of Adventure in the Nineteenth-Century Congo.* New York: Viking, 2002.

Kennedy, Thomas C. *British Quakerism, 1860–1929: The Transformation of a Religious Community.* Oxford: Oxford University Press, 2001.

Klein, Martin A. "Slavery, the International Labour Market and the Emancipation of Slaves in the Nineteenth Century." In *Unfree Labour in the Development of the Atlantic World,* edited by Paul E. Lovejoy and Nicholas Rogers, 197–220. London: Frank Cass, 1994.

Kloosterboer, W. *Involuntary Labour since the Abolition of Slavery: A Survey of Compulsory Labour throughout the World.* Leiden, the Netherlands: E. J. Brill, 1960.

Koss, Stephen. *Fleet Street Radical: A. G. Gardiner and the Daily News.* London: Allen Lane, 1973.

———. *Rise and Fall of the Political Press.* Vol. 2, *The Twentieth Century.* Chapel Hill: University of North Carolina Press, 1984.

Lacey, Jane. "Cadbury's, Sao Tomé and the Gold Coast: A Study of Industrial Involvement in Imperial Problems." Ph.D. diss., University of Sussex, 1970.
Langhorne, Richard. "Anglo-German Negotiations Concerning the Future of the Portuguese Colonies, 1911–1914." *Historical Journal* 16 (1973): 361–87.
Lee, Alan J. "The Radical Press." In *Edwardian Radicalism, 1900–1914*, edited by A. J. A. Morris, 47–61. London: Routledge & Kegan Paul, 1974.
Lee, Sidney. *King Edward VII*. Vol. 2. New York: Macmillan, 1927.
Leventhal, F. M. *The Last Dissenter: H. N. Brailsford and His World*. Oxford: Clarendon Press, 1985.
Lewis, Becky W. "Henry Woodd Nevinson." In *Dictionary of Literary Biography*. Vol. 135, edited by William B. Thesing, 255–61. Detroit: Gale Research, 1994.
Lewis, Philip. *Gatley on Libel and Slander*. 8th ed. London: Sweet & Maxwell, 1981.
Livermore, H. V. *A History of Portugal*. Cambridge: Cambridge University Press, 1947.
Lockhart, J. G., and C. M. Woodhouse. *Cecil Rhodes, the Colossus of Southern Africa*. New York: Macmillan, 1963.
Lorimer, Douglas A. "Race, Science and Culture: Historical Continuities and Discontinuities, 1850–1914." In *The Victorians and Race*, edited by Shearer West, 12–33. Aldershot, UK: Ashgate, 1996.
Louis, Wm. Roger. "Great Britain and German Expansion in Africa, 1884–1919." In *Britain and Germany in Africa*, edited by Prosser Gifford and Wm. Roger Louis, 3–46. New Haven, Conn.: Yale University Press, 1967.
Louis, Wm. Roger, and Jean Stenger. *E. D. Morel's History of the Congo Reform Movement*. Oxford: Clarendon Press, 1968.
Lovejoy, Paul E., ed. *Africans in Bondage: Studies in Slavery and the Slave Trade*. Madison: University of Wisconsin Press, 1986.
———. *Transformations in Slavery: A History of Slavery in Africa*. Cambridge: Cambridge University Press, 1983.
Lovejoy, Paul E., and Nicholas Rogers, eds. *Unfree Labour in the Development of the Atlantic World*. London: Frank Cass, 1994.
Lowe, C. J. *The Reluctant Imperialists: British Foreign Policy, 1878–1902*. 1st American ed. New York: Macmillan, 1969.
Lowe, C. J., and M. L. Dockrill. *The Mirage of Power*. Vol. 1, *British Foreign Policy, 1902–14*. London: Routledge & Kegan Paul, 1972.
Lutz, Hermann. *Lord Grey and the World War*. Translated by E. W. Dickes. New York: Alfred A. Knopf, 1928.
MacKenzie, John M. "Empire and Metropolitan Cultures." In *The Oxford History of the British Empire*. Vol. 3, *The Nineteenth Century*, edited by Andrew Porter, 270–93. Oxford: Oxford University Press, 1999.
MacQueen, Norrie. *The Decolonization of Portuguese Africa: Metropolitan Revolution and the Dissolution of Empire*. London: Longman, 1997.
Manokha, Ivan. "Modern Slavery and Fair Trade Products: Buy One and Set Someone Free." In *The Political Economy of New Slavery*, edited by Christine van den Anker, 217–34. Basingstoke, Hampshire, UK: Palgrave Macmillan, 2004.
Marjoriebanks, Edward. *Carson the Advocate*. New York: Macmillan, 1932.
Marks, Shula. "Southern and Central Africa, 1886–1910." In *The Cambridge History of Africa*.

Vol. 6, *1870 to 1905*, edited by Roland Oliver and G. N. Sanderson, 422–92. Cambridge: Cambridge University Press, 1985.

Marques, A. H. De Oliveira. *History of Portugal*. Vol. 2, *From Empire to Corporate State*. New York: Columbia University Press, 1972.

Marsh, Peter T. *Chamberlain: Entrepreneur in Politics*. New Haven, Conn.: Yale University Press, 1994.

Martin, Phyllis M. "The Violence of Empire." In *History of Central Africa*, edited by David Birmingham and Phyllis Martin. Vol. 2, 1–26. London: Longman, 1983.

Matthew, H. G. C. *The Liberal Imperialists*. Oxford: Oxford University Press, 1973.

Matthews, Noel. *Materials for West African History in the Archives of the United Kingdom*. London: Athlone Press, 1973.

McCaskie, T. C. "Cultural Encounters: Britain and Africa in the Nineteenth Century." In *The Oxford History of the British Empire*. Vol. 3, *The Nineteenth Century*, edited by Andrew Porter, 665–89. Oxford: Oxford University Press, 1999.

Meacham, Standish. *Regaining Paradise: Englishness and the Early Garden City Movement*. New Haven, Conn.: Yale University Press, 1999.

Messiant, Christine. "Angola: The Challenge of Statehood." In *History of Central Africa: The Contemporary Years since 1960*, edited by David Birmingham and Phyllis Martin, 131–65. London: Longman, 1998.

Miers, Suzanne. *Britain and the Ending of the Slave Trade*. New York: Africana Publishing, 1975.

———. "The Brussels Conference of 1889–1890: The Place of the Slave Trade in the Policies of Great Britain and Germany." In *Britain and Germany in Africa*, edited by Prosser Gifford and Wm. Roger Louis, 83–118. New Haven, Conn.: Yale University Press, 1967.

———. *Slavery in the Twentieth Century: The Evolution of a Global Problem*. New York: AltaMira Press, 2003.

Miers, Suzanne, and Igor Kopytoff. *Slavery in Africa: Historical and Anthropological Perspectives*. Madison: University of Wisconsin Press, 1977.

Miers, Suzanne, and Richard Roberts, eds. *The End of Slavery in Africa*. Madison: University of Wisconsin Press, 1988.

Mikell, Gwendolyn. *Cocoa and Chaos in Ghana*. New York: Paragon House, 1989; Washington, D.C.: Howard University Press, 1992.

Miller, Joseph C. "A Marginal Institution on the Margin of the Atlantic System: The Portuguese Southern Atlantic Slave Trade in the Eighteenth Century." In *Slavery and the Rise of the Atlantic System*, edited by Barbara L. Solow, 120–50. Cambridge: Cambridge University Press, 1991.

———. "The Paradoxes of Impoverishment in the Atlantic Zone." In *History of Central Africa*, edited by David Birmingham and Phyllis Martin. Vol. 1, 118–59. London: Longman, 1983.

———. *Way of Death: Merchant Capitalism and the Angolan Slave Trade, 1730–1830*. Madison: University of Wisconsin Press, 1988.

Minter, William. *Portuguese Africa and the West*. Baltimore, Md.: Penguin Books, 1972.

Mintz, Sydney W. *Sweetness and Power: The Place of Sugar in Modern History*. New York: Viking Press, 1985.

Monger, George. *The End of Isolation*. London: Thomas Nelson and Sons, 1963.

Morton, Marcia, and Frederic Morton. *Chocolate: An Illustrated History*. New York: Crown Publishers, 1986.

Munro, J. Forbes. *Africa and the International Economy, 1800–1960*. London: J. M. Dent & Sons, 1976.

Nartey, Robert Nii. "From Slave to Serviçal Labor in the Plantation Economy of São Tome and Principe, 1876–1932." Ph.D. diss., University of Illinois, Chicago, 1986.

Neilson, Keith. "'Control the Whirlwind': Sir Edward Grey as Foreign Secretary, 1906–16." In *The Makers of British Foreign Policy: From Pitt to Thatcher*, edited by T. G. Otte, 128–49. New York: Palgrave, 2002.

Newbury, C. W. *The Western Slave Coast and Its Rulers*. Oxford: Clarendon Press, 1961.

Newitt, Malyn. *Portugal in Africa: The Last Hundred Years*. London: Longman, 1981.

Newman, Sir George. *Quaker Profiles*. London: Bannisdale Press, 1946.

Nicolson, Harold. *The Congress of Vienna*. New York: Harcourt Brace Jovanovich, 1946.

Nightingale, Robert T. *The Personnel of the British Foreign Office and Diplomatic Service, 1851–1921*. London: Fabian Society, 1930.

Northrup, David. *Indentured Labor in the Age of Imperialism, 1834–1922*. New York: Cambridge University Press, 1995.

Nowell, Charles E. *A History of Portugal*. New York: D. Van Nostrand, 1953.

Nwaka, Geoffrey I. "Cadburys and the Dilemma of Colonial Trade in Africa, 1901–1910." *Bulletin de l'Institut Fondamental d'Afrique Noire* [Université de Dakar] 42 (October 1980): 780–93.

Nworah, Kingsley Kenneth Dike. "Humanitarian Pressure-Groups and British Attitudes to West Africa, 1895–1915." Ph.D. diss., London University, 1966.

Nzongola-Ntalaja, Georges. *The Congo from Leopold to Kabila: A People's History*. London: Zed Books, 2002.

Oliver, Roland. *Sir Harry Johnston and the Scramble for Africa*. London: Chatto & Windus, 1957.

Oliver, Roland, and J. D. Fage. *A Short History of Africa*. Harmondsworth, UK: Penguin, 1962.

Oliver, Roland, and G. N. Sanderson, eds. *The Cambridge History of Africa*. Vol. 6, *1870 to 1905*. Cambridge: Cambridge University Press, 1985.

Othick, J. "The Cocoa and Chocolate Industry in the Nineteenth Century." In *The Making of the Modern Diet*, edited by Derik Oddy and Derik Miller, 77–90. London: Croom Helm, 1976.

Owen, David. *English Philanthropy, 1660–1960*. Cambridge, Mass.: Belknap Press of Harvard University Press, 1964.

Pakenham, Thomas. *The Scramble for Africa: The White Man's Conquest of the Dark Continent from 1876 to 1912*. London: Weidenfeld and Nicolson, 1991.

Paquette, Robert L. "Revolts." In *A Historical Guide to World Slavery*, edited by Seymour Drescher and Stanley L. Engerman, 334–44. New York: Oxford University Press, 1998.

Patterson, Orlando. *Slavery and Social Death: A Comparative Study*. Cambridge, Mass.: Harvard University Press, 1982.

Phillips, William D., Jr. "The Old World Background of Slavery in the Americas." In *Slavery and the Rise of the Atlantic System*, edited by Barbara L. Solow, 43–61. Cambridge: Cambridge University Press, 1991.

Platt, D. C. M. *Cinderella Service: British Consuls since 1825*. London: Longman, 1971.

———. *Finance, Trade, and Politics in British Foreign Policy, 1815–1914*. Oxford: Clarendon Press, 1968.
Pomeranz, Kenneth. *The World That Trade Created*. Armonk, N.Y.: M. E. Sharpe, 1999.
Porter, Andrew, ed. *The Oxford History of the British Empire*. Vol. 3, *The Nineteenth Century*. Oxford: Oxford University Press, 1999.
———. "Trusteeship, Anti-Slavery, and Humanitarianism." In *The Oxford History of the British Empire*. Vol. 3, *The Nineteenth Century*, edited by Andrew Porter, 198–221. Oxford: Oxford University Press, 1999.
Porter, Bernard. *Critics of Empire: British Radical Attitudes to Colonialism in Africa, 1895–1914*. New York: St. Martin's Press, 1968.
———. "The Edwardians and Their Empire." In *Edwardian England*, edited by Donald Read, 128–44. New Brunswick, N.J.: Rutgers University Press, 1982.
Reading, Marquess of. *Rufus Isaacs, First Marquess of Reading*. New York: G. P. Putnam's Sons, 1940.
Redmayne, Paul, and Thomas Insull. *Cocoa and Chocolate*. London: Oxford University Press, 1939.
Reynolds, Edward. *Stand the Storm: A History of the Atlantic Slave Trade*. London: Allison & Busby, 1985.
Richardson, Tim. *Sweets*. London: Bloomsbury, 2002.
Ritner, Peter. *The Death of Africa*. New York: Macmillan, 1960.
Robbins, Keith. *Sir Edward Grey: A Biography of Lord Grey of Fallodon*. London: Cassell, 1971.
Roberts, Andrew. "Portuguese Africa." In *The Cambridge History of Africa*. Vol. 7, *1905 to 1940*, edited by A. D. Roberts, 494–537. Cambridge: Cambridge University Press, 1986.
Roberts, Bechhofer. *Sir John Simon*. London: Robert Hale, 1938.
Robinson, Ronald, and John Gallagher. *Africa and the Victorians: The Official Mind of Imperialism*. 2nd ed. paperback. London: Macmillan, 1981.
Rodney, W. "The Colonial Economy." In *General History of Africa*. Vol. 7, *Africa under Colonial Domination, 1880–1935*, edited by A. Adu Boahen, 332–50. London: Heinemann, 1985.
Rodrigues, José Honório. *Brazil and Africa*. Translated by Richard A. Mazzara and Sam Hileman. Berkeley: University of California Press, 1965.
Rogers, T. B. *A Century of Progress, 1831–1931: Cadbury Bournville*. Privately printed, 1931.
Rotberg, Robert I. "Plymouth Brethern and the Occupation of Katanga, 1886–1907." *Journal of African History* 5 (1964): 285–97.
———. *The Rise of Nationalism in Central Africa*. Cambridge, Mass.: Harvard University Press, 1965.
Rowlinson, Michael. "Cadbury World." *Labour History Review* 67 (April 2002): 101–19.
———. "Cadburys' New Factory System, 1879–1919." Ph.D. diss., University of Aston, Birmingham, 1987.
———. "The Early Application of Scientific Management by Cadbury." *Business History* 30 (October 1988): 377–95.
———. "Quaker Employers." *Historical Studies in Industrial Relations* 6 (Autumn 1998): 163–98.
Rowlinson, Michael, and John Hassard. "The Invention of Corporate Culture: A History of the Histories of Cadbury." *Human Relations* 46 (1993): 299–326.

Russell, A. K. *Liberal Landslide: The General Election of 1906*. Hamden, Conn.: Archon Books, 1973.

Ryder, A. F. C. *Materials for West African History in Portuguese Archives*. London: Athlone Press, 1965.

Saunders, Kay, ed. *Indentured Labour in the British Empire, 1834–1920*. London: Croom Helm, 1984.

Sawyer, Roger. *Casement, the Flawed Hero*. London: Routledge & Kegan Paul, 1984.

———. *Slavery in the Twentieth Century*. London: Routledge & Kegan Paul, 1986.

Schuchard, Ronald. "'An Attendant Lord': H. W. Nevinson's Friendship with W. B. Yeats." In *Yeats Annual No. 7*, edited by Warwick Gould, 90–130. London: Macmillan, 1990.

Schwab, Peter. *Africa: A Continent Self-Destructs*. New York: Palgrave, 2002.

Scott-Bayfield, Julie A. *Defamation: Law and Practice*. London: FT Law & Tax, 1996.

Searle, G. R. *The Quest for National Efficiency: A Study in British Politics and Political Thought, 1899–1924*. Berkeley: University of California Press, 1971.

Seibert, Gerhard. *Comrades, Clients and Cousins: Colonialism, Socialism and Democratization in São Tomé and Príncipe*. Leiden, the Netherlands: Leiden University, 1999.

Shaw, Caroline, comp. *São Tomé and Príncipe*. Oxford: Clio Press, 1994.

———. "São Tomé and Príncipe." In *The Post-colonial Literature of Lusophone Africa*, edited by Patrick Chabal, 234–47. Evanston, Ill.: Northwestern University Press, 1996.

Sideri, S. *Trade and Power: Informal Colonialism in Anglo-Portuguese Relations*. Rotterdam, the Netherlands: Rotterdam University Press, 1970.

Simmons, John, ed. *Cocoa Production: Economic and Botanical Perspectives*. New York: Praeger, 1976.

Smith, Alan K., and William Gervase Clarence-Smith. "Angola and Mozambique, 1870–1905." In *The Cambridge History of Africa*. Vol. 6, *1870 to 1905*, edited by Roland Oliver and G. N. Sanderson, 493–521. Cambridge: Cambridge University Press, 1985.

Smith, Chris, John Child, and Michael Rowlinson. *Reshaping Work: The Cadbury Experience*. Cambridge: Cambridge University Press, 1990.

Smith, Dennis. "Englishness and Liberal Inheritance after 1886." In *Englishness: Politics and Culture, 1880–1920*, edited by Robert Colls and Philip Dodd, 254–82. London: Croom Helm, 1986.

Smith, Simon C. *British Imperialism, 1750–1970*. Cambridge: Cambridge University Press, 1998.

Solow, Barbara L., ed. *Slavery and the Rise of the Atlantic System*. Cambridge: Cambridge University Press, 1991.

Southall, Roger J. "Cadbury on the Gold Coast, 1907–1938: The Dilemma of the 'Model Firm' in a Colonial Economy." Ph.D. diss., University of Birmingham, 1975.

"St. Thomas." *Encyclopedia Britannica*. 11th ed. Cambridge: Cambridge University Press, 1910.

Steiner, Zara S. *Britain and the Origins of the First World War*. New York: St. Martin's Press, 1977.

Stenton, Michael, and Stephen Lees, eds. *Who's Who of British Members of Parliament*. Vol. 2, *1886–1918*, and Vol. 3, *1919–1945*. Atlantic Highlands, N.J.: Humanities Press, 1978 and 1979.

Stewart, A. T. Q. *Edward Carson*. Dublin: Gill and Macmillan, 1981.

Stone, Glyn A. "The Official British Attitude to the Anglo-Portuguese Alliance, 1910–1945." *Journal of Contemporary History* 10 (October 1975): 729–46.

———. *The Oldest Ally: Britain and the Portuguese Connection, 1936–1941*. Woodbridge, UK: Boydell Press, the Royal Historical Society, 1994.

Stranz, Walter. *George Cadbury: An Illustrated Life of George Cadbury, 1839–1922*. Aylesbury, UK: Shire Publications, 1973.

Street, C. J. C. *Lord Reading*. London: Geoffrey Bles, 1928.

Sundiata, Ibrahim K. *From Slaving to Neoslavery: The Bight of Biafra and Fernando Po in the Era of Abolition, 1827–1930*. Madison: University of Wisconsin Press, 1996.

Swaisland, Charles. "The Aborigines Protection Society, 1837–1909." In *After Slavery: Emancipation and Its Discontents*, edited by Harold Temperley, 265–80. London: Frank Cass, 2000.

Tams, Georg. *Visit to the Portuguese Possessions in South-Western Africa*. 1845; reprint, New York: Negro Universities Press, 1969.

Taylor, A. J. P. *English History, 1914–1945*. Oxford: Oxford University Press, 1965.

Thomas, Donald. *The Victorian Underworld*. London: John Murray, 1998.

Thomas, Hugh. *The Slave Trade: The Story of the Atlantic Slave Trade, 1440–1870*. New York: Simon & Schuster, 1997.

Thomas, Nicholas. *Colonialism's Culture: Anthropology, Travel and Government*. Princeton, N.J.: Princeton University Press, 1994.

Thomas, Roger. "Forced Labour in British West Africa: The Case of the Northern Territories of the Gold Coast, 1906–1927." *Journal of African History* 14 (1973): 79–103.

Thornton, John. *Africa and Africans in the Making of the Atlantic World, 1400–1680*. Cambridge: Cambridge University Press, 1992.

Tilley, John, and Stephen Gaselee. *The Foreign Office*. London: G. P. Putnam's Sons, 1933.

Tinker, Hugh. *A New System of Slavery: The Export of Indian Labour Overseas, 1830–1920*. London: Oxford University Press, 1974.

Titterton, W. R. *A Candle to the Stars*. London: Grayson & Grayson, 1932.

Torp, Jens Erik, L. M. Denny, and Donald I. Ray. *Mozambique, São Tomé and Príncipe: Economics, Politics and Society*. London: Pinter, 1989.

Turley, David. *Slavery*. Oxford: Blackwell, 2000.

Turner, Howard. *Africa South of the Sahara*. 2nd ed. Harlow, UK: Longman, 1994.

Urquhart, Duncan. *Cocoa*. 3rd ed. London: Longmans, Green, 1956.

Uzoigwe, G. N. *Britain and the Conquest of Africa: The Age of Salisbury*. Ann Arbor: University of Michigan Press, 1974.

Vail, Leroy, and Landeg White. *Capitalism and Colonialism in Mozambique: A Study of Quelimane District*. London: Heinemann, 1980.

Van Hall, C. J. J. *Cacao*. London: Macmillan, 1932.

Viet-Wilson, J. H. "Paradigms of Poverty: A Rehabilitation of B. S. Rowntree." In *Retrieved Riches: Social Investigation in Britain, 1840–1914*, edited by David Englander and Rosemary O'Day, 201–37. Aldershot, UK: Scholar Press, [1995].

Vincent-Smith, J. D. "The Anglo-German Negotiations over the Portuguese Colonies in Africa, 1911–1914." *Historical Journal* 17 (1974): 620–29.

———. "The Portuguese Republic and Britain, 1910–14." *Journal of Contemporary History* 10 (October 1975): 707–27.

Vipont, Elfrida. *Arnold Rowntree.* London: Bannisdale, 1955.

Wagner, Gillian. *The Chocolate Conscience.* London: Chatto & Windus, 1979.

Walker-Smith, Derek. *Lord Reading and His Cases: The Study of a Great Career.* London: Chapman & Hall, 1934.

Walvin, James. *The Quakers: Money and Morals.* North Pomfret, Vt.: John Murray, 1997.

———. *Slavery and the Slave Trade: A Short Illustrated History.* Jackson: University Press of Mississippi, 1983.

Ward, A. W., and G. P. Gooch, eds. *The Cambridge History of British Foreign Policy, 1783–1919.* Vol. 1, *1783–1815,* Vol. 2, *1815–1866,* Vol. 3, *1866–1919.* 1922–1923; reprint, New York: Octagon Books, 1970.

Ward, W. E. F. *A History of Ghana.* London: Allen and Unwin, 1966.

Warhurst, Philip R. *Anglo-Portuguese Relations in South-Central Africa, 1890–1900.* London: Longmans, 1962.

Wheeler, Douglas L. "The Portuguese Revolution of 1910." *Journal of Modern History* 44 (June 1972): 172–94.

Wheeler, Douglas L., and C. Diane Christensen. "To Rise with One Mind: The Bailundu War of 1902." In *Social Change in Angola,* edited by Franz-Wilhelm Heimer, 53–93. Munich, Germany: Weltforum Verlag, 1973.

Wheeler, Douglas L., and René Pélissier. *Angola.* New York: Praeger, 1971.

Whitehouse, J. Howard. "Henry Nevinson." *Contemporary Review* 161 (January 1942): 44–47.

Wickizer, V. D. *Coffee, Tea and Cocoa: An Economic and Political Analysis.* Stanford, Calif.: Stanford University Press, 1951.

Willequet, Jacques. "Anglo-German Rivalry in Belgian and Portuguese Africa?" In *Britain and Germany in Africa,* edited by Prosser Gifford and Wm. Roger Louis, 245–73. New Haven, Conn.: Yale University Press, 1967.

William A. Cadbury, 1867–1957. Privately printed, 1958.

Williams, Iolo A. *The Firm of Cadbury, 1831–1931.* New York: Richard R. Smith, 1931.

Wilson, Charles. *A History of Unilever: A Study in Economic Growth and Social Change.* Vol. 1. London: Cassell, 1954.

Woolf, Leonard. *Empire & Commerce in Africa.* 1920; reprint, New York: Howard Fertig, 1968.

INDEX

APS Aborigines' Protection Society
BFASS British and Foreign Anti-Slavery Society
PWA Portuguese West Africa